Teaching Language Arts

TEACHING LANGUAGE ARTS

Barbara D. Stoodt
UNIVERSITY OF NORTH CAROLINA—GREENSBORO

HarperCollins*Publishers*, New York
Cambridge, Philadelphia, San Francisco, Washington,
London, Mexico City, São Paulo, Singapore, Sydney

Photo Credits   Page 1, © Elizabeth Crews; 18, © Elizabeth Crews; 24, Bellerose, Stock, Boston; 46, © Fortin, Stock, Boston; 63, © Elizabeth Crews; 73, © Jean-Claude Lejeune; 91, © Elizabeth Crews; 116, © Elizabeth Crews; 128, © Jean-Claude Lejeune; 134, © Crews, Stock, Boston; 146, © Elizabeth Crews; 162, © Elizabeth Crews; 172, Holland, Stock, Boston; 197, Vandermark, Stock, Boston; 209, © Elizabeth Crews; 222, © Elizabeth Crews; 231, © Jean-Claude Lejeune; 257, © Elizabeth Crews; 276, © Menzel, Stock, Boston; 285, © Elizabeth Crews; 299, Vandermark, Stock, Boston; 321, © Elizabeth Crews; 355, © Elizabeth Crews; 359, © Elizabeth Crews; 389, © Elizabeth Crews; 399, © Steve & Mary Skjold.

Sponsoring Editor: Alan McClare
Project Editor: Lauren Shafer/Ellen MacElree
Text Design: Rita Naughton
Cover Design: Wanda Lubelska Design
Cover Photo: Monkmeyer Press (Paul Conklin), Teacher & Pupils, Alexandria, VA.
Text Art: Fine Line Illustrations, Inc.
Photo Research: Mira Schachne
Production Manager: Jeanie Berke
Production Assistant: Beth Maglione
Compositor: ComCom Division of Haddon Craftsmen, Inc.
Printer and Binder: R. R. Donnelley & Sons Company
Cover Printer: NEBC

Language Arts Methods

Library of Congress Cataloging in Publication Data

Stoodt, Barbara D.
  Teaching language arts.

  Includes index.
  1. Language arts (Elementary)—United States.
I. Title.
LB1576.S799 1988   372.6'044   87–31040
ISBN 0–06–04656–9

90 91 9 8 7 6 5 4 3 2

To my students—past, present, and future
who teach me so much

Contents

Preface

Teaching Language Arts emphasizes integrated language arts instruction while recognizing that separate subject instruction is necessary in some instances. More effective teaching is the primary goal of this book. It is designed to help teachers and prospective teachers create warm, literate environments that are both stimulating and disciplined, and that offer students many varied opportunities for language use. This text was written to help teachers and prospective teachers teach fast-paced, businesslike lessons, ask questions that stimulate children's thinking, and communicate ideas clearly. The fortunate children in these teachers' classrooms will acquire enthusiasm for language.

This book integrates theory and practice to help teachers and prospective teachers acquire the foundations of instructional excellence. Moreover, this text reflects the belief that teachers need to know the *why, what, how,* and *when* of teaching language arts, so that they will know what to do when they get into classrooms. Classroom teachers do not have time to stop and look up answers in a book or search their memories for lists of skills they learned for an examination. They are on the "firing line" of teaching, and they must have the know-how to teach language arts.

Practical understanding is developed in part through vignettes based on actual incidents in elementary school classrooms. The vignettes help develop practical insights regarding language arts instruction. They demonstrate how teachers can integrate effective instruction to meet individual needs.

Additional special features of this book include introductory sections that help students focus on key concepts; many practical teaching suggestions and applications of theory; troubleshooting sections based on surveys of experienced teachers who identified common language arts problems along with suggested solutions; thought questions at the end of each chapter that help students review main ideas; and a glossary at the end of the book that gives students an immediate reference for terminology used in the text.

This book includes one optional chapter, Chapter Six, which addresses reading skills. It is optional because the vast majority of colleges and universities offer courses in reading that are separate from language arts courses. However, it was included because reading is clearly an important aspect of the language arts. Instructors may choose to use the chapter as a survey of developmental reading or they may omit the chapter because the topic is addressed in other courses.

An instructor's manual accompanies *Teaching Language Arts.* It contains teaching suggestions, identification of issues pertinent to each chapter, objective and subjective test items, and additional related readings.

A number of people have been involved in producing this book and deserve recognition for their contributions. Alan McClare, the sponsoring editor, has cheerfully supported the author and provided insightful advice. Lauren Shafer, the project editor, has patiently collaborated with the author.

One reviewer, Leo Schell, Kansas State University, went far beyond the call of duty in analyzing the manuscript. His detailed analysis of the manuscript and his suggestions have helped enormously. In addition, the following reviewers read the manuscript carefully, and their thoughtful suggestions contributed much to this book: Ruth Beeker, University of Arizona; Edward Paradis, University of Wyoming; and Donna Wiseman, Texas A & M University.

Barbara D. Stoodt

Part ONE

Foundations of the Language Arts

Chapter **One**

The English Language Arts

CHAPTER OVERVIEW

This chapter introduces the English language arts through classroom vignettes that illustrate the practical exigencies of teaching listening, speaking, reading, and writing. As you examine these teaching situations the interrelationships among the language arts, thinking, and experience become apparent. The classroom scenarios also create a frame of reference for understanding the role of language in life and in learning.

Anticipation Guide

Before you read this chapter, think about the following question. What do you know about the language arts? As you read, try to answer the guiding questions below.

1. Why are listening and reading considered receptive language arts?

2. What are the expressive language arts?

3. How is literature related to language arts instruction?

Key Concepts

language arts	speaking
listening	reading
writing	expressive language arts
receptive language arts	

INTRODUCTION

Language is central to human life. Human beings find self-identity through language, shape their knowledge and experience through language, and depend on language as a lifelong resource for sharing feelings and information (NCTE, 1983). Our language evidences our culture, abilities, attitudes, geography, and values. Our ability to become self-sufficient and to lead productive lives is influenced by our language proficiency. Speaking, listening, reading, and writing comprise the **language arts.** However, thinking is central to each of the language arts and could be considered the fifth language art. The language arts are basic academic competencies, as well as the media of human communication.

Language is a process. Language has no inherent content. It is the vehicle used to encode and decode data that we derive from thought and experiences. Listening and reading are the sources of data that we decode to understand. We encode, communicate, our ideas and experiences in speaking and writing.

Children learn language in natural contexts for their own purposes. Research tells us that children learn to speak, listen, read, and write to fulfill meaningful functions in their lives (Read, 1971; Clay, 1975; Bissex, 1980).

Language learners begin with a need to get something done that requires language; then they develop the language competence necessary to fulfill that function. Consequently, effectively teaching the language arts requires teachers to create stimulating, language-rich environments that give children genuine and meaningful purposes for speaking, listening, reading, and writing (Auten, 1985).

A language-rich school environment is portrayed in the following vignette. As you read this sketch, identify the stimulating contexts that are provided for speaking, listening, reading, and writing instruction in this group of 28 six-year-olds.

VISIT TO A FIRST-GRADE CLASS

Terry B. looked over her busy classroom, observing that every child in the room was engrossed. Her idea for a "monster" unit evolved from the children's favorite book, *Liza Lou and the Yeller Belly Swamp* by Mercer Mayer. This book intrigued the children so much that they chose it for reading aloud every time they had a chance. Wisely, Terry chose it as the stimulus for the unit.

To initiate the language arts unit, Terry seated the children in a circle for "talking time." Then her request to describe their favorite monsters resulted in a lively discussion. As the children talked, she wrote the descriptive words they used on chart paper. The list looked like this:

ugly	silly	scary	green
one-eyed	spooky	friendly	dumb
frightening	mean	big-nose	angry
bony	bone-head	greedy	nasty
sly			

After the pupils finished their discussion, Terry asked them to look at the words while she read them aloud. She asked the children to think about what these words told about a monster. After a discussion that included some inappropriate responses, the children decided that the words told how the monster looked and acted. Terry explained that these words would help them understand what the monster looked like in their favorite stories.

Next, she read *Liza Lou and the Yeller Belly Swamp* aloud. As she read the story, the children listened to determine whether the author had used any of their words. They were delighted to find that Mercer Mayer had used many of these words. After she finished reading the story, Terry asked her students to tell the part of the story that they especially liked. In particular, the children identified the monsters' tricks as their preferred part of the book. Some of the more gregarious children stood and acted out their favorite trick as they explained it to the class.

While the list of words was on the chalkboard and the story was fresh in their minds, Terry elicited a cinquain poem from the children. She started with a noun, *creature.* Then she asked the children to describe the monster and they agreed on the descriptive phrase, *greedy giant.* They described the monster's actions in the third line, *walks around laughing.* When they composed the fourth line of the cinquain, they decided to write, *mean, green, selfish, bonehead.* Finally, the children concluded the poem with the word, *monster.* Then Terry explained that this five line poem was called a cinquain poem. At another time, the children would learn more about cinquain poetry.

Creature—

Greedy giant

Walks around laughing

Mean, green, selfish, bonehead

Monster—

By the time the students finished composing their cinquain, several children were clamoring to write their own monster stories. Terry reminded them that they could use the words on the chalkboard, the words in their personal files, the picture thesaurus, and the picture dictionary to help write their ideas about monsters. She told the children to pick up writing paper from the writing center for their stories. Two children chose to use the typewriters located in the back of the classroom for writing their stories.

Several first graders were able to compose excellent stories, but they were not able to write their ideas. Instead, they used tape recorders to dictate their stories for later transcription. For some children, the process of composing did not come easily, so four of the students drew their stories. When they completed their drawings, she had a conference with each one giving them an opportunity to dictate a story or a picture caption. She noted with some satisfaction that these students copied monster words from the charts on their pictures. When "writing time" was completed, some of the children wanted to read their stories aloud. They enjoyed the "monster stories" so much that they asked to continue reading and talking about monsters the following day.

On the next day, Terry prepared for language arts class by arranging an array of reading materials including trade books, basal reading materials, and stories written by the children. Following is a list of the reading materials the children used.

Stories written by the children in the class.

Steven Kellogg. *The Mystery Beast of Ostergeest.* Dial Press, 1971.

Mercer Mayer. *Liza Lou and the Yeller Belly Swamp.* Parents Magazine Press, 1976.

Walter Dean Myers. *The Dragon Takes a Wife*. Bobbs-Merrill, 1972.

Maurice Sendak. *Seven Little Monsters*. Harper & Row, 1975.

Tomi Ungerer. *The Beast of Monsieur Racine*. Farrar Strauss, 1971.

The Monster Books, Set 1 by Bowmar/Noble Publishers Inc., 1981.

For reading instruction, Terry used *The Monster Books, Set 1*. She presented the new vocabulary to the children in sentences on the chalkboard. After they decoded and discussed the new words, she gave the children an opportunity to read the words in sentences. Then they discussed the monster they would be reading about and she posed three silent reading questions to the children. When the children completed reading the story silently, they discussed the silent reading purposes. Terry's questions led the children to compare the monster in their reader with the monsters in the *Liza Lou* story. The children supported their answers by reading appropriate content from their book. Each pupil had an individual chalkboard to use during reading group to write words and answers to questions. Terry frequently asked students to explain the meaning of the words and phrases they were reading and writing. They used consonant sounds they had learned and context clues as aids to decoding unknown words. In this lesson, Terry introduced the initial cluster *sn* in this lesson and reviewed the initial clusters *gl* and *bl*. After participating in direct instruction during the reading group, every child chose a book to read independently at their desk. Each reading group in the classroom was patterned after this one.

When the students completed their independent reading, they wrote or drew stories to add to their writing files. Several of the children proposed that they make monsters as an art project, to which Terry readily agreed.

The objectives for this language arts unit which were developed during two consecutive days of instruction were:

Students will participate in a discussion.

Students will recall details (regarding monsters).

Students will listen to a story for specific purposes.

Students will use descriptive words.

Students will participate in a group composition of cinquain.

Students will write, dictate, or draw a story.

Students will read stories written by classmates, trade books, and basal readers.

Students review the initial clusters *gl* and *bl* and will learn the initial cluster *sn*.

LISTENING, SPEAKING, READING, AND WRITING

In the preceding vignette, language is used in many different ways for a variety of purposes. The stimulating environment created by the teacher encouraged children to develop **listening, speaking, reading,** and **writing.** Terry believes that children learn to listen by listening, to speak by speaking, to read by reading, and to write by writing; therefore she cultivates an environment that stimulates a wide range of language uses. Because she believes that language should grow out of children's experiences, she builds on the students' existing experiences and introduces additional experiences to motivate their speaking, listening, reading, and writing. Terry views literature as an imaginative use of language which has a natural place in language arts instruction. She agrees with Manning (1985) that, "There is increasing evidence of the importance of children's literature and library reading in school reading programs." Consequently, she reads aloud every day and includes trade books in daily instruction.

Terry believes that children learn to use and understand language as they relate it to their experiences and interests. This is why she selected one of the children's favorite stories as a stimulus for the language arts unit. As they listened, talked, read, and wrote about monsters they were relating language to their thoughts. These students had opportunities to express meaning through speaking and writing **(expressive language arts)** and they had opportunities to understand the meaning of others through listening and reading **(receptive language arts)** (Halliday, 1975). They were using language to think and to understand.

Listening

Listening for specific purposes focused students' attention as the teacher read *Liza Lou and the Yeller Belly Swamp.* Listening to stories helps children develop a sense of story—that is, a story grammar that contributes to understanding and remembering stories (Mandler and Johnson, 1977). Reading and telling stories to children also develops their appreciation and enjoyment of literature. Listening for descriptive words in the story enhances listening vocabulary. Like many first graders, Terry's students have many opportunities for listening to directions and carrying them out.

Listening is the primary language skill. Chronologically children listen before they manifest any other language skills. Listening is central to all learning (Devine, 1982). In spite of this fact, many teachers complain about their students' listening skills; this important skill is often neglected. Perhaps this occurs because children have already learned a great deal through listening and they demonstrate listening skills in the classroom. Actually, this command of listening skills merely demonstrates that children have the basis for developing and refining these existing skills. However, it is important that young children have opportunities to refine existing listening skills and alleviate poor habits through meaningful practice.

Speaking

The class discussion enabled pupils to advance their speaking skills (oral language). Children develop oral speech when they use language to sort and interpret their experiences (Vygotsky, 1978). Children in first grade have a continuing need for oral language experiences to ensure total language development. Dictating words that described monsters expanded their oral language and enriched their vocabulary. As the children wrote, they shared their thoughts informally with one another. Some youngsters elected to read monster stories aloud. Each of these types of experiences enhanced oral language.

Reading

In the lesson described, Terry's pupils developed and practiced their reading skills through reading the stories they wrote, the words on the chalkboard, basal readers, and trade books. Personal stories, textbooks, and trade books are essential components of the language arts program. Literacy develops when children experience printed language in a variety of forms such as fiction, nonfiction, and poetry. Terry varies the reading program through incorporating many types of material with the basal reader. Children experience greater reading success when the content motivates and interests them. Since personal stories address familiar thoughts and words and are inherently interesting, they play an important role in learning to read. Classroom discussions of the stories they read contribute to reading comprehension. The children who told about their favorite parts of the story and who acted out the monsters' tricks were demonstrating their understanding of written language.

Word recognition instruction is also an important aspect of reading acquisition. Direct instruction in sight words, context clues, structural analysis, and phonics helps children become independent readers—that is, they can decode unknown words without assistance (Anderson et al, 1985).

Writing

Writing skills were developed as Terry's pupils composed the cinquain poem as well as their individual compositions. This, in turn, helped them understand that written symbols (words) represent meaning. As the children wrote their own ideas or watched the teacher write their dictated stories, they became aware of writing conventions such as spelling, capitalization, and punctuation. These conventions are subskills of writing. When they wrote stories, the children were practicing handwriting skills which are best developed out of a personal need to write (Moffett, 1979).

The preceding section of this chapter examined language arts instruction in a first-grade classroom. This section will explore language arts instruction in a fifth-grade classroom. Pupils at the fifth-grade level are relatively independent users of language arts skills, which permits them to use listening, speaking, reading, and writing to learn. However, they have need for a continuous language arts instruction. Examine how this teacher provides speaking, listening, reading, and writing instruction for 28 fifth-grade students.

VISIT TO A FIFTH-GRADE SCIENCE CLASS

Carolyn smiled at her fifth graders as she returned their "Microbe Mania" stories. She felt successful when she thought about the excellent stories they had written. The "Mania" began when she initiated a science unit on microbes. She introduced the science unit by brainstorming words associated with the concept, microbes. Carolyn's students could think of only a few words which indicated their limited knowledge about microbes. Therefore, she decided to develop a study guide to steer them through the important ideas presented in the textbook. The study guide appears on page 11.

Before reading the chapters, Carolyn's pupils discussed the key vocabulary, study guide questions, and the chapters. After reading and completing the study guide, she found that they had learned quite a lot from the assignment. She allowed them to brainstorm microbe concepts and they generated many words this time. After the students listed all of the words they could think of, Carolyn told them to study the words and to think of categories for the words. They suggested the following categories: types of microbes, reproduction, parts of microbes, infectious diseases, and useful microbes. Then she divided the class into groups and each group sorted the list of words into categories. When they finished this activity, the various groups compared their lists and discussed the reasons for the different sortings which led to some categorization changes.

For homework, Carolyn instructed the students to create comic strips illustrating one aspect of a microbe's life. She reminded them that the words they brainstormed would be useful in creating comic strips. They handed in the comic strips the following day. Carolyn assigned the students to editorial teams for editing their comic strips. Two people were assigned to each team. The members of the editorial teams were responsible for editing each other's writing. They were expected to use standardized editorial symbols, to locate misspelled words, to identify grammatical errors, and to identify any places where the content did not make sense. They were very interested in reading each other's comic strips; many of the errors they identified demonstrated their understanding of microbes. After the necessary revisions were completed, the comic strips were bound into a class book.

Carolyn's students were intrigued by Leeuwenhoek, Jenner, Spallanzanni, and Pasteur. They asked a number of questions about these scientists such as "how they were able to discover microbes so long ago." The accidental nature of the scientists' work also interested them. Carolyn asked them how they could find out more about the scientists and their

Study Guide for Microbe Unit

Part 1: Vocabulary

Find a meaning for each of the following words as you read this unit. Make notes on your study guide to help you remember the word meanings.

All of the following are types of microbes:

algae	viruses
bacteria	protozoa
fungi	rickettsiae

All of the following words are related to microbes:

pathogens	paramecium
infectious diseases	spirilla
toxins	cilia
amoeba	flagellum
euglena	

Part 2: Read these questions before you read Chapters 3 and 4. Answer these questions after you read the chapters.

1. How many types of microbes are there?

2. List the types of microbes discussed in these chapters.

3. How do microbes move?

4. Do all microbes reproduce the same way?

5. How do microbes reproduce?

6. How are microbes related to microscopes?

7. How is the work of Jenner, Leeuwenhoek, and Pasteur related to the study of microbes?

8. Identify the discoveries of these scientists: Jenner, Leeuwenhoek, and Pasteur.

Part 3: Think about these questions after you read the chapters; then write a paragraph to answer each question.

1. Are microbes useful? Why or why not?

2. Are microbes harmful? Why or why not?

3. How are microbes related to disease?

4. What do microbiologists do?

5. How are microbes related to life in outer space?

6. How can you use the information in this unit in your life?

discoveries which led to a review of library skills. She had already taught them how to take notes, so she took the class to the library to do research. They gathered information regarding each of the scientists. Six of them were grouped together because they had difficulty reading and locating information, and she worked directly with them while the other children worked independently.

After completing their library work, the pupils returned to their classroom where Carolyn explained how to proceed to the next stage of their project. She placed several copies of *Ben and Me* by Robert Lawson and *Mr. Revere and I* by Robert Lawson on the reading table because she wanted the children to use these books as models, for their writing project. She had read these books aloud to the class earlier, but she thought some of the students might like to refresh their memories. She explained that everyone would write a story about one scientist's discoveries. She told them to create stories that told about the scientific discoveries from the point of view of an animal similar to those in Lawson's fictionalized biographies. They studied point of view previously in their basal reading series and in the stories that she read aloud to her class daily. Carolyn reminded the pupils that all of their information had to be accurate; the only fictional aspect of the story was to be the animal and its point of view. As the children composed, they were allowed to consult many types of books—reference, trade, science, language, readers, spelling, thesaurus, and dictionaries. During the writing process, all of the children worked independently except the group of six pupils whose language skills were lagging behind. These students worked as a group with the teacher's direct guidance, composing an experience story which they edited together. One pupil in the group typed the story into the computer and printed copies for each group member.

As the pupils completed the first drafts of their stories, they worked in editorial teams refining their writing to a publishable stage. Publishable in this situation simply means that the material is refined to a stage where it can be shared with others. Carolyn's students usually bind their publishable stories into hardback books. When the first draft was edited, the children rewrote their stories. They could word process on the classroom computer, type it on available school typewriters, or hand write the stories. Then the editorial teams went to work again. In some instances, the children found it necessary to rewrite their stories due to editorial work, while some children changed their minds about what they wanted to say. When all the stories were edited to the students' satisfaction, they illustrated the stories. Then the stories were bound into hardback books and cataloged for the library. An example of this type of story is shown in Figure 1.1. This unit of study consumed approximately 90 minutes of class time each day during a two-week period.

Carolyn's objectives for her fifth-grade class were as follows:

1. To develop basic concepts regarding microbes through listening, speaking, reading, and writing.

2. To develop meanings for the vocabulary associated with microbes.

3. To understand expository content and identify the important ideas expressed in this content.

4. To use literature as a writing model for expressing point of view.

5. To use the writing, editing, and rewriting process to prepare a completed writing project.

6. To practice locating information using card catalogs, tables of contents, and indexes.

7. To practice using note-taking skills.

8. To communicate the acquired knowledge regarding microbes in a comic strip and biographical fiction format.

LISTENING, SPEAKING, READING, AND WRITING

The students in the preceding vignette are refining and developing language arts skills. By fifth grade, many students have well-developed language skills; however, some may lag behind in this important area. The students in this sketch are using language skills to acquire new knowledge. They are acquiring new ideas from listening and reading while they are expressing their ideas through speaking and writing. Figure 1.2 illustrates this aspect of the language arts. Carolyn believes that children actively seek understanding when they have a real need for information. Furthermore, she believes that exploration leads to understanding. This accounts for activities like completing a study guide, researching the lives of scientists, and writing comic strips and fictionalized biographies (Busching and Lundsteen, 1983). Recent studies of language learning stress the critical influence of the learning situation, demonstrating that language flourishes in settings where children are exposed to mature language models and have opportunities to create and receive messages in many different tasks (Busching and Lundsteen, 1983). What these students say and write (expressive language) grows from what they hear and read (receptive language). This sketch demonstrates the relationship between the language arts and the content areas in middle-school classes.

Listening

Listening is an important source of information for fifth-grade students; they receive many directions through listening. To listen to the literature read aloud daily affords them a mature language model. Listening vocabulary is expanded as the pupils participate in brainstorming. Carolyn encourages concentration through purposeful listening situations. During the school year she uses listening activities from which she develops guidelines for effective listening. Critical listening activities are also developed with her students.

Alexander J. Little

Hi! I'm Alexander J. Little.
You may not understand me when I tell
you I am the real man-I mean, mouse-
behind pasteurization. You see, it was
like this, I was running around, getting

1

some food for my son, when this guy
Louis Pasteur came in and started
mixing all this stuff together.

    There was a stove in the corner
of the room with a pot of milk on it,
M-m-m, oh yes, back to the Pasteur fellow.

2

    After he left for the day, I
read what he had written down.
Then I saw what he was doing. He
was trying to kill germs in milk,
so it would be safe to drink!

3

Figure 1.1 *Alexander J. Little*
Source: A composite of students' work in Carolyn Herman's classroom in Winston Salem
Forsyth Schools.

I thought about it, and then added on to what he had already written. After 8 hours of work, and no sleep, I figured it out.

4

If he were to heat the milk to a certain temperature for a certain amount of time, it would kill the germs!

5

When Louis came in the room he saw the milk boiling. He turned the stove off and took a drop of milk and looked at it under a microscope. He saw that the germs were gone.

6

Maybe they should call it littlezation instead of Pasteurization!

7

Figure 1.1 (*Continued*)

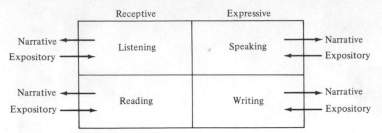

Figure 1.2   The Expressive and Receptive Language Arts Related to Types of Written Content

Speaking

Class discussion of the study guide and the science chapters the students read provide opportunities to translate ideas into oral language. Brainstorming provided additional opportunities for refining oral language. Students developed conversational skills as they categorized words and discussed their editorial work. The small group of pupils whose development is lagging had opportunities to refine speaking skills as they composed the language experience story. Reading their personal writings and language experiences stories aloud helped students refine oral language skills. Speaking skills continue in importance at this grade level because students must communicate ideas to an audience whether the audience includes one person or many persons.

Reading

Like the majority of fifth-grade students, these children have many opportunities to read. Their teacher created a series of purposeful reading situations whereby students used reading as a vehicle for learning new ideas and information while researching their reports. They not only read a science textbook, but also trade books and reference materials to obtain knowledge. Reading the study guide helped them attach meaning to new vocabulary and identify important ideas in the chapters. Information location skills enabled the pupils to find appropriate information in the card catalog, the table of contents, and the index. Proofreading skills were essential as they edited the comic strips and stories. They then read the completed comic strips and stories created by classmates.

Writing

Writing gave these students another means of organizing and expressing ideas. They wrote their ideas as they worked through the study guide. The comic strips required an expressed science concept. After they made written notes for research in preparing a fictionalized biography, they prepared biographical drafts for their editor. Each writing task involved the components of writing: spelling, punctuation, grammar, and handwriting. Editorial work further involved use of these skills. Working through this writing project to the point of publication helped students develop respect for their language and their ability to use their language.

LANGUAGE ARTS INSTRUCTION

Any discussion of language arts instruction must begin with the understanding that there is no one way to teach language arts in all classrooms. Teachers are individuals who have a variety of skills and talents. However, they must consider the nature of children, language development, language types, and language functions in their instruction. Teaching the language arts includes inspiring children to think and to share their thoughts by talking about them.

Creating a Language-Rich Environment

Language setting or environment is a powerful factor in language development (Auten, 1985). Immersing children in a language-rich environment exposes them to oral as well as written language and introduces them to the form and function of language. A language-rich environment is a warm, literate environment which stimulates interchange and interaction. Children learn language from each other as much as they learn from the teacher, making opportunities for interchange and interaction very important (Britton, 1985). As children discuss books, plays, and shared experiences they are developing both language and thought processes. Through interaction they build flexibility, fluency, and precision of expression. When students record the behavior of a guinea pig, explain why dry ice doesn't melt, or write a story about how children lived in Abraham Lincoln's time, they are shaping their own understanding and developing the language resources for an increasing range of purposes. Aquariums, terrariums, classroom pets, group projects, experiments, and field trips stimulate language interchange. Language develops throughout the day—including lunch and recess.

Such meaningful and purposeful activities contribute to language growth and encourage language production. Authentic language activities are based on writing letters to "real" people or writing stories about actual experiences; such enterprises lead children to produce language. Language development results from indirect, ongoing activities, as well as from direct instruction.

Language flourishes in settings where children are exposed to mature language models (Busching and Lundsteen, 1983). Teachers should therefore model language use for their students. Teachers who express themselves clearly and who exhibit an appreciation of language are creating excellent learning environments for children. An appreciation of language might include reading to children daily. Teachers can savor language by repeating

Immersing children in a language-rich environment.

especially appealing passages. To draw students' attention to the lovely and unusual things, events, or behaviors around them stimulates children to think, talk, listen, read, and write about their environment and experiences. For instance, teachers may point out butterflies, birds, flowers, rain, acts of consideration for others, or cooperative undertakings for students to discuss, read, and write about.

Classrooms should also provide a variety of supplemental materials. Students should have access to materials that stimulate language exploration. They should be able to select from trade books written at many readability levels, which address a wide variety of interests. Newspapers, magazines, brochures, almanacs, games, video cassette recorders, and computers should be available for use. It is particularly helpful for schools to have media centers that include books, film, tapes, and so forth. Students who are limited to textbooks, workbooks, and worksheets do not achieve as well as those who have opportunities to explore many kinds of media (Leinhardt, Zigmond, and Cooley, 1981; Rosenshine and Stevens, 1984).

The physical environment encourages language development when children's work is displayed on the bulletin boards. Bright charts around the classroom, displays of trade books, interest centers, chalkboards, computers, and typewriters invite children to listen, speak, read, and write. In addition, the classroom arrangement should give students' easy access to the many resources in the classroom; for example, students should be able to obtain paper, pencils, paints, or paste without interrupting the teacher. Classroom arrangement should provide places for students to work in groups of various sizes. At times students will work individually, while other situations will arise when they may function as members of a large group, a small group of five or six, or in triads or pairs. Figure 1.3 shows a sample room arrangement for an elementary classroom.

Literature and the Language Arts

No language arts program is complete without extensive experiences with literature. Literature is an imaginative use of language; as such it provides the linguistic and conceptual input so important to language growth. For example, all writers are readers; many writers believe the only way to learn to write is to read (Weiss 1979). Literature provides a model for both oral and written language; *Swimmy* by Leo Lionni is a picturebook masterpiece which illustrates ways of using language to describe events and feelings. In this book, there is an "eel whose tail is almost too far away to remember." Literature has many other values for students including enjoyment, developing imagination and thought, vicarious experience, insight into human behavior, cultural background, literary awareness, and appreciation. "Literature enables us to live many lives and to begin to see the universality of human experience. It provides a record of all that people have thought or dreamed of throughout the ages" (Huck, Helper, and Hickman, 1987).

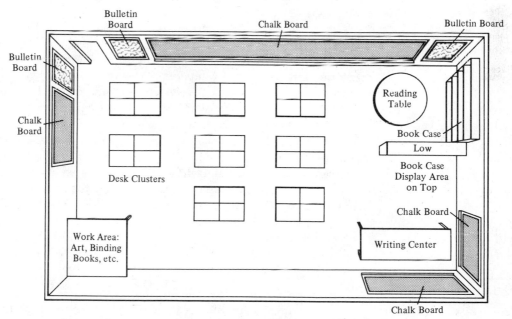

Figure 1.3   Sample Room Arrangement in an Elementary Classroom

LANGUAGE ARTS AND MULTICULTURAL EDUCATION _____

Multicultural education imparts greater sensitivity to the needs of all people. Through reading, discussing, thinking, writing, and listening, children build respect for other cultures and an understanding of the universality of human experience. People are alike no matter what their color or language. Furthermore, multicultural studies heighten the self-esteem of cultural minorities. "Multicultural education is designed for all children—and educators—not just dark-skinned pupils in inner cities, on reservations, or in *barrios.* It is also for the pupils living in solidly middle-class, upwardly mobile, homogeneously white communities who will grow up to live in an increasingly multicultural and multilingual society which suffers tensions because of those differences" (Dillon, 1986). In order to participate actively in their culture, human beings must understand the worldwide systems driving the culture: physical, biological, social, political, communicative, and economic (Boulding, 1985). Multicultural education is essential for the national and international understanding that will lead to peace.

Traditionally, the United States has represented a melting pot of culture, and it grows more varied in culture and language each year. Recently, groups like the Vietnamese and Cambodians have added to our cultural mix. In addition, we are exporting both the English language and culture at a rapid rate. We can no longer speak of English as if it were one language—there are too many varieties of English to do so. The Japanese form of English is *Japlish* and includes a 20,000 word dictionary. Japlish represents the Japanese absorption of American trade, culture, and language. Such cross-cultural exchanges create greater need for understanding.

Language is culture and to teach a language is to teach a culture (Hansen-Krenig, 1986). English teachers are teaching English culture. Culture is a particular, socially determined way of seeing the world including the categories into which we lump people, events, things, and ideas: a set of operating principles by which we've come to understand how things work in life (Dillon, 1986). In other words, American English speakers share certain ways of viewing the world because we share a language; however, our world is smaller and more varied than in the past, which means that we must learn about the other cultures comprising our world. Puerto Ricans, Cubans, and American Indians have cultural backgrounds and values that are important to our understanding. As we come to appreciate the contributions of various cultural groups, we acquire increased respect for individuals.

Literature offers many values to multicultural education according to Norton (1987), Jenkins (1973), and Carlson (1972). These values are summarized in the following list.

1. Literature enables minority children to learn about their cultural heritage. They learn to appreciate the contributions of their culture to the country and the world. This knowledge develops a sense of pride and cultural identity.

2. Learning about other cultures helps children understand that people belonging to other cultural groups have feelings, emotions, and needs like their own.

3. Reading about other cultures helps children realize that all people have contributed to American and world culture.

4. Through literature children can learn that people must live in harmony in spite of different personal beliefs and values.

5. Children can broaden their understanding of history, geography, and natural history as they read about the rest of the world.

6. Literature helps children learn about social change.

7. Literature helps children learn about problem-solving strategies that can help them in the future.

8. Literature exposes children to notable members of minority groups who can serve as life models for others.

SUMMARY

Speaking, listening, reading, and writing comprise the language arts. These skills are developed and refined during language arts instruction to give children opportunities to speak, listen, read, and write for a variety of purposes. The teachers described in this chapter created environments that invited language use. Their instruction evolved out of the students' interests, while addressing the objectives established by the school systems. Through careful use of such resources as time, materials, and equipment these teachers were able to address students' individual needs. Multicultural education is developed through language arts skills; students listen, speak, read, and write in order to understand their own and other cultures.

Thought Questions

1. Discuss the fact that human beings continue to develop language arts skills throughout life. Think of examples to support this idea such as ways that the elderly use language skills.

2. Describe an environment that would be most conducive to developing language skills.

3. How is children's literature related to language arts instruction?

4. Think of a question that you would ask each of the vignette teachers if you were to meet them.

5. In your own words explain multicultural education.

Enrichment Activities

1. Examine the teacher's edition of an elementary language arts text for any grade level. Read the philosophy of the text which you will find in the introductory section of the book. Compare the ideas expressed there with those presented in this chapter. How are they similar and how are they different?

2. Visit an elementary school or university media center and view some of the available software for teaching language arts and for word processing.

3. Choose an issue of *Language Arts,* a journal published by the National Council of Teachers of English. Read the entire journal.

Selected Readings

Bissex, Glenda (1980). *GNYS at WRK: A Child Learns to Write and Read.* Cambridge, MA: Harvard University Press.

Busching, Beverly A., and Judith I. Schwartz (eds.) (1983). *Integrating the Language Arts in the Elementary School.* Urbana, IL: National Council of Teachers of English.

Clay, Marie M. (1986, April). "Constructive Processes: Talking, Reading, Writing, Art, and Craft." *Reading Teacher. 39,* 764–770.

Dyson, Anne Haas, and Celia Genishi (1983, September). "Research Currents: Children's Language for Learning." *Language Arts, 60,* 751–757.

Genishi, Celia (1984, January). "Research Currents: What Is a Context for Learning Through Language?" *Language Arts, 62,* 52–58.

Halliday, M. A. K. (1975). *Learning How to Mean: Explorations in the Development of Language.* London: Edward Arnold.

Heath, Shirley Brice (1983, November/December). "Research Currents: A Lot of Talk About Nothing." *Language Arts, 60,* 999–1007.

Lindfors, Judith (1980). *Children's Language and Learning.* Englewood Cliffs, NJ: Prentice-Hall.

Squire, James (1983). *Instructional Focus and the Teaching of Writing.* Columbus, OH: Ginn, p. 3.

Wagner, B. J. (1985, September). "ERIC/RCS Report: Integrating the Language Arts." *Language Arts, 62,* 557–560.

References

Anderson, Richard, Elfrieda Hiebert, Judith Scott, and Ian Wilkinson (1985). *Becoming a Nation of Readers.* Champaign, IL: Center for the Study of Reading.

Auten, Anne (1985). "ERIC/RCS Report: Building a Language-Rich Environment." *Language Arts, 62,* 95–100.

Bissex, Glenda N. (1980). *GNYS at WRK: A Child Learns to Write and Read.* Cambridge, MA: Harvard University Press.

Boulding, K. (1985). *The World as a Total System.* Beverly Hills, CA: Sage.

Britton, J. (January, 1985). "ERIC/RCS Report: Building a Language-Rich Environment." *Language Arts, 62,* 95–99.

Busching, Beverly, and Sara Lundsteen (1983). "Curriculum Models for Integrating the Language Arts." In *Integrating the Language Arts in the Elementary School,* Beverly Schwartz and Judith Schwartz (eds.). Urbana, IL: National Council of Teachers of English, pp. 3–27.

Carlson, R. (1972). *Emerging Humanity: Multiethnic Literature for Children and Adolescents.* Dubuque, IO: Brown.

Clay, Marie M. (1975). *What Did I Write?* Exeter, NH: Heinemann.

Devine, T. G. (1982). *Listening Skills Schoolwide.* Urbana, IL: National Council of Teachers of English.

Dillon, David (September, 1986). "Editorial," *Language Arts 63,* 5.

Halliday, M. A. K. (1975). *Learning How to Mean: Explorations in the Development of Language.* London: Edward Arnold, p. 65.

Hansen-Krenig, J. (September, 1986). "China, The United States: Communication, Culture, and Conflict." *Language Arts 63,* 5.

Huck, C., S. Helper, and J. Hickman (1987). *Children's Literature in the Elementary School,* 4th ed. New York: Holt, Rinehart and Winston.

Jenkins, E. (May, 1973). "Multi-Ethnic Literature: Premise and Problems." *Elementary English, 50,* 693–699.

Leinhardt, G., N. Zigmond, and W. W. Cooley (1981). "Reading Instruction and Its Effects." *American Educational Research Journal, 18,* 343–361.

Mandler, Jean M., and Nancy S. Johnson (1977) "Remembrance of Things Parsed: Story Structure and Recall." *Cognitive Psychology 9,* 111–151.

Manning, John C. (1985) "Integrating Reading with Other Subjects." *Reading Today 3,* 3.

Moffett, John (1979). "Integrity in the Teaching of Writing." *Phi Delta Kappan 6,* 276–279.

National Council of Teachers of English, Executive Committee (1983). "Essentials of English," *Language Arts, 60,* 244–248.

Norton, D. (1987). *Through the Eyes of a Child* (2d ed.). Columbus, OH: Charles Merrill.

Read, Charles (1971). "Pre-School Children's Knowledge of English Phonology." *Harvard Educational Review, 41,* 1–34.

Rosenshine, B., and R. Stevens (1984). "Classroom Instruction in Reading." In *Handbook of Reading Research,* P. D. Pearson (ed.). New York: Longman, 829–864.

Tiedt, Iris M., SuzAnne Bruemmer, Sheilah Lane, Patricia Stelwagon, Kathleen Watanabe, and Mary Williams (1983). *Teaching Writing in K–8 Classrooms.* Englewood Cliffs, NJ: Prentice-Hall, p. 41.

Vygotsky, Lev (1978). *Mind in Society: Development of Higher Psychological Processes,* Michael Cole (ed.). Cambridge, MA: Harvard University Press.

Weiss, M. Jerry (ed.) (1979). *From Writers to Students.* Newark, DE: International Reading Association.

Chapter **Two**

Teaching the English Language Arts

CHAPTER OVERVIEW

This chapter is concerned with helping teachers and prospective teachers create effective instruction. After introducing curriculum and instruction, the chapter identifies the qualifications for teachers of the English language arts. Then we examine the integrated, separate subjects, whole language, and combined approaches to language arts instruction. Instructional concerns are introduced through a model of the instructional cycle; then approaches for guiding students' learning are examined. Effective teaching research has contributed to our understanding of how teachers can increase student achievement; therefore we examine the strategies that teachers can use to increase language growth. Finally, we examine evaluation in general terms.

Anticipation Guide

Before reading this chapter think about what you know about curriculum and instruction. Can you define these terms? Then read the following questions and try to answer them as you read this chapter.

1. Into what categories do the qualifications for English language arts teachers fall?

2. Identify the major characteristics of an integrated English language arts curriculum.

3. Identify the major characteristics of a separate subjects English language arts curriculum.

4. What teacher activities are associated with increased student achievement?

Key Concepts

curriculum approach

separate subjects approach

integrated English language arts

instruction process

INTRODUCTION

Language develops naturally during the preschool years. When children enter school, however, they are introduced to systematic instruction designed to nurture continued language growth. This planned set of learning experiences is the **curriculum.** Another definition of curriculum is the program of study in a school. Language arts curriculum is composed of the skills needed to communicate. To learn communication skills students need many opportunities to apply them in meaningful content. The English language arts curriculum refers to the objectives of the planned learning experiences and the sequence of these objectives. The overall goal of the English language arts curriculum is to enable students to use language effectively to communicate. Since language is central to learning students must be taught to use it as a facilitator of learning.

Curriculum development is influenced by the nature of the English language arts. The fact that the English language arts is a **process** is an important factor in designing the curriculum. Processes, such as speaking, listening, reading, and writing are learned through use. In other words, one learns to talk by talking, to listen by listening, to read by reading, and to write by writing. But, each of these processes includes knowledge as well. In order to communicate through oral language, the speaker must have knowledge about the audience and must have something to say and a reason to say it. The listening process needs a foundation of knowledge to help listeners understand what they are hearing. They need knowledge about word meanings as well as phonics, structural analysis, context, and sight words. The preceding is merely a sample of the knowledge related to English language arts.

The following vignettes exemplify separate subjects and integrated language arts instruction. Many authorities reject the instruction in the separate subjects vignette, but it will seem most familiar to many of you because it is the instruction you experienced in school. As you read these vignettes, identify the instructional activities that are process oriented and those that are knowledge oriented. Can you identify an effective teaching behavior?

SEPARATE SUBJECTS VIGNETTE

Rose Butler glanced at the classroom clock and noted that it was 10:15, so she put the spelling book down and picked up the English text. Then she turned to her fourth-grade class and said, "Boys and girls put your spelling books away and take out your English book. Today we are going to study the agreement between a subject pronoun and the verb of a sentence. Think about this sentence, 'The birds fly.' Does it remind you of anything that we studied last week?" Michael raised his hand and responded, "It's like the subject and verb in a sentence must agree." "Good answer Michael. Are the subject and verb singular or plural in this sentence?" One of the students replied that they were plural. Then Rose asked them to make the sentence singular. She asked the students to think of reasons that a pronoun subject and a verb needed to agree. Several of the children recognized that pronouns replace nouns, and therefore, a pronoun and a verb would have to agree just like a noun and a verb. After this discussion, Rose told her students to look at the practice exercises in the textbook. After one of the students read the directions aloud and they practiced some example sentences, the students were given 20 minutes to complete the assignment.

INTEGRATED LANGUAGE ARTS VIGNETTE

In the classroom next door, David King told his fourth-grade students to get their writing folders from the file. After they sat down with their folders, he explained that they were to choose a piece from the folder to revise. He went on to explain that they were going to talk about noun and verb agreement, as well as sentence combining. Then he told the children to look at their compositions and select sentences that illustrated proper noun and verb agreement and to explain why the sentence showed noun and verb agreement. A number of the students read their sentences aloud and explained the noun and verb agreement. Most of them understood the concept after the discussion and they proceeded to revise any sentences that did not reflect correct noun and verb agreement.

Vignette Discussion

As you have already realized, the objective in each vignette was to develop student understanding of noun and verb agreement and pronoun and verb agreement. In the first vignette, the teacher was giving the students instruction in grammar knowledge and she was teaching process when the students filled in the correct answer in the exercise. The teacher was using the **separate subjects approach.** Implementing **integrated English language arts instruction,** the teacher in the second vignette taught grammar knowledge as well, and he provided experience with language arts processes through the students' compositions. In subsequent sections, these approaches to English instruction are explained in greater detail.

WHAT DO ENGLISH LANGUAGE ARTS TEACHERS NEED TO KNOW?

Recently the National Council of Teachers of English established a committee to identify teachers' qualifications for teaching the English Language Arts (NCTE, 1986). Following is a listing of these qualifications.

Knowledge

1. That growth in language maturity is a developmental process.

2. How students develop in understanding and using language.

3. How speaking, listening, writing, reading, and thinking are interrelated.

4. How social, cultural, and economic environments influence language learning.

5. The processes and elements involved in the acts of composing in oral and written forms (e.g., considerations of subject, purpose, audience, point of view, mode, tone, and style).

6. Major developments in language history.

7. Major grammatical theories of English.

8. How people use language and visual images to influence the thinking and actions of others.

9. How students respond to their reading and how they interpret it.

10. How readers create and discover meaning from print, as well as monitor their comprehension.

11. An extensive body of literature and literary types in English and in translation.

12. Literature as a source for exploring and interpreting human experience—its achievements, frustrations, foibles, values, and conflicts.

13. How nonprint and nonverbal media differ from print and verbal media.

14. How to evaluate, select, and use an array of instructional materials and equipment that can help students perform instructional tasks, as well as understand and respond to what they are studying.

15. Evaluative techniques for describing students' progress in English.

16. The uses and abuses of testing instruments and procedures.

17. Major historical and current research findings in the content of the English curriculum.

Pedagogy

1. Select, design, and organize objectives, strategies, and materials for teaching English language arts.

2. Organize students for effective whole-class, small-group, and individual work in English language arts.

3. Use a variety of effective instructional strategies appropriate to diverse cultural groups and individual learning styles.

4. Employ a variety of stimulating instructional strategies that aid students in their development of speaking, listening, reading, and writing abilities.

5. Ask questions at varying levels of abstraction that elicit personal responses, as well as facts and inferences.

6. Respond constructively and promptly to students' work.

7. Assess student progress and interpret it to students, parents, and administrators.

8. Help students develop the ability to recognize and use oral and written language appropriate in different social and cultural settings.

9. Guide students in experiencing and improving their processes of speaking, listening, and writing for satisfying their personal, social, and academic needs and intentions.

10. Guide students in developing an appreciation for the history, structure, and dynamic quality of the English language.

11. Guide students in experiencing and improving their processes of reading for personal growth, information, understanding, and enjoyment.

12. Guide students toward enjoyment, aesthetic appreciation, and critical understanding of literary types, styles, themes, and history.

13. Guide students toward enjoyment and critical understanding of nonprint forms.

14. Help students make appropriate use of computers and other emerging technologies to improve their learning and performance.

15. Help students use oral and written language to improve their learning.

Attitudes

1. A recognition that all students are worthy of a teacher's sympathetic attention in the English language arts classroom.

2. A desire to use the English language arts curriculum for helping students become familiar with diverse peoples and cultures.

3. A respect for the individual language and dialect of each student.

4. A conviction that teachers help students grow by encouraging creative and responsible uses of language.

5. A willingness to seek a match between students' needs and teachers' objectives, methods, and materials for instruction in English language arts.

6. A willingness to respond critically to all the different media of communication and a willingness to encourage students to respond critically.

7. A commitment to continued professional growth in the teaching of English language arts.

8. A pride in the teaching of English language arts and a willingness to take informed stands on current issues of professional concern.

9. A sensitivity to the impact that events and developments in the world outside the school may have on teachers, their colleagues, their students, and the English language arts curriculum.

The knowledge, skills (pedagogy), and attitudes identified by the National Council of Teachers of English are addressed throughout this book. These qualifications will enable teachers to effectively teach the English language arts. The model shown in Figure 2.1 illustrates the processes that comprise the English language arts.

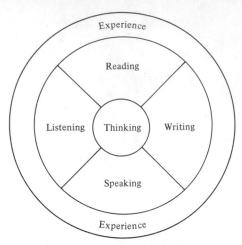

Figure 2.1 Processes that Comprise the English Language Arts

DESIGNING ENGLISH LANGUAGE ARTS INSTRUCTION _____

Language arts instruction is concerned with giving students meaningful situations for learning and applying language arts skills. The instructional content includes language arts knowledge and processes organized around objectives or instructional focus points. Language arts processes can be applied to many types of content since the content is not inherent to the process. Thus, the students' own language and children's literature are often sources of the content. The instruction used to develop these processes can be presented in several ways. Four approaches appear most frequently in contemporary schools—integrated, separate subjects, whole language, and a combination of the preceding. These instructional approaches are discussed in the following sections.

Integrated English Language Arts Instruction _____

What is integrated language arts instruction? Instruction refers to the procedures or actions that teachers use to help students learn. **Integrated English language arts instruction** is child centered. It is based on the concept that speaking, listening, reading, and writing are interrelated and reciprocal (Brown, 1973; Halliday, 1975; Dale, 1976; Harste, Burke, and Woodward, 1981). Instruction in one language process enhances the learning of the other language processes (Chomsky, 1972; Boutwell, 1983; Squire, 1983). Children do not develop one aspect of language independently of the others. Reading is learned through appropriate oral and written activities; writing is learned by attending to reading as a writer would—composing orally, reading drafts to peers, and engaging in related activities. Oral language is learned in the context of rich opportunities for receiving and producing written language (Wagner, 1985). An integrated approach is a holistic approach which addresses language as a whole rather than dividing it into smaller discrete parts.

Holdaway says that the language arts flow naturally one into the other in integrated instruction (Holdaway, 1979).

Characteristically, integrated instruction gives children opportunities to interact as they develop language skills. Language skills develop as children make sense of their world. They listen to others, talk with others, read language, and write language as they make sense of their world. In an integrated approach, learners and their interests are the focus of instruction. "Integrating the language arts means providing natural learning situations in which reading, writing, speaking and listening can be developed together for real purposes and real audiences" (Wagner, 1985).

Earlier in this chapter you read two vignettes. The teacher in the second one demonstrated integrated language arts instruction. This teacher used the students' writings to teach grammar (noun and verb agreement) and revision. The students read their own compositions, identified sentences that exemplified noun and verb agreement, read the sentences aloud, and explained why they demonstrated pronoun and verb agreement. They listened to one another explain their sentences. They wrote as they revised their compositions. Thus, the students were speaking, listening, reading, and writing.

In Chapter One, Terry clearly demonstrated the integrated curriculum in the first-grade vignette. Language arts skills were developed in an interrelated manner as the children talked about monsters, listened to stories about monsters, read about monsters, wrote about monsters, and created monsters through various media. In fact, Wagner (1985) suggests that "a good way to integrate language arts is to focus on something else—the study of flight, or cats, or the water cycle, or energy-giving foods, or Boston in 1773 for example." She also suggests that "when focusing on something other than language, the teacher needs to provide an environment rich with resources for making language connections."

Instruction like that described in the preceding paragraphs gives children opportunities to make language connections. For example, if they have opportunities to dictate stories and observe their teacher writing their words, then they can read what the teacher has written. Language connections are promoted when students have opportunities to discuss ideas and concepts before reading, when they have questions to guide their reading, writing, and research, when they participate in editing and peer editing of writing, and when they discuss common experiences, role playing, and classroom drama.

Scheduling Integrated Language Arts Instruction   Integrated language arts instruction takes place in schools where scheduling provides for long periods of speaking, listening, reading, and writing. Teachers in these schools model the integration of language arts as they engage in these activities with their students. They often write with their students, read with their students, listen to their students, and converse with their students. Language flourishes in settings where children are exposed to mature language models (Graves, 1984). A daily schedule for an integrated language arts program might look like the following.

8:30 Introductory activities, greet students

8:45 Language arts including speaking, listening, reading, and writing (grammar, spelling, and handwriting are taught during this period)

10:30 Physical education

10:45 Social studies/science/health

12:00 Lunch

1:00 Read to students (carefully selected literature)

1:25 Mathematics

2:15 Break/recess

2:30 Music/art

3:00 Dismissal

Integrated Instruction Research   Research regarding the effect of interrelated language arts instruction is sparse. However, Hillocks (1984) reports that integrated instruction improves achievement. Read (1971) and Bissex (1980) report observations of children that support the belief that children learn language in natural contexts for their own purposes. Graves (1984) demonstrated that children learn to read through writing. Studies by King and Rental (1981) and Clay (1975) demonstrate the relationship between reading, writing, and oral language. Veatch (1978) found that language arts activities, including creative writing, influenced reading achievement. Stauffer and Pikulski (1974) produced significant improvement in students' writing through increased use of oral language and reading. They provided students with opportunities to dictate stories, to hear stories, and to reread stories they had created. Research supports the contention that students have stronger motivation to write, more ideas to write about, and greater success in writing when composition is taught in conjunction with other language arts activities (Weaver, 1978). Disabled readers can also experience success when they have opportunities to speak, dictate stories, listen to stories, and write their own stories (Stoodt, 1985). Further research is needed to determine the value of integrated language arts instruction.

Integrating Language Arts with Content   Language arts can be integrated with other subjects in the elementary curriculum (Busching and Lundsteen, 1983). This seems to be a logical approach. After all, since children must speak, read, write, and listen about something, why not use language to learn content area concepts? In this approach, children have opportunities to use language in meaningful contexts. Integration is both efficient and effective because one subject matter aids in learning another (Roehler, 1983). Certainly, the fifth-grade vignette in Chapter One exemplified this approach.

Strengths and Weaknesses of Integrated Instruction _____

The strengths of integrated English instruction are varied. For instance, it is a natural approach that is very similar to the way that children acquire language during the early years of life. This instruction is related to the fact that speaking, listening, reading, and writing are interrelated even when they are not taught in an integrated fashion. Students must use all of the language arts to complete their assignments. Focusing on the interrelatedness of the language arts permits teachers to design instruction that fits the developmental stages of their students. Integrated instruction is based on children's interests and experiences, as well as authentic purposes for language use. Children's literature plays an important role in this approach since teachers often rely on children's trade books for reading content and discussion, and as models for writing. Elementary language arts textbooks also contain many references to literature. The role of literature in language arts instruction will be discussed in Chapter Eight.

However, there are some weaknesses. One of the most formidable weaknesses is the demand that integrated instruction places on teachers. This instructional approach is predicated on the notion of a well-prepared teacher who has planning time and a wealth of materials readily available. The longer blocks of scheduled language arts time are difficult to obtain in some schools. In spite of the fact that integrated instruction is a natural approach, some children do not have success with it.

Separate Subjects Approach to Language Arts Instruction _____

A **separate subjects approach** to language arts instruction is at the opposite end of the continuum from integrated language arts instruction. Students are taught the separate subjects that comprise the language arts. Proponents of this approach contend that the subprocesses of English are in operation even when they are not apparent. Instruction is based on specific learning objectives which determine what the learner will do. "The focal point of instruction is the 'content' of language as stated by the objectives" (Hemphill, 1981). An example of such an objective is, "Each student will correctly write the initial letter *d* in the words *do* and *dog* and the initial letter *c* in the words *cat* and *can.*"

After students learn the skills comprising the separated subjects included in the English curriculum, they have many opportunities to practice these skills. The goal of practice is to enable students to integrate English skills into a *process.* Students need many opportunities to practice the English skills, so they can integrate them without conscious attention. In many instances this practice occurs in workbooks, work that the students copy from textbooks or the chalkboard, and photocopied exercises. In addition, many computer materials present English content for skills practice.

Separate Subjects Schedule   Ordinarily a separate subjects approach to instruction is organized around language arts subject areas; however, this organization is not essential to a separate subjects approach. The classroom schedule in a separate subjects approach is planned around periods of time designated for the study of specific subject areas. A sample separate subjects schedule is shown below.

8:30 Introductory activities

8:45 Reading

9:45 Spelling

10:00 Social studies

10:30 Physical education or recess

10:45 Handwriting

11:00 Grammar

11:15 Writing (composition)

11:45 Lunch

12:45 Read to students

1:00 Mathematics

2:00 Science

2:30 Art (M, W, F and Music T, Th)

Separate Subjects Research   Most of the data regarding separate subjects instruction has been gathered in direct instruction research projects. Brophy and Good (1986) show that teachers can enhance academic growth through direct instruction. In reading, research shows clearly that teaching phonics skills increases achievement (Anderson et al., 1985).

Strengths and Weaknesses of Separate Subjects Instruction

Separate subjects instruction has strengths. First, it can be based on children's interests and experiences and on children's literature. Separate instruction fits into the direct instruction model, which has a proven success rate. In this approach, teachers can focus on fewer objectives at a time rather than coordinating many skills at once. They can teach the skills students need gradually and give them opportunities to practice and review these skills.

Perhaps the most significant weakness of separate subjects instruction is the fact that this approach fragments the language arts. It does not help children understand the interrelatedness of the language arts. This factor may inhibit children's language development. The separate subjects approach is subject centered rather than child centered, which some authorities assert will stifle children (Schweinhart et al., 1986). Separate subjects instruction also tends to focus on the text rather than on teacher creativity; hence, students can end up reading the language of others and filling in blanks in workbooks rather than composing their own written language.

Whole Language Approach

According to the proponents of the whole language approach to English instruction it focuses on meaningful, active learning. This approach is simply a variation of the integrated approach. It has been articulated by such scholars as Smith (1978), Goodman and Goodman (1979), Graves (1984), and Moffett and Wagner (1983). Although, conceptions of a whole language program vary from researcher to researcher (DeFord, 1981; DeStefano, 1981). The principles of whole language instruction reflect effective language instruction. Furthermore, it is difficult to find distinctions between integrated language arts instruction and whole language instruction. The following list summarizes the basic tenets of whole language instruction.

1. A totally integrated approach to language instruction.

2. Focus on students' experiences and interests. Students self-select materials that have special meaning.

3. Students engage in writing regularly; they write about topics that are meaningful and interesting to them. Students' compositions become an integral part of the language arts program.

4. Students engage in oral language activities more frequently than they do in traditional classrooms.

5. Teachers are language models who participate in classroom language activities and read to children regularly.

6. The teacher as a researcher who observes students' learning as a basis for developing generalizations about how children learn the language arts.

A Combination Language Arts Program

Each approach to language arts instruction is valuable and has been successful with many students, while failing with some others. For example, integrated language arts instruction that encourages children to write about the ideas and vocabulary presented in reading clearly advances comprehension (Wittrock, 1975). Children read and understand ideas best when they have listened and talked about the ideas included in the written content. Actually, it is literally impossible to separate the language arts, even when they are taught as separate subjects. Integration occurs because children listen, talk, read, and write in each separate subject. Language permeates the school day. Children listen to gather information, they talk to express their ideas to others, they read to gain ideas and concepts, and they write to share their ideas with others.

Nevertheless, there are times when teachers should plan direct instruction to teach specific skills students need to develop in order to communicate effectively. For instance, many children must learn to capitalize appropriate words in sentences, to use appropriate punctuation marks when writing, and to decode words in reading content. Experienced teachers have found that achievement is enhanced when needed skills are taught directly to the students. They also benefit from opportunities to apply these skills to their own language activities in the longer periods of uninterrupted work that characterize an integrated approach to instruction. The theme of this text, therefore, is to combine the best aspects of each instructional approach to help students learn effectively.

A combination approach to language arts instruction provides both a student centered focus and an emphasis on developing communication skills. The learning activities center on broad areas of interest that make the most of the existing relationships among the language arts. However, this program includes teaching students specific skills that will help them use language processes most effectively. For example, Terry's monster unit represented a broad area of interest that focused on the interrelated language arts. Although this was not discussed in depth in the vignette, in actual practice Terry used direct skills instruction derived from the teacher's edition of the basal reading series to teach the students decoding skills. The students completed a few practice exercises so she could determine whether they understood the principle she was teaching. Then Terry guided them as they applied the skill in decoding unknown words occurring in the trade books they were reading. After the children wrote their own thoughts about monsters, the revising and editing process gave Terry an opening to teach punctuation skills that the children could apply in all of their writing. This enhanced their understanding of punctuation in the written language they read.

Instruction that develops language arts skills identified in the curriculum may be based on materials from the teacher's edition of a text and/or the student's edition of a language arts series (such as the page shown in Figure 2.2). Of course, it is important to transfer these skills to children's own language and the bulk of skill practice should take place with the students' language and be based on activities that they find interesting and meaningful.

Examination of Figure 2.2, a second-grade teacher's edition page reveals that the objective is: "Capitalize titles and initials and follow them with a period." This is a common objective for second-grade students and this skills centered, separate subject material can be coordinated with an integrated approach to instruction. The teacher could use the suggested lesson up to the point of *Follow-up.* Then the teacher might ask students to complete the exercise provided in the text or the students could practice by writing their parents' names with appropriate titles. Then the students could examine trade books and their own writings to find additional instances of this skill.

Research and Language Arts Instruction   In addition to the research related to integrated language arts and to separate subjects instruction, researchers have explored other aspects of language arts and instruction. A summary and analysis of this research supports the following conclusions.

Teaching

Objective

- Capitalize titles and initials and follow them with a period.

Motivation

Ask volunteers what their middle names are. Write each child's entire name on the board, using an initial for the middle name. Point out the initial, and explain to the class that parts of people's names can be written in this way. Pupils will learn about this in today's lesson.

Lesson Sequence

Guide pupils as they read this lesson. Make sure they understand that *Dr.*, *Miss*, *Mr.*, *Ms.*, and *Mrs.* are titles. Ask whether they know how to pronounce the words for which *Dr.* and *Mr.* stand. Point out the example name, and have pupils explain why it is necessary to write this name with a period and three capital letters. Then write item 1 on the board, and have children tell where capitals are needed. Children can complete the exercise independently. You may wish to have some pupils work at the board as the class corrects the exercise together.

Follow-Up

Reteaching

Write the following names on the board: *Dr. Sam L. Lowen, Mr. George D. Sym, Ms. Ruth Brian, Mrs. Lowe.* Explain the use of each capital letter and period. Then erase the periods and replace the capital letters with lowercase letters. Have pupils come to the board and rewrite the names correctly.

Target Skill 8

- Capitalize titles and initials and follow them with periods.

---

15 Writing Titles and Initials

Titles of people begin with a capital letter.
A period comes at the end of most titles.
You do not need a period after **Miss** in a title.

[Dr. Roy] [Miss Ho] [Mr. Lee] [Ms. Gray] [Mrs. Poe]

An **initial** takes the place of a person's name.
An initial is always a capital letter.
A period comes after each initial.

[Tara B. Day]   [R. J. Diaz]

Tara Betty Day   Robert John Diaz
Tara B. Day   R. J. Diaz

Write these titles and names correctly.

- dr nan ross

  Dr. Nan Ross

2. mr lin l chu

4. mrs jan orn

1. miss rita cruz

3. ms sue more

5. mr ted huff

60   Grammar/Mechanics: Writing Titles and Initials

Additional Activities *for Lesson 16*

Easy   Write the following incomplete sentences on the board: *My name is _____ . My address is _____ . The name of my school is _____ .* Have volunteers come to the board and complete the sentences. Be sure pupils use capital letters correctly.

&

Additional Resources

- *Related Activities* Teacher's Edition pages 45A-B
- **Workbook** page 29
- **Test and Practice Masters**
  Practice Master 18
- **Teacher's Resource Book**
  Extra Practice Worksheets 8a, 8b, 8c
  Reteaching Chart 8

Figure 2.2   Language Arts Textbook Exercise

Source: Ronald Cramer et al., *Language: Skills and Use*, 2d ed., TE, Grade 2, pp. 59 and 60. Copyright © 1986 by Scott, Foresman and Company. Reprinted by permission.

1. The language processes are developmental. They grow gradually over a period of years (Chall, 1983).

2. Balanced attention to all of the language arts is critical. Speaking and listening are traditionally neglected in schools. Reading instruction has tended to overwhelm the other language arts. In recent years, writing has begun to attract the attention it merits.

3. It is important for writing experience to occur early in children's schooling. Graves has demonstrated that the average first grader is capable of two or three pieces of independent writing per week (1973). Even kindergarten children can express their thoughts in writing (Stoodt, 1985).

4. Language arts can be developed across all curricular areas. Students can develop language arts skills as they study social studies, science, mathematics, and so on. They can use language arts skills to learn content in the curricular areas.

5. Thematic units offer children opportunities to repeatedly use a core of concepts and vocabulary terms in reading, writing, speaking, and listening over a period of weeks. In this approach to instructional planning, the basic thematic ideas serve, in effect, as advance organizers for the instructional activity that is to follow (Squire, 1983).

THE INSTRUCTIONAL CYCLE

Figure 2.3 illustrates the instructional cycle that has been derived from research in teaching and learning (Wittrock, 1986).

The first instructional function in the cycle is *reviewing and checking homework* which includes reteaching any skills and knowledge that are necessary.

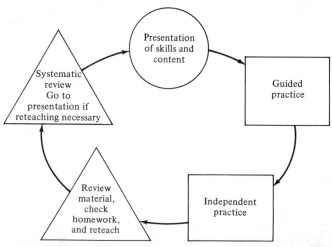

Figure 2.3   The Instructional Cycle

The second function is *presentation* of the content or skills that are to be learned. Effective presentations have the following characteristics: identification of objectives, clarity of presentation, highlighting of main points, and demonstrations when appropriate. Students should understand exactly what they are to do and why. After the presentation the teacher provides *guided practice,* answers questions and checks students' understanding. During this phase of instruction, the teacher should make sure that every student has an opportunity to respond. Teachers use informal assessment such as observation and checklists to monitor student progress. Guided practice continues long enough to permit students to gain independence. Throughout the instructional cycle, teachers should give students feedback so they can repeat what they are doing right and correct any systematic errors. Students should receive specific praise for behavior that meets the lesson's objectives. General praise does not tell students what they have done well and therefore should continue doing. After students demonstrate the desired knowledge or skill, they should have *independent practice* that is directly relevant to the skills or content taught. Following independent practice, the teacher reviews the material and *checks homework* if it was assigned. Homework review should be followed with reteaching if this appears necessary. Finally teachers should provide *systematic review* of previously learned material. Assessment of skills and knowledge during reviews and on tests reveals material that needs to be retaught.

English language arts instruction should incorporate the knowledge acquired from effective teaching research. The following section summarizes this research as it relates to the instructional cycle.

Direct Instruction

Overwhelming support exists for direct teaching of skills and concepts (Rosenshine, 1979). "Direct instruction means an academic focus, precise sequencing of content, high pupil engagement, careful teacher monitoring and specific corrective feedback to students" (Duffy and Roehler, 1982). "In direct instruction, the teacher, in a face-to-face, reasonable formal manner, tells, shows, models, demonstrates, teaches the skill to be learned. The key word here is *teacher,* for it is the teacher who guides the learning situation and leads the lesson, as opposed to having instruction 'directed' by a worksheet, kit, learning center, or workbook." Teachers may provide direct instruction to the entire class or to individuals through conferences. Most of the behaviors attributed to effective teachers are included in the direct instruction paradigm. Teaching functions identified by researchers and included in the instructional cycle are:

Review the previous day's work and/or homework and reteach as necessary

Present the new content and skills

Guide student practice with feedback

Independent practice

Periodic reviews (including tests)

When initiating a lesson, make certain that the students understand its purpose and the exact nature of the task. Building background information, introducing vocabulary, establishing reading purposes, and explaining the nature of the expected outcomes helps students understand what they must do to complete the task. When students understand why they are doing a task, they become active participants in the learning process.

Direct instruction usually focuses on teaching skills and textbooks are frequently used. However, teachers can use direct instruction when integrating language arts instruction. They focus on students' experiences, needs, and interests, which creates student centered instruction. Students can discuss, listen, read, and write during direct instruction rather than fill in blanks on worksheets.

Academic Engaged Time

Another concept emerging from effective teaching research is academic engaged time. Academic engaged time refers to quality time—the time when students are actively engaged in learning. Classrooms in which students are actively engaged in learning for a large proportion of time are characterized by high achievement in basic skills (Rosenshine and Berliner, 1978). The essential ingredient is *involvement.* Students have to be involved with the teacher or with the content. The more time students spend in direct contact with the teacher, the better their chances of learning the material. The time that students spend engaged in learning should be devoted to listening, speaking, reading, and writing. This enables students to practice the language arts which is important since students need both instruction and opportunities to use their language skills.

The fact that spending more time on learning results in greater achievement seems obvious since we are more likely to learn what we are taught. However, each of us can attest to the fact that we have at some time failed to learn what we were taught. In some classrooms, students spend too much time waiting for the teacher to get organized, or waiting for the teacher to reprimand students who are misbehaving. Children who are completing seat work while the teacher directly instructs a reading group are not actively engaged in learning. In fact, you would find it very useful to select one child in a classroom and follow that youngster for a day to learn exactly how many minutes the student is actively engaged in a learning situation. The outcome will surprise you.

Questioning

Teachers use questioning strategies to actively engage students in learning. "Talking—asking and answering questions—often reveals our thoughts and feelings to us as well as to others. This experience, in turn, clarifies our views and focuses our thinking" (Christenbury and Kelly, 1983). Questions are important teaching tools because they facilitate thinking. Students manifest their understanding of oral and written language when they respond to questions. Their answers to questions give teachers data that helps them know whether to reinforce students' answers or to help them rethink the situation. At times, students' answers reveal that they need more data in order to understand information or concepts. Far too often, both at home and in school, we behave as if talking and listening (or reading and writing) will automatically result in understanding (King, 1984). Questions help teachers identify whether communication has succeeded or failed.

During recent years educators have directed their attention to hierarchies of questioning based on the theory that questions formulated to represent various levels of thinking stimulated students to think at those same levels (Redfield and Rousseau, 1981; Christenbury and Kelly, 1983). Earlier researchers suggested that teachers spent too much time asking lower level questions implying that questions at certain cognitive levels were of greater value than others (Christenbury and Kelly, 1983). Recent research raises questions about strict adherence to hierarchies as a means of increasing learning (Winne, 1979).

QUESTIONING HIERARCHY

Instructional questions are often organized into hierarchies that reflect the levels of thinking because questions are used to promote students' thinking. Following is a simple hierarchy that is accompanied by sample questions.

Literal Level Questions

Literal questions address the information and meanings that the author or speaker explicitly state. The listener or reader must be able to comprehend the speaker's or author's meaning. At this level, the listener or speaker is concerned with the question *What did the author say?* Questions at this level are concerned with the identification and recall of main ideas and details. The listener or reader must reproduce meaning that is close to the author's intended meaning. Thus the listener or reader must have a thorough understanding of word, sentence, and paragraph meaning. Literal level questions can be answered by quoting directly from the content. The literal level of understanding is basic to understanding subsequent levels of questions.

Interpretive or Inferential Questions

Interpretive or inferential questions are at a higher level of understanding than literal questions. These questions are concerned with meanings that are *not* stated by the speaker or author. The speaker or author suggests and hints at ideas rather than states them directly, and the listener or reader must use background experiences to figure out what the speaker or writer intended to convey. In order to answer inferential questions, the listener or reader must relate facts, generalizations, definitions, values, and skills to the content that is heard or read. The answers to these questions are not always right or wrong because students' backgrounds vary, leading to varying answers.

Critical or Evaluative Questions

Critical or evaluative questions require listeners and readers to make judgments about the quality, value, and validity of the content being read. Evaluative thinking is very much dependent on the ability to think at the literal and inferential levels. Listeners and readers must evaluate the accuracy of content, synthesize information, make comparisons and inferences, and suspend judgment to avoid jumping to conclusions. Critical listeners and readers must be able to recognize the speaker's or author's purpose, point of view, and use of language. They must be able to distinguish fact from opinion. Critical listeners and readers should test the speaker's or author's assertions against their own observations, information, and logic.

Creative Questions

Creative questions are concerned with imaginative, original thinking that requires the reader to think beyond the lines of print. Creative listening and reading are efforts to use the information and ideas heard or read as a basis for arriving at new ways in which to view the world. Creative responses should reflect flexibility and open-mindedness. Creative students may be able to come up with several ways of solving a problem by synthesizing previous knowledge with new ideas and information.

Sample Questions

The sample questions are designed to be used with fourth-grade students. They are based on the book *Thor Heyerdahl—Viking Scientist* by Wyatt Blassingame (E. P. Dutton, 1979). The sample questions are derived from the part of this book that tells about the Kon-Tiki voyage from South America to the Polynesian Islands.

Literal questions

What was used to build the raft?

Why did Heyerdahl make the voyage?

What did the crew most fear on the voyage?

Inferential questions

Why did Heyerdahl feel responsible for the five men with him?

Why is the voyage compared to a scientific experiment?

Why do you think Thor Heyerdahl and his crew risked their lives to make the voyage?

Critical questions

Can you think of other men and women who have had adventures like those of Thor Heyerdahl?

Do these people have any unique characteristics? What are they?

What characteristics are essential to people who are so adventuresome?

Creative questions

Would you like to make a voyage or have an adventure like this one? Where would you go or what would you do?

Do you have an important dream?

The following guidelines are helpful to teachers who are preparing questions that will cause students to think.

1. Use questioning hierarchies as guidelines rather than adhering strictly to them. Using these guidelines, write out questions in advance. This is especially important for the novice teacher.

2. Before creating questions examine the content and identify the important ideas and concepts toward which you are guiding students. Then ask questions about these important ideas that will lead students to understand them.

3. Be flexible—do not expect the discussion to go exactly as you preplanned. Listen carefully to students making sure you hear their entire response. Sometimes their incorrect response is better than the one you expected. At times, students' answers will indicate their interests or concerns which the teacher may choose to explore with additional questions.

4. Ask questions that have more than one right answer (Spiegel, 1980). Questions having only right and wrong answers do not stimulate much thinking. The really stimulating questions are the ones that have several appropriate responses. These questions also give students more opportunities to experience success. Also, ask questions that require multiple word answers. Questions that require elaborate answers tend to foster both language development and cognitive development (Spiegel, 1980). When students offer one-word answers, encourage them to enlarge on their answers.

5. Encourage students to ask questions. Students should feel free to ask questions without fear of embarrassment. Teachers should not be afraid of departing from lesson plans in order to answer students' questions because their questions are worthy of attention. They also give teachers opportunities to tailor instruction to meet students' needs.

6. Allow sufficient "wait time." Hyman (1979) reports that teachers wait only one second for student to respond before asking another student to respond or restating the question. Insufficient "wait time" pressures students to answer to such a degree that they may give an incorrect answer when they knew the correct answer. Hyman (1979) notes that increasing the "wait time" from three to five seconds increases the quality of answers.

7. Avoid asking too many questions. Research shows that teachers who thought they were asking 12 to 20 questions every half-hour were actually asking 45 to 150. This appears to be more of an inquisition than a discussion. Such rapid-fire questioning discourages student participation.

8. Create an atmosphere that encourages students to discuss content with one another. Students should have opportunities to ask and answer each other's questions. Teachers have a tendency to dominate discussion, when student interaction is more appropriate.

INSTRUCTIONAL SCAFFOLDING

An instructional scaffold is an oral or written framework created as two or more individuals interact. In this instance, the scaffold is usually created by a teacher and student or students. The teacher makes statements or asks questions that cue the student to think and contribute to the framework of statements, questions, and answers. This type of interaction helps develop students' language knowledge. Following is a scaffolding script that occurred between a teacher and a second grader when the teacher developed the concept of opposites in sentences that were introduced in the English text.

T: Can you think of something that is the opposite of breakfast?

S: Is it lunch?

T: Can you think of something that is a meal that is farther from breakfast than lunch?

S: Do you mean, dinner?

T: Yes.

T: There are some sentences written on these cards. Read them and make up a sentence that is the opposite of the one on the card.

S: *(Reads)* "Our reports will be bad." *(Composes the sentence)* "Our reports will be good."

Scaffolding activities are usually related to problem-solving situations that involve reading and writing. A number of researchers have established scaffolding as an important aspect of language learning (Clark, 1976; Cross, 1978; Chall and Snow, 1982).

Instructional scaffolding is useful in writing. As teachers and students build scaffolds to solve problems, they can help students in selecting topics, sequencing ideas, or organizing a group of ideas. This kind of scaffolding can be developed through questions like: Which of these topics do you like the best or know the most about? What should come next in this story? What are your main ideas? What details will you use to support these ideas? What organization makes the most sense for presenting these details? Lehr (1985) describes a youngster who is discussing her paper on gorillas: "I don't want it to be just a pile of facts. The kids wouldn't like it and neither would I. But I don't know how to organize all of this." Statements like this help teachers understand the kinds of suggestions students need in order to develop language skills.

Children's learning flourishes in situations where they are allowed some degree of control over their own actions and where they can interact with adults who are receptive. Adults who are less concerned with rightness and wrongness, are more likely to respond to children in ways that stretch thinking. Both research and practice indicate that scaffolding can create opportunities that encourage children to stretch thinking and language.

LESSON PLANNING

Effective teachers plan carefully for teaching so they can make the most of the teaching–learning situations. Hunter (1977) points out that teachers who plan instruction that focuses on identified objectives increase student achievement. In addition, lesson plans help teachers meet individual needs and have successful, interesting lessons. Lesson plans help monitor students' progress. They enable teachers to use time more economically because planning eliminates last minute scrambling to locate materials.

At times teachers have to depart from plans to capitalize on immediate experiences and events; nevertheless, plans help teachers meet their responsibilities as educators. With a plan, teachers can depart from it and return to it, identifying skills that were slighted or that require reteaching or review. Lesson planning should be more detailed for novice teachers; experienced teachers usually need less detailed plans since they are familiar with the lessons. They do need to plan carefully and to identify the focus of their instruction as they continue to improve their teaching performance.

Although lesson plans differ from school to school, the following components, modeled after those introduced by Madeline Hunter (1977), are commonly found in lesson plans. After a discussion of lesson plan components, two sample lesson plans will be given.

Components of a Lesson Plan

Objectives are the first component of the lesson. Objectives should state precisely what students are to do, learn, and/or appreciate. Before teaching, the teacher must ask, "What is the learning objective?" "Where is the

Effective teachers plan carefully.

learner in relation to the learning objective?" "What must the learner do in order to learn this?"(Hunter, 1977). These questions help teachers focus on learning and on the students' state of readiness for acquiring skills or knowledge. The learning objective must be at the correct level of difficulty for the learner. Learning does not occur when lessons are too easy or too difficult. Prior knowledge determines to a great extent what learners should learn next.

The introduction is the second component of the lesson. Active participation of the learners is the goal of this component. In this part of the plan, the teacher states how to introduce the knowledge, skills, or attitudes to the students. The teacher may demonstrate the desired learning outcomes. For example, Anderson et al. (1979) increased reading achievement by presenting the pronunciation of new words. The introduction should motivate students to learn. Successful students generally are those who are highly motivated to learn (Hunter, 1967). The introduction includes ways of activating students' experiences in relation to the lesson, explaining what you are going to do, relating the content to the students' lives, and allowing students to familiarize themselves with the material. At times, novelty is important to introduce the lesson and arouse students' interest.

Actual instruction is the third basic component. This section includes the activities, discussion questions, and practice used to instruct, as well as any variations that are introduced to meet individual needs. Both guided and independent practice are included in this section. Planning the appropriate length for practice sessions is important because these sessions should be long enough to improve learning while maintaining attention. In the practice sessions that immediately follow learning, teachers should avoid fatigue and failure because this discourages students (Weisberg, 1986). The role of practice sessions is clear-cut in achieving effective instruction; massed practice is scheduled at the beginning, with a review in the middle of the lesson and at the end of the lesson (Weisberg, 1986). Follow-up practice is essential for retention (Hunter, 1977). Because the largest amount of forgetting occurs after the skill is no longer practiced, practice should occur on the day after a lesson is taught and on the third and fifth days after that. A lesson that is learned well and practiced regularly is not likely to be forgotten.

Materials that will be used by both teacher and students are listed in this section. This should include text references, trade books, games, practice activities, and materials that students will need, such as pencil and paper. To help students become proficient learners, materials should reflect the appropriate level of difficulty and address students' interests.

The closing section of the lesson plan is synthesis and evaluation. In synthesis, teacher and students review what they have learned. Synthesis creates a basis for evaluating the lesson which increases the effectiveness of students and teachers. When students have completed the planned instruction, the teacher should make them aware of how well they have learned. When students feel successful, they are motivated to learn. Evaluation also helps students realize those skills that require additional practice for mastery. Finally, the teacher should evaluate student progress toward the objectives because this will enable him or her to plan future lessons and to identify those skills that require reteaching.

A SECOND-GRADE LESSON PLAN

Objectives

The students will become aware of describing words.

They will extend their concepts of describing words.

They will identify describing words.

Introduction

Read the book *Swimmy* aloud. Prepare students to listen by giving them a silent reading purpose: Listen for words and phrases that tell how the characters looked and felt. Write the words and phrases identified on the chalkboard. Assign the students to pairs and have them take turns describing their toy or pet.

Have students identify words they used to describe. Write them on the chalkboard. Why do we need describing words? Give each student an apple. They are to eat and think of ways to describe what and how they feel as they eat an apple. Write apple descriptions.

Variation

Students who are not able to write may dictate or record their descriptions on the tape recorder.

Materials

Apples, chalk, paper, pencils.

Synthesis and Evaluation

After the students complete writing the description of their apples, collect them, and read them over quickly to determine whether the students have achieved the objectives. Review the concept of describing words and the uses of describing words. When reading to the children note the use of descriptive words to reinforce the concept. On subsequent days, students may look at trade books, personal journals, and basal readers for additional examples of descriptive words.

A FIFTH-GRADE LESSON PLAN

Objectives

To learn what action verbs are.

To identify action verbs.

To use action verbs in writing.

Introduction

Silently read *It's About Time* by Miriam Schlein. Silent reading question: What does this selection have to do with doing things? Students identify the activities they read about. Identify the words and phrases that tell about the activities. Write their responses on the chalkboard and underline the verbs. Ask them to explain what the underlined words tell. Ask them to read a paragraph in the reading selection omitting these words. What happens? Why are these words so important? Guide them to the understanding that action verbs are very important in listening, speaking, reading, and writing because they make our language more lively and interesting. Understanding and using them will make our language more interesting.

Instruction

Tell students to take out their personal journals and find three action verbs in them. Ask some of the students to read their sentences aloud. As they read, have the class point out action verbs. Explain that an action verb shows what the subject does or did. Ask them to identify the part of the sentence in which the action verb is found (subject, predicate, object). Stress the fact that the main word in the predicate is the verb and that most verbs are action verbs. Ask students to add a paragraph to their personal journal. After they complete the paragraph, ask them to identify the action verb in each sentence. Ask students to change their action verbs to passive. What happens?

Materials

Students' personal journals, chalk, chalkboard.

Synthesis and Evaluation

Ask students to select their best example of an action verb to share with the class. Students who have difficulty will complete the exercises in the text. Observe their personal journals to see that they use verbs appropriately.

SELECTING AND USING INSTRUCTIONAL MATERIALS

Among the curriculum decisions that language arts teachers must make is the choice of instructional materials. As we noted earlier, teachers use many different materials to teach the language arts. These materials must be carefully evaluated since they are used for instruction. Appropriate instructional materials reflect the adopted language arts curriculum, as well as the needs and interests of the students who will use them. The difficulty level of such materials should be appropriate to the students. Furthermore, instructional materials should avoid racial, sexual, and age bias. Unfortunately, some teachers assume that instructional materials were created by authorities in the field; therefore they do not require critical appraisal. The fact that published materials bear the name of an expert does not insure that they will meet the needs of an individual teacher or of a class of children.

Textbooks

Textbooks certainly are an important aspect of most English curricula. Language arts textbooks lend themselves to many instructional uses. Perhaps very capable teachers who have unlimited time and a large variety of instructional materials at their disposal do not need textbooks. But the majority of teachers do not have these resources, and some do not have the education or the experience that permits them to teach without textbooks. Textbooks are not innately "good" or "bad"; teaching without a text is not automatically "good." The text is not the entire program, but rather only one aspect of the total language arts program. A carefully selected textbook can be valuable to the language arts program, especially when a thoughtful teacher tailors it to the individual children in his or her classroom. Textbooks are only one of the materials that teachers use for language arts instruction. Textbooks save time and effort for teachers, freeing them to concentrate on other tasks.

English (language arts) textbooks have strengths to contribute to the curriculum. They can provide an organized, sequential instructional program with a scope and sequence for the language arts curriculum, as well as the supporting materials needed to deliver instruction. Supportive materials may include the activities and practice materials that help students master language arts skills. A well developed language arts text stimulates children to become active language users. Many English textbooks have attractive, novel content that motivates students.

Language arts textbooks also have limitations. They can easily become the entire program themselves unless teachers plan carefully to incorporate many types of materials into language arts instruction. Textbooks do not teach themselves; teachers must fit the lessons to the students in their classrooms. The authors of the textbook have not seen the individual students in a given classroom, so a teacher's education and experience help him or her fit the text to the experiences, strengths, and weaknesses of specific students. Teaching ideas and activities are merely suggestions, a smorgasbord of ideas, so to speak. Teachers must choose those that are most appropriate to their students. Specific textbooks may have shortcomings that make them particularly difficult to teach; therefore, evaluation of language arts textbooks is very important.

Evaluating Language Arts Textbooks   Following is a guide for evaluating English textbooks. This guide may be converted into a checklist and the user may choose to assign points to the various categories as an aid in identifying appropriate instructional materials.

1. What is the copyright date of the materials? Instructional materials are often used for five to seven years; therefore, selecting materials that are already dated means that they will soon be out-of-date.

2. Who wrote the materials? Are the authors experts in the field of English?

3. Do the materials reflect an integrated philosophy of the language arts?

4. Do the materials stress interaction in lifelike situations as a means of developing children's language?

5. Does the content incorporate children's literature?

6. Is the content appropriate to the students' cognitive development, interests, experiences, and language development?

7. Is the language in the students' books clear and natural?

8. Are the language arts balanced in these materials? (Are speaking, listening, reading, and writing stressed equally?)

9. Do the materials encourage creative approaches such as students making up their own statements rather than filling in blanks or completing multiple choice items?

10. Do the materials relate language arts to the content areas?

11. Is the instructional cycle apparent in these materials? (Introduction, practice, evaluation, reteaching when necessary)

12. Does the teacher's manual include suggestions that aid teachers in meeting individual needs?

13. Does the teacher's manual include appropriate teaching methods?

Workbooks

Workbooks and duplicator materials that accompany language arts textbooks are intended to furnish students with opportunities to practice language skills. Practice materials tend to stress correctness of the mechanical skills because practice exercises for these skills are easier to develop than are integrated language activities. Thus, skills such as punctuation, capitalization, usage, and spelling are stressed in practice materials. However, many teachers and language arts authorities believe that these skills are best developed in a functional manner when children are expressing their own ideas through oral and written language for authentic purposes. Whether a workbook can offer actual communication activities that enable students to attain these objectives is a hotly debated question. Admittedly, all teachers experience days when they have difficulty creating interesting, motivating language situations for children. On those days a workbook would be welcome. Teachers can use workbook activities as seatwork with students while they are giving direct instruction to other students. In this instance workbooks may be a better option than some of the usual activities. They are certainly more valuable than some of the faded ditto sheets seen in classrooms.

Workbooks do not have to be difficult, boring, and uninteresting. Workbook activities do not have to be "fill in the blank" or multiple choice; they can be designed to stimulate whole language activities. For example, one fourth-grade language arts workbook suggests that students pretend they are visiting a foreign country and think of what they would say to the first people they met. They are to write a statement, a question, an exclamation, and a command that they would include in their conversation.

In research dealing primarily with reading workbooks, Osborn (1984) identified guidelines for workbook tasks that will help language arts teachers. The following guidelines are based on Osborn's and on Owen's (1986) research.

1. Workbooks should support and strengthen language arts curriculum objectives.

2. Workbooks should furnish appropriate practice materials.

3. Workbooks should incorporate adequate review materials.

4. The language of the workbook should be consistent with the rest of the program and the students who are using it.

5. Instructions to students should be clear, concise, and easy to follow.

6. Students should be able to complete workbook activities independently.

7. Workbook content should be accurate.

8. Workbook content should be interesting.

9. The instructional design of workbook tasks should be carefully planned to avoid confusion.

10. Students should be able to understand what, how, and why they are doing an activity.

Using English Textbooks and Workbooks

Textbooks and workbooks are generally as good as the teachers who are using them. Well-prepared teachers use textbooks and workbooks as reference materials rather than as the total language arts program. They avoid a "cookbook" approach of following the book and the teacher's manual page by page. Covering every page and completing every activity does not necessarily lead to mastering language skills. As children use language, teachers often note areas needing improvement. Then they can refer students to specific materials and exercises in the text or the workbook that will help them overcome these problems.

Teachers can use textbooks to implement the language arts curriculum. They can achieve this through comparing the scope and sequence of the text with those of their curriculum to determine the match between the two. This analysis may reveal that the teacher will need to supplement the text in order to help students achieve the objectives stipulated in local curricula. A case in point is a language arts text that did not identify and introduce the steps to report writing at the fifth-grade level, although the local curricula required that students write several reports. After the teacher noted this discrepancy, he located supplemental materials to develop these skills.

Teachers often discover that they must change the sequence for introducing knowledge, skills, and attitudes in the text in order to implement the curriculum guide. Of course, textbooks should be flexible enough for teachers to make such changes. There is no research to support the notion that any one sequence for introducing language arts curriculum leads to better achievement than another. Teachers should be free to modify the knowledge, skills, and attitudes that they will stress, and the sequence for introducing them. They should choose explanations, activities, and practice materials from the text that are appropriate to their language arts curriculum and their students. They may choose to omit inappropriate aspects of the text and/or accompanying practice materials. Teachers should also capitalize on the opportunities to develop language skills that arise naturally in the classroom. For example, students may bring pets to school, they may share a cocoon found in the yard at home, or the teacher may read a book that arouses children's interests in other books by the same author. Each of these incidents is a natural language situation that is superior to the contrived situations in many textbooks.

Content area textbooks and instructional materials are resources for teaching English also. Content materials are excellent sources of authentic language activities. Students learn the language arts as they participate in debates, discuss social studies and science issues, write descriptions of experiments, and read literature that helps them understand other times and places. Listening, speaking, reading, and writing operate in every area of the curriculum.

Guidelines for Using Textbooks   Many beginning and some experienced teachers find it difficult to know how much time and attention to spend on the language arts textbook. Not everything in the language arts textbook deserves the same amount of attention. In many classes, there is no way to work everything in the textbook into the school year. Furthermore, you will want to include things that are not in the textbook. The following guidelines for using a language arts textbook are based on ones developed by

1. Survey the textbook, identifying the major concepts developed.

2. Rate each chapter or lesson using this scale:
   a. Crucial
   b. Important
   c. Desirable
   d. Helpful

3. Make a rough estimate of the amount of time you believe is appropriate for each chapter. Should you decide to cover three chapters the first nine weeks, then decide how many weeks to devote to each chapter. One chapter may be worth five weeks, a second three, and a third only one.

4. Determine which chapter to begin the year with. Chapter One isn't necessarily the best. Choose something that will motivate students and stimulate their interest in language, as well as one that an inexperienced teacher can teach comfortably while managing the pupils. Avoid excessive skill and drill at the beginning of the year.

5. Determine the sequence of chapters at least until Christmas. Alternate crucial and/or important chapters with desirable and helpful ones.

6. Rate each activity in a chapter using this scale:
   a. Crucial
   b. Important
   c. Helpful
   d. Deletable

7. Use step 6 to proportion your estimated time allotment for this chapter. For example: Chapter 5 in a second-grade text—"Action Words."

Activity	Topic	Rating	Number of Days
1	Calling for help	Important	2
2	Action words	Crucial	2
3	Adding -ed	Deletable	0
4	Using *did, done, gave, given*	Crucial	2
5	Using *saw, seen, went, gone*	Helpful	1
6	Using *ran, run, came, come*	Important	2
6	Using *don't, doesn't, isn't, can't*	Deletable	0
8	Words that name noises	Helpful	1
Review		Important	2
	Total days		12

8. Plan for application activities in most of the chapters. The textbook is the "how to" part of instruction. Application is the use of textbook learnings in other areas of the curriculum, such as incorporating oral reports into science and social studies. Students can learn how to give oral reports in language arts class and actually give them in science and social studies. Application may occur simultaneously with study, immediately following study, or in the near future. Practice probably should occur at each of the times identified.

9. Finally, start to plan how to teach the activities. Introduce the lesson or chapter in an imaginative, interest-arousing way. Don't introduce a lesson or chapter by saying, "Open your textbooks to page 48." Use the textbook for practice or clarification—after introducing and explaining the lesson and providing guided practice.

Selecting Activities and Practice Materials

In addition to the workbooks and blackline duplicating masters that accompany published language arts textbooks, many language arts activities, practice materials, follow-up activities, and games are available for teachers to use. These materials play an important role in many classrooms. However, teachers should avoid using these materials as "busy work" or "time fillers." Teachers should carefully examine and use them only when they give students appropriate reinforcement and practice of skills that are a part of the curriculum. Such activities should encourage students to become active learners. Faded duplicator materials that children can barely see are not appropriate for instruction. Teacher-made materials should be carefully constructed, all the words should be spelled correctly, and any artwork should be clear. Any language and instructions that the teacher writes should be clear and understandable. All practice materials, games, and so forth should be introduced to students with discussion, so students are motivated to complete the activities. Teachers should clarify, extend, and relate the ideas they are developing through these materials.

EVALUATION AND INSTRUCTION

Evaluation is designed to measure the progress of entire classes, or of individual students toward achieving curriculum goals. Evaluation helps teachers and administrators assess the success of the curriculum, of teaching materials, and of methods. Teachers use evaluation data to plan appropriate instruction, to grade students, and to alter instruction to meet students' needs.

Many strategies and instruments are available for evaluating students' progress in the language arts. Experienced teachers usually prefer to use data from several sources, rather than one test score, for evaluating students. Each instrument and strategy can contribute to our understanding of individual students and the entire class. However, only a limited number of instruments and strategies should be used with any individual student in order to avoid student frustration. We will evaluate these in the language arts processes chapters. A list of useful instruments and strategies is given below:

Standardized tests

Informal tests (includes those accompanying published English series, teacher-prepared tests, close procedures)

Diagnostic tests

Checklists (teacher prepared)

Scales (a sample to which the students' work is compared like a handwriting scale)

Conferences

File of each student's work

Systematic observation

Students' journals

Teachers' logs

The instructional cycle is based on teacher knowledge of students including their strengths and weaknesses. These data can be gathered from standardized instruments, observation, and the informal instruments accompanying a published English series. With these data in hand the teacher plans instruction for a student or students. Following instruction, the lesson is evaluated and the teacher determines whether reteaching is necessary.

The following example will help you understand the role of evaluation in teaching. Mary R. has taught fourth grade for the past four years. She has developed a helpful evaluation system. Mary keeps individual files of sample work for each student including an audio tape of each. Her students keep journals. She regularly administers the tests that accompany the adopted English series. Although she does not use all of the text or the workbook with her students, she uses the tests to assess how her students measure up to the curriculum. During the early part of the school year she uses a checklist to guide her observations. Mary's checklist is shown in Figure 2.4. As the year progresses, she finds the checklist is not necessary, although she does observe students continually and makes notes to help her memory.

As a result of analyzing her data, Mary realized that several of her students had serious difficulties with word meanings. They also exhibited problems with the meanings of words like: untidy, exhausted, elated, and fragile. Mary considers word use and word meaning very important skills in the fourth-grade language arts program. Therefore, she identified information and exercises in the textbook that might help these students refine their understanding of word meaning. She also planned to help them transfer the understandings and skills that they used in the exercises to their own reading, writing, and speaking.

SUMMARY

Integrated, separate subjects, whole language, and combination approaches to language arts instruction were examined in this chapter. The merits and the deficits of integrated instruction and subskills instruction were identified and

Name _____   Date _____

Observer _____

_____

Speaking
   voice   participation
   diction   thoughtful
   grammar & usage   vocabulary

Listening
   attention
   comprehension
   courtesy

Reading
   word recognition
   comprehension
   study skills

Writing
   prewriting   spelling
   composition   grammar
   revision   handwriting   Code: + good
   editing   − needs
                                              improvement

Figure 2.4   A Fourth-Grade Student Evaluation Checklist for English

discussed. The characteristics of effective instruction were explained including: review of previous instruction, presentation of new skills/learnings, guided practice, feedback and correction, independent practice, weekly and monthly reviews. Included in the discussion of effective teaching were direct instruction, academically engaged time, and questioning and discussion. The role of evaluation in planning instruction is discussed in the final section.

Thought Questions

1. Describe effective language arts instruction. What are some of the strategies that teachers can use to achieve effective instruction?

2. Explain the concept "academically engaged time."

3. Explain the concept "direct instruction."

4. How can lesson plans help teachers become more effective?

5. How is evaluation useful for both students and teachers?

6. Discuss the stages of teacher development and identify ways to help teachers grow into professionals.

Enrichment Activities

1. Examine the language arts textbook used in a local school district. How do the lesson plans used in it compare to the lesson plan model in this chapter?

2. Create questions to guide students' discussion of a trade book using the guidelines suggested in this chapter.

3. Arrange to observe in an elementary classroom. Which approach to instruction does the teacher use?

4. Using the guide in this chapter, create a lesson plan for a language arts skill.

5. Start a file of pictures from magazines, books, calendars, pamphlets, and so on, for use in teaching the language arts.

6. Obtain a copy of *Language Arts* and of *Reading Teacher* and read several articles in each.

7. Interview two experienced teachers and ask them to look at the checklist of qualifications for language arts teachers found in this chapter. Do they agree with the checklist? Can they suggest any alterations?

8. Ask your instructor whether there is a local association of English teachers or a local council of the International Reading Association. If there are local professional organizations like these, attend a meeting. What value do you think professional teachers could derive from these organizations?

Selected Readings

Busching, Beverly, and Judith I. Schwartz (1983). *Integrating the Language Arts in the Elementary School.* Urbana, IL: National Council of Teachers of English.

Hoffman, James V. (1986). *Effective Teaching of Reading: Research and Practice.* Newark, DE: International Reading Association.

Katz, Lilian G. (November 1985). "Research Currents: Teachers as Learners." *Language Arts, 62,* 7, 778–782.

Katz, Lilian G. (1977). "Teachers' Developmental Stages." In *Talks with Teachers,* L. G. Katz, Ed. Washington, DC: National Association for the Education of Young Children.

King, Martha L. (Summer 1984). "Language and School Success: Access to Meaning." *Theory Into Practice, 23,* 3, 175–182.

Lehr, Fran (October 1985). "ERIC/RCS Report: Instructional Scaffolding." *Language Arts, 62,* 6, 667–671.

Mayher, John S., and Rita S. Brause (March 1985). "Learning Through Teaching: A Structure for Inquiry and Change." *Language Arts 62,* 3, 227–281.

Petty, Walter T., and Jullie M. Jensen (1980). *Developing Children's Language.* Boston: Allyn and Bacon, Chapter 4.

Platt, Nancy (Summer 1984). "How One Classroom Gives Access to Meaning." *Theory into Practice, 23,* 3, 239–245.

Rich, Sharon (November 1985). "Restoring Power to Teachers: The Impact of 'Whole Language." *Language Arts, 62,* 717–724.

Robinson, H. Alan, and Alvina Treut Burrows (1974). *Teacher Effectiveness in Elementary Language Arts: A Progress Report.* Urbana, IL: National Conference on Research in English.

Spiegel, Dixie Lee. (December 1980). "Desirable Teaching Behaviors for Effective Instruction in Reading." *Reading Teacher, 34,* 3, 324–330.

References

Anderson, L., C. Evertson, and J. Brophy (1979). "An Experimental Study of Effective Teaching in First-Grade Reading Groups." *Elementary School Journal, 79,* 193–222.

Anderson, Richard, Elfrieda Hiebert, Judith Scott, and Ian Wilkinson (1985). *Becoming a Nation of Readers.* Champaign, IL: Center for the Study of Reading.

Auten, Anne (1985). "ERIC/RCS Report: Building a Language-Rich Environment." *Language Arts, 62,* 95–100.

Bissex, Glenda N. (1980). *GNYS at WRK: A Child Learns to Write and Read.* Cambridge, MA: Harvard University Press.

Blair, T. R. (November, 1984). "Teacher Effectiveness: The Know-how to Improve Student Learning." *Reading Teacher, 38,* 138–142.

Boutwell, Marilyn (September 1983). "Reading and Writing Process: A Reciprocal Agreement." *Language Arts, 60,* 6.

Brophy, J. and T. Good (1986). "Teacher Behavior and Student Achievement," in *Third Handbook of Research on Teaching,* M. Wittrock (ed.). New York: Macmillan.

Brown, Roger (1973). *A First Language.* Cambridge, MA: Harvard University Press.

Bruner, Jerome (1978). "The Role of Dialogue in Language Acquisition." In *The Child's Conception of Language,* A. Sinclair, R. J. Jarvelle, and W. J. Levelt, (eds.). New York: Springer-Verlag.

Busching, Beverly, and Sara Lundsteen (1983). "Curriculum Models for Integrating the Language Arts." In *Integrating the Language Arts in the Elementary School,* Beverly and Judith Schwartz (eds.). Urbana, IL: National Council of Teachers of English, pp. 3–27.

Chall, Jeanne (1983). *Stages of Reading Development.* New York: McGraw Hill.

Chall, Jeanne, and C. Snow (1982). *Families and Literacy.* Final report to the National Institute of Education.

Chomsky, Carol (1972). "Write Now, Read Later." In *Language in Early Childhood Education,* C. B. Cazden (ed.). Washington, DC: National Association for Young Children.

Christenbury, Leila, and Patricia Kelly (1983). *Questioning a Path to Critical Thinking.* Urbana, IL: National Council of Teachers of English.

Clark, Margaret (1976). *Young Fluent Readers.* London: Heinemann.

Clay, M. (1975). *What Did I Write?* Exeter, NH: Heinemann.

Cross, T. G. (1978). "Mothers' Speech and Its Association with Rate of Linguistic Development in Young Children." In *The Development of Communication,* N. Waterson and T. Snow (eds.). Chichester, England: John Wiley.

Dale, P. S. (1976). *Language Development: Structure and Function* (2d ed.). New York: Holt, Rinehart and Winston.

DeFord, D. E. (1981). "Literacy: Reading, Writing, and Other Essentials." *Language Arts, 58,* 652–658.

DeStefano, J. S. (1981). "Demonstrations, Engagements, and Sensitivity: A Revised Approach to Language Learning." *Language Arts, 58,* 103–112.

Duffy, G., and Laura Roehler (1982). "An Analysis of the Instruction in Reading Instructional Research." In *New Inquiries in Reading Research and Instruction (Thirty-first Yearbook of the National Reading Conference.* J. Niles and L. Harris (eds.). Rochester, NY: National Reading Conference.)

Farmer, Marjorie (1986). "Introduction." In *Consensus and Dissent,* M. Farmer (ed.). Urbana, IL: National Council of Teachers of English Yearbook.

Goodman, Yetta M. (1983). "Beginning Reading Development: Strategies and Principles," In *Developing Literacy: Young Children's Use of Language.* Newark, DE: International Reading Association.

Goodman, K. S., and Y. Goodman (1979). "Learning to Read Is Natural." In *Theory and Practice of Early Reading: Vol. 1,* L. B. Resnick and P. A. Weaver (eds.). Hillsdale, NJ: Lawrence Erlbaum Associates.

Graves, D. H. (1984), *Writing: Teachers and Children at Work.* Exeter, NH: Heinemann Educational Books.

Graves, Donald (1973). *Children's Writing: Research Directions and Hypotheses Based upon an Examination of the Writing Processes of Seven-Year-Old Children.* Unpublished doctoral dissertation, Buffalo, NY: S. Y. S.

Halliday, M. A. K. (1975). *Learning How to Mean: Explorations in the Development of Language.* London: Edward Arnold.

Harste, J. C.; C. L., Burke; and V. A. Woodward (1981). *Children, Their Language, and World: Initial Encounters with Print.* Bloomington, IN: Indiana University, Language Education Department (NIE Final Report #NIE-G-79-0132).

Hemphill, John (September 1981). "Language Arts Instruction: A Continuum of Possible Models." *Language Arts, 58,* 643–651.

Hillocks, G. (1984). "What Works in Teaching Composition: A Meta-analysis of Experimental Treatment Studies." *American Journal of Education, 93* (1), 133–170.

Holdaway, Don (1979). *Foundations of Literacy.* Australia: Ashton Scholastic.

Hunter, Madeline (1967). *Motivation Theory for Teachers.* El Segundo, CA: TIP Publications.

———. (1977). *Resources in Education.* Washington DC ERIC Clearinghouse on Teacher Education.

———. (1979). "Diagnostic Teaching." *Elementary School Journal, 80,* 41–46.

Hyman, Ronald T. (1979). *Strategic Questioning.* Englewood Cliffs, NJ: Prentice-Hall.

King, Martha (Summer 1984). "Language and School Success: Access to Meaning". *Theory into Practice,* 173–182.

King, Martha and Rental, Victor (1981). *How Children Learn to Write: A Longitudinal Study.* NIE final report, Volume 1 (NIE-G-0137 and NIE-G-79-0039).

Lehr, Fran (October, 1985). "ERIC/RCS Report: Instructional Scaffolding." *Language Arts, 62,* 667–672.

Manning, John C. (1985). "Integrating Reading with Other Subjects." *Reading Today, 3,* 3.

Moffett, James, and B. J. Wagner (1983). *Student-Centered Language Arts and Reading, K–13: A Handbook for Teachers* (2d ed.). Boston: Houghton-Mifflin,

National Council of Teachers of English (1986). *Guidelines for Teachers of English Language Arts.* Urbana, IL: National Council of Teachers of English.

Osborn, J. (1984). "The Purposes, Uses, and Contents of Workbooks and Some Guidelines for Publishers." In *Learning to Read in American Schools.* R. Anderson, J. Osborn, and R. Tierney (eds). Hillsdale, NJ: Lawrence Erlbaum Associates Publishers, 45–113.

Owen, S. (1986). "Students' Comprehension of Workbooks." An unpublished doctoral dissertation, Greensboro, NC: The University of North Carolina at Greensboro.

Read, Charles (1971). "Pre-School Children's Knowledge of English Phonology." *Harvard Educational Review, 41,* 1–34.

Redfield, D., and E. Rousseau (1981). "A Meta-analysis of Experimental Research on Teacher Questioning Behavior." *Review of Educational Research, 51,* 237–245.

Roehler, L. (1983). "Ten Ways to Integrate Language and Subject Matter." In *Integrating the Language Arts in the Elementary School,* B. Busching and J. Schwartz (eds.). Urbana, IL: National Council of Teachers of English.

Rosenshine, Barak (1979). "Content, Time, and Direct Instruction. In *Research on Teaching: Concepts, Findings and Implications.,* P. L. Peterson and H. J. Walberg (eds.). Berkley, CA: McMutchan.

Rosenshine, Barak, and David Berliner (1978). "Academic Engaged Time." *British Journal of Teacher Education, 4,* 3–16.

Schweinhart, L. B. Weikart, and W. Larner (1986). "Consequences of Three Preschool Curriculum Model Through Age 15." *Early Childhood Research Quarterly, 1* (1), 15–45.

Smith, F. (1978). *Understanding Reading* (2d ed.). New York: Holt, Rinhart Winston.

Spiegel, Dixie Lee (December, 1980). "Desirable Teaching Behaviors for Effective Instruction in Reading." *Reading Teacher, 34,* 324–330.

Squire, James (1983). *Instructional Focus and the Teaching of Writing.* Columbus, OH: Ginn, p. 3.

Stauffer, R., and J. Pikulski (1974). "A Comparison and Measure of Oral Language Growth." *Elementary English, 51,* 1151–1155.

Stebbins, L. (1976). *Education as Experimentation: A Planned Variation Model, Vol. 111A.* Cambridge, MA: Abt Associates.

Stoodt, B. (1985). *Kindergarten Journals.* Unpublished Paper, Greensboro: UNC-Greensboro.

Teale, William (1981). "Learning About Learning to Read by Observing Parents Reading to Their Children." Paper presented to the Annual Meeting of the International Reading Association, New Orleans.

Veatch, Jeannette (1978). *Reading in the Elementary School* (2d ed.). New York: Wiley.

Vygotsky, Lev, (1978), *Mind in Society.* Cambridge, MA: Harvard University Press.

Wagner, B. J. (September 1985). "ERIC/RCS Report: Integrating the Language Arts." *Language Arts 62,* 557–560.

Weaver, Gail (October 1978). "Integrating Written Composition with Other Language Arts Activities." *Language Arts, 55,* 873–877.

Weisberg, Renee (1986). "The Madeline Hunter Model of Teacher Effectiveness." In *Effective Teaching of Reading: Research and Practice,* James V. Hoffman (ed.). 181–197.

Weiss, M. Jerry, Ed. (1979). *From Writers to Students.* Newark, DE: International Reading Association.

Winne, P. (1979). "Experiments Relating Teachers' Use of Higher Cognitive Questions to Student Achievement." *Review of Educational Research, 49,* 46.

Wittrock, M. (1975). "The Generative Approach to Reading." *Journal of Educational Psychology, 67,* 484–489.

Wittrock, Merlin C., Ed. (1986). *Handbook of Research on Teaching* (3d ed.). New York: Macmillan.

Chapter Three

Foundations of Language

CHAPTER OVERVIEW

The qualifications for English language arts teachers include knowledge of the language processes, language history, as well as understanding of language acquisition. This chapter extends readers' understandings in these areas.

Language is essential to life as we know it. Human beings use language to make sense of their world; this chapter explores the importance of language in our lives. Language and thought are closely related, although our inability to observe thought makes it difficult to understand the precise nature of this relationship. Then the systems that comprise language, morphemics, syntax, and discourse are described and examined. The historical development of English reflects the cultural development of English-speaking peoples. English instruction is founded on understanding the major aspects of its history. Language instruction is further influenced by the growth and development of the language learner; therefore, we analyze children's language acquisition and the factors influencing this process. Language is a central factor in life, but nowhere is this more apparent than in the development of thinking. Thus the relationship between language and thinking must be considered as teachers learn to teach both language and thinking. Finally, we explore children's use of language in their lives.

Anticipation Guide

Brainstorm all of the ways you use language in one day. As you read this chapter compare your list to the ideas in this chapter. Did you know that English is closely related to French? Can you think of a reason for this close relationship? If you cannot, be sure to find out as you read this chapter.

1. How does language influence our lives?

2. How is English related to French?

3. How do synthetic languages differ from analytic languages?

4. How do children acquire language?

Key Concepts

language

phonemes

morphology

syntax

analytic language

semantics

discourse

linguist

language functions

synthetic language

telegraphic language

holophrases

schemata

INTRODUCTION

We tend to take language for granted, attending to the meaning more than the actual words and **syntax.** The following brief language scripts illustrate children's cognitive development and language development at three different stages.

Language and Thinking Incidents

Incident 1

Teacher to preschool child (age four):	"Say these numbers backwards."
Preschool child:	Turns around and looking over his shoulder repeats the numbers.

Incident 2

Kindergarten student:	I don't like *Show and Tell* when the other kids are showing and telling.

Incident 3

Fourth-grade teacher to class:	"In the story you just read, the author describes a solar car. What is the source of energy in a solar car?"
Class:	silence
Teacher:	What makes a solar car go?
Class:	silence
Teacher:	What does solar mean?
Student #1:	Is it a kind of battery?
Teacher:	Well in some instances, this kind of energy is stored in batteries for future use, but think about it some more. Have you ever heard the word *solar* used in reference to anything? Have you heard it on television or read about it in a newspaper or magazine?
Student #2:	I heard about a solar hot water heater.
Teacher:	What heated the water in the solar hot water heater?
Student #2:	The sun, I think.

The student in incident 1 is at a concrete level of thinking; there appears to be only one meaning for the word *backwards.* Of course, this is the age appropriate level of thinking. The student in incident 2 is thinking out loud which is to be expected at that age. Also revealed is the egocentric nature of development at that age—interest in "show and tell" is held only when it is your own turn.

In incident 3 teacher and students are demonstrating the use of scaffolding to develop thinking and language. The teacher gradually led the students to relate their schemata to the new word in order to expand their concept of car and of fuel. The teacher used aspects of both Piaget's and Vygotsky's theories which are explained in the next section.

LANGUAGE'S INFLUENCE

Language so permeates our lives that we rarely recognize how important it is. Virtually every activity of life is conducted in language—it is the medium for delivering service in department stores, for buying groceries, for delivering medical care in hospitals and doctors' offices, for determining justice in the courts, and for educating our children. "In these, and in all other activities of life, language is the essential foundation for exchanging information, offering opinions or advice, determining the facts upon which decisions are made, requesting the unknown, and even reasoning through personal or abstract problems" (Shuy, 1984). Language is either consciously or unconsciously associated with everything we do.

Language is the common element in each of the language arts. Human beings listen to language, speak language, read language, and write language. The language arts are channels for communicating thoughts, feelings, and knowledge to others and they are channels for receiving communication regarding the thoughts, feelings, and knowledge of others. Language is a central tool in all learning. When we think we use language to communicate with ourselves. All of the language processes—listening, speaking, reading, and writing—afford learners the resources for constructing meaning (Strickland, 1985). For instance, when an individual sees a tree, hears the object called a tree, says the word tree, and carries an image of a tree in his or her head, the possibility arises that one can write information about the tree, discuss the tree with another individual who did not see the tree, and think about the tree when it is absent. Anything that can be thought can be communicated through language.

Language gives us access to the world's store of knowledge. For instance, a physician who is treating a patient with unusual symptoms can read about the experiences of other physicians with these symptoms. Students use language to acquire knowledge from books and from teachers. We share current information and events through personal letters and news broadcasts. The world's business is transacted through language. If language were eliminated, life as we know it would disappear from the world.

Language has a powerful influence on our emotions because language has a certain amount of control over thinking. Words can help us overcome fear because it collapses in the presence of experience organized into concepts and expressed in language. Naming, describing, and classifying an experience makes human beings more secure. A good example of this phenomenon occurs when our physician tells us that we have a virus. This generally means we have an unidentified disease, but with a bit of rest we will recover. Nevertheless, most people feel better when the illness is labeled than they would if the physician said they had an unidentified disease. Labeling alleviates our concern, for even in this enlightened era, some people believe in "word magic." There are people who believe that reading the word *communist* in textbooks will lead students to become communists. They are not unlike the primitive peoples who believe they can protect their children by giving them a lowly name that will not attract the attention of the gods.

Language and Thought

Once we acquire a language system, we can communicate an unlimited number of ideas, experiences, and perceptions. By selecting and combining words according to the rules of the language system, we can generate an infinite number of messages. Language makes it possible to imagine, to question, to reason, to problem solve, and to plan. Anything that is thought can be communicated. Language enables us to translate experiences into words, to sort information, to organize experience, and to formulate generalizations. Language enables us to label our experiences and to store them in memory in the form of cognitive structures called **schemata.** When new situations related to existing experiences, ideas, or information are encountered, we retrieve this data from our memory. These schemata enable us to understand. For example, when a teacher introduces a journal writing activity, students should be encouraged to think about their experiences (schemata) with diaries and letters to help them understand what the teacher expects of them.

Language and thought are so intertwined that it is difficult to examine them separately. Language is crucial to the highly sophisticated thinking that distinguishes humans from apes. "Thoughts above the habitual level—and human habit patterns can be quite complex—are so infused with language in longhand or shorthand and so dependent on its load of meaning in word and syntax that language surely is more than a mere carrier of thought. Obviously, in many instances language is thought" (Smith, Goodman, and Meredith, 1976). Some authorities believe that language is necessary to thinking (Bruner, 1966), whereas other authorities believe that thinking is necessary to language (Piaget, 1960).

Piaget on Language and Thought Piaget believed that thinking preceded language and that the child translated his or her thoughts into language. He viewed them as separate entities. Piaget's theories on language and thought stressed the need to avoid teaching too fast. He defined teaching as creating situations where students could discover structure after which they would translate that structure into language (Duckworth, 1964). Thus instructional programs should offer children many opportunities to explore materials and situations to discover structure and then they should have the time to associate language with the structure they discover.

Vygotsky on Language and Thought In contrast to Piaget's theory, Vygotsky emphasized the role of language in thinking and forming concepts (1962). He identified dialog with adults as a powerful factor in developing children's thinking, and he stressed early verbal interaction between children and the adults in their environment. According to his theory, words play a central part in the development of thought. As children acquire words, they acquire the tools of thinking.

Thinking can be classified as *verbal* or *nonverbal*. Nonverbal thinking is manifested when students work some problems in geometry and physics (Smith, Goodman, and Meredith, 1976). Children can show that they understand ideas without words; they do this through manipulating objects in play and problem-solving situations. The verbal aspects of thought are those that students manifest in language. However, most of the thinking in classroom situations involves language structures. Teachers must be concerned with the ways that language and thought work together because language is the major vehicle for teaching thinking. Furthermore, students and teachers must understand the thoughts that others express in language in order for teaching and learning to occur.

Translating Vygotsky's theory into classroom instruction involves giving students opportunities to talk with teachers and students. The scaffolding model presented in Chapter Two provides a model of this approach to instruction. Vygotsky would recommend a strong emphasis on vocabulary development since he views words as thinking tools.

CHARACTERISTICS OF LANGUAGE

Language *is a system of arbitrary symbols used for communication.* This definition, as well as the characteristics of language, should influence the ways that we teach the language arts.

Language is a system. Because language is systematic it follows patterns or rules that are consistent and predictable. These patterns and rules enable us to generate messages that communicate our thoughts to other people who speak the same language.

Language is arbitrary. The word *dog* is an arbitrary set of sounds that English speakers have agreed to accept as a symbol for the four-legged, furry animal that barks. Nothing is inherent in the animal that causes the word *dog* to represent the animal; this symbol-animal relationship is an arbitrary one. In German, the word *hund* symbolizes dog. The fact that we consistently use the same symbol (word) to represent the same specific concept, makes it possible to communicate with others. This fact also makes it possible for people, both native-born and foreign-born to learn the language. Think of the pandemonium that would result if this arbitrary relationship were not consistent—we would literally experience a "Tower of Babel."

Language is symbolic. Words are not things; they are symbols that represent the ideas, objects, animals, people, etc., that we think about, talk about, write about, read about, and listen about. Words enable us to think and discuss abstract concepts such as freedom, as well as concrete objects like dogs. Words allow us to examine things that are absent; without words communication would be restricted because we would have to point to the object or draw a picture of an idea.

Language permits communication. People communicate through language. The need to communicate makes it necessary for us to learn language. Learning a language common to the language group in which one lives enables human beings to communicate with other members of the language group.

Language reflects its environment. Language shows the imprint of its physical environment. For example, Eskimos have many words in their language to classify snow because snow is an important concept to Eskimos. On the other hand, Arabs value the camels in their environment, so they have many words to describe camels in their language.

Language gradually changes. English is a dynamic language that is in continuous use. Words are added to the English language each year, while other words become obsolete. Approximately 3000 new words are added to the English language each year. The pronunciation of words changes over a period of years. For instance, the *k* in *knife* was once pronounced, but now it is silent. Presently, many American English speakers are pronouncing the word *what* as if it were spelled *wat,* which leads us to conjecture that the *h* in *what* will eventually be a silent letter.

Three processes explain language change. The first is variation occurring when new ideas and inventions develop and enter the language. Obviously, there was no vocabulary for computers at the time of the Battle of Hastings because there were no computers, although we have need for an extensive computer vocabulary today. The second language change process is geographic change. Whenever people move to a new location, their language changes as it adapts to new situations. Finally, language changes through importation of foreign words and expressions. For instance, pizza was imported from Italy. My great-grandparents would not recognize the word *pizza* because it was imported after their lifetime (Malmstrom, 1977).

ENGLISH LANGUAGE SYSTEM

As scientists who study language, **linguists** investigate the language system, including phonology, morphology, syntax, discourse, and semantics. Phonology refers to the sounds of a language. Morphology is the study of word forms. Syntax is the study of word order. **Discourse** refers to a group of sentences that are related in some sequential fashion. Semantics are concerned with the meaning of language.

Phonology is concerned with the smallest discrete units of sound in a language which are called **phonemes.** The stream of sounds uttered in oral language can be divided into language units (phonemes) which have been combined into pronounceable sequences (McNeill, 1970). For example, the word *hat* has three phonemes: /h/ /a/ /t/. Each of these phonemes has a distinctly different sound and changing any one of the phonemes would change the word. For example, if one changed the /h/ to a /c/ the word would become *cat;* if the /t/ were changed to a /d/ the word would become *had;* and if the /a/ were changed to an /o/ the word would become *hot.* Approximately 44 phonemes constitute the English language. Phonemes are represented in written language by graphemes. The relationship between phonemes and graphemes is not a one-to-one relationship because two graphemes may represent one phoneme. For example, in the word *boat* the grapheme *oa* represents the /o/.

The phonology of the English language includes *stress, pitch,* and *juncture,* as well as phonemes. Stress is the volume used to pronounce a syllable or a word. The meaning of a sentence is altered when stress is shifted. Notice how the meaning changes when one stresses the word in italics in these sentences:

Is *Susan* going to eat that pie?

Is Susan going to eat *that* pie?

Pitch is the highness or lowness of the sound. Pitch also influences the meaning of words and sentences. How does pitch alter the meaning of the following sentences?

Muffin is coming. (The falling pitch is on *coming,* which is interpreted as a statement of fact.)

Muffin is coming? (The rising pitch is on *coming,* which is interpreted as a question.)

Junctures are the breaks between words. Variations in junctures—the length of pause between words—can change the meaning of an utterance. How does the meaning change in the following sentences when a pause is created by a comma?

Susan Helen's mother bought a new car.

Susan, Helen's mother, bought a new car.

Morphology deals with the meaningful grouping of phonemes (sounds), emphasizing grammatical factors for grouping sounds. Morphemes are the smallest meaningful units of language. Free morphemes may stand alone in a phrase or sentence and bound morphemes must be combined with other morphemes. For example, *dog* is one morpheme that is a free morpheme. *Dogs* is comprised of two morphemes; *dog* is the first morpheme and *s* a bound morpheme is the second morpheme. The *s* represents plurality in this instance.

Syntax is concerned with the arrangement of words into meaningful combinations. The identical vocabulary arranged in different ways can express different meaning. For example:

The flower was on the table.

The table was on the flower.

The study of syntax involves classification of sentences and parts of sentences.

Semantics is the meaning system of a language. The semantics of a language include word meanings, the connotative meanings of words, and the denotative meanings of words, as well as multiple meanings. Denotative meanings are dictionary meanings. Therefore, they are more formal definitions, while connotative meanings are feelings about concepts and experiences that are derived from an individual's personal experiences. For example, individuals who have good experiences with reading are likely to give positive, warm meaning to literature while individuals who have had difficulty learning to read may have negative reactions to anything related to reading. Connotative meanings are more difficult to communicate to others because these meanings tend to be individual and personal.

The syntactic structure of a sentence also influences meaning. As you saw in a preceding example, when the identical vocabulary is arranged in a different sequence the meaning is changed. Scrutinize the following sentences for a shift in meaning.

The dog bit the flea.

The flea bit the dog.

The difference in meaning will have considerable impact on the dog in question.

You have examined the various systems that comprise a language, but language instruction is also influenced by the nature of the language in question. Since you are teaching the English language, you will need to understand the nature and development of English. For instance, a synthetic language should be studied and taught in a different fashion than an analytic language. A **synthetic language** is one that indicates the relationship of words in a sentence by means of inflections. In the case of Old English, a synthetic language, the inflections most commonly took the form of endings on the noun and pronoun, the adjective, and the verb. The distinctive form of these words provided the information necessary to understand a sentence. An **analytic language,** such as modern English, relies on the fixed order of words to show relationships in a sentence. It makes a great deal of difference in English whether we say *The dog bit the man* or *The man bit the dog.* Analytic languages make extensive use of prepositions and auxiliary verbs to show relationships (Baugh, 1963).

Dialect

Dialect is a language variation. The dialect that we speak is influenced by where we live and where we have lived in the past. In fact, both geography and history impinge upon dialect. For example, the country of origin of the original settlers of the community in which we live influences our language. Children acquire the dialect of the people in their immediate speech environment and they alter their dialect somewhat as they move from place to place. Dialect has many implications for language arts teachers, which will be discussed more fully in Chapter 9.

FUNCTIONS OF LANGUAGE

Language can be examined from a variety of perspectives. One of those perspectives is uses or functions. Functions of language are the ways that we use language to communicate orally and in writing. These language functions involve audiences, either listeners or readers (Smith, 1977). Children learn language and its functions at the same time; therefore, the language functions have implications for language arts instruction. Children's language learning is enhanced when they learn language in functional situations based on genuine communication that involves interacting with others (Pinnell, 1985). Understanding the functions of language will help teachers foster functional language instruction in meaningful situations.

Halliday (1975), who considers language acquisition a process of "learning how to mean," has identified seven universal language functions:

Instrumental language is language created to get something the speaker or writer wants or needs. Instrumental language is functioning when the youngster says, "Gimme a cookie!" In language arts instruction this function appears in conversations, discussions, letters, notes, and invitations.

Regulatory language is language used to control the behavior, feelings, or attitudes of others. Regulatory language is functioning when a child says, "Stop that!" In language arts instruction this function appears in oral and written directions, role playing, and persuasive writing.

Interactional language is language used to establish a relationship with others, and it could be considered social language. Interactional language is functioning when a child says, "Will you play house with me?" This function appears in activities like conversation, discussion, letters, and notes.

Heuristic language is used for "finding out" things about the world; this type of language enables children to investigate and to learn. Heuristic language is functioning when a youngster asks, "Where does snow come from?" Activities such as interviews, discussion, role playing, reading textbooks and trade books that answer questions, and writing activities that help children investigate all use heuristic language.

Personal language is used to share the speaker's or reader's feelings and/or point of view; language is used to express individuality. Personal language is functioning when a youngster says, "Red is best." Activities such as panel discussions, debates, readers' theatre, diaries, dramatizations, and activities that reflect a response to literature involve personal language.

Imaginative language is used for fun, for the pleasure of saying words and ideas to entertain or amuse. Imaginative language is creative language. Imaginative language is functioning when a child says, "Let's pretend." Imaginative activities include choral reading, storytelling, dramatization, and writing poems and stories.

Representative language (informative language) is used to convey information to others. This type of language informs, describes, or expresses. Informative language is functioning when a youngster says, "It's raining." This function of language is represented in oral and written reports, as well as in various forms of discussion.

Representative language conveys information.

A BRIEF HISTORY OF THE ENGLISH LANGUAGE

The origin of language in human behavior is debatable; nonetheless it seems clear that language must have begun in some form about one million years ago (Leakey, 1971). Thus, it is safe to say that the English language we use reflects many centuries of development. Our English is quite different from that spoken and written during the early period of English history. The history of a language parallels the history of its users; therefore, the political, social, and cultural history of the English has profoundly influenced the English language. Historical influences have resulted in changes in the phonemes, morphemes, syntax, and semantics of English. Following is the Lord's Prayer written in Old English:

Fæder ūre,
þū e eart on heofonum,
sī þīn nama gehālgod.
Tōbecume þīn rīce.
Gewurþe ðin willa on eorðan swā swā on heofonum.
Ūrne gedæighwāmlīcan hlāf syle ūs tō dæf.
And forgyf ūs ūre gyltas, swā swā wē forgyfað ūrum gyltendum.
And ne gelæd þū ūs on costnunge,
Ac ālȳs ūs of yfele. Sōþlīce.

Old English

English evolved over a fifteen-hundred-year period, from the Anglo-Saxon (Old English) shown in the preceding example to the Modern English that we speak. Linguists divide the history of English into three periods: Old English dating from 450 to 1150 AD; Middle English from 1150 to 1500; and Modern English from 1500 to the present.

The prehistoric inhabitants of the British Isles spoke Celtic and variations of this language survive today in Ireland, Scotland, and Wales. Celtic also survives in place names like the Thames River, a Celtic river name. During the fifth and sixth centuries, the Angles, Saxons, and Jutes invaded England and their Germanic languages became the basis for the grammar and the vocabulary of Old English. In fact, the name England is derived from Anglaland, "the land of the Angles," and the language, "Angle-ish" is from the same source (Bambas, 1980). Many influences impinged on Old English during the 500-year period of its use. The English people of this period traded, worshiped, and fought with peoples who used other languages and these languages influenced Old English. Most notable among these influential languages were: Celtic, Latin, Scandinavian, and French.

The Latin language had a significant impact on Old English beginning with the Roman invasion of England about 43 AD; this influence appears in words like *church* and *bishop.* In 597 AD missionaries came from Rome to convert the Anglo-Saxons to Christianity; they also created the first written records of Old English. Through the missionaries' influence, more Latin words were adopted by the Anglo-Saxons. Traders also adopted languages from other countries. The Scandinavians left their imprint on the English language as they raided and plundered the southern and eastern coastal areas of England (787 AD–850 AD). Words such as *sky, ship, fish,* and *egg* are of Scandinavian origin. The Scandinavian influence is also apparent in place names like *Grimsby* and *Derby.*

Out of all the languages that have altered English, French made the greatest contribution due to the Norman conquest of England in 1066. The Normans spoke French and by the year 1400, 10,000 French words were added to the English language (Bambas, 1980). As a result of the Battle of Hastings, French became the prestige language of the ruling class. For two hundred years following the Norman conquest, French remained the language of ordinary conversation among the upper classes in England (Baugh, 1963). Gradually, the conquered people assimilated the language of the conquerors and French left an indelible mark on the English language. Nevertheless, a great many basic elements of English vocabulary are derived from Old English. We *eat, drink,* and *sleep* in English, we also *work, play, speak, sing, walk, run, ride,* and *leap* in English. Our houses have English *halls, rooms, windows, doors, floors,* and *steps.* Thus, Old English is still with us.

Middle English

During the Middle English period, momentous changes occurred in the English language, changes more extensive and fundamental than those at any time before or after. Many of these changes were the result of the Norman Conquest. Other changes were merely continuations of earlier alterations in Old English. The changes of this period affected both the grammar and the vocabulary of English. At the beginning of the Middle English period which occurred shortly after 1200 AD, English looked like a foreign language; at the end it was Modern English.

The vocabulary of English changed dramatically during the Middle English period. During this period the vocabularies of two languages were assimilated into one language, which led to a duplication of word meanings in certain instances, and unnecessary words died out. Where both the English and French words survived they were usually differentiated in meaning. For example, *ox, sheep, swine,* and *calf* are English words having the same meaning as the French words *beef, mutton, pork,* and *veal.* These words denoted the animal in the original language. However, as a result of changes during the Middle English period, these words are used to distinguish the meat from the living beast in English.

French words were quite rapidly assimilated into English. In fact, English endings were added to French words as freely as to English words. For example, the adjective *gentle* was recorded in 1225 and within five years it was compounded with an English noun to make *gentlewoman.* A little later we find *gentleman, gentleness,* and *gently.* The richness of English synonyms emerged during the Middle English period. Latin, French, and English have mingled to create the words necessary for conveying vivid images, ideas, and emotions. Following are examples of English synonyms that originated in these three languages: *rise* (English), *mount* (French), *ascend* (Latin); *ask* (English), *question* (French), *interrogate* (Latin). By the end of this period the English language looked and sounded very much like it does today.

Modern English

At the beginning of the Modern English period which occurred about 1500 AD, all the long stressed root vowels changed in pronunciation. This is called the "great vowel shift." This change is relatively mysterious because no one understands why this vowel shift occurred in English and not in the continental European languages (Malmstrom, 1977). This shift occurred after printing had more or less frozen English spelling, thus the pronunciation changes are not reflected in spelling. As a result, English is more difficult to spell than Spanish, Italian, and many other European languages.

Modern English pronunciation also changed in other aspects. The *k* in *knob, knot, knee,* and *know* became silent, although it was formerly pronounced. Likewise, the *t* in *listen* and *glisten,* formerly pronounced, became silent in this period. Other silent letters that were once pronounced include the initial consonant sounds in *gnaw, gnat, gnarl, wrap, wreath, wreck,* and *pneumonia.* The *gh* in *night* and *sight* were once pronounced, while the *b* in *lamb* and *comb* was formerly pronounced.

Borrowed Words

Throughout its history, English has shown a strong proclivity to borrow words from other languages. Some examples of English borrowing from other languages are listed below.

American Indian	chipmunk
	hominy
	moose
	skunk
Dutch	cruller
	golf
	measles
	wagon
Italian	balcony
	piano
	umbrella
Spanish	alligator
	cargo
	mosquito
	tornado
	vanilla

Greek	acrobat
	catastrophe
	magic
Russian	steppe
	vodka
Persian	khaki
	sherbert

English Today

English is fast becoming a universal language; we could say that global English is developing (McCrum, Cran, and MacNeil, 1986). Global English is the result of massive English-language training programs, international business, textbooks, language courses, tape cassettes, video programs, and computerized instruction. More people use English than have used any language in human history (Bambas, 1980). The cross-cultural spread of English is unprecedented. It is a multicultural language which is exported along with many other American and British exports. English is the language of computers of medicine, technology, popular entertainment, and international advertising.

The Japanese have borrowed more than 20,000 words since the Second World War. This language is called Japlish and has led to the production of special dictionaries. The French have borrowed from English and their borrowings are called Franglais. It seems that we have come full circle, the French are borrowing back the words that we adopted from them in 1066.

English has a number of assets which facilitate its dissemination including natural gender, inflectional simplicity, and a cosmopolitan vocabulary. First, the gender of English nouns is determined by meaning and does not require a masculine, feminine, or neuter article. Second, English grammar is simple and flexible. Nouns and adjectives have highly simplified word endings. And finally, English has a large vocabulary, 80 percent of which is foreign-born (McCrum, Cran, and MacNeil, 1986).

Although English has many assets, the chaotic nature of its spelling is a problem for many people. The system for spelling English words lacks simplicity and consistency. For example, the vowel sound in each of the following words is spelled differently: *believe, receive, leave.* The apparently erratic spelling conventions for English are the result of the history of English, borrowings from other languages, and the invention of the printing press. As English evolved, pronunciation of certain words gradually changed and letters that had once been sounded became silent. Borrowing words from other languages impacts on spelling because the English speaker may pronounce the word differently than it was pronounced in the original language and may attempt to spell the word as it was spelled in the original language. Finally, the printing press was invented in the 1400s at a time when spelling conventions for English had not been systematized. For example, Shakespeare frequently spelled the same word three different ways on one page. Printers simply selected one spelling which became the convention for spelling that particular word. In spite of a somewhat erratic spelling system, English is a wonderfully flexible, expressive language with a rich cultural history.

We have examined the nature of language, the development of English as a language, and now we will look at children's acquisition of language.

LANGUAGE ACQUISITION

Language acquisition illustrates the almost unlimited potential of the human mind. Gleason (1969) points out that "no one has yet been able to program the most sophisticated computer to turn out the sentences that any five-year old can produce with ease and assurance." Dale observed that "the more we know about language, the less we understand how it works. The acquisition of language is one of the major feats of child development" (Dale, 1976). As teachers and prospective teachers, you must understand language acquisition because language instruction should parallel language acquisition.

As you can discern from the preceding quotations, language acquisition fascinates those who study it. Various theories have been developed to explain the phenomenon of language acquisition. The two major theories are the *behaviorist* theory and the *nativist* or *innate theory.* These theories will be explained in the next few paragraphs.

Behaviorist Theory

According to the behaviorist theory, language is learned entirely through experience. The behaviorists maintain that infants are born with the general ability to acquire language and that language learning occurs as a result of the environment into which the child is born. Individuals acquire language because the significant people in their environment reinforce their language experimentation. Imagine an infant, who, while babbling, accidentally says "mama." Mother, who is nearby, runs to the bed and picks the infant up, hugging him or her, while repeating the sound. Then mother tries to stimulate the child to say "mama" again. The mother tells others that her child is talking. This behavior reinforces the baby who will try to please others by repeating the magic words that created all of the excitement. The behaviorist believes that children talk "baby talk" because they are reinforced for doing this. It is obvious from this discussion that the behaviorist theory is a stimulus–response theory. In other words children learn what is reinforced and eliminate language that is not reinforced. This appears to be an oversimplification of language acquisition.

The greatest weakness of this theory is its failure to explain the fact that children appear to learn a system or a set of rules for creating utterances. They use these rules to create utterances that they have never heard before; therefore, language acquisition cannot be explained through simple imitation. Also the relatively short time period during which children acquire language seems to violate the behaviorist theory because this short time frame would not enable children to be reinforced in all of the language they learn.

Nativist Theory

The nativist or innate theory maintains that youngsters have a biological tendency to learn language. This theory emphasizes the innate factors involved in language acquisition, and while it values the role of environment, it interprets environment differently from the behaviorists. Chomsky (1965) and McNeill (1970) have articulated this view of language acquisition. They believe that the child is born with the "wiring" to learn language; this special wiring has been called a "language acquisition device" (LAD). In addition, they believe that human beings automatically know quite a lot about language that enables them to sort out the language system of the community in which they live. They do not have to learn that one can ask information questions in his or her language, but they have to learn how one asks information questions (Lindfors, 1980).

In the nativist theory, the language environment is important because the child interacts with others in the environment in order to acquire language. According to this theory the environment provides the linguistic data that children use to learn the language system of their "native tongue." They hear and formulate rules that govern language. This explanation of language acquisition relies upon a child who is an active language learner and a seeker of meaning. And this does seem to describe the child's search for the capacity to communicate and it also helps account for the frustration of the deaf youngster who cannot communicate.

At the present time, it appears that no single theory fully accounts for language acquisition. There is no question that we are born with a predisposition to learn language, since humans are the only species that learn to speak. In spite of the fact that the pet lovers among us claim that our pets speak to us, we must admit under duress that our animals do not use human language. Pet animals often live their entire lives in a language environment but, they do not learn to speak. But we also must recognize that there is an element of imitation in language learning. Children emulate the language in their environment, after all infants who live in an English-speaking household do acquire English. They also exhibit familial language traits, such as unique ways of pronouncing words, phonemes, or of sequencing words in phrases or sentences.

Nevertheless, children produce utterances that they have never heard, such as, "see foots." Utterances such as the preceding suggest that children listen to the language surrounding them and generalize rules for inflecting words, sequencing words, selecting words that express the meaning they wish to convey and so forth. The use of "foots" represents overgeneralization of the rule for creating plurals by a youngster who has not learned that there are irregular nouns that are not pluralized by the usual "s" or "es" rule.

Children seem to learn language because they want to understand the world in which they live. Human beings are meaning-seeking creatures (Smith, 1978). Language acquisition is a meaning focused process. Although children's meanings and expression change as they grow, the fact that expression of meaning is the goal of language remains unchanging over time. "The child is thrusting to mean." As they are bathed daily in natural, meaningful interaction, children actively process the workings of language discerning underlying regularities both in how language is structured and how language is used in different social situations (Lindfors, 1979). One of the most significant and dramatic findings of language acquisition research is the fact that adults respond to children who are acquiring language on the basis of the meanings the children are attempting to convey, rather than on the basis of the forms they use. For example, a young girl referred to her mother in the statement, "He a girl" and the mother responded "that's right," because the mother understood the meaning the youngster was expressing (Brown, Cazden, and Bellugi-Klima, 1971).

Children are apparently born meaning-seeking creatures and language is a vehicle understanding. Thus it appears that aspects of language acquisition are innate or nativist. On the other hand, it is undeniable that environment plays an enormous role in language acquisition. Certainly, parents who listen to children speak and respond to their meanings help facilitate language development. This leads to the conviction that language acquisition has elements of both the behaviorist and nativist theories.

LANGUAGE ACQUISITION

Language Development

Talking is one of the most important milestones in a young child's life. Parents and grandparents eagerly await the advent of the child's first word. Perhaps this event is eagerly awaited because parents and grandparents realize how important language will be in the child's life, that the child uses language to make sense of his or her world. Language development is highly individual with considerable variation from child to child; environmental factors as well as innate factors influence language acquisition. However, children do acquire a language system in a remarkably brief period of time. The great majority of language development occurs during the first two years of life. From birth through the age of four-and-a-half children learn the essentials of the English language—its phonemics, morphology, syntax, discourse, and semantics. They acquire language in an orderly sequential pattern, consistently demonstrating that they are learning a language system. Even rudimentary efforts to speak exhibit understanding of the basic aspects of a language system.

By one year, many children say their first word. At approximately 18 months of age a child may produce a two-word sentence, and by three-and-a-half years of age the important rules of language are mastered (Hodges and Rudorf, 1972). Of course, four-year-old children do not talk like adults. Their vocabularies are not as rich and their memories are more limited, but they have acquired the competence to produce and comprehend all the possible forms of sentence construction found in adult speech. Furthermore, they acquire this complex system of communication without instruction.

Apparently, acquisition of the language system begins before birth. "When you place the baby in a bassinet and get two people to stand over it talking in a language the baby never heard before, the baby's arms and legs move in synchrony with the rhythms of the spoken language, despite the fact that it is a language the baby has never heard before. However, if you use a computer to distort the rhythms within the language . . . and create a vocal noise, the baby will not react the same way" (Restak, 1985). The baby appears to have an inborn genetic ability to respond to the meaning expressed in a language whenever two people talk together in a meaningful way. When the noise becomes meaningless, the baby does not respond. This response to meaningful language may be rooted in the infant's prenatal experiences with his or her mother's language. Researchers have found that the fetus responds to sounds before birth (Appleton, 1975).

When babies start to babble at the age of three months, they start with all possible language sounds. At this age it is impossible to distinguish the babbling of a Chinese child from that of a Dutch child, or an American. But, six-month-old babies babble in Chinese, or Dutch, or English because they have gradually eliminated the language sounds that are not used by the people around them (Hodges and Rudorf, 1972). Through babbling, six-month-old babies acquire the majority of the phonemic system of English. There is also evidence that they learn the difference between angry and friendly verbal expression, between male and female voices, between various intonation and rhythm features, and between certain speech segments (Clark and Clark, 1977).

By their first birthday, average youngsters are speaking single words—mama, dada, bye-bye, or drink. These first words are labels for things in the environment. Early word pronunciations are usually simplifications of adult pronunciations, omitting final consonants. *Dad* may be pronounced with a consonant plus a vowel, "Da." Children at this stage of development may have a repertoire of 50 words (Gleason, 1969). At this age, they tend to use the few words in their vocabulary in a general fashion. For instance, Linda has learned the word "doggie," but she does not understand the general classification of animals, so she calls all animals "doggie," including the cows she sees in a field during an automobile drive. Some children call all men "daddy" to their mother's embarrassment. Although one-year-olds speak one word at a time, they often express an entire sentence. For example, when they say "drink" they may be implying the sentence, "I want a drink!" or they may say "mama" expressing "Come here Mother." These one word sentences are called **holophrases**. Quite complex meanings underlie the single word utterances of the holophrase stage of development, signaling that children at this age probably have a concept of syntax that exceeds their ability to produce syntax. Holophrases are words that function as sentences. This stage indicates that youngsters are beginning to develop a sense of syntax or grammar.

By 18 months, many children produce two and three word phrases which usually express more meaning than the individual words indicate. This **telegraphic language** concentrates on nouns, verbs, and descriptive adjectives which have their own semantic content, while omitting words like *my,* *has, and, I, to,* and *at.* Usually the omitted words are function words like prepositions, articles, and conjunctions which are words that have little or no semantic content, but merely show how the content words are related to each other. For instance, "see baby" may mean "I want to see the baby." "Susan's doll" means "that is Susan's doll." Children at this age use words to name, describe, and specify objects or actions that are present in their environment. "Dada run" may mean that Daddy is running in the child's presence. These youngsters comprehend more complex language than they produce; for instance, if Linda's mother says "Drink all of your milk," Linda will understand what her mother wants, although she may choose not to do it.

At two years to thirty months of age, children have approximately 100 words in their vocabulary and they are putting two words together to create primitive sentences. At this stage of development children use their vocabulary in a very direct fashion—to name, to show ownership, to locate, and so on. Words are sentenced to show meaning. They are learning to describe objects and may create utterances like "red ball." They know that some words refer to actions and demonstrate this knowledge in utterances like "Mommy read" when Mommy is actually reading. Children in this stage of development continue to comprehend more complex language than they utter. Their grandmother may say, "Go get your new truck to show Aunt Sharon" which the youngster understands and performs.

Three-year-olds stop sounding like walking telegrams because they learn about the little words in our language. They learn that English has little words and word parts that make a difference in the meaning of our utterances. This understanding advances their control of the English morphological system considerably. They learn to use "the," "a," "in," and "on," the *'s,* the plural *s,* the *-ing* verb form, and two forms of the past tense verb (*ed* as in "walked" and vowel change as in "sing, sang, sung") (Beck, 1983).

Four-year-old children are creatures of their senses; they are concerned with the smell of a thing, the touch of a thing, and the sound of a thing. This sensual awareness begins to take on conceptual dimensions which are expressed in their language (Beck, 1983). As exemplified in the following quotation of a four-year-old who looked out at a dark evening and said it was "as dark as a plum." Another four-year-old who became aware of being naked while bathing said, "Look at me. I'm barefoot all over" (Beck, 1983).

Six-year-old children have quite a sophisticated language system, although it is not an adult language system. At this age, average children have a vocabulary that exceeds over 2500 words (Dale, 1976). Their language and thinking remain quite concrete, relying on word order more than word meaning for understanding. In this concrete stage of thinking, the first word pronounced is the most important and the next is of second importance and so on. They do not consciously understand the conceptual and relational qualities of words; therefore, words like "more" and "less" and "before" and "after" present them with problems (Dale, 1976). Although their word meanings are different from adult meanings, they use their word meanings consistently. A young friend of mine demonstrated this stage of development when his mother in a joking way said, "Your brother has no "class"—he is rooting for the wrong team." To which, Jimmy responded, "Why doesn't Luke have to go to school?" In Jimmy's mind class meant school. By the age of seven, children have a better understanding of semantics, although their semantic system develops throughout their lives.

Children continue to develop and refine their language as they progress through elementary school. Their sentences grow longer and more complex, while they will probably double the size of their vocabulary. An average first grader speaks sentences that are 11 words in length while average sixth graders use 14 words in their sentences (Strickland, 1962). Chomsky found that children continued to acquire syntax during this period (Chomsky, 1970). Mastery of imbedded sentences does not occur until nine or ten years of age. For example, many ten-year-olds would not clearly understand the subject of *to do* in the sentence, "Sharon asked George what to do."

ACQUISITION OF THOUGHT

An important part of language development is the acquisition of thought that parallels language development. In fact, thought can be considered the fifth language art because it is intimately related to listening, speaking, reading, writing, and thinking. As discussed in an earlier section, we do not know which comes first—language or thought. However, it is clear that thoughts are close to language. When we think, we talk to ourselves.

Young children think aloud. Apparently, they acquire the raw materials for thinking—words, concepts, and experiences—from their environment. They acquire these as they listen to the ideas and the explanations of those around them. They also acquire thinking skills from interacting with the people around them. Let us consider Kelly who is in the *other-external speech* stage of development which lasts from approximately age one-and-one-half to three. In this stage children are dependent on others for language that elaborates ideas and the commands leading to complex activity (Vygotsky, 1962). For instance, when Kelly was two-and-one-half her brother refused to let her play with his cars; she told her mother, who said, "Why don't you play with your tricycle?" Kelly's mother is helping her think of alternative activities. Consider what a different thought pattern is modeled for a youngster whose mother might respond, "Go play with your dolls; cars are for boys."

Gradually Kelly will learn to speak for herself. She will begin to encode elaborated ideas and plans for activities into her own speech. She will express her elaborated ideas orally during the stage of *self-external speech* which extends from the ages of three to four and a half. During this period, she will literally think aloud.

At approximately age four-and-one-half, Kelly will begin to internalize speech and be able to think without speaking her thoughts aloud (Vygotsky, 1962). According to Vygotsky, she will be in the *self-internal speech* stage of development. Although her thinking will not be of an adult nature, she will be moving along the continuum toward adult thought. At four-and-one-half her thoughts are still quite concrete, although slowly and gradually she is growing toward more abstract thought. Abstract thought is not developed until roughly the age of 12.

The teaching implications arising from an understanding of children's thought development are manifold. First, according to Vygotsky, children acquire inner speech (thought) from people in their language environment. This notion clearly points to the fact that children must have excellent language and thought models to enable them to achieve the fullest possible development. Vygotsky's work also would indicate that children cannot think in an extremely quiet environment. They must be allowed to talk (think aloud) as they learn in school. It is entirely possible that when we force children to be quiet we are also forcing them *not to think!*

We help children develop thinking skills when we model thinking activities and think aloud so children can follow our thought processes (refer to Chapter Two). Problem-solving activities and literature that demonstrates such activities help children develop thinking skills.

SUMMARY

Language enables us to communicate and to learn. Language makes life as we know it possible; hence, children must acquire language in order to fully participate in the world. Morphemics, syntax, and discourse are language systems acquired by children. Language is a powerful, creative system because once we acquire the language system, we can generate utterances that no one has ever heard before.

Understanding the historical development of the English language enables teachers to teach English more effectively. The fact that English is an analytic language influences the way that it is taught. English has developed through three stages: Old English, Middle English, and Modern English. Because English is in constant use, it is also constantly changing. We are often unaware of these changes because we are living them.

Gradually and systematically children acquire a language system. Although their language system is complete by the time they enter school, their language is elaborated and their utterances grow longer as they mature. They acquire this system through a genetic predisposition to acquire language, through imitation, and through their search for meaning. Children use language for a variety of functions or reasons including: personal, imaginative, heuristic, interactional, regulatory, and instrumental.

Language and thought are interrelated in children's development. Teachers can use this interrelationship to help children refine both language and thought. By modeling thought processes and examining thinking and problem solving in literature teachers can guide students' learning.

Thought Questions

1. How does the fact that English is an analytic language influence the teaching of language arts?

2. Imagine a communication system that does not include spoken language and explain its operation. What functions are the most difficult to perform without spoken language?

3. Compare English with a synthetic language. How are the languages alike? How are they different?

4. Briefly explain the theories of language acquisition.

5. Describe the language of a one-year-old child, a three-year-old child and a five-year-old child.

6. What is the difference between morphology and semantics?

7. Which comes first language or thought?

Enrichment Activities

1. Tape the language of a three-year-old child and a five-year-old child. Contrast the number of words and sentence length for each child.

2. Observe a group of children in a classroom and identify the functions of language you see in use.

3. Obtain a British and/or Australian newspaper or magazine and compare the language with that found in a local newspaper or magazine.

4. Observe a child in nursery school and count both the number of words and the number of different words that he or she uses during a day.

5. Examine history of language concepts included in the students' edition of a language arts series.

Selected Readings

Bambas, Rudolph C. (1980). *The English Language: Its Origin and History.* Norman, OK: University of Oklahoma Press.

Baugh, Albert C. (1963). *A History of the English Language.* New York: Appleton-Century-Crofts.

Beck, M. Susan (1983). *KIDSPEAK: How Children Develop Language Skills.* New York: New American Library.

Dale, P. (1976). *Language Development: Structure and Function.* (2d ed.). New York: Holt, Rinehart and Winston).

Gruenewald, Lee J., and Sara A. Pollak (1984). *Language Interaction in Teaching and Learning.* Baltimore, MD: University Park Press.

Halliday, Michael (1975). *Explorations in the Functions of Language.* London: Edward Arnold.

Hodges, Richard, and E. Hugh Rudorf (1972). *Language and Learning to Read: What Teachers Should Know About Language.* Boston: Houghton-Mifflin.

Jaggar, Angela, and M. Trika Smith-Burke (1985). *Observing the Language Learner.* Newark, DE: International Reading Association.

Lindfors, J. (1979). "Providing Environments That Foster Children's Language Development." *Practical Applications of Research,* American Educational Research Association.

Malmstrom, Jean (1977). *Understanding Language,* New York: St. Martin's Press.

McCrum, Robert, William Cran, and Robert MacNeil (1986). *The Story of English.* New York: Viking.

Smith, E. Brooks, Kenneth S. Goodman, and Robert Meredith (1976). *Language and Thinking in School* (2d ed.). New York: Richard C. Owen Publishers.

Vygotsky, Lev (1962). *Thought and Language.* Cambridge, MA: MIT Press.

Waterhouse, Lynn H., Karen Fischer, and Ellen Ryan (1980). *Language Awareness and Reading.* Newark, DE: International Reading Association.

References

Appleton, T. (1975). "The Development of Behavioral Competence in Infancy." In *Review of Child Development Research,* F. D. Horowitz (ed.). Chicago: University of Chicago Press.

Bambas, Rudolph C. (1980). *The English Language: Its Origin and History.* Norman, OK: University of Oklahoma Press, p. ix.

Baugh, Albert C. (1963). *A History of the English Language.* New York: Appleton-Century-Crofts, 64, 135.

Beck, M. Susan (1983). *KIDSPEAK: How Children Develop Language Skills.* New York: New American Library, pp. 18–33.

Brown, R., C. Cazden, and U. Bellugi-Klima (1971). "The Child's Grammar from I to III," in *Child Language: A Book of Readings,* A. Bar-Adon and W. Leopold (eds.). Englewood Cliffs, NJ: Prentice-Hall.

Bruner, J. S. (1966). "On Cognitive Growth." In *Studies in Cognitive Growth,* J. S. Bruner, R. R. Oliver, and P. M. Greenfield (eds.). New York: Wiley.

Chomsky, C. (Spring 1970). "Language Development After Six," *HGSEA Bulletin, 14* (3), 14–17.

Chomsky, N. (1965). *Aspects of the Theory of Syntax.* Cambridge, MA: MIT Press.

Clark, H., and E. V. Clark (1977). *Psychology and Language.* New York: Harcourt Brace Jovanovich, p. 377.

Dale, Philip (1976). *Language Development: Structure and Function* (2d ed.). New York: Holt, Rinehart and Winston, pp. 166–175.

Duckworth, Eleanor (June 1964). "Piaget Rediscovered," *ESS Newsletter,* Elementary Science Study, Educational Services, Watertown, MA.

Gleason, Jean Berko (1969). "Language Development in Early Childhood." In *Oral Language and Reading,* James Walden (ed.). Champaign, IL: National Council of Teachers of English, p. 16.

Halliday, Michael (1975). *Explorations in the Functions of Language.* London: Edward Arnold, pp. 11–15.

Hodges, Richard, and E. Hugh Rudorf (1972). *Language and Learning to Read: What Teachers Should Know About Language.* Boston: Houghton-Mifflin, 38.

Leakey, R. (November 1971). "Man's Evolutionary Future." In a Symposium at the American Eugenics Society, New York.

Lindfors, J. (1980). *Children's Language and Learning.* Englewood Cliffs, NJ: Prentice-Hall.

Malmstrom, Jean (1977). *Understanding Language,* New York: St. Martin's Press, p. 58.

McCrum, Robert, William Cran, and Robert MacNeil (1986). *The Story of English,* New York: Viking.

McNeill, D. (1970). *The Acquisition of Language.* New York: Harper & Row.

Piaget, J. (1960). *Language and Thought of the Child.* London: Routledge and Kegan.

Pinnell, G. S. (1985). "Ways to Look at the Functions of Children's Language." In *Observing the Language Learner,* A. Jaggar and M. Smith (eds.). Newark, DE: International Reading Association and National Council of Teachers of English.

Restak, Richard M. (Spring 1985). "The Human Brain: Insights and Puzzles." *Theory into Practice,* vols. 91–94.

Smith, E. Brooks, Kenneth S. Goodman, and Robert Meredith (1976). *Language and Thinking in School* (2nd Ed.). New York: Richard C. Owen Publishers.

Smith, F. (1977). "The Uses of Language." *Language Arts, 54,* 638–644.

———. (1978). *Understanding Reading* (2d ed.) New York: Holt, Rinehart and Winston.

Shuy, Roger W. (Summer 1984) "Language as a Foundation for Education: The School Context." *Theory into Practice,* XXIII, 3–30.

Strickland, Dorothy S. (1962). *The Language of Elementary School Children: Its Relationship to the Language of Reading Textbooks and the Quality of Reading of Selected Children.* Bulletin of the School of Education, XXVIII, Bloomington, IN: Indiana University Press.

———. (1985). "Forward." In *Observing the Language Learner.* Newark, DE: International Reading Association, p. v.

Vygotsky, Lev (1962). *Thought and Language.* Cambridge, MA: MIT Press.

Part **TWO**

Language Arts Processes

Chapter **Four**

Teaching Oral Language

CHAPTER OVERVIEW

Oral language is so easily acquired that parents and teachers tend to underestimate its importance. Oral language is the basis for developing listening, thinking, reading, and writing. Being able to communicate effectively through oral language is important in everyone's life. Children share meanings through the various forms of informative oral language—conversation, discussion, interviews, and oral reports. Meaning also is created and shared through aesthetic oral language, such as creative drama, puppets, story telling, readers' theatre, and choral reading. Teachers play an important role in developing oral language. They create opportunities for students to talk in an environment that facilitates oral expression. Teachers design instruction that gives students "something to say," "a reason for saying it," and "someone to say it to."

Anticipation Guide

In your opinion, how important is talk to learning? Why do you think this? Do you think children need to learn how to talk? As you read this chapter think about the following questions.

1. How is oral language related to the other language arts?

2. What are the characteristics of an effective use of oral language?

3. What activities develop oral language?

Key Concepts

oral language (talk)   reader's theater
informative oral language   choral reading
aesthetic oral language   audience

INTRODUCTION

Oral language (talk) is the primary source of all other language forms. Children who have strong oral language facility usually become good readers and they have greater potential for writing (Tiedt et al., 1983). Nevertheless, we take talking for granted (because most children learn to talk without formal instruction). By the time children come to school, they are quite accomplished talkers. They use most of the sounds of English (phonemes); they use the sentence patterns of English (syntax); they string sentences together to express meaning (discourse); they know the meaning of many words (semantics); and they use language for a wide range of functions (purposes).

Although this language facility is quite impressive, students still have to learn effective communication skills. Oral language is essential to the communication process. Ninety percent of our language use is oral. Our friends, colleagues, and prospective employers learn about us from our oral language facility. Nevertheless, most teachers express less than whole-hearted belief in the value of pupils' talk for learning (Wells and Wells, 1984).

TALKING TO LEARN

Talk is important to thinking and learning (Vygotsky, 1962; Britton, 1970). Teachers have long observed that many students do not know what they think with any degree of specificity until they talk through their thinking (Buckley, 1976). Frank Smith (1982) observes that we talk to ourselves as an aid to cognition, emotions and socialization. We learn by talking with others about our ideas (Wilkinson, 1984). Putting our thoughts into words helps us sort out the myriad of thoughts and images impinging on our minds. We assimilate new information through our own words. Our own words are ones that we understand; therefore translating ideas into our own words is a means of understanding (Emig, 1977). This was demonstrated, in a study of kindergarten, first-, and second-grade students who were read a story. Then they were divided into three groups at each grade level to demonstrate their comprehension of the story. One group drew a picture, the second group discussed the story, and the third group dramatized the story. Their understanding was evaluated with a reading comprehension test. The dramatization group scored highest, and the discussion group scored only slightly behind them, but the children who drew pictures had the lowest comprehension scores (Galda, 1982).

Students learn social studies, science, and mathematics by talking about these subjects. Wilkinson (1984) found students who used oral language successfully in communicateing with their peers achieved higher grades. Research shows that teachers promote learning when they encourage students to talk about the task at hand (Thaiss and Suhor, 1984). Thus teachers who encourage students to collaborate increase their achievement.

Talking also helps students learn listening, reading, and writing. Talking is essential to listening skills because it is through listening to others talk and asking them questions to ascertain whether they have understood what they have heard that helps us refine listening skills. Teachers prepare students to read through discussing new words and ideas. They prepare students to write, through discussing ideas prior to writing. In the early stages of writing, children are writing down their oral language. Talk literally surrounds listening, reading, and writing. Talking about writing creates a bridge from oral language to written language.

The objective of teaching oral language is to develop students' ability to express ideas clearly, interestingly and appropriately. Oral language experiences should challenge students to extend, enrich, and elaborate their existing language patterns. Classroom experiences that develop oral language include drama, puppetry, choral speaking, readers' theater, discussion groups, and conversations. Oral language development cannot be confined to the early grades; these abilities should be developed throughout students' school life for the following reasons:

1. Talking is the most common use of language.

2. Oral language is basic to the other forms of language.

3. Oral language is a familiar and secure mode of expression for many students.

Following are two vignettes that demonstrate oral language development in elementary school classrooms.

DEVELOPING ORAL LANGUAGE IN GRADE TWO

Ellen Pearson is the teacher in this classroom of 26 second graders. She schedules three "talking times" a week with her students. One of the "talking time" strategies that she uses is "inner circle." Approximately half of the children in the class are in the "inner circle." This group discusses a problem or topic that is identified by the teacher or the students, while the group outside the circle observes. At an appointed time, the groups exchange places. This strategy permits more active participation than a whole class discussion. On the day of our visit to her classroom, the children are discussing proper nutrition for the rabbit their class has just received as a class pet. The children prepared for their discussion by reviewing sections in their health textbook about nutrition, by asking questions of a person who has pet rabbits at home and by viewing a videotape from the media center. The objectives of their discussion are to identify the correct kinds of food to provide proper nutrition for the rabbit, how much food the rabbit should be given, how often the rabbit should be fed, and who should feed him.

DEVELOPING ORAL LANGUAGE IN GRADE FIVE

Linda Allen's fifth grade "lunch bunch" meets during their lunch hour to discuss books once a week. The group composition of the lunch bunch changes each week, although the teacher always participates. The guidelines for group membership are that each person must have read the book and each must actively participate in the discussion.

Several "lunch bunch" students brought copies of *Sarah Plain and Tall* by Patricia MacLachlan, which was the chosen book. The following discussion ensued.

TEACHER: How would you describe Sarah's personality in this book?

MARY: I liked her.

JANET: Me too.

TEACHER: I'm glad you liked Sarah, but you will have to elaborate more. What was it that you liked so much about her?

DAWN: Well, she is her own person. You know what I mean?

TEACHER: No, tell me.

DAWN: It's hard to put into words, but she was a real person.

MARY: She thought she was O. K. She didn't pretend or try to make herself beautiful.

TEACHER: What makes you think that Sarah did not pretend?

MARY: She said she was "Sarah plain and tall." She didn't make excuses or try to change herself.

ELIZABETH: She enjoyed things.

MARY: She enjoyed different things, like she could bake bread, but she preferred to build bookshelves and paint. She liked color and used color when she described things. Do you remember when she said her brother told her that a fogbound sea was a color that had no name?

DAWN: She was a liberated woman!

CHRIS: Yes, she wore overalls and helped build a barn. And this story happened a long time ago. I don't think women usually did things like that in those days.

GWEN: Well, I liked her because she liked herself.

TEACHER: How do you know she liked herself?

GWEN: She said she was "fast and good" when she worked on the barn. A lot of people are afraid to say things like that because people will think that they are "stuck up."

TEACHER: Was Sarah "stuck up"?

CHORUS: No!

TEACHER: Let's see if we can put together a description of Sarah's character.

As you read this chapter compare the ideas presented about teaching oral language with those in the vignettes.

EFFECTIVE TALKERS

Effective talkers are relatively easy to identify. They exhibit poise and confidence which puts their audience at ease. Their pleasing voice invites others to listen. Their interesting content leads listeners to concentrate. They respect others' ideas. They have a repertoire of language that empowers them to express ideas and information. Their sense of audience helps them select language which their audience understands. But effective talkers listen as well as talk, so they can respond appropriately to questions and comments.

Voice

Speakers should have well-modulated, pleasing voices. They should vary the pitch and rhythm of their voices to express meaning. Their pronunciation is clear, distinct, and correct and the tempo is neither too fast nor too slow. The volume is adjusted to room and audience size. As you can readily discern, these qualities are best developed through practice in talking to various size groups for a variety of purposes. Allowing students to tape and analyze their oral language makes them aware of their voices and our oral expression. Taping speakers whom students admire and analyzing the qualities of these speakers will help us identify characteristics they wish to emulate. Figure 4.1 illustrates a speaker voice analysis.

Teachers may wish to create charts like the one shown in Figure 4.1 for classroom use. Students should have opportunities to develop and practice desirable voice characteristics so they can acquire greater control of their oral language.

Students should learn that careful planning, subject matter knowledge, and language control will help them relax. Relaxation is important because it contributes to voice quality. Tense speakers tend to speak in a shrill, rapid voice which makes listeners uncomfortable. Generally, speakers should avoid any characteristics that lead listeners to concentrate on the voice rather than the message.

Mannerisms

Mannerisms are characteristics like fidgeting, mouth noises, twitching, hand twisting, throat clearing, facial expressions, and nervous movements that may detract from the presentation. Many times speakers are unaware of these mannerisms. But classroom language activities give teachers opportunities to guide students away from distracting mannerisms. Videotaping is an ideal way to help students analyze their own performance and detect any mannerisms they need to correct.

Audience

A sense of audience is important in both oral and written language processes. We speak or write differently depending on the person addressed and our relationship to that person. An elementary teacher speaking to a youngster who disrupted the class said, "That's enough James. Be quiet." However, talking to another teacher in the hall she said, "That kid is driving me nuts." And when she had a conference with James's parents she said, "James is very talkative in class and this is interfering with his learning. He doesn't pay attention to the instruction." Our oral language reflects the relationship be-

Date: _12-31-87_

Time: _6 PM_

Context: _Anchorperson Evening News_

Voice tone: _low pitch, pleasant_

Speaking rate: _fast_

Expression: _raised voice to show excitement; spoke slower at end of broadcast_

Strengths: _pleasing voice tone_

Weaknesses: _looked down too much; did not raise and lower voice very much; not expressive_

Figure 4.1   Speaker Voice Analysis

tween speaker and audience, their respective power and status, the formality of the situation, the importance of the communication, and the kind of response expected.

Middle-grade children can begin to study the audience factors like the following. Audience size influences style of speech. Ordinarily, the larger the audience the more formal the presentation. Of course, the converse is true, the smaller the audience, the more informal the presentation. Small audiences permit greater intimacy among audience members and between audience and speaker. Speakers in small groups may know more about the audience which allows them to respond at a different level. Certainly voice control is indicated by audience size also. Small audiences are easier to address in a conversational manner. On the other hand, a large audience requires the speaker to use a microphone.

Middle-grade students can select language that will communicate with each audience. Audiences differ in their "frame of reference," which is comprised of audience needs, background knowledge, expectations, and experiences (Pinnell and Green, 1986). When there is a mismatch in any of these areas, the speaker must prepare the audience to overcome these differences. For instance, if the class (audience) anticipates the speaker will teach them the important ideas in a social studies reading assignment and the speaker (teacher) expects the students to identify these ideas on their own, there is a mismatch that can frustrate everyone. Therefore, the teacher must change the audience's expectations.

Speakers must be aware when their audience is not responding. Sensitivity to the audience signals enables the speaker to adjust the content or delivery to meet audience needs. In some instances, they need to elaborate on some of the points they have explained, to help audience comprehension. There are situations in which the best speech is a short one, so the speaker needs to cut his or her presentation because the audience is tired.

Content

Content is central to communication. Speakers have a responsibility to have something worthwhile to say. Their ideas should be carefully examined prior to speaking, so they may approach an audience with confidence. Content is gathered from experience, textbooks, class, trade books, and discussions. There are four major aspects of content, ideas, words, sentences, and the organization of the discourse. Students must identify the ideas they wish to communicate, associate the content with words and sentences, and organize their content in a logical fashion that helps them communicate. Content may be organized in many ways. Among the many organizational patterns teachers use are stories, jokes, riddles, cause and effect, comparison, chronological order, and questions and answers.

The idea content of oral language is derived from experiences, television, movies, literature, books, and listening to others' ideas. Discussing the ideas they plan to talk about helps them associate words with their experiences and to organize the information. Obviously, the richer the children's experiences, the richer the store of ideas they have to share as they talk with others. A rich store of ideas helps children listen to others' with greater understanding because they can associate the ideas and words they are hearing with those stored in their memory. Exploring and discussing ideas and experiences helps children organize them and relate them to their schemata thus facilitating recall.

Speaking Vocabulary

Ordinarily, we have four vocabularies. We have a speaking vocabulary, a listening vocabulary, a reading vocabulary, and a writing vocabulary. Many of the same words are found in each vocabulary, but there are differences in these vocabularies as well. For instance, *and, the,* and *but* are probably found in all four vocabularies, while a word like *matrix* may be found in the reading vocabulary only. That means that we recognize it when we read it, but do not use it in conversation. On the other hand, we are not likely to say the word *matrix* when we are talking, perhaps because we are unsure of the pronunciation. Think about your own vocabularies. Can you identify words that you understand when you hear other people use them, but you do not say these words? Are there words that you understand when you read them, but that you do not use when you write?

A large vocabulary is very important because speakers use these words to express their thoughts in precise, interesting ways. Vocabulary is important in early reading because the major task facing beginning readers is that of learning to read the words in their speaking vocabulary. A large vocabulary is associated with intelligence. Many intelligence tests are tests of vocabulary which is understandable, since many of the words in our vocabulary are labels for the concepts we know. Thus, when we speak of vocabulary development, we are speaking of conceptual development. Both vocabulary and conceptual development reflect children's experiences and our interests which suggests that the more experiences and interests they have, the larger their vocabulary.

Vocabulary develops and expands throughout our lifetime. Between the ages of three and five children's vocabulary expands greatly as they label the many features of their experiences. The greatest vocabulary growth occurs during the school years. Their experiences widen during these years and they acquire the words to express new ideas and experiences. Many children use words when they have only partially grasped their meanings. But they will gradually refine their understanding of these words through conversation with adults. As children refine their understanding of words they differentiate the meanings of nouns more closely and use descriptive words with greater precision (Tough, 1981).

Vocabulary reflects interests derived from home and school activities (Tough, 1981). Rapidly developing ten- and eleven-year-old children use many technical words reflecting their interests and increasing knowledge in the content areas. These children are also beginning to appreciate the subtle differences in word meanings, and multiple meanings. They enjoy books like *The King Who Reigned, A Chocolate Moose for Dinner,* and *Amelia Bedelia.* By the age of twelve, many children can think more abstractly about words. For instance, they are more able to separate words from the objects they stand for.

Expanding students' word knowledge improves their oral language. One of the best ways to stimulate vocabulary growth is to extend students' experiences. Another recurring theme is students' interests. As they learn more about their interests such as space travel, building models, or whatever their current enthusiasms are, children acquire the words that label these concepts. For instance, space travel involves such words as solar, blast-off, and weightlessness.

Oral Syntax

Children usually come to school with the ability to combine words into phrases, clauses, and sentences. In fact when children enter school, they use the major sentence structures that occur in English (Loban, 1976). Children's control of syntax continues to grow during the elementary school years. Following is a summary of the types of sentences that elementary school children commonly use.

1. Simple sentences consisting of subject, verb, and object. "The dog went to the park."

2. Compound sentences, consisting of two simple sentences that are joined by a conjunction. "The dog went to the park and the dog barked at the joggers."

3. Complex sentences which are comprised of one or more independent clauses and one or more dependent clauses connected by a subordinate conjunction (the subordinate conjunction may be inferred rather than stated). "The dog who went to the park barked at the joggers."

The use of complex language structure parallels the ability to use cognitive structures (Gruenewald and Pollak, 1984). However, teachers should not assume that children fully understand all of the syntactic structures they use. Comprehension of language often lags behind language use. Language, both written and oral, may be difficult for some children to understand. This is particularly true of the language used in the content areas because it includes complex sentences containing many independent and dependent clauses (Gruenewald and Pollak, 1984).

Oral language instruction should focus on prepositions, conjunctions, negatives, and questions, which research indicates present some problems to children (Loban, 1976; Nilsen, 1983; Athey, 1983). Instruments like the one presented in Figure 4.2 provide teachers with the information they need to guide children's language learning.

TEACHING ORAL LANGUAGE

Oral language activities are divided into two broad groups, **informative oral language** activities and **aesthetic oral language** activities. These categories are based on the type of content that practice within the activity. Therefore, informative oral language activities include conversations, dialogs, discussions, debates, meetings, interviews, and oral reports while aesthetic oral language activities include storytelling, reader's theater, drama, puppetry, role playing, and choral reading. Table 4.1 summarizes the types of activities teachers can use. How literature serves as a pivotal role in both types of oral language activity will be discussed.

Name _____

Date _____

---

1. Student listens to others and responds appropriately.   Yes   No

2. When talking and explaining, the student uses complete   Yes   No
   sentences. (Complete sentences in oral language differ from
   those in written language.)

3. Student had a _____ large _____ average _____ small / speaking vocabulary.

4. When student gives information or explains, others usually   Yes   No
   understand.

5. Student usually pronounces words clearly and correctly.   Yes   No

6. Student uses language to:
   ask permission
   ask for information
   agree
   say what he wants to do
   explain
   give directions
   praise another
   criticize

7. Student uses language to:
   give reports
   participate in discussions
   dramatize
   reader's theatre

8. Student's voice quality (high–low; loud–soft)   Good   Poor

9. Student's speaking rate (fast–slow)   Fast   Slow

Figure 4.2 Student Language Analysis Guide

Several factors have mitigated against talking in classrooms. Lange reports that teachers feel that they lack the class time to develop oral language skills. Also many teachers have insufficient background to instruct children in the development and use of oral language. Finally, talking has a low priority in education (Lange, 1981). Winkeljohann concurs with Lange. She

Table 4.1 Types of Oral Language Activities

Information Activities	Aesthetic Activities
Conversations	Choral reading
Debates	Drama
Dialogs	Puppetry
Discussions	Reader's theater
Interviews	Role playing
Meetings	Storytelling
Oral reports	

reports that teachers are not clear on the purpose of oral language instruction. Furthermore, schools often did not have oral language curricula and consistently paid little attention to the oral language of children (Winkeljohann, 1978).

In the book *The Prime of Miss Jean Brodie* by Muriel Spark, Miss Brodie, a teacher, says, "To me education is a leading out of what is already there in the pupil's soul . . . It is (not) a putting in of something that is not there. . . ." As language teachers we could say the same thing. Children already have language when they come to school—teachers do not put it in their mouths. Teachers guide children as they refine existing oral language. Children learn to talk by talking; therefore, teachers give children many opportunities to practice using oral language. Teachers stimulate oral language development by motivating students, asking questions, and creating an environment that stimulates oral language use.

Language is not so much a subject to be studied as it is a process of thinking that must be used if it is to be mastered (Buckley, 1976). Students need to have something worthwhile to say (experiences, concepts), a way of saying it (semantics, syntax, discourse), and a reason for saying it (pragmatics, functions) to learn language (Gruenewald and Pollak, 1984). Teachers facilitate discussion through assignments that include oral language, for instance, a writing activity may involve peer tutoring or a social studies assignment may incorporate a debate. Through developing the background knowledge for these activities, and involving students in purposeful oral language activities teachers can meet the need to have something to say, a way of saying it and a reason for saying it. The following factors should be considered when planning oral language instruction.

1. Student preparation for talk (something to say, a way to say it, and a reason to say it).

2. Planned, systematic, direct instruction.

3. Clear objectives that are apparent in teaching and in evaluation.

4. An environment that encourages appropriate talk.

5. A teacher who models effective oral language.

6. A teacher who uses effective instructional strategies such as scaffolding and questioning to help children mature in their use of oral language.

Talking Environment

An environment in which people cherish and encourage children's talk challenges them to communicate orally and to use oral language as they think and learn. In a talk-inducing environment, furniture is arranged to give students easy assess to one another. Bright posters, displays, and bulletin boards stimulate children's interests; arrangements of trade books invite them to read. Reference materials enable students to check information and to identify ways of sharing their ideas appropriately.

Modeling Oral Language

Teachers should model appropriate oral language for children. Their appropriate use of language in the classroom has a powerful influence on children. The following example demonstrates an instance of the powerful impact of teachers' language. Some years ago during a teacher shortage in the midwest, a school system recruited teachers from a nearby state. The newly recruited teachers spoke a dialect that was not a prestige dialect in the state to which they emigrated. The children in their classes began to talk like the teachers in a matter of a few weeks which gave rise to many parent complaints. In an open meeting of parents in the school system, many parents complained that their children were using semantics and syntax that were unacceptable in their home. They stated that their children's oral language was "ruined" by the school. They threatened to remove their children to a private school unless steps were taken to improve the teachers' oral language skills. This led to several teachers' decisions to return to their home state rather than deal with the fact that their oral language was unacceptable to their students' parents.

A Listening Teacher

In addition to modeling oral language for children, teachers should listen to students to develop the children's language. Children express themselves better when their teachers are interested in what they say. Teachers who listen attentively to children make them realize that their ideas are worthwhile, which encourages them to continue sharing their thoughts orally. Teachers must avoid distractions like grading papers while a youngster is talking to them. In class, they must listen and respond appropriately to students' comments and avoid cutting them off because the teacher thinks they are giving an incorrect response. Hearing children out helps a teacher understand their thinking. If a response appears to be incorrect, ask the student, "Why do you think that?" Children's oral language helps us understand their cognitive development and since we think through oral language, talking encourages cognitive development. The listening teacher has an immeasurable impact on childrens' language development.

Language Play

Young children enjoy playing with language. Preschool children, kindergartners, and first graders repeat sounds, words, and phrases just because they sound good. Teachers facilitate language play when they allow children to explore language in the classroom. Teachers can read books to children that will stimulate their language play because they enjoy the sound of phonemes, words, or phrases in the book. The rhythm of language also appeals to children and leads them to repeat the expressions they hear. Preschoolers like to point to objects in books and say the words. Kindergarten and first-grade children enjoy looking at alphabet books and saying the letter names and words that start with the letters. Books like the following will stimulate language play.

Hosie's Alphabet by Hosie, Tobias, and Lisa Baskin

My Tang's Tungled and Other Ridiculous Situations by Sara and John Brewton

The Angry Lady Bug by Eric Carle

Tomie dePaola's Mother Goose by Tomie dePaola

Jambo Means Hello: Swahili Alphabet Book by Tom and Muriel Feelings

Millions of Cats by Wanda Gag

The Rain Puddle by Adelaide Holl

A Very Special House by Ruth Krauss

Gobbledygook by Steven Kroll

Big Pig by Dennis Nolan

Faint Frogs Feeling Feverish and Other Terrifically Tantalizing Tongue Twisters by Lilian Obligado

Pierre by Maurice Sendak

The Carsick Zebra and Other Animal Riddles by David Adler

Language Books for Middle Grade/Intermediate Students

Juba This and Juba That by Virginia Tashjian

With a Deep Sea Smile by Virginia Tashjian

Yertle the Turtle and Other Stories by Dr. Seuss

DEVELOPING INFORMATIVE ORAL LANGUAGE _____

Informative oral language is concerned with language that is used to convey information. This category of language includes conversations, dialogs, discussions, debates, meetings, interviews, and oral reports.

Conversations _____

Conversation is an informal, small group activity; however, it is not random activity. Conversation is a reciprocal process with the participants talking about a topic of mutual interest. Conversation gives them an opportunity to discuss feelings and opinions regarding a wide range of topics. Conversation gives children an opportunity to rehearse and organize their knowledge in a nonthreatening situation. Opportunities to participate in conversation help some students overcome self-consciousness and develop confidence when expressing their thoughts and ideas. Conversation may be free-wheeling because the participants can move freely from topic to topic as one participant builds on the contributions of another.

Conversation participants must attend to the topic as they keep up with the conversation and sustain the interchange that occurs during conversation. To do this students need well-developed interests, a variety of experiences, a good memory, and a courteous attitude. Interests and experiences provide the content of conversation. A good memory gives children the basis for remembering the ideas expressed by other participants, as well as their own ideas. Courtesy is a cornerstone of good conversation. Participants should exhibit courtesy as they wait for other participants to complete their thoughts, by avoiding arguments with other participants, and by listening to other individual's thoughts.

Teachers can develop children's conversational skills and abilities by providing a physical setting that encourages conversation. They should schedule conversational time for and with students. Conversation may be scheduled as a time to talk about anything students are interested in, or subjects may be introduced for students conversation.

Informed, thoughtful conversation is a learning experience, as well as an interesting and entertaining one. Conversation may grow into full class discussions. If students exhibit strong interests in topics that emerge during conversation, they may wish to organize a full class discussion of the topic.

Dialogs _____

A dialog is conversation that occurs between two people. Dialog is particularly valuable for children because it presents an opportunity to interact with one person and to obtain feedback. As the youngster talks with another person, failures to communicate are readily apparent. They learn how to communicate meaning to another person because the individual they are talking with can immediately ask for more information if it is necessary to establish understanding. Dialog creates a model for thinking because the participants are thinking aloud with the distinct advantage of immediate feedback when communication fails (Bruner, 1978).

Discussions

Discussion is more formal than conversation because usually there are more participants and more specific goals. Discussion is a dynamic event which requires participants to simultaneously orchestrate a number of language skills (Pinnell, 1984). For instance discussion goals should be clear to all participants, since the discussion continues until the goals are achieved. In a discussion, participants share the responsibility for moving toward a conclusion that achieves the identified goals. The major differences between conversation and discussion lie in the group size, specificity of goals, and the need for a conclusion. Discussion can help students develop thinking skills. For example, Athey (1983) recommends devoting class discussion time to deliberate exploration of the deeper and fuller meaning of selected concepts like happiness, democracy, and probability (mathematics). These are important, abstract concepts which could be developed through discussion with middle-grade students.

The guiding principles for discussion are similar to those of conversation. During a discussion participants should stay on the topic, work toward achieving the goals, and work toward a conclusion. A participant who digresses from the topic is interfering with progress of the discussion toward stated goals. Discussion participants should be prepared to discuss the topic. This means that they may have to read and research in preparation for the discussion. Students should monitor their own participation. They should actively participate in the discussion, but avoid dominating or dropping out of the discussion. A list of discussion guidelines for classroom use follows.

Discussion Guidelines

1. Learn as much as you can about the topic.

2. Support your opinions with facts.

3. Stay on the topic.

4. Listen carefully to the other discussants.

5. Ask them to explain their ideas when you do not understand.

6. At the end of the discussion help the leader identify the most important ideas and summarize them.

The discussion leader has specific responsibilities. The leader opens the discussion and establishes goals for the discussion (see the suggested topics in the following section). At times, the leader will find it necessary to clarify participants' statements and to summarize progress to that point as a basis for continuing productive discussion. Occasionally, discussion leaders will have to handle differences of opinion between participants. They also have to diplomatically cope with the talkative students who attempt to dominate discussions and the very shy students who do not participate sufficiently. Teachers will find it necessary to model discussion leader behavior for students, but all students should have opportunities to serve as discussion leaders so they can develop leadership skills.

Discussion Topics Books are discussion topics. Children may discuss literature from many perspectives. For example, they may discuss plot, theme, characterization, setting, author's style or story subject matter. Peer relations is an interesting subject matter for middle-school children, and this subject is apparent in books like *A Girl Called All, The Young Landlords,* and *Summer of the Swans.* Personal integrity is an important topic for middle-grade children, and this subject is developed in books like *Roll of Thunder, Hear My Cry, Words by Heart,* and *Bitter Herbs and Honey.* Younger children also encounter many discussions as they read or are read to. For instance they learn about children with special needs when they discuss books like *My Friend Jacob, Anna's Silent World,* and *Follow My Leader.* You may refer to the first part of this chapter for an example of a book discussion.

School or class problems are interesting discussion subjects. Discussions may focus on topics like the following:

Planning for field trips

Luncheon menus that are boring

School pride

Ways of helping the handicapped

Friendliness to new students

Panel Discussion Panel discussions are formal discussions designed to present information to an audience. In panel discussions individual participants are assigned topics and information to research. Panel members may be selected because they have an expertise that will make their discussion contribution especially valuable. The panel members discuss a topic before an audience who then usually asks questions. Panel members should prepare and research their information carefully. Participants should support their opinions with facts.

Debates

Debates are a form of discussion or dialog. Debaters present two sides of an issue. The debaters usually present their carefully planned argument; they then respond to the argument presented by the other person and to any audience questions. Many middle-grade children enjoy debating current issues. For example, they may debate the pros and cons of a strike, or a political candidate's platform, or the need for import quotas. It is important that students important to the debate prepare careful notes based on accurate information. Debaters should learn to support their opinions.

Meetings

Middle-grade children can use the skills acquired from conversations, discussions, and debates as they participate in meetings. Many middle-grade classes elect class officers and hold meetings; some middle-grade students belong to interest groups, hobby groups, 4-H clubs, or scout troops. These students need to use oral language as they participate in these groups. They also need to learn about parliamentary procedures so they can participate without embarrassment. Parliamentary procedures are given below.

1. The class or group president calls the meeting to order. Group members should be quiet and pay attention when this is done.

2. The president asks the secretary to read the minutes of the last meeting.

3. The president asks if there are any changes or additions to the minutes. If there are not changes or additions, the president says that "the minutes will be accepted as read."

4. The president asks the treasurer to give a treasurer's report. The president asks for any questions. If there are none, the president says that "the treasurer's report will be accepted as read."

5. The president asks for committee reports.

6. The president asks the group if there is any old business. If there is, a motion is made and seconded; then the group discusses the motion until they are satisfied. The group votes on the motion.

7. After old business is completed, the president asks the group if there is any new business. If there is, motions are made and seconded, and the group discusses the new business until they are ready to vote on the motion or motions.

8. The president of the group asks for a vote to adjourn the meeting. After there is a motion and a second to the motion, the group votes to adjourn the meeting.

Interviews

An interview is a form of oral information gathering. The interviewer may speak with one or two individuals or a small group of people. Interviewers gather information regarding an individual, a group (musical group or political group), or a situation (nuclear accident). The interviewer prepares questions that will obtain the desired information.

Interviewers should make an appointment with the person or persons in advance. They should also learn as much as they can about the person prior to the interview. Publicity materials distributed by press agents, publishing companies, or television networks are sources of information. Additional information may be found in newspapers and magazines. The interviewer prepares questions in advance, usually preparing more questions than necessary because some answers take more or less time than planned. Interviewers often tape interviews, but permission should be obtained before taping. If the interviewee did not permit taping, then the interviewer should carefully record all responses. The interviewer should thank the person or persons interviewed for their time.

Elementary school students may interview people like the following:

school principal	spelling contest winners
teachers	student writers
student artists	school visitors
local high-school athletes	

Oral Reports

Oral reports are a way of sharing information and ideas. Discussions, conversations, and interviews are preparation for oral reports. Students can gain confidence from their experiences talking in groups where the responsibility for communication is shared with others. During the middle grades, students may give short oral reports on topics of interest.

Students should keep in mind the following things about giving oral reports.

1. Choose an interesting topic and study the topic.

2. Make the report short.

3. Your report should have an introduction, a body, and a closing.

4. Include only important ideas—too many details will make the report boring. Arrange the important ideas in a logical order.

5. Prepare note cards for the report, but do not read the cards. Use the cards as a prompt if necessary.

6. Speak so everyone can hear you.

7. Use pictures, objects, models, etc., to clarify your ideas.

The teacher should schedule oral reports carefully, so that the class does not become bored by listening to a large number of reports at one time. Scheduling a few reports at a time is one way to make reports interesting. Oral reporting may be varied by dividing the class into small groups and having the groups listen to reports rather than having all students listen to all of the reports.

Criteria should be established for oral reports and students evaluated relative to their progress toward the criteria. Teacher evaluation should be supplemented by peer evaluation. Teachers may distribute evaluation forms for students to complete.

AESTHETIC USES OF ORAL LANGUAGE

Aesthetic uses of oral language are natural and spontaneous in childrens' lives. In fact, oral language activities are variations and extensions of dramatic play that serve as a bridge from the home into the school. These uses of language include creative or interpretive drama (Heathcote, 1983), puppets, reader's theater, role playing, storytelling, and choral reading. Each of these activities is natural to most children. Children chant words and rhymes that sound good to them, they learn jump rope jingles, and games like "Farmer in the Dell" and "Red Rover, Red Rover." Drama emerges when they play house, and role playing when they pretend they are parents, animals, or monsters. Children use drama and role playing to try out life roles, ways of behaving and preparing for new situations (such as field trips), and solutions to problems. Students enjoy imagining themselves in exciting situations, in other times, and in other places. All these forms of dramatic play serve as primary tools for developing affective and cognitive communication skills in children (Heathcote, 1983).

Values of Aesthetic Language

Dramatic play stimulates language and imagination. Children like to dramatize some of the stories that the teacher reads to them, thus extending their acquaintance with literature. As they act, tell stories, play with puppets, and create choral readings, children are creating oral language scripts. These oral scripts stimulate reading, create listening content, and serve as models for students who are learning to write.

Appropriate content for aesthetic uses of oral language is the same as content for any language activity. The content should be interesting to the audience, participants should be able to identify with the characters and events in the story, and the story should expand their horizons. New concepts, feelings, places, peoples, and situations stimulate children's imaginations. Plots should be simple and have a distinct climax. A story used for any dramatic play activity should be structured with a definite beginning, middle, climax, and ending. Good stories for dramatization rely on the mental images created in the children's minds rather than on illustrations (Cottrell, 1975)

Aesthetic applications of oral language extend students' opportunities to both speak and listen because an audience is involved in most of these activities. Thus, the activities discussed in this section give children opportunities to develop both language skills and audience skills.

Storytelling

Storytelling is an ancient art. The oral literature of long ago is the progenitor of present literature (Frye, 1970). Storytelling is a natural form of dramatic play which children begin to use early in their lives. Children naturally tell stories about daily events in their lives to parents and friends. They retell stories that were read to them and ones that they saw on television. Many teachers will agree that children enjoy retelling television programs especially after ten of their students retell the same program. Teachers who enjoy storytelling foster their students' storytelling activities.

Storytelling in the Classroom The content for storytelling is found almost everywhere. Jokes and riddles are a natural bridge to somewhat longer stories. Perhaps the most important thing to remember when teaching children about storytelling is that they should choose an enjoyable story. Choosing stories that are meaningful to the teller makes it possible to tell them with the sensitivity and enthusiasm that are essential to storytelling. Stories selected for storytelling should fit the occasion. For example, a funny story fits a happy situation, while a sad occasion calls for a more somber story.

The storyteller should know the story well enough to tell it in his or her own words. Stories are not memorized because the teller should adapt them to the audience. The storyteller may include the names of students or use local street and city names to make the story particularly interesting. Sensitivity and enthusiasm as well as a pleasing voice and clear speech are necessary for a successful story.

The storyteller should sit on the floor or on a low chair with the listeners clustered around. Such a physical arrangement creates a more intimate group and enables the storyteller to maintain eye contact with the audience. At the same time, the audience can see the storyteller's face and enjoy both the facial expressions and the vocal nuances. Audience response stimulates the storyteller and enhances the process.

Traditional literature grew out of the oral tradition; therefore, it is natural storytelling material. The following list includes suggested stories; also included is a story this author told a group of students. This story has universal appeal for children because the traditional story line is tailored to a local place and characters. Many traditional stories lend themselves to modernization and you may wish to visit your local library to identify additional stories.

The Three Little Pigs

Little Red Riding Hood

The Gingerbread Boy

"Why North Carolinians Are Called Tarheels"

"Why the Sky Is Carolina Blue"

"Why the Elephant Got a Long Trunk"

"Why the Rabbit Has a Short Tail"

 MY PANCAKE RAN AWAY *OR* THE PANCAKE PICNIC

One Sunday morning, I decided to cook pancakes for Muffin and me. I made several very normal looking pancakes, and suddenly Muffin started barking. She barked and barked, so I turned around to see what was going on. Well, that pancake was sitting up in the pan looking around. Then he jumped out of the pan and ran out the door. Muffin ran after him barking and I ran after Muffin because I didn't want her to get hit by an automobile. Paul and Jo, my neighbors and their dog Randy saw us run out of the house and wanted to know if they could help. I explained that I was chasing Muffin who was chasing a pancake man. They were a little surprised, but Jo, Paul, and Randy joined me. We ran up Holdsworth Court, where we saw Luke and Seth who ran after us to Lake Brandt Road. We could see Muffin and the Pancake Man ahead of us, but they turned onto Old Battleground Road where there were more cars and I was really worried about Muffin. Jo said, "I think they are going to New Garden Road." Sure enough, they did. They ran right past Guilford Battleground Park. Then I heard someone calling me from the park. It was Nancy Randall who was out for her morning jog. She said, "Is something wrong? I just saw Muffin run by." I said, "Come on, I need your help to catch her." So Nancy joined Jo, Paul, Randy, Luke, Seth, and me. We ran along New Garden Road as fast as we could because we could barely see Muffin and the Pancake Man ahead of us. Muffin can really run when she is hungry.

Finally, we came to Guilford College and we saw some Guilford College students jogging around the track. They yelled at us and wanted to know what we were running after. We motioned for them to join us and explained as we ran along. The Guilford College students joined Jo, Paul, Randy, Luke, Seth, Nancy, and me as we ran after Muffin and the Pancake Man. We ran past the airport and saw a van full of Piedmont stewardesses; they rolled down the window and wanted to know what we were chasing. We explained and they got off the bus and joined Jo, Paul, Randy, Luke, Seth, Nancy, the Guilford College students, and me chasing Muffin and the Pancake Man. Then we came to Kernersville and we saw some automobile salespersons at Parks Chevrolet; they ran out to the road and asked us, what we were chasing; we told them and they joined Jo, Paul, Randy, Luke, Seth, Nancy, the Guilford College students, the stewardesses, and me chasing Muffin and the Pancake Man.

Next we came to the Yadkin River. Everyone stopped on the banks of the river because we were winded from running so far and didn't know how to get across the river. While the Pancake Man was catching his breath, Muffin grabbed him by the leg. Then Jo, Paul, and Nancy went into the Little

General store and bought syrup and butter. When they came out, we sat down on the grass and had a pancake picnic. We had so much exercise from all of that running that we didn't have to exercise for a week. Muffin and Randy ate so much pancake that they didn't have to eat for a week. And everyone agreed that the next time I make pancakes we should have another pancake picnic.

Selecting and Preparing to Tell Stories   There are several considerations in choosing stories to tell. The following guidelines are appropriate for teachers who are going to tell stories for students.

1. The story should have a simple plot.

2. The plot should have a beginning, middle, and end.

3. The story should have repetition.

4. The story should be one that you like.

Once you have selected a story to tell, you should prepare to tell it. First, read the story and mentally divide it into episodes or natural breaking points. You do not have to memorize the story; just develop a sequence that will convey the major events in the story. You may include your own characters, places, or expressions in the story.

Props are sometimes useful in storytelling. A flannel board may be used for placing characters that have been backed with sandpaper or flannel. A storyteller may choose to wear different hats while telling a story; stuffed animals, puppets, or other toys make other interesting props.

Reader's Theater

Reader's theater is an oral presentation of drama, prose, or poetry by two or more readers who read clearly and expressively. It is one way of enjoying good literature. Reader's theater is more formal than other ways of sharing literature; therefore it is most appropriate for intermediate or middle-grade students. In reader's theater, characterization is conveyed by the reader and the narrator; the presentation allows the audience to create their own images through the readers performance.

Reader's Theater in the Classroom   The performers in reader's theater must understand what the author has to say so they can structure the character development. Each character is represented by a different person with the narrator filling in the details of plot and setting. Selections should be read clearly and expressively. There is minimal action and the readers do not use props. The readers usually take formal positions behind lecterns and sit on stools. They turn their back to the audience to show that they are absent from a scene. Many literature selections are appropriate for reader's theater.

Reader's theater presentations involve selecting a play or story, reading it, rehearsing, and staging. Manna (1984) identifies five essential characteristics for reader's theatre stories:

1. An interesting story

2. A fast-paced story

3. Recognizable and believable characters

4. Plausible language

5. Distinct style

Many basal readers include play scripts that could be used for reader's theater presentations. Manna suggests stories like the following:

Bradley, A., and M. Bond. *Paddington on Stage* (Boston: Houghton Mifflin, 1977).

Falls, G. A. *The Pushcart War* (New Orleans: Anchorage Press, 1983). (This is an adaptation of Jean Merrill's book.)

Qackenback, D. Hattie, *Tom and the Chicken Witch* (New York: Harper & Row, 1980).

Jennings, C. A. and A. Harris, eds. *Plays Children Love: A Treasury of Contemporary and Classical Plays for Children* (New York: Doubleday, 1981).

Korty, C. *Plays from African Folktales* (New York: Scribners, 1975).

The following selections are merely suggestions.

Bremen Town Musicians

The Sneetches by Dr. Seuss

How the Grinch Stole Christmas by Dr. Seuss

Horton Hatches the Who by Dr. Seuss

The Cat Ate My Gymsuit by Paula Danziger

The Elephant Who Challenged the World by James Thurber

Where the Sidewalk Ends by Shel Silverstein

This Dear Bought Land by Robert Lawson

On the Day Peter Stuyvesant Sailed into Town by Arnold Lobel

Soup by Robert Newton Peck

From the Wings of an Eagle by Hildegard Swift

After selecting a story or script, the students should read it through and discuss it. During the discussion, the teacher should probe students' understanding of the story, so that the children can interpret the characters and the story action. After the children understand the story, characters should be assigned and the children should practice the voice inflections and gestures needed to interpret the story. Then they can rehearse the story trying out their various interpretations. Finally the production is staged, keeping in mind that story interpretation is more important than staging. For reader's theater presentations, the participants usually sit on stools in a row interpreting the story with voice and gesture rather than with movement.

Reader's theater develops children's oral language, but it also prepares them to write their own scripts. After participating in reader's theater, children may think of stories they would like to adapt and create their own scripts for such productions.

Drama

Drama is a natural part of the language arts program. Classroom drama is done for fun, understanding, and learning. Drama is a way of learning and knowing; the actors become participants instead of merely observers (Heathcote, 1983). "Creative drama is an improvisational, nonexhibitional, process-centered form of drama in which participants are guided by a leader to imagine, enact, and reflect upon human experience" (Siks, 1983). As children improvise a story they have read, an episode from a story, or an incident they have observed, they participate in the literature or the incident. Children must comprehend and express the important details of plot and character, word meanings, story sequence, and relationships of cause and effect (Miccinati and Phelps, 1980). For example, students who dramatize the Battle of Guilford Court House or the Battle of the Alamo are deepening their understanding of these events.

Drama makes especially strong contributions to the growth of children's communication effectiveness (Busching, 1981). Creative drama requires logical and intuitive thinking, personalizes knowledge, and yields aesthetic pleasure (Siks, 1983). Drama gives children opportunities to experiment with words, emotions, and social roles. Heathcote (1983) is interested in using drama to expand children's understanding of life experiences, to reflect on particular circumstances, and to make sense out of their world in a deeper way. Through drama children become sensitive, confident communicators.

According to Heathcote (1983) there are two types of drama. *Creative drama* is acting one's own individual interpretation of an idea. This kind of drama is relaxed, informal, and a natural extension of children's creative play. The other type of drama is *interpretive drama* which is more structured. Interpretive drama provides less latitude for creativity and problem solving because the participants are restricted by the script. On occasion, interpretive drama may be an appropriate means of exploring the meaning in a play or a story, but generally creative dramatics offers the richest experiences for elementary school children.

Drama is a way of learning and knowing.

Creative Dramatics in the Classroom   Teachers should create many opportunities for children to participate in short, unstructured dramatic play. This is relatively easy since creative drama does not require scripts, memorization, or elaborate staging. The process of dramatizing is a valuable learning experience for children. Some guidelines for developing such activities are given below.

1. Props are not necessary, but many teachers gather together objects and clothing that can serve as props in dramatic play. Jewelry, fabric, hats, canes, clothing, and Halloween costumes are among the props that children enjoy using.

2. Select a good story or have the children select a favorite story. A story requiring a large number of characters or with many crowd scenes gives all or most children a chance to participate.

3. Discuss the main events with the students. Identify and sequence the events to be included in the drama. You may wish to outline this part of the drama.

4. Discuss the action in each scene. Children may practice pretending to walk in heavy boots, to walk happily, sadly, or so forth. Pantomime is a way of preparing students to act and move in expressive ways. As a whole class, children can pantomime getting ready for school or making a peanut butter sandwich or any ordinary activity (Miccinati and Phelps, 1980).

5. Identify the characters in the story. Discuss the characters' actions, attitudes, and feelings. Explain that they should act the way they think the character walked, talked, etc.

6. Assign character roles to class members. Ask the participants to think about and visualize the character. Children who do not want to participate can be directors or stage managers.

7. Give the audience a purpose for watching the play. (For example, the students may observe characterization and character development or plot development.)

8. Dramatize the story.

9. Discuss what the participants and the audience learned from the activity.

10. Recast the characters and play the story again.

Any story, episode, or event that children have enjoyed is a likely subject for dramatization. Perhaps, a few suggestions may stimulate you to think of others. Young children enjoy dramatizing many traditional stories they have heard over and over like *Jack and the Beanstalk* and *Little Red Riding Hood.* They also enjoy dramatizing books like *Gone Is Gone* and *Millions of Cats* by Wanda Gag. Many of John Burningham's cumulative tales lend themselves to dramatization like *Mr. Grumpy's Outing.* Middle-grade students enjoy stories like *Bunnicula* by James and Rebecca Howe, *The Pushcart War* by Jean Merrill, and *The Book of Three* by Lloyd Alexander.

Drama can be used in all areas of the curriculum. For instance social studies students could dramatize situations like the following:

Immigrants arriving in this country. Why did they leave their homeland? What did they bring with them? What do they expect to do in the United States? What will they have to do to become citizens of this country?

The life of a famous person. An incident in the life that contributed to the fame or infamy of someone.

Local problems. Are there roads or extensions of a road that are projected or even under construction? How do the people in various parts of the city feel about the road? What kinds of problems are precipitated by these events?

A presidential visit to students' hometown. Why is the President coming? What is the reason for the visit? What will the President be served? Where will the visitor stay? What special arrangements must be made?

Historical books. *Johnny Tremain* by Esther Forbes, *Zeely* by Virginia Hamilton, and *Ben and Me* by Robert Lawson are valuable social studies dramatizations.

Science students might dramatize these types of subjects:

A scientific discovery, such as the polio vaccine. Answer questions like who, how, where, or when, and the effects on our lives today.

Scientific problems like methane gas or a local chemical spill. Dramatize the discovery and its effects on the people.

Science fiction. Dramatize the scientific advancements needed for the future and how they will change our lives.

A book like *The Wump World* by Bill Peet.

Puppetry

Puppet shows are dramas in which the actors are puppets. Most children thoroughly enjoy making and manipulating puppets, as well as watching puppet shows. Puppetry is an advantageous activity for some shy children because they can express themselves with the puppet. Puppetry is also especially effective with children who are reluctant to participate in creative drama (McCaslin, 1984). The simplest puppet show is one in which a youngster kneels behind a table and moves an object along the edge of it. Students may make puppets or they may use commercially produced puppets. Puppets can be made from many common materials. Figure 4.3 shows some of the more popular types of puppets that children can construct.

Stick puppets can be made from tagboard, cardboard, paper plates, or construction paper. After the character is drawn and the puppet is decorated with yarn, sequins, tissue paper, and so forth, it is attached to a stick, tongue depressor, or dowel for manipulation.

Paper plate puppets are created by drawing faces on paper plates and gluing the plates on sticks, dowels, or rulers. These puppets can be decorated with scrap materials like yarn for hair.

Sock puppets are made from socks by adding yarn hair, button eyes, felt bits for a nose, etc. Then the sock puppet is pulled over the child's hand for manipulation.

Styrofoam cup puppets are made by decorating the cup and attaching the completed puppet to a stick for manipulation.

Cloth puppets are made from fabric which can be sewn together to fit over the child's hand and then decorated to create a character.

Paper bag puppets are made from paper lunch bags. These can be made in two ways. The character may be drawn on the bag and the youngster can put the bag over his or her hand to manipulate it. The second way is to put stuffing in the bag and decorate it, and then to attach it to a stick, dowel, or ruler for manipulation.

Stick Puppet

Paper Plate Puppet

Sock Puppet

Styrofoam Cup Puppet

Cloth or Hand Puppet

Paper Bag Puppet

Figure 4.3   Student-Made Puppets

Puppetry is a dramatic event, but it has other values as well. Puppetry stimulates the imagination of many children as they create puppets and plan to dramatize a story. Children have opportunities to practice cooperation as they work with others often in close quarters. Thus puppetry is a multifaceted activity.

Puppetry in the Classroom   Activities like the following will encourage children to use their puppets.

1. The teacher's puppet may tell a story or teach the children a new skill. When teaching first grade, this author used a puppet to introduce phonemes to children. They became so engrossed in the puppet and telling their parents about its antics, that some of the parents did not realize their children were talking about a puppet. One parent called to find out about Mr. Soloman; imagine her surprise to learn he was a puppet.

2. Encourage children to play with their puppets. They may have a conversation with their puppet or have the puppet help them review their spelling words.

3. The children may practice having their puppet demonstrate anger, excitement, shyness, happiness, or hunger.

4. The children may imagine that their puppet is angry and talk to him or her to find out what is wrong.

5. The children may imagine that the puppet is speaking for them in a conversation with their teacher, another child, or their mother.

6. The children can compose stories for their puppet to act.

Role Playing

Role playing is a form of drama and an extension of dramatic play. In role playing the participants assume a role or roles for a particular reason. Usually, the purpose is to understand another person or a situation. Role playing can help children solve social or emotional problems, overcome anxieties, and develop greater control in a given situation. When children assume the role of other children, teachers, or parents, they can better understand different perspectives in given situations. For example, children can overcome fears of a trip on an airplane through role playing. They can gain comfort and reassurance from role playing (McCaslin, 1984).

Role playing situations arise from everyday events and situations. New situations that students have not encountered previously or that make them anxious are good material for role playing. Assuming the teacher's role when they do not understand a rule or decision helps them understand better that rule or decision. When the teacher is introducing a new form of instruction or class organization like individualized reading, role playing will help the children function more smoothly.

Choral Reading—Voice Chorus

A choral reading activity is one in which a group of children read a selection in unison, although it may include smaller group or solo parts. McCracken (1983) believes that chanting and singing are two of the easiest ways to teach children some complete units of meaningful language. Choral reading requires students to listen and respond to language. Through participating in choral reading students become aware of the sounds of language, predictable language patterns, and the rhythm and melody of language that can help them understand the meaning of text (Miccinati, 1985). After choral reading experiences children are better able to predict the words and phrases that follow one another. The purpose of choral reading is to convey meaning through sound, stress, duration, and pitch.

There are four common choral reading types: refrain, line-a-child, antiphonal, and unison (Miccinati, 1985). The easiest to learn is refrain; in this type the teacher reads most of the lines and the students read the refrain. The line-a-child type allows individual students to read specific lines, while the entire group reads the beginning and ending of the selection. Antiphonal or dialog choral reading is most appropriate for middle or intermediate level students. This type of choral reading enables students to explore pitch and duration of sound. Boys, girls, and groups with varying voices speak different parts of the selection. Unison is the most difficult choral reading approach because the entire group speaks all of the lines. The participants must practice timing so that they are producing words and sounds simultaneously.

Choral Reading in the Classroom   When initiating a choral reading activity, the teacher should prepare the students by giving them a silent reading purpose and giving them time to read the material silently. After silent reading, the teacher leads a discussion to determine whether the students understand the selection. When the discussion is completed, the teacher may assign parts and/or explain clearly which groups and individuals will read the lines in the selection. Once the students understand the instructions, they may practice reading. The teacher may choose to vary the approach with a single selection to help students understand the various ways of expressing meaning.

Material for choral reading should be meaningful, have strong rhythm, have an easily discernable structure, and perhaps rhyme (McCracken and McCracken, 1983). A list of suggested selections for choral reading is given below.

> "The Pickey Fence" by David McCord. In *Far and Few, Rhymes of Never Was and Always Is,* Little, Brown, 1952.
>
> "The Umbrella Brigade" by Laura Richards. In *Time for Poetry,* Scott Foresman, 1959.
>
> "Godfrey, Gordon, Gustavus Gore" by William B. Rand. In *Time For Poetry,* Scott Foresman, 1959.
>
> "Two Fat Cats" by Nancy Briggs. In *Storytelling and Drama,* 2nd ed., William C. Brown, 1979.
>
> "Yak" by William Jay Smith. In *Oh, That's Ridiculous,* Viking Press, 1972.

A more complete list of suggestions is found in Jeannette Miccinati's article "Using Prosodic Cues to Teach Oral Reading Fluency," *The Reading Teacher* (November, 1985), 206–212.

WRITING SCRIPTS

Many children will enjoy writing scripts for puppet shows, dramas, and reader's theater. This activity offers teachers an excellent opportunity to integrate the language arts because in order to write scripts children will read, discuss, write, and then produce their work. Frequently, children enjoy working together to write scripts. Most script writing occurs in the middle grades; however, primary grade children can frequently create their own scripts as well.

Students can study play scripts to learn the format and writing conventions used in preparing scripts. Then they should choose stories that they particularly enjoy. The stories that are most appropriate for scripts:

1. Have a definite beginning, middle, and end.

2. Have a few, well-developed characters.

3. Have a climax.

4. Do not require elaborate staging.

After students complete their script, they should try it out and then make any revisions they wish. One of the best ways to try out a script is to read it through in a reader's theater situation and make notes for revision. Then it should be ready for production.

LEARNING TO BE AN AUDIENCE

Oral language activities give children an opportunity to both speak and listen. An **audience** is a group of students assembled to experience a dramatic presentation, to participate in or observe a panel discussion and other oral language activities. An audience may be any size. The children who are sitting together on the floor to watch a drama unfold are receiving input that can stimulate their thoughts and imagination. During oral language activities the participants, whether they are discussants, actors, or interviewers, are sharing information and modeling ways of sharing thoughts and feelings for the audience.

Teachers should prepare children to function as an audience. Audience learning experiences should be carefully planned (Siks, 1983). The audience should focus on specific objectives—for example, they may observe character development or plot line or compare stories. The teacher should write the objectives on a chalkboard so children can review objectives as needed. Following the presentation, the audience should have an opportunity to discuss their objectives and to ask any questions that they would like answered.

Courtesy is an important audience skill. Audience members should be in their seats (even when the seat is on the floor) before the presentation begins. The audience listens quietly, and waits until intermission to discuss the drama with friends. Any comments for the actors should occur during the final discussion. Children should leave the audience only in cases of an emergency (the teacher should provide this information prior to the presentation).

TROUBLESHOOTING

Several common oral language problems have been identified.

1. Children who talk too much and do not listen. Teachers can help some of these children by giving them specific purposes for listening and then discussing these purposes after the oral language event. These children need specific listening instruction and activities to help them learn to concentrate (see Chapter Five). A successful concentration strategy might teach children to stop, listen, and think before they hold up their hand. Making individual stop signs might help them remember the three steps of stop, listen, and think before participating in discussion. After they learn this strategy, they begin to monitor each other to be sure that everyone thinks before they talk.

2. Children who do not talk. Sometimes we think that the nontalker is a blessing, but unfortunately children need to talk in order to learn. To have children tape record their thoughts helps some of them overcome shyness. This gives the teacher an opportunity to assess oral language development without upsetting shy children. Some children will talk through a puppet or as a participant in a drama where they are pretending to be another person. Children are very surprising; some shy children bloom when they talk through a puppet.

3. Children who speak so softly that they cannot be heard. Many girls go through a stage of talking very softly. We must urge them to hold their heads up and to project their voices. Some children speak softly in order to get attention; therefore we need to give guidelines. Some students may need to practice projecting. Activities like choral reading, reader's theater, and panel discussions provide opportunities to project.

4. The difficulty in finding time to implement oral language activities which are less valued by many adults and are not assessed in standardized testing programs. Teachers feel pressure to teach the skills that they know will be measured in their annual testing. This is a difficult problem to handle because teaching oral language effectively will prepare children to do well on standardized tests; but it is difficult to convince teachers of this.

SUMMARY

Both informative talking and aesthetic talking make significant contributions to children's growth and development. Informative talking includes activities like conversation, discussion, interviews, and so on. Aesthetic oral language activities include storytelling, reader's theater, creative dramatics, puppetry, and choral reading. Children share meanings through both forms of oral language. However, many adults take talking for granted and fail to give proper attention to the oral language curriculum. Talking (oral language) is fundamental to the development of the other language arts. Teachers play important roles in oral language development because they must not only create situations that encourage oral expression, but they must also model appropriate oral language. Classroom activities can encourage children to express their thoughts and ideas. As they express themselves, children create an oral composition which develops speaking, listening, reading, and writing skills.

Many children naturally tell stories, role play, act out their favorite stories, and talk through their puppets, so the aesthetic oral language activities are a natural part of their learning experience. These activities are truly learning experiences which develop thinking skills, concepts, and a way of exploring ideas; therefore, they are not frills in the language arts curriculum. In addition to acting in dramatic activities, children should learn appropriate audience skills.

Thought Questions

1. Explain how oral language functions as the foundation for listening, reading, and writing.

2. Identify the three components of any oral language situation.

3. Discuss why some teachers tend to neglect oral language instruction.

4. How can teachers facilitate oral language development?

5. Compare informative oral language activities with aesthetic oral language activities.

6. Write a defense for including storytelling, reader's theater, drama, puppetry, and choral reading in weekly lesson plans. This defense should identify the values of oral language.

7. How does children's literature fit into oral language instruction?

Enrichment Activities

1. Join with another member of the class to plan and present a reader's theater production.

2. Make a file of possible discussion topics for the grade level you teach or plan to teach.

3. Make arrangements to observe in an elementary classroom. Use the language checklist in this chapter (Figure 4.2) as a guide for assessing one child's oral language.

4. Interview an elementary school teacher regarding oral language instruction. How many oral language class activities does this teacher have each week?

5. List situations or stories for children to dramatize (at a grade level that you teach or plan to teach).

6. Look at some of the children's books suggested in this chapter. Select a character and make a puppet you can use to dramatize the story. Arrange to present your drama to a group of elementary school children.

7. Design three oral language experiences for a specific grade level.

8. Choose a favorite speaker and evaluate their oral language to identify the traits that are especially appealing.

Selected Readings

Busching, Beverly (March 1981). "Readers Theater: An Education for Language and Life." *Language Arts, 58,* 330–338.

Cottrell, June (1975). *Teaching with Creative Dramatics.* Skokie, IL: National Textbook Co.

Heathcote, Dorothy (September 1983). "Learning, Knowing, and Languaging in Drama: An Interview with Dorothy Heathcote." *Language Arts, 60,* 695–701.

Heinig, Ruth Beall, and Lyda Stillwell (1981). *Creative Drama for the Classroom Teacher.* New York: McGraw-Hill.

McCaslin, Nelli (1984). *Creative Drama in the Classroom* (4th ed.). New York: Longman.

McCracken, Robert, and Marlene McCracken (1983). "Chants, Charts, an 'Chievement." In *Teaching Reading Through the Arts,* J. Cowen (ed.). Newark, DE: International Reading Association, pp. 69–77.

Miccinati, Jeannette L. (November 1985). "Using Prosodic Cues to Teach Oral Reading Fluency." *Reading Teacher, 39,* 206–212.

Ross, Ramon (1980). *Storytelling* (2d ed.). Columbus, OH: Charles Merrill.

Roth, Rita (February 1986). "Practical Use of Language in School." *Language Arts, 63,* 134–142.

Siks, Geraldine Brain (1983). *Drama with Children* (2d ed.). New York: Harper & Row.

Taylor, Mary (1983). "Readers Theater in the Classroom." In *Teaching Reading Through the Arts,* J. Cowan (ed.). Newark, DE: International Reading Association, pp. 6–10.

Watson, Ken, and Bob Young (February 1986). "Discourse for Learning in the Classroom." *Language Arts, 63,* 126–133.

Wells, Gordon, and Jan Wells (1984). "Learning to Talk and Talking to Learn." *Theory into Practice, 23,* 190–197.

References

Athey, Irene (1983). "Thinking and Experience: The Cognitive Base for Language Experience." In *Developing Literacy: Young Children's Use of Language,* R. Parker and F. David (eds.). Newark, DE: International Reading Association, pp. 19–33.

Britton, James (1970). *Language and Learning.* Hamondsworth, England: Penguin.

Bruner, Jerome (1978). "The Role of Dialogue in Language Acquisition." In *The Child's Conception of Language,* A. Sinclair, R. J. Jarvelle, and W. J. Levelt (eds.). New York: Springer-Verlag.

Buckley, M. (September 1976). "A Guide for Developing an Oral Language Curriculum." *Language Arts, 53,* 621–627.

Busching, Beverly (March 1981). "Readers Theater: An Education for Language and Life." *Language Arts, 58,* 330–338.

Cottrell, June (1975). *Teaching with Creative Dramatics.* Skokie, IL: National Textbook Co.

Emig, Janet (May 1977). "Writing as a Mode of Learning." *College Composition and Communication 28,* 122–128.

Frye, Northrup (1970). *The Educated Imagination.* Bloomington IN: Indiana University Press.

Galda, Lee (October 1982). "Playing About a Story: Its Impact on Comprehension." *Reading Teacher, 36,* 52–55.

Gruenewald, Lee, and Sara Pollak (1984). *Language Interaction in Teaching and Learning.* Baltimore: University Park Press.

Heathcote, Dorothy (September 1983). "Learning, Knowing, and Languaging in Drama: An Interview with Dorothy Heathcote." *Language Arts, 60,* 695–701.

Lange, Bob (September 1981). "ERIC/RCS Report: Directing Classroom Communication." *Language Arts, 58,* 729–733.

Loban, Walter (1976). *Language Development: Kindergarten Through Grade Twelve.* Urbana, IL: National Council of Teachers of English.

Manna, A. L. (1984). "Making Language Come Alive Through Reading Plays." *The Reading Teacher, 37,* 712–717.

McCaslin, N. (1984). *Creative Dramatics in the Classroom* (4th ed.). New York: Longman.

McCracken, Robert, and Marlene McCracken (1983). "Chants, Charts, and 'Chievement." In *Teaching Reading Through the Arts.* J. Cowen (ed.). Newark, DE: International Reading Association.

Miccinati, Jeannette L. (November 1985). "Using Prosodic Cues to Teach Oral Reading Fluency." *Reading Teacher, 39,* 206–212.

Miccinati, Jeannette, and Stephen Phelps (December 1980). "Classroom Drama from Children's Reading: From the Page to the Stage." *Reading Teacher, 34,* 269–272.

Nilsen, A. (February 1983). "Children's Multiple Uses of Oral Language Play." *Language Arts, 60,* 194–201.

Pinnell, Gay Su (Summer 1984). "Communication in Small Group Settings." *Theory into Practice,* 246–254.

Pinnell, Gay Su, and Judith Green (April 1986). "Research Currents: Learning from Language Research to Talk About Education." *Language Arts, 63,* 384–389.

Siks, Geraldine (1983). *Drama with Children* (2d ed.). New York: Harper & Row.

Smith, Frank (September 1982). "The Unspeakable Habit." *Language Arts, 59,* 550–554.

Thaiss, Christopher, and Charles Suhor, Eds. (1984). *Speaking and Writing K–12.* Urbana, IL: National Council of Teachers of English.

Tiedt, Iris M., SuzAnne Bruemmer, Sheilah Lane, Patricia Stelwagon, Kathleen Watanabe, and Mary Williams (1983). *Teaching Writing in K–8 Classrooms.* Englewood Cliffs, NJ: Prentice-Hall.

Tonyes, May and Zintz, M. (1981). *Teaching Reading/Thinking/Study Skills in Content Classrooms.* Dubuque, Iowa: William C. Brown.

Tough, Joan (1981). *Talk for Teaching and Learning.* Plymouth, England: Ward Lock Educational.

Vygotsky, Lev (1962). *Thought and Language.* Cambridge, MA: MIT Press.

Wells, Gordon, and Jan Wells (1984). "Learning to Talk and Talking to Learn." *Theory into Practice, 23,* 190–197.

Wilkinson, L. (February 1984). "Research Currents: Peer Group Talk in Elementary School." *Language Arts, 61,* 164–169.

Winkeljohann, Rosemary (1978). "Oral Language Instruction in the United States: The State of the Art. A paper presented at the Annual Meeting of the International Reading Association World Congress in Hamburg, Germany.

Chapter **Five**

Listening to Learn

CHAPTER OVERVIEW

We hear, but do we listen? Listening skill is the source of much of the information, knowledge, and pleasure that we experience in life. People commonly assume that the ability to listen is a natural gift requiring no instruction. Unfortunately, this is not true. Listening can and should be taught. This chapter addresses the cognitive processes involved in listening comprehension. A planned instructional program is recommended, including teaching strategies, lesson plans, and activities for developing the art of listening in elementary classrooms. Troubleshooting suggestions are included to assist teachers in coping with specific listening problems. Suggestions are included to guide assessment of listening abilities.

Anticipation Guide

Are you a good listener? How do you know you are a good listener? Have you ever had a problem listening? What caused it? Think about these ideas as you read this chapter. Also try to answer the following questions when you finish reading this chapter.

1.   How is listening skill related to attention?

2.   How is listening related to the other language arts?

3.   What causes poor listening?

Key Concepts

listening comprehension	kinesics
listening	anaphoric terms

INTRODUCTION

The world's most important affairs are conducted around conference tables. One person talks and others listen. We climb aboard great airliners that fly through murky skies with our lives depending upon the listening abilities of the pilot. Every day we are bombarded by spoken language from radios, televisions, telephones, robots, tapes, records, and even automobiles who remind us to "buckle up." We are a society of listeners. "We listen a book a day; speak a book a week; read a book a month; and write a book a year" (Lundsteen, 1978). Listening is both the most common and most mysterious of the language arts. Wilt (1950) discovered that children spend almost 60 percent of their classroom time listening. In social studies classes, students spend 75 percent of their time listening (Herman, 1967). Recent research confirms that students spend a major portion of school time listening (Devine, 1978). Listening also influences employment; white-collar workers receive some 40 percent of their salaries for listening (Nichols and Stevens, 1983). Listening is so common that we are in danger of omitting it from our teaching, yet we listen with only 25 percent efficiency (Nichols and Stevens, 1983).

Listening is primarily an activity of the mind, not of the ear. **Listening** is converting spoken sounds to meaning in the mind. Listening at its most basic level is simply a matter of processing incoming sounds into words and phrases so that the listener can make sense of the sounds. For instance, when you lift the telephone receiver, you hear a stream of words that you must process into a message; unless you understand what you hear, you will not know how to respond. Listening involves thinking and reasoning, therefore more intelligent students listen more effectively than students with less intelligence. Effective listeners quickly and consistently approximate speakers' meanings in a variety of spoken material. Listeners comprehend best when their language is very similar to that of the speaker.

Listening and reading are receptive language arts concerned with understanding language. In one instance the language is spoken and in the other it is written. Listening skill is acquired before reading and it is important to learn to read. Students prefer listening to reading as a means of learning until they achieve sixth- to seventh-grade reading level; after that they begin to prefer reading for learning. Listening skill enables children to associate spoken words and written words which is basic to word recognition.

Skillful listening also undergirds the development of reading comprehension, since in both listening and reading comprehension the student is associating meaning with language. Through listening children acquire the semantics, syntax, and phonology needed for speaking and writing. Youngsters who lack hearing acuity and/or listening skill have difficulty acquiring skill in language use.

As you read the following vignette, see if you can identify factors that could interfere with listening. How well do you think the students listened in this vignette?

LISTENING IN A FOURTH-GRADE CLASSROOM

On a dark, rainy October morning, the boys and girls in Mark Richards fourth-grade class clamored into the classroom shaking rain from their umbrellas and raincoats with a great deal of noise and confusion as they chattered about the heavy rainstorm. Mark was working at his desk. He tersely greeted the students with a stream of instructions. "Go back to your lockers, hang up your coats, place your boots in the locker, and put your umbrellas up to dry. Then copy the assignments that I have written on the chalkboard—when you are finished copying, quietly go the library shelf and select a book that you want to read. Go to your seat and read it, while I prepare this report for the principal."

Mark, a second-year teacher, was very discouraged with the results of his instructions. Seven of the twenty-nine students asked him to repeat the instructions, while five others ignored his instructions and continued talking. When he asked them why they were talking, they explained that they were asking their friends what he had said. Several youngsters selected books to read rather than copying the written material on the chalkboard. Mark was especially concerned about this incident because he had noted on several occasions that his students appeared to lack listening skills. After thinking about the problem, he talked with Mrs. Stevens, his principal. She suggested that they call the supervisor of language arts, Mrs. Brown, for assistance.

WHAT IS INVOLVED IN LISTENING?

Five factors that influence listening emerge from most analyses (Lundsteen, 1979). They are:

1. Previous knowledge and experience.

2. Listening material.

3. Physiological activity (hearing, sensation, perception).

4. Attention or concentration.

5. Thinking and reasoning.

6. The speaker.

Each of these factors is discussed in subsequent sections of this chapter.

Previous Knowledge and Experience

Background knowledge about a topic is one of the most important variables influencing listening (Samuels, 1984). If listeners lack the background or experience to understand the message they may hear it, but not comprehend it. Lack of background knowledge makes inferencing very difficult for students. Prior knowledge may include facts, ideas, information, attitudes, schemata, and language. An instance of this is seen in a classroom where the teacher is discussing conservation with a group of students who have no related experiences, so they do not understand what the teacher is saying. Students who have knowledge and experience related to the topic can anticipate what is going to be said; they can think along with the teacher.

Language   Language is included in the background knowledge that students bring to the listening task. Successful listening is predicted on the listener's ability to segment and analyze spoken language into appropriate morpheme and syntactic units. We need only recall how when we have to listen so carefully to identify the words and phrases of a spoken foreign language that the message is lost.

Listeners need command over the key components of language, phonology (sound structure), syntax (sentence structure), semantics (word meanings and the relationships among meanings) (Pearson and Fielding, 1983). Students have to be able to discriminate between /bad/ and /bat/. They must be sensitive to the pitch (rising or falling), stress (loudness), and juncture (where one word stops and another begins) in listening to spoken language. At the syntactic level, listeners must be able to see how words are strung together to make sense and to recognize cues to meaning such as the positions of words in sentences. At the semantic level, listeners need to know word meanings and to have a large store of concepts derived from experience. Another requirement of effective listening is knowledge of the speaker's vocabulary. For example, in a discussion about cows, listeners need to know that a cow is a mammal that moos, gives milk, has four legs, a tail, and so forth. There are many types of cows—some are used for meat while others are dairy animals. Among the classification of dairy cows are included Gurnseys, Jerseys, and so on.

Anaphoric terms are a common source of comprehension difficulty (Pearson and Johnson, 1978). Anaphoric terms are words used as a substitute for a preceding word or group of words—for example, *it* in "Give it to me" and *them* in "Muffin and Randy are outside. Please bring them in." When listeners fail to connect anaphoric terms with appropriate referents they cannot comprehend.

Listeners can comprehend better if they know how the text is structured. Listeners who have a sense of story grammar understand that a story has a setting (time, place, and characters), a problem, an attempt to solve the problem, and a resolution (Mandler, 1978; Stein & Glenn, 1979). (The concept of story grammar will be illustrated later in this chapter in Figure 5.1.) This knowledge enables students to anticipate what is going to occur next in a story. Informative literature (exposition) is usually structured around main ideas and supporting details. Knowing this makes it possible for listeners to anticipate a main idea and to expect details that support the main idea.

Before introducing a listening activity, analyze students' background. If you find inadequate background build the necessary background to enhance listening comprehension. Pictures, films, records, books, resource persons, and discussion help build background. Advance organizers are often used in reading, but they are equally effective in listening. An advance organizer is simply a short paragraph that identifies the important ideas to be presented. Advance organizers enable teachers to preview content and let students know what they can expect to gain from listening, thus establishing a purpose for listening.

Listening Material

The content of the listening material greatly affects student comprehension. Lundsteen (1979) has classified listening materials into the following categories:

Self-expression (emotive, affective).

Expository (informative, newspapers, content textbooks, and so on).

Literary (narrative, drama, poetry).

Persuasive (designed to influence as in commercials, advertising, and so forth).

Sensitivity to the purposes of content helps readers understand. As stated in the preceding section, listeners comprehend content that is related to their knowledge and experiences. Well-structured content is easier to understand than disorganized content (Mandler, 1978; Stein & Glenn, 1979). Complicated sentence patterns and technical jargon interfere with understanding. Content that is related to listeners' interests is easier to understand. For example, students hear their teachers much better when they announce a class party than they do when teachers announce the weekly spelling test.

Students have to listen to content that is less than ideal and that is poorly presented, so we must prepare them to overcome these obstacles. Students may impose their own organization on content that is unorganized. When content is uninteresting, students should list ways that the content could be useful to them, in other words, they should search for values in the content to increase listening comprehension.

Physiological Activity

Listening begins with hearing speech sounds uttered by a speaker. The listener discriminates one sound from another, then analyzes and sequences the message. We have little control over hearing. Sounds are conducted through the air and through our bones; the only way we can stop receiving sound waves is to cover our ears or use earplugs. However, we have more control over listening than over hearing. We can consciously screen out background noise and/or messages that we do not want to hear. Listening involves more conscious thinking than hearing does. The components of physically hearing a message include (Lundsteen, 1979):

Auditory acuity (no hearing loss is present).

Discrimination (the ability to identify likenesses and differences in sound)

Analysis (unconsciously "taking apart" pitch, tone, and rhythm)

Auditory sequencing (recall of sound in proper time order)

The physiological component of listening can be enhanced by having students' hearing tested. Also, teachers can use science content to teach students about the physical aspects of listening which makes them more sensitive to use their hearing efficiently. Exploring noise pollution in the environment

Attention is essential to listening skill.

makes students aware of the need to screen out sounds that interfere with listening comprehension.

Teachers and students should be aware that a noisy environment can detract from listening comprehension. Noisy environments cannot always be controlled, however; the control must come from within the listener who can deliberately focus on the message and screen out distractions.

Attention or Concentration

Listeners can process ideas faster than speakers can state them; therefore, attention is essential to listening skill. Interest enables us to put forth the effort necessary to listen well. Interest motivates listeners to screen out background noises so they can concentrate on the communication. Interest enables listeners to focus on the message and track it, since a listening episode may extend over an indeterminate period of time. Interest and knowledge about a topic enable listeners to anticipate content contributes to understanding.

Thinking and Reasoning

Listening comprehension should occur at four cognitive levels: literal, interpretive (inferential), critical, and creative.

Literal comprehension is recalling the information the speaker stated. In the chapter vignette, Mark's students had to remember the directions so they could respond appropriately. In order to achieve this they had to remember details in sequence. They also had to remember another detail, which was to "work quietly." This level of understanding is relatively easy for students because everything they have to understand is stated by the speaker. If they do not understand a word used by the speaker, they can ask for more information.

Interpretation (inference) is more complex than literal comprehension. The listener must be able to understand what the speaker's statements meant. In the earlier vignette, the students had to understand at the literal level (remember the information in sequence) and to process that information further in order to understand what their teacher meant by what he said. They had to understand that they should obtain pencils and paper without specific directions to do so. These pupils were required to infer a main idea. In this situation, they had to infer the importance of copying material from the chalkboard. The basis for this inference was the teacher's statement that they were to complete copying the work from the chalkboard before they selected a book to read. They also had to infer that Mark told them that he was working on a report for a specific reason. In order to reach this conclusion they had to understand the relationship between the tasks he assigned them and the fact that he told them he was completing a report. Then they had to think critically about the situation.

Critical listening is based on literal comprehension and interpretation. Listeners must evaluate or make judgments about what they have heard. In this instance, the pupils who listened critically evaluated the situation and realized that their teacher was working on a report. Then they concluded that they should not interrupt their teacher. These students went beyond the teacher's statements; they evaluated the situation and made a decision about what they should do.

Creative or appreciative listening is concerned with pleasurable listening. Listeners experience an aesthetic response to spoken language when they listen appreciatively. Children listen appreciatively to stories, radio, plays, television, and records. The vignette in this chapter did not involve appreciative listening.

Students' social and emotional adjustment and attitudes influence listening comprehension. Individuals who are socially and emotionally well-adjusted tend to listen more accurately than those who are distracted by problems (Ross and Thomas, 1978). Although teachers cannot prevent social and emotional maladjustment, they can be aware of these interferences and use teaching strategies that help students focus on the message.

The Speaker   Teachers must be sensitive to their impact on students' listening. They must be aware of listeners' needs, the amount of information they have on a topic, their intellectual level, and their interest in the topic. When listeners lack background knowledge, the speaker helps them bridge the gap between the known and the unknown by providing necessary background information. If listeners are uninterested, the speaker motivates them. Listeners who are intellectually slow need a slower presentation, so the information and ideas do not move too fast for them.

The speaker's delivery of content influences listeners' understanding. Verbal factors like speaking tempo, voice quality, and enunciation influence listening comprehension. Talking too fast or too slow impedes listening. Mannerisms or voice inflections that detract from the content interfere with understanding. Nonverbal communication signals are called **kinesics**. These signals—facial expressions, eye contact, direction of gaze, hand gestures, posture, and body motions—all convey meaning and are part of communication. Both speakers and listeners use nonverbal signals; listeners may signal that they are bored and a sensitive speaker will note this and change the delivery or draw the presentation to a close.

When the speaker's and the listener's dialects differ, greater demands are placed on the listener's processing. These demands severely interfere with listening comprehension (Samuels, 1984). When the speakers realize their dialect differs significantly from that of the audience, they should extend extra efforts to help the audience understand what they are saying—for example to speak slightly slower and explain terms that listeners may misunderstand.

LISTENING INSTRUCTION

Research shows that students who have listening instruction comprehend better than students who have not had this instruction (Devine, 1982). Elementary students who received direct training in listening improved their listening comprehension (Early, 1960; Duker, 1969). Research with middle school students produced equally positive results (DeSousa and Cowles, 1967).

Pearson and Fielding (1983), summarizing listening instruction research, reached the following conclusions:

1. Listening training in the same skills typically taught in reading comprehension curricula tends to improve listening comprehension.

2. Listening comprehension is enhanced by various kinds of active verbal responses on the part of students during and after listening.

3. Listening to literature tends to improve listening comprehension.

4. Certain types of instruction primarily directed toward other areas of language arts (e.g., writing or reading comprehension) may improve listening comprehension as well.

5. Direct teaching of listening strategies appears to help children become more conscious of their listening habits than do more incidental approaches.

Listening instruction begins in kindergarten and continues through high school. Indeed, there are indications that college students need listening instruction. The same listening skills are taught to all students. The major differences in listening instruction at the different grade levels is in the instructional content. Naturally, more sophisticated content is used for junior and senior high-school students. For instance, high-school students listen to science content about DNA and RNA, while elementary school children listen to information about measuring temperature. Content time for older students is longer. Due to the length of listening selections, middle-grade, junior high-school, and senior high-school students must learn to take notes to strengthen their memory for the main points.

Listening Skills

Specific listening skills are not as important as the strategies that help children become more effective listeners. In general, listening skills parallel reading skills. Devine (1978) suggests that teachers examine the reading skills listed in one of the popular basal reading series because each basic reading skill can be translated into a basic listening skill. More recently, Devine (1982) developed a scope and sequence of basic listening skills that parallel reading comprehension skills. This text will focus on the strategies that can be used to teach children listening. The basic strategies and activities included are appropriate for teaching any basic listening skills, such as listening for main ideas, listening for supporting details, or listening for cause and effect.

Designing Listening Instruction

Listening instruction must be systematic if it is to improve students' listening ability. To increase listening comprehension it should be a part of daily and weekly lesson plans, and not a "one shot" infrequent activity. Five to ten minutes each day of listening instruction or listening practice is more effective than longer, less frequent lessons.

Listening instruction will focus on teaching students strategies they can use to listen, while listening activities are included to give students opportunities to practice these skills in various settings. Listening instruction should provide for transfer of listening skills from practice situations to actual use in the classroom. For example, listening for main ideas in practice materials should be transferred to social studies or science content.

Successful listening instruction directs students to listen to fulfill their own needs, interests, and desires. For instance, students who are listening to complete an assignment, create a project for the science fair, or simply listening to a good story for pleasure have listening purposes that are very real to them. The suggested teaching strategies develop both active listening and oral or written responses because research shows that such responses result in listening skill development.

Listening Instruction Develops Thinking Skills

The following teaching suggestions will help students develop thinking skills through listening.

Literal Understanding   This level of thinking occurs when listeners follow directions, understand stated sequence, and identify stated main ideas and stated details. The lesson plan below is an example of how to teach literal comprehension.

LESSON PLAN FOR LITERAL COMPREHENSION (GRADES THREE THROUGH EIGHT)

OBJECTIVES

Students will remember the details read to them in a short mystery and solve the mystery.

INTRODUCTION

Ask children what mysteries are. Then have them identify examples of mysteries and discuss how they are solved. Explain that you will read a short mystery aloud. They are to listen for clues (details) that will help them solve the mystery. They may make notes if they wish. After the story is finished, students solve the mystery by relating the clues until they solve the mystery.

VARIATIONS

Mystery and clues can be compared to main ideas and details.

MATERIALS

Mystery stories such as:

Joseph Rosenbloom. *Maximilian You're the Greatest.* New York: E. P. Dutton.

Joseph Rosenbloom. *Maximilian Does It Again.* New York: E. P. Dutton.

M. Masters. *Long-Lost Cousin and Other Mysteries.* Deephaven, MN: Meadowbrook Press. This book is part of a series called *Can You Solve the Mystery?*

SYNTHESIS AND EVALUATION

Ask the students to listen to a paragraph containing a number of details. Have the students write down the details they remember.

Literal Listening Suggestions

1. Select content that has a strong sense of sequence, either fiction or nonfiction. Read the selection to the students. Write the major events or steps on sentence strips (cards, strips of tagboard, or chart paper containing one sentence) and place these in a pocket holder or tape them to the chalkboard. The students then rearrange the strips until the order is correct.

2. This activity is similar to the preceding one except that students must compose the steps or events in the sequence. This is more appropriate for middle-grade students.

3. Read students a paragraph that includes a main idea. Write three sentences on the chalkboard and ask students to identify the one that best states the main idea. Younger children can choose the picture that best represents the main idea. Be certain to ask students to explain "why" they think a particular statement is the main idea.

Inferential Listening Suggestions

Listeners use their background experience and knowledge to think at an inferential level because the speaker does not state everything for them. Activities like the following will reinforce this skill.

1. Riddles are ever popular listening and reading activities for children. They make children remember details and infer answers.

2. By reading stories that require pupils to interact with the story, they should be able to explain why they chose a particular answer. Books such as the following are good for this activity: Titles from the *Choose Your Own Adventure Series* by Bantam-Skylark; titles from the *Pick a Path Series* by Scholastic; titles from *Fantasy Gamebooks* by Laurel-Leaf Library (a division of Dell).

3. Select a story to read and write three possible outcomes for the story on the chalkboard. Tell the children, " I have written three possible outcomes for this story on the chalkboard. While I am reading the story to you, think about how the story might turn out. I will stop reading before the end of the story, so you can choose one of the outcomes. Then I will finish reading the story, so you can see if you were right." This activity may be varied by having the children vote on the outcomes. They should be able to explain why they selected a particular outcome.

Critical Listening

Television programs and commercials provide much raw material for critical listening. Listeners must evaluate and judge the veracity of such messages. Critical listeners are problem solvers—they use listening skills to gather the data necessary for solving problems. The activities described below encourage critical listening.

1. Read statements to students and have them identify statements of fact and statements of opinion. For example, "I have the most beautiful dog in the world." "I live at 606 Pleasant Drive." "My father is an accountant." "My mother is the best golfer in the state of Ohio." Use newspaper or magazine articles for this activity when doing it with middle-grade students.

2. Read stories that are real and make-believe to children and ask them to identify which are real and which are make-believe. They should explain why they identified specific stories as real or make-believe.

3. Teach students the common propaganda devices. Explain each type of propaganda, give examples of each type, and have students identify examples of each in television and radio commercials. The propaganda devices most commonly used follow:

    Bad Names: When disagreeable words are used to create distaste—for example, a candidate who uses the epithet "communist" to describe an opponent.

    Glad Names: When agreeable words are used to create a pleasant feeling about the person or thing—for example, a diet aid that is guaranteed to make you "slim" and "trim."

    Plain Folks: The propagandist tries to appear like the person next door. This is an avoidance of "fancy" sophisticated trappings—for example, the candidate who attempts to appear just like a neighbor.

    Transfer: This propaganda attempts to transfer the respect we have for certain concepts to a product or a person. For instance, the American flag and the American eagle are sometimes used in the background of advertisements that have nothing to do with the flag or the eagle.

    Testimonial: This technique is based on a well-known person recommending the product. Many times athletes appear in commercials for shaving products. This is an example of testimonial propaganda.

    Bandwagon: This type of propaganda tries to convince us that "everyone is buying the product or voting in a certain way." Since we usually like to be on the winning side, there is a tendency to go with the crowd.

    Card Stacking: This propaganda usually deals with complex information or ideas. The speaker gives correct information, but they only tell one side of the situation. For example, an insecticide may work very well for controlling pests, but it may have side effects for animals and people.

4. Listen to campaign speeches by candidates seeking elected office. Identify the types of propaganda they use.

5. Teach students to use a guide for evaluating content likely to contain propaganda. These sample questions can guide students' evaluation of propaganda.

What propaganda technique is used?

Who composed the propaganda?

Why was the propaganda created?

To what listener interests, emotions, and prejudices does the propaganda appeal?

Will I allow myself to be influenced by this propaganda?

Appreciative Listening

Listening to ghost stories around a campfire is one form of appreciative listening. Listening that involves a creative response to the message is another aspect of appreciative listening. The following activities give students opportunities to practice their appreciative listening skills.

1. Read a poem or a story and have students identify the mood created by the selection.

2. Listen to recorded music such as Chopin's "Dirge" for sad music or "Whistle While You Work" from *Snow White and the Seven Dwarfs* for happy music. Ask the children to identify the moods created by the music.

3. Read scary stories to the students and have them identify the words that frighten them.

Listening instruction should focus on strategies that will help students understand and remember the content they hear. Opportunities to practice listening to interesting content (such as the books that teachers read to students) enhance understanding. Following the lesson plan format introduced in Chapter Two (objectives, introduction, variation, materials, synthesis, and evaluation) will help you develop effective instruction. These lessons should include modeling (showing children), guided practice, independent practice, and many opportunities to apply their skills.

Strategies

Instruction should develop the following listening strategies.

1. Asking questions of the content. Ask questions before listening because they will focus thought and encourage students to anticipate content. These questions are actually purposes that guide listening. You may want to use the questioning guidelines in Chapter Two for reference.

2. Looking for the structure of the content. Brain researchers tell us that human beings naturally seek patterns and structure in their experiences (Hart, 1975). These patterns help us understand and remember. Story

grammar (which is discussed in subsequent sections) structures fiction; nonfiction is structured by main ideas and details which may be organized in various ways such as comparison, cause and effect chronological order, and so forth (this is discussed later); and poetry for children is structured as lyric, narrative, ballad, limerick, free verse, Haiku, and concrete poetry. Identifying the structure will help students remember.

3. Categorize, relate and associate ideas. When ideas are linked they are easier to remember. Categorizing also helps students identify structure. For example, if one goes to McDonald's restaurant to order an apple pie, cheeseburger, coke, Big Mac, fries, Chicken McNuggets, coffee, cherry pie, and an ice cream sundae, it is easier to remember sandwiches, dessert, beverages, and Chicken McNuggets than to remember the separate items. Students can relate the content to their own lives. They can ask questions like: How does this concern me? How does this relate to what I already know? What does it remind me of? How does it relate to my life outside school? How can I apply this information?

4. Summarize periodically. In summarizing, the speaker's main ideas are identified and restated briefly. Students can stop and summarize in their minds or on paper up to that point. This strategy is most effective with middle-grade students; however, teachers can help younger children by summarizing for them, so that as more experienced students they can do it independently.

5. Make oral or written responses to content (Samuels, 1984). This helps students become active listeners. Encourage students to listen with pencil in hand. This gives them a minimal structure for response and allows for physical involvement. Link listening with note taking. Students may complete activities such as the following.

1. After the talk (oral presentation), list five main ideas.

2. Write a two-sentence summary of the presentation.

3. After listening, fill in blanks like the following.

The main character was _____.

In this story the setting was _____.

The problem in this story was _____.

The solution to the problem was _____.

4. What was the author's purpose (persuade, inform etc.)? How do you know this was the purpose?

This chapter develops the strategies, materials, and practice activities for implementing appropriate listening instruction. You will find that children's literature is involved in many of the listening strategies and practice activities. Literature functions in several important ways in listening instruction. Literature can be used to learn about listening, and to sensitize children to the importance of listening and the science of listening. The literature in the following list can be used to teach children about listening. Suggested grade levels for using these materials are included with each item.

Adoff, Arnold. *MAN DA LA.* New York: Harper, 1971. *Primary.*

Baylor, Byrd. *Plink Plink Plink.* Boston: Houghton-Mifflin, 1971. *Primary.*

Baylor, Byrd, and Peter Parnall. *An Other Way to Listen.* New York: Scribners, 1978. *Middle grades.*

Blaine Marge. *The Terrible Thing That Happened at Our House.* New York: Parents Magazine Press, 1975. *Upper primary and middle grades.*

Bodecker, N. M. *It's Raining Said John Twaining: Danish Nursery Rhymes.* New York: Atheneum, 1973. *Primary and middle grades.*

Branley, Franklyn. *High Sounds, Low Sounds.* New York: Crowell, 1967. *Upper primary and middle grades.*

Carley, Wayne. *Is Anybody Listening?* Champaign, IL: Garrard, 1971. *Primary.*

Carlson, Bernice Wells. *Listen! And Help Tell the Story.* New York: Abingdon Press, 1965. *This collection of stories, finger plays, action stories, action verses, and poems is very helpful to teachers of both primary and middle grades.*

DeReigniers, Beatrice. *It Does Not Say Meow.* New York: Seabury, 1972. *Primary.*

Elkin, Benjamin. *The Loudest Noise in the World.* New York: Viking, 1954. *Primary.*

Gaddert, Lou Ann. *Noisy Nancy Norris.* New York: Doubleday, 1971. *Primary.*

Gaddert, Lou Ann. *Noisy Nancy and Nick.* New York: Doubleday, 1971. *Primary.*

Guilfoile, Elizabeth. *Nobody Listens to Andrew.* Chicago: Follett, 1957. *Primary.*

Hann, Jacquie. *That Man Is Talking to His Toes.* New York: Four Winds Press, 1976. *Middle grades.*

Hutchins, Pat. *Don't Forget the Bacon.* New York: Greenwillow, 1976. *Primary.*

Mayer, Mercer. *What Do You Do With a Kangaroo?* New York: Four Winds Press, 1973. *Primary.*

O'Neill, Mary. *What Is That Sound?* New York: Atheneum, 1966. *Middle grades.*

Pienkowski, Jan. *Gossip.* Los Angeles: Price/Stern/Sloan Publishers, 1981. *Primary.*

Shulevitz, Uri. *Oh What a Noise!* New York: Macmillan, 1971. *Primary.*

Slepian, Jan, and Ann Seidler. *The Silly Listening Book.* Chicago: Follett, 1967. *Primary.*

Spier, Peter. *Crash! Bang! Boom!* New York: Doubleday, 1972. *Primary.*

Spier, Peter. *Gobble Growl Grunt.* New York: Doubleday, 1971. *Primary.*

Withers, Carl. *The Tale of a Black Cat.* New York: Holt, Rinehart and Winston, 1966. *Primary.*

Literature also provides the content for listening comprehension activities; however, these activities will work equally well with textbooks and newspaper and magazine articles. Well-written materials written about topics that interest students give them content that has significance. They have opportunities to hear excellent language that will serve as a model for their own oral and written language. Strickland (1971) found that students' ability to listen increased when teachers read to them. When children listen to literature, they are practicing listening skills with interesting content. Following are guidelines for selecting books to read aloud which are based on those suggested by Trelease (1986).

1. Is it a fast-paced book?

2. Does the book have well-developed, three-dimensional characters? This means that characters' strengths and weaknesses are revealed. Some types of books do not have characters, such as informational and reference books, but if there are characters, they should be three dimensional.

3. Is the dialog easy to read? Books with extensive use of dialog are difficult to read.

4. Does the book have long descriptive passages? If it does and is a appropriate choice otherwise, can the description be cut out or reduced?

STORY GRAMMAR

The concept of story grammar was mentioned earlier. A simplified story grammar is explained in the next section and the explanation is followed by a completed story grammar form based on the book *A Toad for Tuesday* by Russell E. Erickson. This particular activity was completed by a third-grade class.

A story grammar provides structure for reading comprehension and for the composing aspect of the writing process. Figure 5.1 is a story grammar design that can be used in guiding reading and writing.

When teaching children about story grammar, your lesson plan should

The Setting

Who, where, when

The Problem

The problem or conflict that the protagonist encounters and attempts to solve.

Events

A series of attempts to solve the problem.

The Resolution

The problem or conflict is solved and the story winds down. In an episodic story, each chapter has a story grammar. A novel may include a series of interlocking episodes, each with its own story grammar.

Story Grammar Diagram

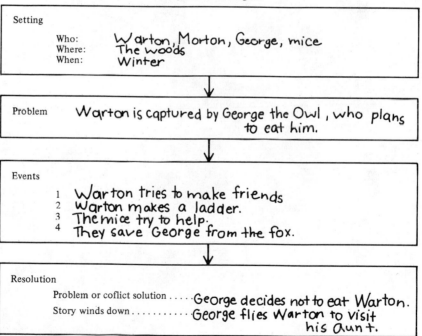

Setting

Who: Warton, Morton, George, mice
Where: The woods
When: Winter

Problem   Warton is captured by George the Owl, who plans to eat him.

Events

1 Warton tries to make friends
2 Warton makes a ladder.
3 The mice try to help.
4 They save George from the fox.

Resolution

Problem or coflict solution . . . . . George decides not to eat Warton.
Story winds down . . . . George flies Warton to visit his aunt.

Figure 5.1   Story Grammar Design Based on *A Toad for Tuesday* by Russell E. Erickson

include the following ideas and concepts. Read a story to the students, then explain that stories have parts and identify the parts of the story. You can use a chart with pictures to explain to primary-grade children, and use words with older students. Then read another short story and have the children identify the parts (directed practice). Point out that they can use the story

Children spend many of their waking hours listening.

"parts" to help them listen to stories, remember stories, read stories, and write stories. On subsequent days, practice identifying story parts. You may have younger children draw pictures to illustrate story grammar, while older students can complete a diagram like the one in Figure 5.1 or create their own diagram. Be sure to have students apply the story grammar when they are reading and writing, so they are fully aware of its applications.

Oral and Written Strategies   Listening is enhanced by strategies that involve oral and written responses. In Chapter Four you learned about dramatizing stories, puppets, and so forth, which are oral responses to listening and reading. In Chapter Seven you will learn more about written responses to listening. Books also encourage children to draw as a result of listening.

For children in the primary grades *The Tale of a Black Cat* by Carl Withers provides a good listening activity for directions. Children follow directions as they listen to the story and those who listen carefully and follow the directions correctly will produce a black cat. You will find interesting drawings in Ed Emberley's books that you build similar kinds of stories around. When reading *Mr. Grumpy's Outing* by John Burningham the listeners could draw the boat and each animal's head as it makes an appearance in the story (see Figure 5.2). This story can be easily adapted to the flannel board by creating the boat, the animals, and Mr. Gumpy.

Another response to listening activity involves listeners creating a map of the places that the characters in the story visited. Figure 5.3 shows a map that students could make based on the story *Rosie's Walk* by Pat Hutchins. To help children listen and understand content, the teacher could introduce a

Figure 5.2   Sample Written Response to Reading Content for *Mr. Gumpy's Outing*

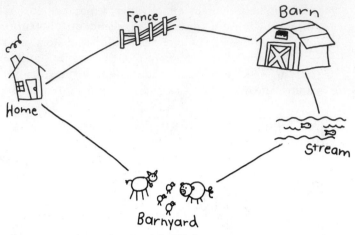

Figure 5.3 Map for *Rosie's Walk*

trade book to a second-grade class by saying, "The title of this book is *Fossils Tell of Long Ago.* It was written and illustrated by Aliki. It explains what fossils are and how they are formed. After you listen to the story, you may discover that you have seen fossils." This brief introduction helps focus students' attention and helps them anticipate the information they will hear and focuses their attention.

A teacher who was introducing *Another Way to Listen* to a fourth-grade class said, "The title of this book is *Another Way to Listen.* The authors are Byrd Baylor and Peter Parnall. This book is about a special kind of hearing that people who are close to nature do. This kind of listening makes it possible to hear such things as wildflower seeds burst open, rocks murmuring, and hills singing. While I read this story, listen to determine what 'the other way to listen is.' " After listening to the story, the students discuss their responses to the listening purpose. A teacher who planned to encourage students' thinking used these questions.

DISCUSSION QUESTIONS

1. Vocabulary: What does *natural* mean in the phrase "the most natural thing"?

2. Literal: What did the old man answer when the boy asked him how he learned to hear the corn?

3. Inferential: Why did the boy say that he never said a word while the old man was listening?

4. Critical: How did the boy learn to hear the hills singing?

5. Creative: What other things could a listener like the old man hear that people do not ordinarily hear?

Listening Lesson for Nonfiction and Textbook Content   The strategies suggested throughout this chapter will work with nonfiction and textbook content; however, students need to have opportunities to examine the
structural patterns found in nonfiction because they are expected to acquire
concepts and information for listening to such materials.

Main ideas and supporting details are most important in structuring
nonfiction and text content. The following lesson description is based on
main ideas and could be expanded to encompass supporting details. Explain
that the objective is to listen for main ideas and ask students if they remember
what a main idea is. Review and clarify their concept of main idea. Then
explain that they will be listening to newspaper articles to identify main
ideas. Read a short selection and ask students to state the main idea and then
to explain why they think this is the most important idea in the selection.
Practice this skill by reading three or four short newspaper selections for them
to state the main idea. If students have difficulty stating the main idea, you
can write three possible main ideas on a chart or chalkboard and have them
identify the correct one. This instruction can be transferred to social studies
or science textbooks by showing students how the main ideas of sections in
these textbooks are like those in a newspaper article. You may make audio
tapes of yourself reading sections from the textbook for students to state the
main ideas. Instruction should be followed by three or four practice sessions
a week over a period of two or three weeks.

A similar introduction can be used in teaching the various ways that
nonfiction is structured, such as main idea, cause and effect, comparison,
chronological order, and examples. You may also use diagrams like the one
in Figure 5.4, which the children complete as they are listening or immediately following a listening experience.

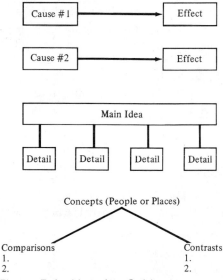

Figure 5.4   Listening Guide

Listening for expressions that signal the structural patterns discussed in this section helps students identify them. Speakers tend to use certain words and expressions to move from one part of their presentation to another. Knowing these key expressions helps listeners understand what the speaker is saying. Reading and writing also use signal expressions; therefore, learning these expressions helps students in all areas of the language arts. The activities suggested in this chapter for developing listening vocabulary can be used to help students learn the meaning and function of these expressions. A list of signal expressions is given below.

Words that signal comparison and contrast
but, however, in contrast, in comparison, similarly, on the other hand, nevertheless

Words that signal cause and effect
the causes, the effects, as a result, so, accordingly, therefore, thus

Words that signal addition
in addition, also, furthermore, moreover, another example

Words that signal time and/or sequence
first, second, third, meanwhile, next, finally, at last, today, tomorrow, soon

Words that indicate examples are presented
for example, for instance, thus, in other words, as an illustration

Listening Study Guide   Middle-grade students must learn to listen with pen or pencil in hand because they have to listen to longer selections. Taking notes make listeners more attentive and accurate. Listening study guides, structured note taking, and listening frames focus students' attention on the main ideas and the plan of the presentation. The following listening study guide can be used with classroom reading, radio speeches, television speeches, and classmates' reports. Teachers may tape class presentations or radio and television materials for the students to use when practicing the use of a listening study guide. This listening study guide is based on a television debate by two candidates for the U.S. Senate. The italicized sections indicate the material printed on the listening study guide. The content not underlined represents the responses of an individual completing the guide.

 LISTENING STUDY GUIDE

1. Date, class (social studies, English, etc.)

2. *What was the topic?* Debate between senatorial candidates regarding who would represent the state of North Carolina most effectively.

3. *How was content organized?* (Commonly used organizations include cause and effect, comparison, sequential pattern, main ideas with supporting examples.) Question and answer style was used in the debate with supporting examples given by debaters.

4. *Did the speakers (content) stick to the point?* No, one candidate particularly failed to answer questions and switch to points he wanted to make.

5. *Do you agree with the ideas (information) given?* I agreed with some of the points made.

6. *Why do you agree or disagree?* I felt that candidate 1 evaded addressing questions and important points made by candidate 2. When given questions to answer, candidate 1 talked about subjects to address rather than answer the question, and gave inaccurate statistics several times during the presentation.

7. *Write the main points in no more than three sentences.* The main points debated were campaign costs, tobacco supports, and experience with foreign affairs.

Listening Frames   A very simple listening guide is a series of frames with blanks which the instructor or speaker prepares in advance so the listener can complete them during or after the listening activity. Listening frames help students understand the parts of a story in fiction, and help them recognize common patterns of discourse in nonfiction. The following example shows a simple series of frames to use with fiction. The underlined answers were composed by a group of fourth graders after they listened to the story, *The Midnight Fox* by Betsy Byars.

LISTENING FRAMES FOR FICTION (PLOT ANALYSIS)

In the story *The Midnight Fox* by Betsy Byars identify at least three events that led to the climax.
First event: <u>Tom admired the fox.</u>
Second event: <u>Tom was afraid to climb the tree.</u>
Third event: <u>The fox killed some chickens.</u>
Fourth event: <u>The fox was captured.</u>

What was the climax of this story? <u>Tom released the fox from the cage.</u>

LISTENING FRAMES FOR FICTION (CHARACTER ANALYSIS)

In the story *The Midnight Fox* by Betsy Byars the main character is <u>Tom.</u> Tom is <u>shy.</u> He is <u>not interested in sports.</u> Tom's big problem in this story is <u>how to get along on the farm until his parents come back.</u> Why is this a problem? <u>Because he is shy and afraid.</u>

Listening frames can be used with text materials. In teaching these patterns, explain them, read illustrative examples, and have children find additional examples. Completing listening frames gives students additional practice with organizational patterns. The following listening frames were written for elementary science content illustrating a cause-and-effect pattern.

LISTENING FRAMES FOR SCIENCE

The topic is <u>how matter changes.</u> The speaker's (reader's) main points were:

1. <u>Adding heat changes matter.</u> Heat causes <u>matter to change from a solid to a liquid.</u>

2. <u>Taking heat away changes matter. Taking heat away</u> causes <u>matter to change from a liquid to a solid.</u>

THE DIRECTED LISTENING-THINKING ACTIVITY (DLTA) _____

This strategy, which is modeled after Stauffer's (1975) Directed Reading-Thinking Activity may be used at any grade level. This activity encourages active listening to fiction and nonfiction. Students use their thinking abilities and their prior experiences as they listen. This activity may be used with an entire class or with a small group. Teachers who are striving to develop students' listening abilities will find it useful to do several Directed Listening-Thinking Activities each week. Following are the steps to use in the directed listening-thinking activity as it is applied to fiction.

1. Select a story that has a strong plot structure. The story should include conflicts or problems to be overcome. Stories used with middle-grade children should be short because longer stories read to them over a period of time would make this strategy ineffective. Primary children would enjoy books like: *Mary of Mile 18* by Ann Blades, *Fish Is Fish* by Leo Lionni, *There's a Nightmare in My Closet* by Mercer Mayer, and *Alexander Who Used to Be Rich Last Sunday* by Judith Viorst. Middle-grade students should enjoy the following books: *The Biggest Bear* by Lynd Ward, *Fantastic Mr. Fox* by Roald Dahl, *Jim and the Beanstalk* by Raymond Biggs, and *Black Folktales* by Julius Lester.

2. Read through the selection and identify places to stop reading. These stopping places should occur just prior to an event in the story so that the listeners can predict what will happen next. Avoid stopping too frequently as this will fragment the story. The number of stops depends on story length, but two to four stops usually work best. For example, when reading *Mr. Grumpy's Motor Car* by John Burningham to a first-grade class, the teacher might choose to stop when the rain clouds appear and when the animals refuse to help push the car.

3. Introduce the story by telling the children the title, the author, and by allowing them to see the cover or the first illustrations in the book. If any students indicate they have heard the story, ask them to keep the outcome a secret until the other students have heard it.

4. Read the story, stopping at each point selected. When you stop, ask children to tell what has happened to this point (briefly), ask them to

predict what might happen next, and to explain why they think so. This encourages students to listen carefully, to think, to predict, and to support their answers. Avoid judging students' responses by stating "right" and "wrong" answers. You may encourage all of the children in the class to participate by asking everyone who agrees with the prediction made to hold up his or her hand. After the predictions are completed continue reading so the students can determine which responses were closest to the story line.

With nonfiction, the teacher uses essentially the same DLTA procedure as with fiction. However, the teacher should introduce the ideas to be explored in the selection in addition to the book title (or the selection title) and the illustrations. For instance, in a selection about the Western United States, the teacher should write the states to be discussed on the chalkboard and compare and contrast their geography with that of the local area. Ask the students to predict what the author will say before reading the selection. Continue this activity by stopping at the selected places for review and prediction.

LISTENING AND THE MASS MEDIA

Our listening skills are used most frequently with the mass media. Children spend a large portion of their waking hours listening to television, radio, tapes, and records. Research shows that children watch television an average of 20 to 36 hours a week until age 11. The hours of television viewing decline after the age of 11. Does watching television for so many hours improve listening skills? Research data is unclear on the relationship between television viewing and listening; however, it appears that there is little if any listening improvement. This is probably true because listening to television is a passive activity while effective listening is an active process.

Teachers should take advantage of the wealth of interesting and stimulating material available for students through the mass media. We can call students' attention to some excellent programs that are scheduled. We can send information to parents regarding quality children's programs and movies. Classroom discussions of good programs and movies helps make children more discriminating in their choice of programs and movies.

Teachers can help children think critically about the shows they are watching by using the critical listening activities listed in this chapter. Teachers can help students derive the most from the mass media by following these guidelines:

1. Preview the material if possible. Television scripts or synopses are sometimes available for this purpose. Television guides are helpful.

2. Present background information, concepts, and key vocabulary to students prior to using the film, television show, radio program, or record.

3. State listening purposes for the students or help them develop their own listening purposes.

4. After the experience discuss the listening purposes and clarify any concepts or ideas that require clarification. Answer students' questions regarding the experience.

5. Use follow-up activities to reinforce important listening skills and content concepts.

ASSESSMENT OF LISTENING SKILLS

Standardized tests and informal tests are used to evaluate students' listening skills. Informal listening tests are used most frequently because so few standardized listening tests are available. Three standardized listening tests are described below.

Standardized Listening Tests

1. *Durrell Listening-Reading Series Test* New York: Harcourt, Brace and World, 1969. This test is published in a primary form (grades 1–2) and an intermediate form (grades 3–6). The primary level examines vocabulary listening, vocabulary reading, sentence listening, and sentence reading. The intermediate level test examines vocabulary listening, vocabulary reading, paragraph listening, and paragraph reading.

2. *Stanford Achievement Tests* New York: Harcourt Brace Jovanovich, 1981. This test battery includes a listening subtest for both the primary and intermediate grade levels. To administer this test, the teacher reads materials and the students mark answer sheets.

3. *The Sequential Tests of Educational Progress* (Listening Comprehension Test) Englewood Cliffs, NJ: Educational Testing Service, 1956. This test measures students' listening skills from fourth grade through college level. These tests examine ability to comprehend main ideas, memory of significant details, understanding the implications of ideas and details, and evaluating and applying material presented. This test is administered by an examiner reading aloud from the test manual as students check off answers on the answer sheet.

Informal Assessment

Observation is a form of informal assessment. Teachers can prepare simple checklists to guide observation and evaluation of listening skills. Figure 5.5 demonstrates such a checklist.

Teachers may prepare taped listening tests by recording paragraphs and selections from children's reading books and content textbooks with accom-

Name of Student _____

Date _____

Listening Strategy

1. Thinking skills

    Literal

    Inferential

    Critical

    Creative

2. Oral response to listening
    (can repeat what is heard, dramatize, report, follow directions)

3. Written response to listening
    (completes study guide, story grammar, etc., follows directions)

Checklists can also be created by making a grid and filling in all of the students' names on one axis and the listening behaviors on the other, which permits a quick summary of the listening skills of the class.

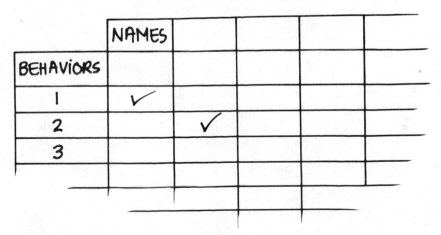

Figure 5.5   Teacher Observation Checklist

panying questions. Answer sheets can be duplicated so children merely mark the answers as they listen to the tape.

Metacognitive Strategies

Metacognitive strategies refer to self-monitoring and self-regulatory mechanisms used by an active problem solver who wishes to achieve a goal (Samuels, 1984). In this instance the active problem solver is a listener who wishes to understand a message. Metacognitive (self-evaluative) skills help students become responsible for knowing when he or she has understood and when they have failed to understand. When students monitor their own understanding, they can ask the speaker for additional information to insure comprehension. Students may ask themselves questions like the following:

Why am I listening to this message (information)?

Is this information important?

What are the major points the speaker has made?

What minor points has the speaker made?

Do I need more information to understand?

What is the structure of this message?

Self-Evaluation Questionnaire

In the primary grades, self-evaluation can be a group project occurring as part of a class discussion on listening skills. Children in grades three through eight may complete self-evaluations similar to the one in Figure 5.6.

TROUBLESHOOTING

Some students exhibit listening difficulties in spite of excellent instruction and many opportunities to practice listening skills. Some of the most common listening problems found among elementary school students and some suggested remedies are discussed here.

1. Some children may be inattentive in the classroom and fail to listen accurately. These children may have a hearing problem (auditory acuity). Hearing problems are subtle to identify and they are often overlooked. The first step in helping an inattentive youngster who seems not to listen is to refer this child for further testing by a specialist to determine whether there is a hearing loss. While waiting for test results, seat the child in the front of the classroom and make certain that he looks at the teacher while listening.

Read the following questions and answer yes or no on the blanks.

1. I concentrated on the speaker. _____

2. I ignored all of the sounds except the speaker's voice. _____

3. I had a listening purpose. _____

4. I thought about the things that I knew that were related to the topic. _____

5. I was able to select the speaker's main ideas. _____

6. I listened for signal words. _____

7. I identified the speaker's organization. _____

8. After the speech I agreed with the speaker. _____

9. After the speech I disagreed with the speaker. _____

Figure 5.6   Self-evaluation of Listening Skills

2. Perhaps the most common listening problems in classrooms, come from youngsters who *always* ask teachers to repeat the directions. These students often ask teachers to repeat directions several times. They frequently fail to complete assignments complaining that they did not understand what was expected. These students often are simply insecure. They understand the directions, but they are afraid they will make a mistake. Help them by assigning a partner to assist them with directions. They should repeat the instructions to the partner to be sure they listened accurately. Then they may proceed with the task. A partner reassures them that help is available if they forget. Gradually, they will overcome the need for this reassurance. However, this is a long, gradual process.

3. Some students in the middle grades have particular difficulty listening to nonfiction selections and classroom lectures. This difficulty is probably the result of listening to dramatized stories on television and reading fiction in basal readers. These experiences have not prepared students to listen to informational materials. Writing the topic, main ideas, and key words on the chalkboard in the order of occurrence in the selection helps these students follow the speaker.

4. Listening and taking notes is a problem for some middle-grade students. This difficulty is often caused by lack of composition skills. These students can take notes by making simple drawings with stick figures to help them remember important points.

5. Some middle-grade youngsters have difficulty identifying the organization of content. Giving these students a checklist to complete for each listening selection helps them. A sample checklist follows:
   Cause and effect _____
   Question and answer _____
   Comparison and contrast _____
   Main idea and examples _____
   Sequential order _____
   Enumeration _____

SUMMARY

Listening is very important in our society. Listening is concerned with understanding spoken language. Listeners must translate spoken words into meaning. In order to understand spoken language, students must hear (receive the sound waves), they must discriminate one word from another and they must comprehend. Comprehension is based on cognitive activity at four levels: literal, interpretive, critical, and appreciative. Literal understanding is based upon what the speaker has stated, the listener must simply understand the words and the syntax of the sentences. Interpretive (inferential) understanding requires the listener to think beyond the stated ideas and information. The listener must relate previous experiences and information stored in his or her brain to the information heard. To listen critically, the listener must evaluate and judge the message. Appreciative listening is concerned with listening for entertainment.

A planned instructional program will improve listening comprehension. Listening instruction should be offered on a daily basis. Lessons of five to ten minutes in length are generally adequate for developing and refining listening skills. The listening curriculum should develop strategies such as: directed listening-thinking activity (DLTA), identifying frames or patterns of organization, and identifying signal words. In addition, specific listening skills should be developed. These skills include listening vocabulary, literal listening, inferential listening, critical listening, and appreciative listening.

Listening achievement can be evaluated through standardized tests and informal tests. However, informal tests are used most frequently because there are few standardized listening tests. Teachers may observe students' listening skills and record their observations on a checklist. Students may self-evaluate their listening skills by answering questions.

Thought Questions

1. Why is listening the most basic language arts skill?

2. How are listening and reading related?

3. How does a listening purpose function to improve listening comprehension?

4. Describe a listening program for an elementary school.

5. Discuss the statement, "Listening is both the commonest and the most mysterious of the language arts."

6. How is metacognition related to listening?

7. Describe three listening strategies that can be used to increase listening comprehension.

Enrichment Activities

1. Ask an elementary teacher to describe the listening program used in his or her school.

2. Examine an elementary language arts textbook to determine what listening skills are taught and how they are taught.

3. Read two of the "Related Readings." Explain ways in which the two readings are alike and different. How do the readings compare with the ideas expressed in this chapter?

4. Create a listening study guide to accompany a middle-grade content textbook. If possible use the study guide in an actual classroom to determine the students' reaction to it.

5. Prepare an introduction and a set of questions to accompany a trade book (fiction or nonfiction) that could be used in a primary classroom. If possible introduce the book to a class and lead a follow-up discussion.

6. Examine a standardized listening test. Identify the skills assessed by the instrument. If possible administer the test to a student.

Selected Readings

Adler, Mortimer J. (1983). *How to Speak/How to Listen.* New York: Macmillan.

Crowell, Doris, and Kathryn Au (January 1979). "Using a Scale of Questions to Improve Listening Comprehension." *Language Arts, 38,* 38–43.

Cunningham, Patricia M. (November 1975). "Transferring Comprehension from Listening to Reading." *Reading Teacher, 29,* 169–173.

Devine, Thomas G. (1982). *Listening Skills Schoolwide: Activities and Programs.* Urbana, IL: National Council of Teachers of English.

Lundsteen, Sara (1979). *Listening: Its Impact at All Levels on Reading and the Other Language Arts.* Urbana, IL: National Council of Teachers of English.

Monteith, Mary K. (January 1979). "Listening/Speaking Skills—The Art of Interactive Communication." *Language Arts, 38,* 61–65.

Moore, David W., and John E. Readence (April 1980). "Processing Main Ideas Through Parallel Lesson Transfer." *Journal of Reading, 23,* 589–593.

Pearson, P. David, and Linda Fielding (September 1982). "Listening Comprehension," *Language Arts, 59,* 617–627.

Russell, David H., and Elizabeth F. Russell (1979). *Listening Aids Through the Grades,* Revised Ed., by Dorothy G. Hennings. New York: Teachers College Press.

Samuels, Jay (Summer 1984). "Factors Influencing Listening: Inside and Outside the Head." *Theory into Practice, 33,* 183–189.

References

Applebee, Arthur (1978). *The Child's Concept of Story.* Chicago: University of Chicago Press.

DeSousa, A. M., and M. Cowles (February 1967). "An Experimental Study to Determine the Efficacy of Specific Training in Listening." Paper presented at the American Educational Research Convention.

Devine, Thomas G. (1982). *Listening Skills Schoolwide: Activities and Progress.* Urbana, IL: National Council of Teachers of English.

Devine, Thomas G. (1978). "Listening: What Do We Know After Fifty Years of Research and Theorizing?" *Journal of Reading, 21,* 296–304.

Duker, Sam (1969). "Listening." In *Encyclopedia of Educational Research* (4th ed.), R. L. Ebel, ed. London: Collier-MacMillan Ltd.

Early, Margaret (1960). "Communication Arts." In *Encyclopedia of Educational Research* (3d ed.), C. W. Harris (ed.). New York: Macmillan Co.

Hart, L. (1975). *How the Brain Works.* New York: Basic Books.

Herman, Wayne (March, 1967). "The Use of Language Arts in Social Studies Lessons." *American Education Review Journal, 4,* 117–124.

Lundsteen, Sara (1978). *Children Learn to Communicate.* New York: Holt, Rinehart and Winston.

Lundsteen, Sara (1979). *Listening: Its Impact at All Levels on Reading and the Other Language Arts.* Urbana, IL: National Council of Teachers of English.

Mandler, J. M. (1978). "A Code in the Node: The Use of Story Schema in Retrieval." *Discourse Processes 1,* 14–35.

Nichols, Ralph, and Leonard Stevens (February 1983). "Are You Listening?" *Language Arts, 60,* 164–165.

Pearson, P. David, and Linda Fielding (September 1983). "Listening Comprehension." *Language Arts, 59,* 617–627.

Pearson, P. David, and Dale Johnson (1978). *Teaching Reading Comprehension.* New York: Holt Rinehart and Winston.

Ross, M., and Thomas G. Ross. *Auditory Management of Hearing-Impaired Children: Principles and Prerequisites for Intervention.* Baltimore, MD: University Park Press, 1978.

Samuels, Jay (Summer 1984). "Factors Influencing Listening: Inside and Outside the Head." *Theory into Practice, 33,* 183–189.

Stauffer, R. (1975). *Directing the Reading Thinking Process.* New York: Harper & Row.

Stein, N., and C. G. Glenn (1979). "An Analysis of Story Comprehension in Elementary School Children." In *New Directions in Discourse Processing,* R. Freidle, (ed.). Norwood, NJ: Ablex.

Strickland, Dorothy (1971). *The Effects of a Special Program on the Oral Language Expansion of Linguistically Different, Negro Kindergarten Children.* Unpublished doctoral dissertation, New York University.

Trelease, J. (1986). *The Read-aloud Handbook* (2d ed.). New York: Penguin.

Wilt, Miriam (April 1950). "Study of Teacher Awareness of Listening as a Factor in Elementary Education." *Journal of Educational Research, 43,* 626–636.

Chapter **Six**

Reading Is a Language Skill

OVERVIEW

The goal of this chapter is to give students an overview of the reading process since the majority of teachers and prospective teachers who use this text will take a separate reading course. This chapter emphasizes the total reading program in the elementary school—including developmental reading, content reading, recreational reading, literature, and reading for students with special needs. The major goals of developmental reading instruction are to help students acquire the reading readiness skills, word recognition skills and reading comprehension that will enable them to understand and interpret written language. Students must learn how to read different types of content including narrative, exposition, and poetry. These types of literature comprise basal reading materials. We must recognize that language skills are developed and refined through use; therefore reading materials should invite students to read. The recreational reading program should motivate students to read for pleasure. Content reading instruction is concerned with teaching children to understand their content textbooks.

Anticipation Guide

What do you think occurs during the reading process? Why are we obsessed with reading in our culture? Think about these ideas and the following questions as you read this chapter.

1. What is reading?

2. How is language related to reading?

3. What are the components of a total reading program?

4. Why is content reading instruction important?

Key Concepts

language experience approach   DRTA
basal reading approach   comprehension
decode   content reading
reading readiness   developmental reading

INTRODUCTION

We teach children to read so they will have an important tool for learning and relearning. In our futuristic culture, knowledge is accumulating so fast that we must constantly update our information. Computer technology has increased the need for literacy rather than reducing it. "Our society places a very high value on learning to read. . . . Children who do not learn to read cannot lead normal lives in our society" (Heilman and Holmes, 1978). Reading is one of the receptive language arts. We receive information and ideas from reading. When we read we are processing written language in order to understand what the author is saying to us. Readers engage in mental dialog with a writer during the reading process. Readers use information from texts along with their own experiences and knowledge about events, places, things, and people in order to understand written language. Of course, they must recognize words and their meanings in order to process the written language. These aspects of reading comprehension are illustrated in the following passage.

> The mail carrier arrived at Susan's door and handed her several letters. Among them was the one she had eagerly awaited. She rushed to the desk to answer it.

After recognizing the first few words of this passage, readers are alerted to the fact that they are reading about mail which should activate their existing knowledge of mail delivery. The words *mail carrier* activate their associations and experiences with mail carriers. For example, many readers would expect the passage to relate to letters or packages after seeing the words *mail carrier.* Readers use their own knowledge to infer information and ideas the author did not include. "No text is completely self-explanatory. In interpreting a text, readers draw on their store of knowledge about the topic of the text" (Anderson and Armbruster, 1985). In the preceding passage, readers infer that Susan took the letters from the mail carrier, looked through the letters perhaps reading return addresses to identify the one she wanted, went indoors, read the letter, then went to the desk and took out paper and pen to write a response. Although, none of this data is expressly stated in the text. The differences in readers' knowledge leads to different interpretations of the same text.

The following sketches illustrate approaches to classroom reading instruction. In the first-grade vignette, the teacher demonstrates language experience reading instruction. She uses language experience at the beginning of the school year; later when the children are reading more she uses language experience two days a week and basal readers on the other days. In the fourth-grade vignette, the teacher utilizes a typical basal reader lesson format. As you read the vignettes compare basal reading instruction with language experience instruction.

A FIRST-GRADE VIGNETTE

After sending the attendance report to the principal's office, Susan Jordan called her first-grade class to order. The first graders sat on rugs while she read *Brown Bear, Brown Bear* by Bill Martin to them. She told them to listen for words that were repeated in this story. When the story was completed, the children identified the repeated words and phrases and Susan wrote them on the chalkboard.

Then Susan asked the children to think of other animals that they could use to make up a story with the same pattern. They started naming the animals that had appeared in the story, but Susan reminded them that they were to think of different animals. Then Anne said "zebra," which started them naming different animals. After they named as many animals as they could, they identified colors. Susan wrote the animals and colors on the chalkboard.

With the completion of the word lists, Susan said, "Now, we are ready to make up our own story in the pattern of *Brown Bear, Brown Bear.* Who has the first line? Allison responded with this sentence, "Red Cow, Red Cow, what do you see?" Susan wrote this sentence on the chalkboard. Later she would transfer the story to a chart. "Can someone think of a sentence that tells what the red cow saw?" Jimmy offered the sentence, "I see a purple giraffe looking at me." As Susan wrote the sentence on the board, she said the words aloud.

Then she read the story aloud with the children joining in on the parts they recognized. Then the children found animal and color words in the story. Using colored chalk, the children drew yellow lines under color words and blue lines under animal words. Susan instructed them to find words that began with *B* and *R,* which were the phonemes that the children were studying. She handed the children sight word cards to match with words in the story. Finally, she had the children count the number of times each word was used in the chart. The words that were used five times were high frequency words that they added to the class word bank.

Later, Susan made copies of the story for each child. The children enjoyed rereading the story and most of them illustrated their personal copies.

A FOURTH-GRADE VIGNETTE

Mark Holden, a fourth-grade teacher, has been participating in an effective teaching workshop sponsored by the school system. In his lesson he implements some newly learned strategies.

Mark is teaching reading to the whole class in order to increase direct teaching time and time on task. This approach decreases the amount of seat work that students must complete while the "other kids" are reading. But he finds that he must work hard to keep all of the students involved in the lesson.

Mark explained that the class was going to read the story "My Robot Buddy" by Alfred Slote. He further explained that their objectives for this story were to review story setting and story theme, and to identify synonyms for some words. Then he introduced the new words for the story. The children silently read the sentences containing new vocabulary in their readers, decoding unknown words independently. After they read the sentences, Mark gave synonyms for the new vocabulary and the students identified the word he was referring to. For example, he asked them to identify the word that means the same thing as a gift which of course was *present*. The children found the new vocabulary for this story relatively easy to understand.

Mark explained that they were going to read a science fiction story about robots. He asked the children what they knew about robots and found that they knew quite a bit. Then he asked the students to predict what the robot in this story would do. They predicted that he would do homework, clean house, and so forth. Mark told them to read the first four pages of the story silently to find out the purpose of the robot in the story. After they read this portion of the story, they discovered that the robot was designed to be a friend of the main character. Mark asked them to predict what the story problem in this story might be. Several of the students predicted "robotnapping" because the author had foreshadowed this idea. Mark told them to read the next two pages silently to see if they were correct. After they discussed the story problem. He asked them to finish the story to find the solution to the problem. During the postreading discussion, they summarized the story and discussed the theme.

When the students completed the story and discussion, they talked about how useful robots would be in their lives. They enjoyed this idea so much that Mark told them to imagine what they would have a personal robot do and then to draft a story about their robot. When the students completed their stories, they put them in their writing files, so they could revise and edit them later. An example of their stories is shown in Figure 6.1.

Language Experience Approach

Susan very successfully used the combined basal reader and language experience approach. The **language experience approach** is based on reading content that is created by writing down children's thoughts. The four language arts—listening, speaking, reading, and writing—are integrated in the language experience approach. Reading materials are thus created for the class from the stories, experiences and ideas that the children dictate to the teacher. Children can record their own ideas for later reading. Research substantiates the value of the language experience approach. Five basic dimensions of a language experience approach are listed below.

1. Children can talk about their thoughts.

2. What children talk about can be expressed in painting, writing, or some other form.

3. Anything the child writes can be read.

4. Children can read what they write as well as what other people write.

5. As children record the sounds that they make in speech, they use the same letters over and over again.

Charlie
Feb 26, 1986

If I had a robot I would name him Harvey. Harvey could do many things like play basketball, soccer, baseball. Because when I'm lonely I like to play. I would also like Harvey to help with my chores so we could have more time to play together. I would tell Harvey help me with my homework. Harvey would also help me clean up my room.

He would have green hair, he would wear a pink shirt and yellow pants. I would fix his knees so they could bend. Harvey would turn into a Porsche 911 so he could drive me to school. When he is a Porsche he would be red, white, and blue. He would be able to go 600 m.p.h. so I would be on time for places I had to be. I think it would be neat to have a robot like Harvey.

Figure 6.1   Sample fourth-grade story and illustration.

A Basal Reader Lesson _____

Mark used a standard **basal reader approach** to teach developmental reading in the fourth-grade vignette. He followed the directed reading–thinking activity (**DRTA**) format in teaching this lesson. The components of the DRTA are listed below (Stauffer, 1980).

1. Surveying and purpose setting: The readers examine the title, illustrations, and/or the first portion of a selection to elicit predictions about the selection.

2. Students silently read a portion of the selection. They stop at a preselected point just prior to an important event to confirm or modify predictions.

3. Students predict upcoming events and reevaluate previous predictions based on additional information. This process is repeated until the selection is completed.

4. The postreading discussion includes a summary of story events and students self-evaluate their use of story clues and predictions.

Mark follows his teachers' manual rather closely in teaching reading. However, his principal indicated on Mark's last evaluation that he needed to develop content reading and recreational reading in his classroom. But Mark is unsure of how to proceed, so he is considering a graduate reading course at the local university.

TOTAL READING PROGRAM

A sound reading program combines skills mastery with reading for personal pleasure and information (Winograd and Greenlee, 1986). In such a program, students read many different kinds of written content for a variety of purposes. They acquire the word recognition and comprehension skills that will enable them to use textual information and their own experiences. A total elementary reading program includes instruction in the following aspects of reading: developmental, content, literature, recreational, and students with special needs.

Developmental Reading

The teachers in the vignettes were teaching **developmental reading** which is the reading instruction designed for students who are making average progress in learning to read. Reading readiness skills, word recognition skills, and comprehension skills are included in the developmental reading program. As you read this chapter notice how heavily we rely on speaking, listening, and writing as a means of developing reading skills.

Reading Readiness   **Reading readiness** is achieved when the child's maturity, knowledge, skills, and experiences and the instructional strategies used in the classroom make it possible for the student to acquire effective reading skills. Reading readiness is a developmental process in that it gradually "unfolds" as the child matures. However, readiness is influenced by parents and teachers.

Research concerned with reading readiness is extensive. Some of these findings are summarized below (Durrell and Murphy, 1963; Frazier, 1983; Robinson, Strickland, and Cullinan, 1978).

1. Children who have broad experiential backgrounds are more successful in beginning reading than children whose backgrounds have been limited.

2. Children who have a rich language background tend to fare better in beginning reading.

3. Children who are emotionally and socially mature are more ready to learn to read. Self-concept, an important aspect of emotional development, is a significant factor in reading readiness.

4. Intelligence (cognitive development) is found to be another significant factor in learning to read. A high intelligence level, however, does not always ensure reading success.

5. Physical development is correlated with success in reading. Girls physically mature more rapidly than boys and also experience greater success in beginning reading.

6. Motivation and the desire to learn to read are two very important aspects of beginning reading achievement.

7. Poor health and visual or hearing impairments are detrimental to learning how to read.

8. Children who know letter names when they enter kindergarten are more successful in learning to read.

9. Concepts of written language influence beginning reading.

The preceding research summary should have alerted you to the fact that reading begins in the home. Children who acquire wide knowledge at home have greater chances for success in learning to read. However, wide experience is not enough. Parents must talk to their children about their experiences because discussing experiences extends children's store of concepts and increases their vocabulary (Olson, 1984). When parents ask children about experiences that the parents did not participate in, they are encouraging children to reflect on experience, to construct meaning, and to exercise their memories.

Parents and teachers who read aloud to children and then engage them in discussing the story read are helping children learn about language, written language, and the enjoyment derived from reading. Furthermore, they are letting children know that reading is an important skill. Children who have access to chalkboards, chalk, pencils, paper, crayons, magic markers, magnetic letters, puzzles, books, and newspapers exhibit greater reading readiness than children who lack these materials (Dunn, 1981).

Developing Reading Readiness   Kindergarten children have an extraordinarily wide variation in reading readiness. For example, Suzanne came to school reading at a second to third grade reading level. She could write her name and alphabet letters. On the other hand, Michael came to the same classroom never having seen or held a book. He did not know colors and he had never held a crayon or pencil. Kindergarten and first-grade teachers must plan programs to meet the needs of both children.

Reading readiness instruction should develop and enhance the skills and abilities that lead to reading success. The skills identified in the following list form a foundation for learning to read.

1. Auditory discrimination, the ability to tell one sound from another, is a learned skill.

2. Visual discrimination, the skill of seeing likenesses and differences in written letters and words, is a learned skill.

3. Knowledge of letter names.

4. Knowledge of letter sounds.

5. A sense of story (story grammar).

6. The desire to read motivates children to exert the effort to learn to read.

Literature and Readiness   Many experiences with written and oral language help kindergarten children acquire these skills and abilities. For instance, reading to children from excellent literature daily, and following it with discussion builds motivation to learn to read, as well as developing comprehension skills. As children listen to stories and discuss them, they develop the foundations of reading **comprehension**—they acquire word meanings, a sense of story (also called story grammar), and inferencing skill. They also learn to use their sense of story to make inferences about plot and character. For example, a kindergarten teacher could read *The Temper Tantrum Book* and follow the oral reading with a discussion of what makes youngsters angry and happy. A follow-up activity might have students draw pictures of things that make them mad and glad. Then the teacher might ask children to dictate phrases or sentences about their pictures. The following day, the teacher could read *Alexander and the Terrible Horrible No Good Very Bad Day* by Judith Viorst, so that the children could compare it with *The Temper Tantrum Book.*

Stories that have repeated phrases help children learn about language. After they hear the repeated phrases a few times, children can join in with the refrain which develops concepts of reading and auditory discrimination. Stories like *Chicken Little, The Little Red Hen,* and *The House that Jack Built* include repeated phrases.

The Shared Book Experience   Many of us remember a "big book," which the teacher used in teaching first graders reading. In that instance, the big book was a large preprimer; however, in contemporary use a big book is used more extensively and is based on literature rather than basal reader stories. Holdaway (1979) describes the shared book experience as an extension of parents reading to their children. Big books are enlargements of stories the children enjoy hearing, which becomes the basis for learning to read. With the use of big books children see a clear association among the words on the page, illustrations, and spoken words. Reading the stories repeatedly leads students to understand, to anticipate words and ideas, and to recognize words. The children frequently read along with the teacher as they become familiar with the stories; later they read the big books independently. Big books capitalize on the fact that children enjoy listening and relistening to favorite stories as well as reading and rereading these stories.

The "shared book" experience may be initiated in several ways. Holdaway (1979) suggests placing a big book on an easel where all of the children can see it and then reading the story aloud. Beasley (1986) reads a story to children several times from a trade book, and then writes the story on large pages with a magic marker; the children illustrate the story for use in classroom shared book experiences. During the oral reading of the big book, the teacher points to the words and later the children will point to the words as they read.

After the children hear the story, the teacher leads them in discussing story ideas, story grammar, characters, plot, and so forth. Then the children can identify words, phrases, and letters. For instance the teacher may instruct children to identify a specific word or phrase with their eyes, then ask an individual child to "frame" the word with his or her hands. Children can also place a word card under the word that looks exactly like the word written on the card. They can find all of the words that begin like a target word such as *boy*, which will help them learn phonics.

Any book can be enlarged into a "big book," although many teachers lead toward predictable books and ones with rhythmic language. Perhaps the most important criteria is that stories enlarged into big books be ones that children particularly enjoy. Many teachers include nursery rhymes, poems, and favorite songs in their repertoire of big books. Books like the following are good for big books.

Hutchins, Pat. *Rosie's Walk.* New York: Macmillan, 1968.

Hutchins, Pat. *Good-Night, Owl!* New York: Macmillan, 1972.

Krauss, Ruth. *The Carrot Seed.* New York: Harper & Row, 1945.

Krauss, Ruth. *A Very Special House.* New York: Harper & Row, 1953.

Lionni, Leo. *Little Blue and Little Yellow.* New York: Astor-Honor, 1959.

Martin, Bill. *Monday, Monday, I Like Monday.* New York: Holt, Rinehart and Winston, 1970.

Martin, Bill. *Brown Bear, Brown Bear, What Do You See?* New York: Holt, Rinehart and Winston, 1983.

Tolstoi, A. *The Great Big Enormous Turnip.* New York: Watts, 1968.

Teachers who have used this approach recommend using child-illustrated stories, teacher prepared "big books," and commercially prepared ones.

The materials for enlarging books include chart pages or pages of tagboard, magic markers (felt tipped marking pens), and rubber cement for gluing on the children's illustrations. Gluing the illustrations on the prepared pages saves having to redo pages due to mistakes. Many teachers have their big books laminated to preserve them. Beasley (1986) has created forty of them for use in kindergarten and first grade. When preparing to use this approach, you may refer to *Foundations of Literacy* (1979) by Holdaway and an excellent article by Slaughter (1983) which is found in *The Reading Teacher*.

Writing and Readiness   Readiness instruction should provide children with many opportunities to write. Dictating stories, sentences, and phrases to the teacher helps children learn to put their thoughts into words. Children should have many opportunities to compose and dictate language experience stories in kindergarten and first grade. This activity also develops concepts of print—for example, top and bottom of the page, left to right progression of print, word, and letter. Children's beginning writing efforts include scribbling, drawing, writing their name, writing letters, and keeping kindergarten journals (Chomsky, 1979; Dyson, 1984) which all help them develop reading skills and learn to compose (Harste, Burke, and Woodward, 1982).

Children need to know letter names and sounds if they are to have reading success. Research indicates that children who have this knowledge are better readers than children who do not (Anderson and Armbruster, 1984). Handwriting instruction can be combined with letter name instruction,

Developmental reading instruction.

so that students learn the letter name as they learn to form the letter. Children naturally develop an interest in writing letters at about the same time that they learn to identify letters (Mason, 1984). Many activities are available to teach children letter sounds. They can sort objects representing different initial consonant sounds. For example, they would put a toy dog, a miniature door, and a toy duck in a box with a *D* on the front of it.

Developmental Reading Instruction

Developmental reading instruction can be divided into word recognition and comprehension. Word recognition refers to the ability to associate pronunciation and meaning with the printed word. One of the cornerstones of skilled reading is fast, accurate word identification (Perfetti and Lesgold, 1979). According to *automaticity* theory, a fluent reader decodes text automatically—that is without conscious effort (LaBerge and Samuels, 1974). In the beginning stages of reading, students are learning to recognize in print words that are in their listening and speaking vocabularies. In the middle grades (intermediate), the focus shifts from recognition of known words to expanding the students' store of word meanings. Word recognition skills are the foundation on which middle graders learn new words. Readers use four basic approaches to **decode** (identify) words.

1. Sight words (memory).

2. Context clues.

3. Structural analysis.

4. Phonics.

A well-balanced reading program provides instruction in each of these word recognition skills. An overreliance on any one skill could impair reading progress. Word recognition instruction must include repeated opportunities for students to read meaningful texts so they develop automaticity in word recognition and reading fluency.

Sight Words (Memory)   Sight words are words that readers can identify because they have memorized them. Sight words are learned through seeing words repeatedly in print.

Sight words should be introduced to children in a meaningful context, since meaning helps them retain words. An instance of this is seen in the sentence, *Mary hit a run in the softball game.* The word *run* derives its meaning from the words *baseball game.* Nouns and verbs are usually easier for children to learn because these words are concrete words that name objects and actions.

Students must be able to look at the details within a word that make it look different from another word. Visual discrimination skills help them identify words. They also must be able to see the distinctive difference between *coat* and *boat* and between *sat* and *sit*. In each of the preceding set of words, only one letter is different which will make these words more difficult to discriminate than others. For example, the length of the word *grandmother* makes it distinctive from the word *in*. Ascending letters like *l* and *t* are distinctive. Descending letters like *g* and *y* create a difference in words.

The major task in teaching sight words is *meaningful repetition,* which facilitates memorization. The following steps should be used when teaching sight words.

1. Present the word in a context. The context may be a sentence or a phrase. Phrases and sentences should be written in manuscript, the new word should be underlined, and copies should be made. Students should have the words they are learning in front of them because looking back and forth to the chalkboard or to charts is difficult for many youngsters.

2. Children should examine the new word closely, looking at its unique characteristics (length, ascending and descending letters). The teacher should say the word aloud.

3. The students should repeat the word following the teacher's pronunciation.

4. Have the students silently read several sentences in which the word appears. All the words in the sentences should be familiar to the class except the new word that is being introduced. Then they may read the sentences aloud.

5. Games and activities should be used to reinforce the new word. These may incorporate the practice of several new words at the same time.

6. Do not introduce words that are easily confused in a single teaching session. This would include such words as *went* and *want, saw* and *was,* and *this* and *that.*

Context Clues   When a reader does not recognize a sight word, the next step is to look for context (meaning) clues. Writers often help readers understand the words they use. Such clues may appear in the same sentence as the unknown word, in the preceding sentence, in the succeeding sentence, or anywhere in the paragraph. In the example, *I stepped in one of the _____ to get my feet wet,* the missing word is *puddles,* while *stepped* and *wet* are context clues for *puddles.*

Listening activities prepare children to use context clues. The teacher can read selections aloud to the children, omitting a word or words and have the children suggest a word for the word omitted. In the example *Rosa is using _____ energy, too. She uses the sun's energy to grow vegetables. Rosa keeps her plants in a sunny window in her room. She depends on direct _____ to make the plants grow tall and strong.* The word missing from the first sentence is *solar* and the word missing in the fourth sentence is *sunlight.*

Children should understand that written language is supposed to make sense. The following strategy suggests using context to make sense.

1. Read the entire sentence and substitute any word (such as *candy* or *moon-beam*) for the unknown word.

2. Go back and think of a word that would make sense in the context of that sentence. For example, in reading the sentence the child might not recognize the word, and might insert the word *moonbeam* for the unknown word.

3. The child should reread this sentence and determine if this word actually makes sense in the sentence.

Structural Analysis   When students use *structural analysis,* they are using the structure of words in order to identify them. Structural analysis includes the use of prefixes, suffixes, root words, compound words, inflected endings, and contractions to identify words. Each word part is described in the following section.

Prefixes are a letter or letters that precede a root word and that change the meaning of the word. The word *unusual* means not usual. *Un* is the prefix and *usual* is the root word.

Suffixes are a letter or letters added to the end of a root word that change the meaning of the word. *Joyful* means full of joy. *Ful* is the suffix meaning full of while *joy* is the root word.

A *root word* is a part of the word that conveys the majority of the word's meaning. Adding prefixes, suffixes, or combining a root with another word will alter the meaning of the root itself. *Preview* means view before because the prefix *pre* means before and the root *view* means view (or see).

Compound words are two words joined together to make a new word. *Football, rainfall,* and *grandfather* are compound words.

Inflected endings consist of a letter or letters that are added to the end of a root word to indicate case, gender, mood, number, person, or tense. Table 6.1 shows how various parts of speech are inflected. Children commonly use inflected endings in their oral language, so they easily understand them when they occur in reading content. The children who are most likely to have difficulty with inflected endings are those who speak nonstandard dialects.

Contractions are a combination of two words written in a shortened form. The deleted letter (or letters) is indicated by an apostrophe. *Can't* is the equivalent of *can not.* Children frequently use contractions in their oral lan-

Table 6.1

Part of Speech	Meaning	Inflected Words
Nouns	Number	Girls
	Gender	Actor
	Possession	Linda's
Verbs	Tense	Plays, played, playing
Adjectives	Comparison	Little, littler, littlest
Adverbs	Comparison	Slower

guage; therefore, in reading, all they have to do is recognize the written form for contractions.

Structural analysis is most useful in word identification when it is combined with other word recognition strategies—for example, to learn prefixes, root words, suffixes, contractions, compound words and inflected words as sight words. Context clues can be combined with structural analysis, too. In the example *Bill threw the basketball at the hoop,* a reader who did not know the compound word could use the context clues *threw* and *hoop* to help figure out the word. If the reader knew *basket* and *ball* as sight words he or she could identify the words comprising the compound word as a means of reading the word.

Phonics   When the reader cannot identify a word as a sight word, through context clues or with structural analysis, he or she should attempt to analyze the word phonetically. Phonics is an essential component of a beginning reading program. All the major published reading programs include phonics as a decoding skill. This is appropriate because English is an alphabetic language in which there are consistent, though not entirely predictable, relationships between letters and sounds (Anderson and Armbruster, 1984). When children learn these letter-sound relationships, most words in their spoken language become accessible to them. Classroom research shows that, generally speaking, children who are taught phonics get a better start in reading than children who are not taught phonics (Johnson and Baumann, 1984; Williams, 1985).

Phonics is most valuable in the beginning reading program, and should be taught in conjunction with sight words, context clues, and structural analysis. The majority of children will begin learning phonics in kindergarten and they will complete phonics by the end of third grade. In planning phonics instruction, teachers should avoid teaching too many letter-sound relationships; programs that attempt to teach all of the rules and all of the exceptions to the rules will drag instruction out over too many years (Anderson and Armbruster, 1984).

Which approach to phonics, analytic or synthetic, is used most frequently? Analytic phonics is based on teaching students sound by associating them with a known word; synthetic phonics teaches the separate sounds of letters in isolation. A recent research study revealed that teachers who were using analytic phonics programs relied on synthetic strategies because they had children pronounce sounds separately (Durkin, 1983). When queried about this practice, the teachers responded that the children heard the speech sound better that way. Both synthetic and analytic phonics have some problems. Children who study analytic phonics have difficulty segmenting the speech sounds in words. Children who study synthetic phonics may have difficulty blending words and they may distort words when pronouncing the sounds that comprise a word, as in the sounding of *cat* which may sound like *cuh-ah-tuh.* However, these problems can be overcome with some modifications of instruction.

1. Teach children to use phonics to help them approximate word pronunciation. They should think whether the word sounds like a word they have heard.

2. Teach children to associate the separate sounds they learn with a word, thus giving the sound a meaningful context.

3. Teach children to decode words in the English language rather than nonsense words.

4. Teach children to pronounce sounds softly to avoid distortion.

5. Provide direct instruction of blending skills.

6. Teach children to use phonics skills in combination with sight words, context clues, and structural analysis.

Following is a suggested scope and sequence for teaching phonics skills.

Sequence of Phonics Skills

1. Consonant sounds should be introduced because they have more consistent phoneme-grapheme correspondences than are vowel sounds. In addition, children who know consonant sounds can use them in combination with context clues to identify new words.

2. Blends, or consonant clusters, are two or three consonants that appear together but retain the same sound as when they occur separately. Some blends occur at the beginning of words like the *gr* in green, while others like *nk* in sink occur at the end.

3. Introduce the soft *c* (s sound). C has a soft sound when it is followed by *e, i,* and *y*—as in *cent, city,* and *cycle.* Introduce the soft *g* (j sound). G has a soft sound when followed by *e, i,* and *y*—as in *gentle, giant,* and *gym.*

4. The regular consonant digraphs should be presented. A *digraph* is a combination of two letters that represents a single sound. Some examples are *sh* as in *ship,* voiceless *th* as in *thank,* voiced *th* as in *them, wh* as in *why, ch* as in *chime, ng* as in *song.*

5. Introduce the long vowel sounds that are represented by the *macron* (‾), such as the *a* in *lāke,* the *e* in *sēat,* the *i* in *tīe,* the *o* in *cōat,* the *u* in *cūbe,* and the *y* in *crȳ.*

6. Introduce the short vowel sounds that are represented by the *breve* (˘), such as the *a* in *hăt,* the *e* in *bĕt,* the *i* in *hĭt,* the *o* in *hŏt,* and the *u* in *sŭn.*

7. Vowel digraphs are two vowel graphemes that represent one sound. In vowel digraphs, both letters lose their individual sound and produce a new sound. Some examples of vowel digraphs are *ai* (pail), *ea* (beach), *oa* (boat), *ee* (feet), *ay* (may), *oo* (food), and *oo* (look).

8. Vowel dipthongs are sounds that consist of a blend of two vowels. Some examples are *ou* (count), *oi* (coil), *oy* (toy), and *ow* (low).

9. Introduce the concept of *r-controlled vowels* to the class. When vowels are followed by an *r,* they do not have a long or short sound, but an *r-controlled* sound. Some examples are *ar* (car), *er* (her), *ir* (fir), *ur* (fur), and *or* (for).

10. Introduce the concept of one-syllable words. A *syllable* is the basic unit for decoding words. Each syllable must have one vowel; the vowel may stand alone or it may be attached to one or more consonants. When a one-syllable word has one vowel that vowel, is usually short as in *cat* and *sit.* When a one-syllable word has two vowels, the first vowel is usually long and the second vowel is usually silent as in *cape* and *seat.*

11. Introduce the syllabication of words with two or more syllables. Explain that each word has as many syllables as vowel sounds. Students should learn that prefixes, suffixes, root words, and inflected endings are usually a separate syllable.

12. Words that contain consonant digraphs, vowel digraphs, blends, dipthongs, and r-controlled vowels must be divided into syllables without separating these sound units.

13. Words can be divided into syllables by vowel and consonant patterns: V/CV-spi/der; VC/CV-can/dy; VC/CCV-en/try.

Blending   Children must be able to blend sounds in order to use phonics skills in decoding words. Sounds should be said softly when blending in order to avoid distortion. Begin blending instruction with short words. Students should be taught to blend the first two letters and then to add the final letter as in these examples:

ca͡ t͡ (cat)
ba͡ t͡ (bat)
si͡ t͡ (sit)
ra͡ n͡   (ran)
ch͡ cho͡o se͡   (choose)
sh͡ shee͡ t͡   (sheet)

After children develop proficiency in blending short words, they should proceed to longer words.

The following books will help with phonics instruction:

Durkin, Dolores (1976). *Strategies for Identifying Words.* Boston: Allyn & Bacon.

Ekwall, Eldon E. (1985). *Locating and Correcting Reading Difficulties.* Columbus, OH: Charles Merrill.

Heilman, Arthur W. (1985). *Phonics in Proper Perspective* (5th Edition). Columbus, OH: Charles Merrill.

READING COMPREHENSION

Comprehension of written content is the purpose of reading instruction. In fact comprehension is reading, unless a reader understands he or she is not reading. **Reading comprehension** is described in the introduction to this chapter. You may want to reread that section as a basis for understanding the comprehension process. Factors that influence reading and listening comprehension are factors within the reader, within the text, and instructional factors. Table 6.2 summarizes the kinds of factors important in reading comprehension.

Table 6.2 Reading and Listening Comprehension Factors

Comprehension Factors Within Reader	Comprehension Factors Within Text	Instructional Comprehension Factors
Experiential background	Organization	Reading purpose
Concepts and vocabulary	Author's language	Vocabulary and concepts
Thinking skills	Author's sense of audience	Discussion questions
Metacognitive skills		Main ideas and details
Reading fluency		Text structure
Sense of story (story grammar)		Opportunities to read
Visualization ability		

Reading Comprehension Instruction

From the very beginning of reading instruction, children should be given all of the elements necessary for constructing meaning. Children should learn early that meaning is central to the reading process. The teacher must help children utilize background knowledge and textual information to construct meaning. An exact scope and sequence of reading comprehension skills is not available because comprehension skills develop throughout the reader's life. Furthermore, comprehension skills are very similar from grade level to grade level since these skills are taught and applied in progressively more difficult content. Table 6.3 is a scope and sequence chart for reading comprehension skills.

The instructional steps to develop students' comprehension include:

1. Teach children the vocabulary used in the selection. Research shows vocabulary is basic to reading comprehension. Instruction should include the meanings of new or difficult vocabulary.

Table 6.3 Scope and Sequence Chart for Reading Comprehension Skills

Comprehension Skills	Teacher's Edition	Teaching Master	Workbook	Practice Master	Tested
Selection comprehension			1, 4, 7, 12, 15, 18, 25, 28, 31, 35, 38, 42, 50, 53, 57, 62, 65, 68, 75, 79, 82, 86, 89, 92, 99, 102, 105, 110, 113, 116, 123, 126, 129, 132, 135, 138		
Synonyms, antonyms	83			15	
Referents	155, 182, 227, 294, 328	24, 30	37	36, 57	○
Context clues	339, 366, 408, 481	50, 56	85, 120	67	○
Main idea	19, 43, 58, 98	1, 8	3, 23	9	○
Inferred comparison and contrast	20, 32, 97	2		1	○
Predicting outcomes	119			19	
Inferred characterization	142, 167, 215, 293	22, 28	34, 72	33	○
Inferred sequence (flashback)	214, 243, 256, 294	31, 37	52, 73	42	○
Drawing conclusions	241, 268, 313, 389	35, 41	59	51, 52	○
Inferred main idea	255, 281, 328, 390	38, 44	64	56	○
Inferred analogy	267, 313, 328	40, 46	67	55	
Inferred cause and effect	501, 520, 547, 573	73, 78	125, 143	92	○
Supporting generalizations	519, 533	77, 80	131		
Literal and figurative language	31, 45–47, 58, 83, 98	4, 11	6	6, 7, 13	○
Simile, metaphor	69, 119, 129, 194	12, 18	17, 47	21	○
Author's purpose	32, 58, 97	5	22	8	○
Theme, mood	128, 156, 182, 195	19, 25	30, 48	31	○

Table 6.3 (*Continued*)

Comprehension Skills	Teacher's Edition	Teaching Master	Workbook	Practice Master	Tested
Suspense, foreshadowing	141, 167, 182, 195	21, 27	33	32	○
Story mood	169–171			29, 30	
Story setting, story plot	338, 366, 380, 390	49, 55	84, 96	63	○
Fact and opinion	379, 417, 447, 482	57, 62	94, 121	74	○
Author's purpose (persuasion)	407, 434, 447, 482	59, 65	101, 122	75	○
Genre (myth, legend)	416, 447, 469, 482	61, 67	104	78	○
Genre (mystery)	457, 502, 520, 572	68, 74	115	88	○
Author's purpose (exposition, narration)	468, 510, 533, 559–560, 573	71, 76	118, 142	90, 91, 95, 96	○
Colons, semicolons	280, 328, 353	43, 48	70	59	
Punctuation review	32			4	

Study Skills	Teacher's Edition	Teaching Master	Workbook	Practice Master	Tested
Diagrams	327, 353, 380, 390	47, 53	81, 98	64, 65	○
Comparing bar, circle, and line graphs	432, 449–451, 458, 469	63, 69	107, 108	76, 77, 79, 80	
Time lines	509, 547, 557, 573	75, 82	128, 144	93	○
City maps	546	81	137		
Test-taking strategies	42, 70, 119	7, 14	10, 11	17, 18	
Making study plans	82, 129, 156	15, 20	20	24	
Previewing	166, 215, 227	26, 32	40, 41	37, 38	
Outlining from a single source	226, 256, 281, 294	33, 39	55, 56	47, 48	○
Outlining	229–231			39, 40	

Table 6.3 (*Continued*)

Study Skills	Teacher's Edition	Teaching Master	Workbook	Practice Master	Tested
SQRRR	312, 315–316, 340, 353, 390	45, 51	77, 78, 97	53, 54, 60, 61	○
Outlining from multiple sources	433, 458, 502	64, 70	109	82, 83, 84	
Completing forms	181, 227, 256	29, 34	44, 45	43, 44	
Critical TV viewing	352, 380, 417	52, 58	88	71, 72	
Signs, symbols	446, 469, 510, 573	66, 72	112	86, 87	○
Transportation schedules	532, 557	79, 84	134		
Special reference books	20, 32	3		2, 3	
Library card catalog	43, 58	9		10, 11	
Dictionary entries	118, 143, 156, 195	17, 23	27	25, 26	○
Thesaurus	556	83	140		

Language Skills	Teacher's Edition	Practice Master
Listening		
Vocabulary	33, 71, 144, 244, 269, 354, 381, 418, 459, 511, 534	
Comprehension	168	
Writing		
Metaphors	21	
Personal letters	33	5
Poetry	44, 59, 228, 548	12
Journal	84	16
Point of view	120, 329, 435	20, 58
Experiences	130	23
Jokes with puns	157	
Letters	168	28
Advertisements	183	
Memoir	216	35

Source: Leo Fay et al., *Previews Teachers Edition,* The Riverside Reading Program. Chicago: The Riverside Publishing Company, 1986. Reprinted by permission.

2. Activate students' schemata (background of experience) by asking students questions which help them relate their experiences to the information in a reading selection. For example, if the reading selection were "Time for Mime" (Fay et al., 1986) the teacher might ask "What does a mime do?" to activate students' background knowledge. The children discuss what a mime is and what a mime does. Some students might recall seeing mimes on television and in circuses and may demonstrate mime for the class. Students think of words that describe a mime, such as mannequin, robot, clowns, funny, silent movies, actor, and Marcel Marceau. Then the teacher asks what skills a mime would need—muscle control, facial expressions, and lots of practice. After this discussion the teacher explains they are to read about mime.

3. "What are some of the most difficult things that a mime has to do?" was the silent reading purpose for this selection. In developmental reading class, students should always read a selection silently before reading aloud.

4. Discuss the reading purpose as well as the following questions: How do mimes express ideas and feelings? (literal level) What are some important things that a good mime must be able to do? (inferential level) Who are some famous mimes? (literal level) How are acting and mime different? (inferential) What would you like to mime? (critical level) The students read sentences and paragraphs from the selection aloud to support their answers. They can create a map (graphic organizer) to illustrate the structure of a selection (see Figure 6.2).

Guiding Comprehension with Questions

Reading instruction should develop students' cognitive skills. Questions are the major instructional tools for guiding students' comprehension. In planning comprehension instruction, teachers should create questions that help students acquire a holistic understanding of selections rather than a fragmented one. Teachers questions should:

1. Direct students' attention to the significant aspects of the selection. Discussion should focus on the main ideas rather than trivial details.

2. Activate students' schemata that are related to selection. Students do not automatically associate their experiences to reading content; therefore, teachers should ask questions during prereading activities, for silent reading purposes and follow-up discussion, that lead students to relate appro-

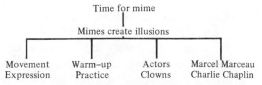

Figure 6.2   Graphic organizer (map) for a mime selection.

priate experiences to ideas and information they read. Pearson (1982) suggests that teachers establish a set of "What if . . ." questions like the following:

a. Have you ever found yourself in a situation where you felt that you could not tell the truth or you would get a friend in trouble? What did you do? What happened?
b. What would you do if you knew that friends of yours were doing something dangerous that might injure them?
c. Jim, the protagonist in this story, is afraid to tell on his best friend. What do you think will happen?
d. What would you do if your best friend were seriously injured?

After the students read the text, they can compare their predictions with the protagonist's actions.

3. Develop students' thinking skills. Cognitive skills usually are related to cognitive levels such as literal, inferential, critical, and creative which are discussed in a later section.

Think-alouds to Develop Cognitive Skills

Children should have models of thinking. For example, a teacher (or another student) can do a think-aloud activity to show students how to think about written language. The following think-aloud example is based on a story adapted from *Blackout* by Anne and Harlow Rockwell.

Text: It was cold, and all the trees were covered with ice. Every branch of every tree was shining with ice.

Teacher: This sounds like an ice storm. The ice can make tree branches break and power lines come down, so that the electric is out. I can almost feel the cold air.

Text: How pretty the trees look!

Teacher: Ice does make everything look beautiful, especially with the sun shining on it, but ice is dangerous.

Text: . . . The wind began to blow, and the ice began to crack, and soon the branches of the trees began to break. CRASH! One big branch fell down.

Teacher: I imagine that the crashes will continue, then the lights will go out and the heat will go off. I have been through this many times.

Notice how the teacher uses her schemata to understand the written text and to predict what will happen next.

Literal thinking is concerned with ideas that are directly stated in reading content. These questions can be answered by quoting the content. The main types of literal thinking are recognizing and recalling main ideas, recognizing and recalling details, recognizing and recalling sequence, following directions, recognizing cause and effect, and paraphrasing content. The following literal level questions are based on *Blackout.*

What caused the power outage?

Why did the mother in this story go out to get wood instead of the father?

Why was it so important to get wood?

Inferential thinking is concerned with deeper meanings. The answers to these questions are not stated in the content, although the author may hint at the answers. Readers must infer because authors cannot tell their readers everything. They have to go beyond the information stated in the reading selection. To infer, students must use their experiences to fill in the missing pieces. The main types of inferential thinking are recognizing relationships, drawing conclusions, making generalizations, predicting outcomes, and understanding figurative language. Comparing and contrasting, as well as citing examples to support answers, help students learn to infer. The following inferential level questions are based on *Blackout.*

Why do you think this story is called *Blackout?*

Explain why the family turned off the water, cooked in the fireplace, conserved the radio battery, and slept in sleeping bags?

What ended the emergency?

Critical thinking requires readers to make judgments about content, such as a character's actions, the author's point of view and purpose, as well as the validity of the content. To think at this level, readers must be able to think at the literal and inferential levels. Readers must approach reading content with an objective attitude and they should suspend judgment until they have enough information to evaluate the content. The following critical thinking questions are based on *Blackout.*

Which of these emergencies would you face if this storm happened in your neighborhood?

Do you think the family members acted wisely? Why? or Why not?

What emergency supplies do you have in your home?

Creative thinking is a deliberate effort to go beyond the information to find new ways of viewing ideas, incidents, or characters that may stimulate novel thinking and production. Creative thinking may result in the form of a new idea, a new story or design, or an improved product or method. The following creative level questions are based on *Blackout.*

What kind of music do you think the radio station would play in an emergency?

What kind of information would the radio station provide in an emergency?

Draw a picture of how you think the ice looked?

Which emergency would you have handled differently? How?

CONTENT READING

Content reading instruction, a special case of comprehension, could also be called reading across the curriculum. Content reading instruction is concerned with helping students read to develop and remember content area concepts which are basis for subsequent learning. "Subject matter textbooks pose the biggest challenge for young readers being weaned from a diet of simple stories" (Gallagher and Pearson, 1983). Content textbooks are largely exposition, while basal readers contain more realistic or narrative fiction; basal readers, therefore, do not prepare students for the content textbooks.

Expository content is organized differently from narrative content and more information is packed into each sentence. Content textbooks are usually written at a more difficult readability level than reading textbooks, in addition the authors of content textbooks often devote more attention to details than to big ideas like goals and outcomes (Anderson and Armbruster, 1984; Herman, 1984). Table 6.4 compares narrative and expository content.

Teaching Content Reading

Research shows that learning is facilitated when critical concepts or skills are directly taught (Baumann, 1984; Patching et al., 1983; Palinscar and Brown, 1984). Unfortunately, content reading is rarely taught (Durkin, 1979; Neilsen et al., 1982). Directly teaching content reading skills with content textbooks increases understanding. Direct instruction in content reading means explaining the steps in a thought process that leads to comprehension. The instruction should include explaining why and how to use a strategy. Successful content reading strategies are listed below.

1. Direct instruction of technical vocabulary, using vocabulary files, crossword puzzles, discussion, and so forth.

2. Teaching students to predict what the author will say.

3. Teaching students to summarize content using, precise outlines, notes, graphic organizers, and semantic mapping.

4. Teaching students to develop questions about the content.

5. Developing metacognitive strategies (students monitor their own understanding).

6. Teachers model inferencing (make their thinking public).

Table 6.4   Comparison of Narrative and Expository Content

Narrative	Expository
Tells story; has characters plot, theme and setting	States information
Provides descriptions and repeats vocabulary	Uses specialized and technical vocabulary that is not often repeated
Reader identifies with character	Reader must interact with content
Plot holds attention	Reader must attend to organization of facts
Single book or story	Uses supplementary materials and references
Concrete concepts related to experiences	Unfamiliar, abstract concepts
Elaborate writing style	Terse writing style
Entertaining	Presents information
Conveys meaning through	Wide use of graphic aids
Rapid reading rate	Adjustable reading rate, slower
Consistent reading level	Wide variation in reading level, overall higher reading level

7. Teaching and having students practice to the level of automaticity study methods such as SQ3R (Survey, Question, Read, Review, and Reread).

8. Prepare study guides for students to use as they read content textbooks. A sample study guide is shown in Figure 6.3.

LITERATURE, RECREATIONAL READING, READING FOR STUDENTS WITH SPECIAL NEEDS

Literature, recreational reading, remedial reading, and gifted reading are the remaining aspects of the total reading program. Literature is the content that students read. Basal readers, which are the springboards into reading, are comprised largely of children's literature today. Literature is more fully discussed in Chapter Nine.

Recreational reading is the program that encourages students to read for pleasure. In this situation, students acquire the habit of reading for their own purposes. Children who are introduced to the joys of reading early in their lives read for pleasure more than those who do not have this experience (Trelease, 1986). Teachers and parents who read aloud to children introduce them to recreational reading. The teacher's role in this dimension of the

I. Literal Understanding
   A. What planets are found in the solar system?
   B. Why is the system that includes the planet Earth called the solar system?
   C. Identify one unique characteristic for each planet in our solar system.

II. Interpretive Understanding
   A. How are Mars and Earth alike?
   B. What things make Earth different from other planets?
   C. Why does the author say that Mercury might have been dreamed up during a nightmare?

III. Applied Understanding
   A. Which planet is most likely to be inhabited? Explain why it is possible for this planet to sustain life.
   B. What adaptations would be necessary for life to survive on the planet you choose?

Figure 6.3   Three-level study guide for a science text.

reading program is motivating children to read for pleasure, as well as including recreational reading time in their teaching plans because many children do not have time to read outside of school. In today's world, many children go from school to daycare facilities, to a babysitter, or to home alone to watch television. Children who are in daycare or with a babysitter often only have time at home for dinner, homework, and bed—there is simply no time in their daily lives for pleasure reading. Two of the most successful recreational reading programs are Uninterrupted Sustained Silent Reading (or USSR) and Drop Everything and Read (DEAR). These programs are based on the concept of everyone in a classroom or an entire school reading at a specific time during the day. Teachers, principals, visitors, secretaries, etc., join in reading.

Several programs fit into the category of reading for students with special needs. For instance, gifted students need a reading program that addresses their needs as do children who are unable to make progress in the regular reading program. Students who are learning English as a second language (ESL) have unique needs as they learn to read English. Students who are in classes for the learning disabled, EMH (educable mentally handicapped), or deaf and blind require specialized instruction. These programs are discussed in more detail in Chapter Thirteen.

A remedial reading program is designed for students who are not acquiring reading skills at the expected rate. The remedial reading program is a "pull out" program where the student leaves the classroom to go to a specialized reading teacher for instruction. Corrective reading is remedial instruction provided in the regular classroom. For more information on these topics you may refer to specialized texts—for example, Albert Harris and Edward Sipay (1985), *How to Increase Reading Ability* (Eighth Edition), New York: Longmans.

COMPUTERS AND READING INSTRUCTION

Reading and computers are interrelated. First, we must read the computer monitor and this has increased our need for sophisticated reading skills. Computers programs can be used to teach reading, as well as to provide students with skills practice. Computers can be used in language experience reading programs as writing tools, and they also have the capacity to make multiple copies of student's language experience stories.

Reading computer monitors presents problems for some individuals. Certain people find that the color of computer print is difficult for them to see. We also know that readers cannot read as fast when they read data on the computer monitor. Some individuals find reading the computer monitor very fatiguing; therefore they must read computer materials for only short periods of time.

Effective computer-based reading instruction is the product of understanding the reading process and the ways that computers can facilitate learning. In the past, teachers have questioned the value of computers for learning to read. However, when computers are used along with trade books, basal readers, content textbooks, language experience stories and students' writing, and word processing operations to build connections between the acts of reading and writing. For example, note taking is simpler when readers use the word processor to write summaries of chapters in content textbooks. Students can create vocabulary files on the computer to quickly look up word meanings. The relationship between oral and written language is strengthened by programs like *The Talking Page* and *Magic Wand Books* which produce speech.

Word identification is the most popular domain for computerized reading instruction, although, some programs exist for developing comprehension skills and content reading skills. Comprehension instruction is the most challenging kind of computerized instruction because students must learn that reading is a "meaning getting" process. Computer program designers find it more difficult to design effective comprehension programs.

Programs like CARIS, for children ages 10 to 14, use computer animation to introduce the meaning of simple noun-verb sentences formed by students. Once the child has selected a noun-verb combination, the computer generates a cartoon depicting the meaning of the sentence formed.

In this program, children dictate stories to a teacher or aide who types them into a computer. The computer then provides a typed copy of the story for the student, followed by an alphabetical list of all the words in the story. DOVACK serves as a teacher resource, maintaining a lot of the stories and all the words used by each student. The teacher can use these word lists to

COMPUTER SOFTWARE EVALUATION FORM:
READING INSTRUCTION

Program title:

Publisher:

Computer compatibility: (Apple IIe, TRS 80, IBM PC)

Copyright date:

Price:

Instructional objective/s: (what the student is expected to learn such as:
    initial consonant sounds, story grammar, word meaning)

Grade level/s:

Use: (developmental, remedial, enrichment)

Time: (amount of time student needs to complete program)

Program content: (answer each item with yes or no)
    A.   Accurate: (i.e., phonics rules accurate, word definitions accurate)
    B.   Are word identification skills taught in the context of words?
    C.   Is comprehension an apparent goal of instruction?
    D.   Does the text have a story grammar (fiction)?
    E.   Is the text structured with main ideas and supporting details?
          (nonfiction)?
    F.   Is fragmentation of the reading process avoided?

Figure 6.4   Computer software evaluation form: reading instruction.

compose weekly vocabulary tests. The *word banks* (file of words used in language experience stories) used by many teachers can be adapted easily to a
computer. A word bank file can be created for each student. It is as useful for
reading, spelling, and composition activities. Children can ask the computer
to pull up all of the words containing a certain letter or letter combination.

The software for comprehension skills is much more limited than it is
for word identification skills. Although computer programs purport to develop comprehension, many programs are limited to presenting content for
the student who reads it and the accompanying questions. Then the student
selects answers to questions from a set of multiple-choice responses. Some
programs do not offer story content; they merely provide questions and
possible answers. Reading comprehension is much more complex than asking
and answering questions. Programs like *The Story-Maker* and *Textman* which

G. Can the student respond correctly without reading and understanding content?

H. Fits with philosophy of adopted reading program?

I. Instructionally sound?

J. Appropriate to student level?

K. Is there evidence of race, ethnic, or sexual bias?

Comments:

Format

A. Clear directions?

B. All content requires left-to-right progression?

C. Illustrations recognizable? (can you tell that that drawing is supposed to be a tree?)

D. Color and sound appropriate? (if used)

Documentation and instructions for teachers

A. Clear and easy to follow?

B. Technical language defined?

Purchase recommended: Yes or no

Comments to support decision:

Figure 6.4 *(Continued)*

were developed by Andee Rubin demonstrate the complexity of comprehension better than the usual question-answer process.

The cloze procedure is one of the more effective procedures for helping students improve their attention to language cues as they read. In this activity, words are periodically omitted from the text and replaced by blank spaces. The reader must infer the missing word from the surrounding context. Deleting every fifth word is the most frequently used cloze pattern. The word-processing capacity of computers makes it easy to create cloze procedures for students to complete.

Selecting computer software to complement reading instruction is a complex task due to the wide variety of reading software available to schools. Figure 6.4 illustrates an evaluation instrument which can be used to guide selection.

Teachers Use Computers

Computers make it easy for teachers to analyze the readability of reading materials. Software for readability formulas are commonly available for computers, for example MECC School Utilities, Spache, Dale-Chall, Fry, Raygor, Flesch, Gunning-Fog all supply computer software. However, teachers should be aware that computerized readability analyses are merely estimates of readability because computers make the analyses appear scientific.

Teachers can use computers to monitor student progress and to help diagnose students' strengths and weaknesses.

TROUBLESHOOTING

Reading problems are so complex that we cannot fully discuss them at this juncture. *How to Increase Reading Ability* by Harris and Sipay lists common reading problems and suggestions of ways to treat these problems.

However, there are some significant instructional problems in reading. The greatest of these problems is the fact that many people never choose to read after they leave school and are no longer forced to read. Armchair diagnosis is impossible, but in many cases the cause of this aversion to reading is the result of excessive fragmentation of skills during instruction. Another factor to be considered is the overuse of artificial reading exercises. When students fill in blanks in exercises, they are not experiencing the pleasure that can occur from reading interesting, well-written content. Children should have many opportunities to develop their skills through reading meaningful discourse. Instruction should make the relationship between reading and language apparent to student.

Teachers and students are frequently criticized because students are not learning to read well enough to satisfy current standards. We should be aware that one must read at a higher level today in order to be successful than ever before. The reading skills required of people in any field of endeavor are extremely sophisticated. We must realize that reading skill is acquired over a *20-year* period. Unless reading is viewed as a skill that is developed over an extended period, our students will never achieve the highest levels of reading skill.

SUMMARY

Reading is an important aspect of the language arts. In order to read, students use their schemata with the written content to construct their understanding. Children should participate in a total reading program to acquire reading skill. A total reading program includes: developmental reading, content reading, literature, recreational reading, remedial reading, and gifted reading. Developmental reading instruction is designed for students who are making normal progress in acquiring reading skills. Reading readiness, word recognition, and comprehension instruction comprise the developmental reading program. Reading readiness instruction develops students' auditory discrimination, visual discrimination, knowledge of letter names and letter sounds, and concepts of written language. It enhances their desire to read because these skills facilitate students' reading development. Word recognition instruction develops students' skills to identify words through sight (memory), context, structural analysis, and phonics; these skills may be used together or separately. Reading comprehension instruction develops students' ability to use their experience with textual information to develop thinking skills. Content reading skills and study skills help students read and remember the concepts developed in their content textbooks.

Thought Questions

1. Explain how reading is related to the other language arts.

2. What are the components of a total reading program?

3. Explain the reading process in your own words.

4. Create a map or graphic organizer of this chapter.

5. How does effective reading instruction involve the other language arts?

6. What skills are developed in the reading readiness program?

7. What is the value of content reading instruction?

Enrichment Activities

1. Study a basal reading series and compare the readiness skills, word recognition skills, and comprehension skills in that program with those discussed in this chapter.

2. Visit a primary classroom to observe language experience reading instruction.

3. Read one of the phonics texts listed in this chapter. Does the author recommend a synthetic approach or an analytic approach?

4. Using the plan for comprehension in this chapter, make a plan for helping children understand a selection.

5. Create a three-level study guide for a content textbook.

6. Compare a narrative selection with an expository selection on the same topic.

Selected Readings

Cohen, R. (April 1983). "Self-generated Questions as an Aid to Reading Comprehension." *The Reading Teacher, 36,* 8, 770–775.

Gambrell, L. (1980). "Think-time: Implications for Reading Instruction." *The Reading Teacher 34,* 2, 143–146.

Guzzetti, B. J. and R. Marzano (1984). "Correlates of Effective Reading Instruction." *The Reading Teacher, 37,* 8, 754–758.

Heilman, A. and E. Holmes (1978). Smuggling Language into the Teaching of Reading. Columbus, OH: Charles Merrill.

Kitagawa, M. (1982). "Improving Discussions or How to Get the Students to Ask the Questions." *The Reading Teacher, 36,* 42–45.

Pearson, P. D. (1985). "Changing the Face of Reading Comprehension Instruction." *The Reading Teacher, 38,* 5, 724–738.

Sadow, M. (1982). "The Use of Story Grammar in the Design of Questions." *The Reading Teacher, 35,* 5, 518–522.

Sanders, N. (1966). *Classroom Questions: What Kinds?* New York: Harper & Row.

Slaughter, J. (April, 1983). "Big Books for Little Kids: Another Fad or a New Approach for Teaching Beginning Reading? *The Reading Teacher, 36,* 8, 758–763.

Stauffer, R. (1980). *The Language-Experience Approach to the of Reading* (rev. ed.) New York: Harper & Row.

References

Anderson, T. H., and B. Armbruster, (1984). "Content Area Textbooks." In *Learning to Read in American Schools: Basal Readers and Content Texts,* R. C. Anderson, J. Osborn, and R. J. Tierney (eds.), Hillsdale, NJ: Erlbaum, pp. 193–226.

Baumann, J. F. (1984). "The Effectiveness of a Direct Instruction Paradigm for Teaching Main Idea Comprehension." *Reading Research Quarterly, 20,* 93–115.

Beasley, T. (1986) "Using Big Books." Lecture at the University of North Carolina at Greensboro.

Chomsky, C. (1979). "Approaching Reading Through Invented Spelling." In *Theory and Practice of Early Reading,* Vol. 2, L. B. Resnick and P. A. Weaver (eds.). Hillsdale, NJ: Erlbaum, pp. 43–65.

Dunn, N. E. (1981). "Children's Achievement at School-Entry Age As a Function of Mothers' and Fathers' Teaching Sets." *Elementary School Journal, 81,* 245–253.

Durkin, D. (1978–79). "What Classroom Observations Reveal About Reading Comprehension Instruction." *Reading Research Quarterly XIV,* 4, 481–533.

——————— (1983). *Is There a Match Between What Elementary Teachers Do and What Basal Readers Manual Recommend?* (Reading Ed. Rep. No. 44). Urbana: University of Illinois, Center for the Study of Reading.

Durrell D., and H. Murphy (December 1963). "Reading Readiness Research in Elementary Education 1933–1963." *Journal of Education, 146,* 3–10.

Dyson, A. H. (1984). "Reading, Writing, and Language: Young Children Solving the Written Language Puzzle." In *Composing and Comprehending,* J. M. Jensen (ed.). Urbana, IL: National Conference on Research in English and ERIC Clearinghouse on Reading and Communication Skills, pp. 165–175.

Frazier, J. (ed.). (1983). "Early Childhood Education Today," in *Classroom Relevant Research in the Language Arts.* Washington D.C.: Association for Supervision and Curriculum Development.

Gallagher, M. C., and P. D. Pearson (1983). "Fourth Grade Students Acquisition of New Information from Text." Paper presented at the National Reading Conference, Austin, Texas.

Harste, J. C.; C. L. Burke; and V. A. Woodward (1982). *Children's Language and World: Initial Encounters with Print.* In J. Langer and M. Trika Smith-Burke (eds.). Reader Meets Author/Bridging the Gap, pp. 105–131. Newark, DE: International Reading Association.

Heilman, Arthur, and Elizabeth Holmes (1978). *Smuggling Language into the Teaching of Reading.* Columbus, OH: Charles Merrill.

Herman, P. A. (December 1984). "Incidental Learning of Word Meanings from Expository Texts That Systematically Vary Text Features." Paper presented at the National Reading Conference, St. Petersburg, FL.

Holdaway, D. (1979). *The Foundations of Literacy.* Australia: Ashton Scholastic.

Johnson, D. D., and J. F. Baumann (1984). "Word Identification." In *Handbook of Reading Research,* P. D. Pearson (ed.). New York: Longmans, pp. 583–608.

LaBerge, D., and S. J. Samuels (1974). "Toward a Theory of Automatic Information Processing in Reading." *Cognitive Psychology, 6,* 293–323.

Lesgold, A.; L. B. Resnick; and K. Hammond (1985). "Learning to Read: a Longitudinal Study of Word Skill Development in Two Curricula." In *Reading Research: Advances in Theory and Practice* (Vol. 4), T. G. Waller and G. E. MacKinnon (eds.). New York: Academic Press, pp. 107–138.

Mason, J. M. (1984). "Early Reading from a Developmental Perspective." In *Handbook of Reading Research,* P. E. Pearson (ed.). New York: Longmans, pp. 505–543.

Neilsen, A. R.; B. J. Rennie; and A. Connell (1982). "Allocation of Instructional Time to Reading Comprehension and Study Skills in Intermediate Grade Social Studies Classrooms." In *New Inquiries in Reading Research and Instruction,* J. A. Niles and L. Harris (eds.). Rochester, NY: National Reading Conference, pp. 81–84.

Olson, D. R. (1984). "See! Jumping! Some Oral Language Antecedents of Literacy." In *Awakening to Literacy,* H. Goelman, A. Oberg, and F. Smith (eds.). Exeter, NH: Heinemann, pp. 185–192.

Palinscar, A. S., and A. L. Brown (1984). "Reciprocal Teaching of Comprehension-Fostering and Comprehension-Monitoring Activities. *Cognition and Instruction, 1,* 117–175.

Patching, W.; E. Kameenui; R. Gersten; D. Carnine; and G. Colvin (1983). "Direct Instruction in Critical Reading Skills." *Reading Research Quarterly, 18,* 406–418.

Pearson, P. D. (1982). *Asking Questions About Stories.* Ginn Occasional Paper Number 15. Columbus, Ohio: Ginn and Company.

Perfetti, C. A., and A. M. Lesgold (1979). "Coding and Comprehension in Skilled Reading and Implications for Reading Instruction." In *Theory and Practice of Early Reading* (Vol. 1), L. B. Resnick and P. A. Weaver (eds.). Hillsdale, NJ: Erlbaum, pp. 57–84.

Robinson, V., D. Strickland, and B. Cullinan (1978). "The Child: Ready or Not?" in *The Kindergarten Child and Reading,* L. Ollila (ed.). Newark. DE: International Reading Association.

Slaughter, J. (April 1983). "Big Books for Little Kids: Another Fad or a New Approach for Teaching Beginning Reading." *The Reading Teacher, 36,* 8758–8763.

Stauffer, Russell (1980). *The Language-Experience Approach to the Teaching of Reading* (Rev. Ed.). New York: Harper & Row.

Trelease, J. (1986) *The Read-Aloud Handbook* (2d ed.). New York: Penguin Books.

Williams, J. P. (1985). "The Case for Explicit Decoding Instruction." In *Reading Education: Foundations for a Literate America,* J. Osborn, P. T. Wilson, and R. C. Anderson (eds.). Lexington, MA: Lexington Books, pp. 205–213.

Winograd, Peter, and Marilyn Greenlee (April 1986). "Students Need A Balanced Reading Program." *Educational Leadership,* 16–21.

Chapter **Seven**

Foundations of Writing Instruction

CHAPTER OVERVIEW

Writing instruction is presented in two chapters because the current emphasis on elementary composition is a relatively recent phenomenon in the language arts curriculum reflecting greater changes than preceding areas of the language arts. Writing is the culmination of speaking, listening, and reading development. Chapter Seven creates perspectives for understanding the writing process and children's acquisition of this ability. Chapter Eight explores writing instruction, teachers' roles in the acquisition of the process, and evaluation.

"Writing is an important medium for self-expression, for communication, and for the discovery of meaning—its need is increased rather than decreased by the development of new media for mass communication" (NCTE, 1983). In Chapters Seven and Eight, writing instruction is approached from a process orientation. Classroom scenarios are presented to help readers understand the nature of writing development. The four dimensions of the writing process—prewriting, composing, revising, and editing—are explored, as well as the instructional process for each phase.

Anticipation Guide

Think about these questions and ideas before reading this chapter. How well do you think you write? How much time do you spend writing aside from assigned writing and reports? Do you enjoy writing? Read the following questions and try to answer them as you read this chapter.

1. How is oral language related to the writing process?

2. What is the nature of the relationship between reading and writing?

3. Identify the four stages of the writing process and explain what happens in each stage.

Key Concepts

prewriting	model
editing	revising
revising	conferences

INTRODUCTION

Writing is finally coming into its own. Both educators and parents are aware of the importance that writing skill has for people who are living in an information age (Naisbitt, 1984). Unfortunately, "most American students cannot write well enough to make themselves understood and only a fraction demonstrate the skills necessary to succeed in school, business or the professions" according to data gathered in the National Assessment of Educational Progress (1986).

Writing is a complex task requiring children to synthesize many abilities. What happens on paper is only a small part of the process; it is the outward manifestation of inward thinking. Professional writers often say that writing is an act of discovery for them, a way to discover what they want to say (Murray, 1978). Writing is complex for many teachers because they are not comfortable with the writing process themselves.

The long-range goal of writing (composition) instruction is developing students' ability to effectively communicate through written language. All humans have a basic need to write. Carol Chomsky (1970) tells us that children want to write, in fact need to write, before they want to read. "When we tell others or ourselves what has happened to us it makes that happening more real and often understandable. We need both to record and to share, both to talk to ourselves within the enormous room of the mind and to talk with others. Children—and some professors—think out loud; but for most of us, thought is socially suppressed, done silently. Since we continue to talk to ourselves within the privacy of our skulls, some of that talking, if made public, is writing" (Murray, 1982).

"Writing is inseparable from thinking, reading, speaking, listening, and studying. Though it has its own norms and uses its own pedagogy, it is part of a circle of connected activities" (Fadiman and Howard, 1979). Oral language activities set the stage for writing; both are language activities, one oral and the other written. Listening and reading give children a feeling for the style and flow of English speech that is essential to good writing. As children write they read and reread their written language to think about what to write next. They also read and reread in order to revise and edit their writing.

The writing process is comprised of **prewriting, composing** (writing), **revising**, and **editing**. Students compose narrative, exposition, drama, and poetry, choosing the writing style that expresses their thoughts and ideas. Perl (1979) found that writers invent or discover the specific details, words, syntactic structures, and perhaps larger structures as they write. As they compose, students learn to use words with the precision necessary to express their thoughts and ideas. They also learn to create sentences and paragraphs that communicate their ideas to the people who will read them (audience).

Teachers need the knowledge, skills, and strategies to guide children who are acquiring writing competence. They must create a learning environment that fosters writing because children learn to write by writing. Children's experiences should be extended through reading, viewing movies, field trips, television, and discussion because these experiences are the raw materials for writing.

As you read the following vignettes identify the experiences the teachers use as a foundation for writing. Also you will want to look for evidence of the four aspects of the writing process: prewriting, writing, revising, and editing.

A KINDERGARTEN VIGNETTE

As we walk into the kindergarten classroom, we hear Angela reading her journal page to the class. When she finishes reading about her visit to *Water World,* her classmates eagerly ask questions. They are particularly interested in the "wave machine." Adam asks whether the waves were really eight feet high. Then Jane wants to know how the wave machine works. After the discussion is completed, Judy explains to the visitors that two of the students share their journals each day. At the beginning of class she identifies the students who will share that day.

Although Judy Ross has taught kindergarten for five years, she had never tried to teach composition. After reading an article about kindergarten journal writing (Hipple, 1985), she decided to try it.

Using the guidelines suggested in the article, Judy set up a program that allocated the first half-hour of each day to journal writing. The journals consisted of five newsprint pages stapled together, one page for each day of the week. At the beginning, she taught the children to write on only one page a day and to write their names and the date on each page. They copied the date from the chalkboard. The children could write whatever they wanted in their journals and some children drew their ideas instead of writing. Any of the children who wanted to could dictate their ideas to Judy.

While the children wrote, Judy circulated around the classroom. She frequently said, "Tell me what you have written." Then the youngster would tell or read what was written. This process stimulated the thinking of the reader, as well as the other children in the class. When children had difficulty thinking what to write next, Judy asked "how" and "why" which seemed to get their ideas going. Mark stopped Judy and asked how to write "pat" and she asked him if he knew how it began, to which he responded "puh." She told him to write the beginning sound and then helped him think of the other letters.

A FIFTH-GRADE VIGNETTE

Rick Johnson picked up a copy of *The Kids' Book of Lists* by Margo McLoone-Basta and Alice Siegel. His fifth-grade students enjoyed reading the book, so he decided to use it for writing motivation. Rick walked to the chalkboard and wrote two guiding purposes:

1. Which of the things that you read about would you most like to do?

2. Write about something that you would like to be the first person to do.

After the children read these purposes, they discussed some of the outstanding people in the book. Then Rick suggested that they think about the purposes for a few minutes and, if they wanted, make some notes. He told them that they could discuss their ideas with a partner. After about ten minutes, most of the children settled into their writing.

Rick circulated around the classroom, asking and answering questions. Ronald held up his hand. When Rick asked what he wanted, Rick responded, "I can't think of anything that I want to do." Rick then suggested that Ronald select the person that he most admired from the book and write about why he admired that person. Ronald did not like that idea, so Rick firmly told him to choose the feat that he liked best and to write about how to perform it.

Then Marcia announced that she couldn't think of anything else to write. Rick discussed her topic with her and asked some questions that got her started again.

After 30 minutes of writing, Rick told the children to conclude their writing. Then they filed their compositions in individual writing files. Later in the week, they would have time to edit and rewrite.

Vignette Discussion

Composition evolves naturally when students talk about their experiences—oral language is the foundation of writing. In each scenario, the students participated in group discussion prior to writing (prewriting). Class discussion of experiences and ideas stimulates thinking and helps children put their thoughts into words thus readying them to write. Each vignette showed students who were speaking, listening, and reading as a basis for writing. Writers read their own compositions and others' writings as they revised and edited; they listened as classmates read their writings; and they talked during prewriting discussions and listened to classmates' comments. Table 7.1 shows the interrelated nature of the language arts as they relate to writing.

Table 7.1   Integration of the Language Arts in the Writing Process

Writing Process	Speaking	Listening	Reading	Writing
Prewriting	Discuss, ask questions, brainstorm	Listen to classmates' discussion, listen to teachers' instructions	Research	Notes, diagram
Composing (drafting)	Conferences	During conferences	Drafts	Drafting
Revising	Conferences	During conferences	Reread, read aloud	Rewrite
Editing	Discuss with teacher or peer editor	To teacher, peer editor	Reread, look up spelling words, look up meanings, look up punctuation and capitalization, read finished product aloud	Rewrite handwriting

Each of the language arts plays an important role in the writing process. During prewriting, students discuss, ask and answer questions, they listen to others comments and to teachers instructions, they read to acquire more background and information, and they make notes and diagrams about their compositions. During drafting, they have conferences that involve talking and listening, they read their drafts as they write. During revision, they speak and listen as they confer with the teacher and other students, they reread their own drafts and rewrite as necessary to refine their written expression. Finally, during editing, they again speak and listen with the teacher and peer editor. They reread, look up word meanings and spellings, and may look up punctuation and capitalization generalizations. They then rewrite the composition in readable handwriting. This final rewriting may be done on a computer or typewriter when available.

The writing instruction in both vignettes demonstrates the four stages of the composing process that researchers have identified. The following sections examine these stages of the composing.

The Writing Process

Writing is a thinking process. As writers compose they discover what they think. The thinking-writing connection is often apparent in classes when students are asked to spend ten minutes writing about the "subject about which they know the most." After several minutes of industrious writing, a student will raise his or her hand and ask, "is it all right if I change my subject, I just realized that I really know more about a different topic." Gaining courage from this student's query, a dozen other students will chime in "yes, I need to change too." Generally the students will change topics two or three times before they are satisfied that they have identified the topic about which they know the most. This exercise appears to clarify the need to write in order to discover what one knows. Isn't it amazing that individuals do not know "what they know most about" until they think through their writing to discover that topic?

Writing is a complex process requiring writers to translate their thoughts, experiences, memories, and feelings into words, sentences, and paragraphs. They spell the words, write the words, and punctuate the written language. Because written language does not flow from the pen in finished form, writers think about their ideas, draft their ideas, edit, revise, and rewrite until the composition is polished more to their liking. The writing process is very much the same for children as for professional writers (Emig, 1971).

THE COMPOSING PROCESS

Each of the four stages of the composing process is discussed in the following sections.

Prewriting

The majority of researchers define *prewriting* as the period of time between giving the assignment and the time writing begins. Most researchers agree that the prewriting stage is relatively brief probably lasting from two to five minutes (Hillocks, 1986). The thinking that occurs during the prewriting period is more important than the length of time.

Prewriting can be considered a "warm-up" period. During this stage students think and discuss writing topics and ideas to include in their compositions. Young students often draw their prewriting ideas, which is a form of pictorial note taking. As they prepare to write they ask the teacher questions and talk with friends; writing is not a quiet sedentary activity. Children and adults need to be free to move around as they think. Calkins describes a prewriting strategy which she observed in a kindergarten classroom; the teacher told the children that they had very interesting topics and that she would like each of them to stand and tell their topic in one sentence. This reinforced the children's motivation to write about their topic and helped those children who had not thought of a topic to think of one (Calkins, 1986). Young children often like to look at books and pictures which can serve as models for their own compositions.

The prewriting period in the middle grades is very similar to that in the primary grades; however, middle-grade students' development permits them to hold ideas in mind while they select related ideas and eliminate unrelated ideas. Middle-grade pupils may decide they need to gather more information and ideas during this exploratory period, so they read books and magazines, watch television programs and movies. The thinking that occurs during prewriting helps students decide on a focus and a form for the projected composition. Form may be story, poem, letter, article, biography, or poster. Some children use the prewriting period to think of various ways to compose the opening sentence.

Several researchers found that writers had the major elements of what was to be written in mind when they began writing (Hillocks, 1986). This may be true because writing is the culmination of many experiences. For example, an individual who is writing about natural resources, uses knowledge acquired from watching television, reading books and newspapers, listening to lectures, talking with others, and observing natural resources in one's environment.

Research reveals that professional writers generally do not outline during prewriting; they prepare brief lists of words or phrases to guide their composing rather than any kind of detailed outline (Emig, 1971). This research raises questions about the practice of requiring note taking and outlining of students. In fact Stallard's (1973) subjects believed that the content often dictated writing form. Formal outlines are unnecessary for the majority of writers. Furthermore it is entirely possible that requiring students to prepare outlines makes them avoid writing.

Prewriting Instruction   Prewriting experiences may take many different forms. During this phase of composition, teachers must give students a writing purpose or assignment. Writing purposes often grow out of students' activities and interests, and should be clear to the students and related to things they know about. Teachers can use strategies that develop students' background experiences thus giving them ideas they can use in writing. Experiences can come from field trips, pictures and posters, resource speakers, reading materials, television, movies, and class discussions.

Talk helps children develop ideas and thoughts. Teachers can develop the oral language that should surround the writing process through talking with children or assigning conversational partners. Hillocks found that children write more when they are prompted by a conversational partner. Class discussion of a story the teacher has read or a shared experience helps children formulate the ideas they want to write. Brainstorming words that can be used to describe a character, concept, picture, or poster gives children vocabulary and ideas that can be written. A very effective prewriting technique for groups or individuals is "clustering," in which words and phrases are clustered around a central subject (Rico, 1983; Tiedt et al., 1983). Figure 7.1 is an illustration of the clustering technique. After clustering, students can compose a paragraph, composition, or story about an appealing aspect of the topic.

To create a cluster, the writer begins with a nucleus word, circled. Then he or she allows any connections to come to mind and writes them down rapidly, each in its own circle, radiating outward from the center in any direction. Each new word or phrase is connected with a line to the preceding

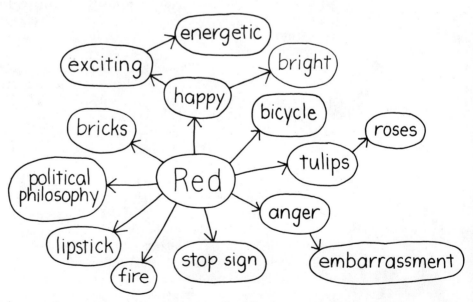

Figure 7.1   Writing cluster based on "red."

circle. When something new and different occurs to the writer, it begins again at the central circle and radiates outward until these associations are exhausted. Rico (1983) states that the writer knows when to stop clustering because he or she will have an urge to write.

When the writer is ready to compose, the next step is to scan the clusters, which will stimulate the first sentence. The writer writes from the pattern of meaning the cluster creates. The following paragraph is based on the "red" cluster shown in Figure 7.1.

Red is an exciting color. It is the color of fun, brightness, and energy. Beautiful flowers like tulips and roses are red, lipstick is red, but so are stop signs, fire, and anger. Red says, "notice me, I am here, I have something to say."

To stimulate prewriting thought, teachers can prepare children to ask themselves questions like the following.

1. What subject do I know the most about?

2. How many words can I think of for this subject?

3. What subject excites me?

4. What books, magazines, and newspapers do I need to learn more about this subject?

5. How can I start the composition?

6. What is the first sentence that I want to use?

The teacher can model thought processes during prewriting by thinking aloud. This approach is demonstrated in the following example.

To **model** (demonstrate) the thinking processes that occur during prewriting, teachers may think aloud while writing on an overhead transparency. Following is a script of the thoughts a fifth-grade teacher shared with his class.

Teacher: I have to write a paper and I need to think about the subject. This is a history paper, so I could write about Guilford Battleground Park because I like to read the markers and look at the statues there. I know a good bit about the Battle of Guilford Court House which was fought there. On the other hand, I know a lot about Thomas Jefferson because he is my hero. I think I know more about Thomas Jefferson because I visited his home three times and I read several biographies about him.

Teacher: Now, what do I want to say about Thomas Jefferson? He was very intelligent, he wrote the constitution, he invented a lot of things. I think this will be my opening sentence, "Thomas Jefferson was a smart man." No, I think I'll change that sentence to, "Thomas Jefferson was a genius."

Modeling makes the prewriting process very clear to students and demonstrates how to make a transition from prewriting to writing. Yatvin (1981) believes that five minutes of silent thinking time should be mandated during the prewriting process. This five-minute period of sustained silent thinking can come at the end of prewriting just before the students begin their actual compositions. Certainly, the teacher should notify students that they must bring their thoughts (or drawings, etc.) to a close, so they can begin composing.

Writing, Composing, Drafting

The second aspect of the writing process is composing. During this stage writers compose, write, and draft compositions. They are getting ideas on paper, changing and rearranging ideas as they go. Uncertainties about spelling, capitalization, and punctuation are overlooked until revision, although some students use a code to identify words, capitalization, or punctuation marks that need to be checked. For example they might draw a triangle around those words that will need a spelling check. Students should be encouraged to take chances with spelling and punctuation, rather than to interrupt their thought processes at this stage.

Teachers function as facilitators during the composing process. They help stalled students get going again, look over drafts and ask questions, and tell students not to worry about spelling at this time. Teachers encourage children to think of more precise words or to say a phrase or a sentence in a better way. At the close of a drafting period, the teacher collects students' papers, and keeps them a day or two. Students are thus permitted to get some distance from their work.

Revising

In revision, writers change and shape the text to make it say what they want. They must decide whether they have communicated with their audience, if not, they identify the changes that will enhance understanding. To do this, they must stand back from the text and become critics—that is, act as if the text were written by someone else (Smith, 1982). Students need to understand that revision is a *rewriting process,* a time when the writer rewrites to get a point across. In revising, writers become critical readers of their own work, who search for ways of extending and improving written expression in the revision process. Calkins describes revision as "having a conference with yourself" (Calkins, 1986). During these conferences writers examine content, word choice, voice, tone, and rhythm. They may decide to replace or delete words; alter sentences, delete, add, or recast sentences to communicate meaning. They focus on content rather than mechanics.

Writers in the elementary grades make the majority of their revisions in words and sentences (Hillocks, 1986). First and second graders tend to revise by adding to their existing composition. Third graders are just beginning to grasp the nature of composition in terms of inserting words and sentences or altering previously written text.

Student–Teacher Conferences   Conferences are the major vehicle for helping children revise. They give teachers occasions to reinforce the positive aspects of students' writing and give the teacher a chance to stimulate children to rephrase, to clarify, and to expand.

Conferences can be either spontaneous or planned. Spontaneous conferences occur when children ask questions that require immediate or nearly immediate responses from the teacher. On the other hand, teachers should plan conferences so that they meet with each student at least once every two weeks. Teachers usually review children's writing files in preparation for conferences to identify areas they need to discuss.

Conferences may have various purposes such as process, focus, expansion, and editing. A process conference focuses on students' processes, increasing their awareness of what they have done and what they will do next. Expansion conferences are necessary when students write one or two sentences and say they are "finished." Focusing conferences are necessary when students are having difficulty narrowing their subject. By focusing on a narrower topic, students create more manageable units of meaning. Expansion conferences help students think about what they have written and elaborate the content. An editing conference is concerned with polishing a piece of writing to the stage of publication. Language conventions are a focal point in editing conferences because writing content is usually in good order prior to editing conferences.

Conferences should focus on writing content. The teacher is more a listener than a judge. Some teachers ask students to read their writing aloud to open the writing conference. Then they stimulate students' discussion of their writing with open-ended questions. For example, a good opening question is, "What do you think of this piece of writing?" A follow-up question is "Why do (or don't) you like it?" As students discuss their compositions they are thinking and refining their work. Teachers should refrain from expressing reactions to students' writing until the later part of the conference. Then they may point out the interesting aspects of the writing and ask questions that will lead students to expand ideas, organize thoughts, and clarify points. For example, the teacher might say, "If you wanted to add more ideas or information, what could you do?" Fleming (1982) suggests saying, "If you could wave a magic wand and revise this paper in one minute, how would you do it?" This query points children toward revision. Teachers should make certain that students are aware of the good points in their writing, so they will repeat these positive factors.

Conference Questions   Since questions are teaching instruments for conferences, teachers should focus on asking questions that stimulate writing and serve as models for the questions students will ask themselves later as they self-evaluate. Students must learn to ask each other questions during peer conferences. Examples of questions for writing conferences are given below.

1. How is your writing going?

2. What are you writing about now?

3. Where are you now in your draft?

4. What do you think you'll do next in your draft?

5. I notice that you changed your lead? It is much more direct. How did you do that?

6. If you were to put that new information in here, how do you go about figuring what to do?

7. When you don't know how to spell a word, how do you go about figuring what to do?

8. How do you figure out where one sentence ends and another one begins?

9. What will you do with this piece when you are finished with it?

10. What changes have you made in this piece of writing?

11. Since you have finished this piece of writing, what are you going to write next? (This starts the prewriting phase of the next piece of writing by encouraging the student to rehearse about an upcoming writing project.)

Planning Writing Conferences   Students should participate in a student-teacher writing conference at least once every two weeks. Students who need more frequent conferences should be able to request them. Conferences can be rather brief, often taking only three to five minutes. While the teacher is conferring with a student, the other students are writing; therefore, the conference does not interrupt work. After the conference, the teacher should take notes for future reference.

Peer Writing Conferences   Two students are paired for peer writing conferences. Each student reads his or her writing aloud; then they discuss the writing, modeling their questions after the teacher's questions. Peer writing conferences should occur at least once a week and more frequently if a student requests a conference. Sometimes a peer writing conference is especially helpful to a student because the peer can ask questions and make comments that appear less threatening to the student. A peer writing conference can be substituted for a student-teacher conference if the teacher is unable to meet with a student.

Group Writing Conferences   Fleming (1985) recommends that students have a group conference before they publish a manuscript. She models the four- to

Group writing conferences help students.

six-member group conferences after the format suggested by Peter Elbow (1973). The conferences followed this pattern:

1. The writer reads his or her writing to the group.

2. The students tell the writer what they like in the piece of writing.

3. The listeners tell the writer what the piece of writing is about. The writer hears a brief summary from each listener. This helps the writer realize whether the composition is sufficiently focused and whether he or she has said what they wanted to.

4. The listeners ask the writer for more information or clarification.

5. The writer questions the listeners. The writer can ask about any parts that seemed troublesome.

In addition to conferences, teachers can give children written guidelines to help them think through their compositions.

Revision Checklist for First Grade

1. Does every sentence tell something?

2. Do my sentences make sense?

3. Are my sentences in order?

Revision Checklist for Sixth Grade

1. Did I stay on the topic?

2. Do all of the sentences relate to the topic?

3. Is the beginning interesting?

4. Are the sentences in a sensible order?

5. Did I use interesting words?

6. Did I use a variety of sentence styles?

7. Is the ending interesting?

8. Now make the changes and when you are finished have another conference with yourself or the teacher.

Teachers can demonstrate revision strategies while writing on an overhead transparency. They can think aloud during the revision process, asking themselves questions like those in the preceding paragraph. To respond to those questions demonstrates revision to their students. Teachers should cross out words rather than erase when they revise, so children learn to do the same. Crossing out words helps children understand that written language does not flow from the pen (or computer) in finished form; thinking is an important part of the revision process.

Students should choose at least one selection from their writing file each week for revision. This piece should be one that they like because revisions take considerable time. Writers often find it necessary to revise several times.

Children need to understand the qualities of good writing as a basis for critiquing their own compositions. They learn about good writing when teachers read from excellent literature and from their own reading. They learn about good writing when they are exposed to a well-developed character, a unique plot, or a richly described setting. Children emulate the literature they read when they write (Graves, 1983; Calkins, 1986). They also learn about good writing from writing. When they write an especially pleasing sentence, description, beginning, or ending their understanding of the qualities of good writing grows.

Editing

Editing is the final phase of the composing process. When writers complete and revise their drafts, it is time to edit. Children need to understand that compositions are not considered complete until they are edited; however, not all pieces are refined to the point of editing. The goal of editing is not to change the text, but to make it optimally readable. In order to do this, writers examine the conventions of language, proofreading for spelling, punctuation, grammar, and capitalization. When the written product is handwritten, authors must use their best handwriting, so that it is readable.

Three approaches to editing are commonly used in elementary writing programs. First, children edit their own writing with the guidance of checklists like those in the following examples. Second, students may edit one another's papers for clarity, completeness, and sequence, as well as the mechanics of spelling, punctuation, and capitalization. Third, the teacher may identify specific points for improvement.

Second-Grade Editing Checklist

1. Does each sentence begin with a capital letter?

2. Is the correct mark at the end of each sentence?

3. Are all of the words spelled correctly?

4. Is the writing neat?

Fifth-Grade Editing Checklist

1. Have you capitalized the beginning of each sentence?

2. Have you capitalized all proper nouns?

3. Are all of the words spelled correctly?

4. Does each sentence have the correct punctuation mark at the end?

5. Have you used quotation marks where they are needed?

6. Have you indented each paragraph?

7. Is your handwriting neat?

During editing the teacher may identify common weaknesses in the students' writing, such as specific punctuation or capitalization problems. A demonstration of appropriate punctuation or capitalization should be followed by student practice. An excellent form of practice is to apply the principles taught in editing their own papers.

Children should learn to use proofreading marks when they edit. Proofreading marks are both efficient and motivating for students.

Proofreading Marks

≡ Capital letter

⊙ Add a period

Sp. Check spelling

⋏ Comma

⋀ Add a word or words

℘ Take out

Publishing

Publishing is the final step in the writing process, wherein students' writing is made public. This is another way teachers and parents can encourage and support students' writing. Publishing can take the form of student-made hardback books. After students draft and revise their writing and edit it with teacher or peer assistance, they may type their text or use a computer and printer to produce the copy. Finally they bind their books. Then the librarian can catalog the books and place them in the library. Children enjoy reading each other's work.

Some students may wish to submit their writing for professional publication. Certain magazines publish children's work and some organizations like International Reading Association Councils publish compilations of children's work and hold Young Author's Conferences. Elementary schools should publish yearly compilations of children's writings and hold their own young author's conferences.

Fleming (1985) suggests the following uses of children's published writings. Make recordings of student authors reading their own writings; mood music can be used as a background. Students may give their own publications as gifts. Reviews of children's writings can be included in school newspapers. Writings can be posted on bulletin boards; posting all of the drafts that the writing passed through is very interesting and helpful to students. Students can read their own writings for assembly programs. Some students can have classmates dramatize their writings for presentation at an assembly or to other classes in the school.

Publication of Children's Writing   Some publishers specialize in children's original writings. You may refer to *Writer's Market,* a publication found in public libraries, for a comprehensive listing of publishers' addresses and other descriptive information. Following are some of the publications specializing in children's work.

Cricket
Cricket League
Box 100
LaSalle, IL 61301

Ebony Jr.
820 S. Michigan Avenue
Chicago, IL 60605

Fun Publishing Company
P. O. Box 40283
Indianapolis, IN 46240

IMED
1820 Cotner Avenue
Los Angeles, CA 90025

Jack and Jill
P. O. Box 567B
Indianapolis, IN 46206

Kids Magazine
Box 3051
Grand Central Station
New York, NY 10017

Stone Soup
Journal of Children's Literature
Box 83
Santa Cruz, CA 955063

PRACTICAL CONCERNS OF THE WRITING PROCESS

Writing with Typewriters

Typewriters are invaluable aids to students because they make it possible for writers to get their ideas on paper faster. This is especially important for those writers who may be struggling with letter formation. Typewriters have many of the advantages of computers, and they are often more available for classroom use because they cost less. Students can develop writing skills with typewriters that they can later transfer to computers; in fact electronic typewriters can function as typewriters or as computer printers.

Classrooms rarely have the space for a typewriter for each student even if the money were available to buy one for each pupil. Therefore, teachers may find it useful to use numbers to assign students to typewriters. This technique is described in greater detail in the following section.

Writing with Computers

Word processing is the most exciting application of computer technology for classrooms. Composing with word processing programs enables writers to focus on the writing process because computers can handle many of the language conventions (spelling, handwriting, punctuation, and grammar) which frees children to concentrate on ideas. This puts the writer in control of the process—choosing what to write about, choosing what to say and choosing how to say it, deciding when to ask for feedback, and determining when they will revise and edit a piece of writing. Most children easily learn word processing programs like Applewriter, Bank Street Writer, etc. Word processing programs usually include dictionaries that can be used to check the spelling of words in children's compositions. Programs are also available to check the grammar, punctuation, and capitalization of compositions. Most word processing programs include "search" commands that make it possible to identify words that have been overused in a composition. Furthermore, a "search and replace" command enables writers to replace one word with another to improve written expression. In short, word processing programs make writing easier.

Recently, computers with word processing programs have been introduced into primary level language arts programs. These programs enable young children to overcome constraints that limit their writing. For example, children starting to write compose at a rate as slow as 1.5 words per minute. This agonizingly slow pace can lead to loss of interest. Computers also help children overcome messy looking compositions. Unfortunately, neatness is sometimes equated with quality. It is possible that the word processor will help us discover a whole new population of writers.

Recent applications of writing research and knowledge to software has produced programs like QUILL (Collins, Bruce, and Rubin, 1982) which enables children to write and to understand the writing process.

QUILL is the forerunner of a new generation of open-ended software that moves beyond the electronic workbooks designed for drill and practice. Open-ended programs allow for and encourage students' active involvement and collaboration of students and teachers. QUILL includes an information storage and retrieval system, an electronic mail system, and a program to help students plan and organize their thoughts. It also uses a text editor. QUILL allows for peer-peer interaction in composing and revising, and encourages students to write to other students in the class. In addition to writing, this program encourages students to read their peers' compositions.

Although computers are a boon to writers, they cannot replace teachers. In fact, teachers must know just as much to teach writing with a computer as to teach without a computer. Computers can bring about major changes in learning environments, but their use requires substantial support from teachers. Unfortunately, teachers have had little help in choosing computers and computer software for use in their classrooms. Writing with computers often leads to alterations in classroom procedures.

Computer Constraints   Computers are seductive because the content we see on the moniter looks so polished that we may think revising and editing are unnecessary. However, this problem is offset by the ease with which one can erase, move, and revise print with the computer. In fact, children who were reluctant to revise prior to using computers are more willing to revise because it does not involve erasing, crossing out, and rewriting.

There are those who believe there is something about handwriting that is sacred to the composing process, that putting the computer between thought and word will inhibit writers' development. However, most people who use computers agree that they must print out draft copies of their work to edit it. Writers report that they frequently print draft copies of their work three or four times in order to edit it to their satisfaction (Stoodt, 1986). Although the majority of classrooms do not have enough computers to permit students to print three or four draft copies, it seems that the computer makes it easier to draft rather than eliminate that step of the writing process.

Availability of computers for students' use is a problem because they are expensive. Therefore, teachers often share computers with other teachers, with only very fortunate teachers having one or more computers in their classrooms. Sharing computer time forces teachers and students to be organized and focused in their planning. Some schools address this problem by creating computer labs and scheduling students for the lab; students can use the computer only at scheduled times, which may not permit adequate time for writers to explore. In this situation, students should complete the prewriting phase before going to the lab and, depending on the time available, they may need to draft the composition before lab.

HOW CHILDREN GROW AS WRITERS

Stages of Writing Development

Composition is a developmental skill. Children mature in writing ability throughout the elementary school years. Therefore, the writing of kindergarten children differs significantly from that of fifth graders. In subsequent paragraphs, we will examine writing as it occurs at various age levels.

Preschool children are surrounded by print. Television, billboards, cereal boxes, newspapers, grocery store labels, and candy wrappers all have print. Seeing print in their everyday environment leads children to draw, scribble, and copy letters, numbers, and words to represent things in their environment. They draw letters and numbers in the sand at the beach, they write with chalk on sidewalks, they even write in the dust on furniture. They like to use magic markers, crayons, and pencils on large newsprint. Chalkboards, computers, and "magic slates" are motivating writing implements for preschoolers. They may try to write such things as names, house numbers, parents' names, and labels like Coca-Cola, as well as other names and numbers in their environment. Preschoolers often ask their parents to read what they have written demonstrating that they expect their writings to have meaning. Many preschool children can look through a stack of mail and identify those pieces that are addressed to them. They often ask parents to write their names because they like to see their own name in writing. Many young children draw stories and tell elaborate stories to accompany their illustrations. All these activities develop readiness for writing.

Kindergarten

Many parents and teachers are amazed at the notion of teaching kindergarten children to write; however, writing is a very natural activity for them. Most children come to school knowing a handful of letters, which they use to write stories, letters, and captions. They learn to write by writing. Kindergarten children surround their written language with talk as they explain drawings and writings with oral language. Five year olds use pictures, words, letters, scribbles, and numbers to record ideas and experiences that they will record in written language as they grow older. For example, a five-year-old friend of mine gave me a page of scribbling as I left her home. She explained it was a list of items that she wanted to buy at a store and included candy, magic markers, roller skates, and a bicycle seat. The following item is an example of a five-year-old boy's writing.

B   A   L   5

He explained, "That's for my street which is Barrett Court (B). My sister's name is Amanda (A) and my brother's name is Luke (L). That's how old I am (5)."

In the preceding examples, the children are learning that it is possible to write one's thoughts and experiences. Children acquire this concept as they observe their parents and teachers. Parents write shopping lists and personal letters. Teachers write language experience charts that translate children's experiences into written language. Children experience the composing process when they dictate ideas for the teacher to write in the form of language experience stories or picture captions.

First Grade

First graders are noisy writers. They talk as they write and try out or rehearse what they want to say. They also read what they have written aloud to see how it sounds. These young writers have many messages to communicate. They adopt sequences of letters and erase their mistakes wearing holes in the paper as they erase and revise (Graves, 1983). First-grade students have to relate words to their thoughts, then think of letters to represent the words, then get their hand to form the letters. Therefore, writing is a complex task for them.

Early in the first-grade year, students usually write initial consonants to represent words (Calkins, 1986). As they develop, they use the initial and final consonant; somewhat later they begin to add letters in medial positions. Then they progress to using a letter for each sound in the word, although these letters may not represent accepted spelling conventions. If too much stress is placed on spelling in the early stages of writing, children will continually interrupt their writing to search for a correct spelling or to worry that they do not know how to spell. This concern with spelling, capitalization, and punctuation causes children to focus on the conventions of writing too early in the process and inhibits their ability to say what they want. You may refer to Chapter Nine to learn more about spelling development.

Many six-year-olds have not learned word boundaries. Because they do not know where words begin and end they run phrases and sentences together in their writing. As they acquire concepts of letter, word, and sentence they will have a better sense of word boundaries.

First graders whose parents and teachers have read to them have a "sense of story" or "story grammar" (Applebee, 1978). They know that stories have characters and settings and they know how to begin a story. However, they do not know how to end stories which is the reason their stories end abruptly with "The End." During first grade, students begin to notice punctuation marks like exclamation marks and quotation marks and use these conventions in their own writing (Calkins, 1986).

Writing is a pleasurable activity for many first graders, who enjoy the process more than the actual product. They write for themselves rather than an audience. These prolific writers often write several stories at one sitting—if they have five pages of paper, they usually write five stories. They enjoy writing about books, lists, telling about their experiences, a television program, or a new toy. The opportunity to write daily leads frequently to spontaneous writing. They become impatient when something or someone interferes with their writing. This author recently visited a first-grade classroom to read aloud. After one story, some children said, "Please let us write, we don't want to talk any more." I told them to go ahead with their writing, while I read another story to the other children. Later in the morning, when the teacher told them it was time for recess, one of the children said, "Do I have to go to recess? I want to write."

Although first graders are prolific writers, they are not very good at revising and editing. They prefer writing a new composition to revising. But teachers can help them with revising and editing during conferences, which are discussed later in this chapter.

Second Grade

Second-grade writers are moving from writing for personal pleasure to writing for an audience. They are becoming more interested in the final product; therefore they will spend more time revising and editing. Their concern for audience and the audience's perception of their writing causes them to make many false starts. They tear up many sheets of paper saying, "That's a dumb story, I'm starting over." Their growing concern for correctness creates "writers' blocks." Second graders' written products tend to be less creative and interesting than those of first graders (Calkins, 1986). If one did not understand child development, it would appear that the children are moving backward rather than forward. But they are "in a stage" which will pass with more writing experience and an understanding instructor.

Because second graders are less self-assured, they need guidance during the prewriting stage. This should be a time for overcoming writers' block, for identifying and exploring topics, and for thinking of what one wants to say about the topic. Second graders are more ready to use discussion as a prewriting activity than first graders who generally prefer drawing (Calkins, 1986). Second-grade teachers must spend more time in writing conferences with children; otherwise students spend more time erasing and editing than they do writing.

Second graders' writing is detailed like their talk. If you ask a second grader to tell about his or her birthday party, you will hear every detail of the party (often learning more than you really wanted to know). This concern for detail appears in their writing.

Second graders are developing an awareness of patterns which they use in writing and oral language. They derive patterns from listening to oral language, literature, and television. Every sentence in a composition may follow the same pattern like the following:

I like cats.

I like dogs.

I like gerbils.

I like frogs.

Third Grade

Third-grade writers are very much like second-grade writers, only more so. They are concerned about the writing conventions and with correctness in their compositions. Third-grade compositions are conventional and wooden when compared to the exuberance of first-grade compositions. Third graders choose giant topics like my life, my pets, my friends, or my family. They also write about their experiences in a one-track, systematic fashion (Calkins, 1986). Third graders tend to overdo. When they use a question mark, they often write five or six question marks to emphasize the question's significance. They also like long compositions incorporating action, sound effects, and conversation. Therefore, a sentence like, "Crash, bang, boom went the thunder" appears in their compositions. They focus on details rather than on wholes, telling their audience every minute detail they experienced.

Teachers need to help third graders focus and limit their topics. When teachers invest effort and understanding, they can spark third graders' energy for writing and help them understand that writing is an opportunity to express their thoughts. They can learn to select the most important details and to become more **holistic** in their outlook. When teachers use writing conferences to help them revise and edit their compositions, the third grade becomes a time for tremendous writing growth.

Middle Grades

Fourth, fifth, and sixth graders are grouped together as middle graders because writing development in these grades reflects steady, gradual growth toward greater sophistication. Students in the middle grades manifest considerable individual variation in their development. The developmental stage of some youngsters will be more like first grade than fourth grade, while the development of others will be more like that of second graders. During the middle grades children develop the ability to read, to reread, to reflect on their writings, and to revise and edit them. Their cognitive development enables them to select starting points rather than starting at the beginning. Their compositions may start in the middle of a story. For example, middle-grade writers may choose to tell about a special Thanksgiving visitor without telling every detail of the entire holiday and all of the food on the Thanksgiving Day menu.

They can think of alternative ways of writing a sentence or a paragraph and select the most effective of the alternatives. Experienced middle-grade writers are able to compose in their heads, so they can remember and plan ahead during the prewriting period. In short, middle-grade students acquire more control over their writing processes. They have an improved sense of audience and the ability to write from different perspectives, such as that of a Martian seeing earth for the first time or the way a pair of shoes views things.

TROUBLESHOOTING

The greatest difficulty that teachers may face in teaching writing is encountering students who have not been exposed to the writing process in earlier grades. These youngsters will tend to be overly concerned with spelling or punctuation rather than with expressing their ideas. They have not had opportunities to learn that their ideas are valuable and that they can express them in writing.

Patience is the only solution to this problem. Providing students with many opportunities to write and reinforcing their success will help them learn they can write. They may need more writing ideas and conferences during the initial stages of writing.

The second problem that teachers encounter in the early phases of writing is parental concern for spelling and punctuation. The solution to this problem is communication. Share your writing goals with the parents and explain that the children will learn the appropriate conventions of writing, but that will occur over an extended period of time.

SUMMARY

Writers at all levels move through the phases of the writing process, prewriting, composing, revising, and editing; however, they do not move through these phases in a linear fashion. Prewriting develops through one's lifetime; one writer may not consciously spend time on a prewriting phase, while another may spend a long period of time on prewriting and very little time on actual composition. Revision and editing may be accomplished at the same time in some instances.

Conferences are an important aspect of helping children grow into writing. As teachers guide children through conferences, they learn to critique themselves and to participate in peer conferences. Conferences are particularly helpful in the revision stage of the writing process because they help students learn to analyze their thoughts and written expression rather than merely look at the mechanics of their writing (which should occur during editing).

Computers and typewriters are tools of writing, but in many classrooms students do not have unlimited access to them, which means that planning is an important aspect of their use.

Finally, children grow into writing. They grow from the writing experience, from knowing what good writing is like, and from instruction.

Thought Questions

1. Discuss each aspect of the writing process.

2. Compare the writing instruction you received as an elementary school student with the writing process described in this chapter.

3. Discuss the pros and cons of the current emphasis on writing instruction.

4. How are speaking and writing related?

5. How are reading and writing related?

Enrichment Activities

1. Observe a writing session in an elementary classroom noting the following things. How was writing initiated? Did the teacher have conferences with the students? Do the students have writing files? What phases (prewriting, writing, revision, and editing) of the writing process did you observe?

2. Locate a computer (many colleges and universities have computer labs for student use). Learn how to use a word processing program; many word processing programs have self-instructional lessons that will lead you through the program.

3. Interview children at various grade levels to determine how much writing they do in class and whether they enjoy writing.

4. Prepare a series of questions to use in guiding a writing conference and use these with a youngster.

5. Read the book *The Art of Teaching Writing* by Lucy Calkins. This book was published by Heinemann, Portsmouth, New Hampshire in 1986.

Selected Readings

Baghban, M. (1984). *Our Daughter Learns to Read and Write.* Newark, DE: International Reading Association.

Calkins, L. M. (1986). *The Art of Teaching Writing.* Portsmouth, NH: Heinemann.

Fadiman, C. and J. Howard (1979). *Empty Pages.* Belmont, CA: Fearon Pitman Publishers.

Haley-James, S. (1981). *Perspectives on Writing in Grades 1–8.* Urbana, IL: National Council of Teachers of English.

Hillocks, G. (1986). *Research on Written Composition.* Urbana, IL: National Conference on Research in English.

Hoot, J. L. (1986). *Computers in Early Childhood Education.* Englewood Cliffs, NJ: Prentice-Hall.

Murray, D. M. (1982). *Learning by Teaching.* Montclair, NJ: Boynton/Cook.

Thaiss, C., and C. Suhor (eds.) (1984). *Speaking and Writing K-12.* Urbana, IL: National Council of Teachers of English.

References

Applebee, A. N. (1978). *The Child's Concept of Story: Ages Two to Seventeen.* Chicago: University of Chicago Press.

Calkins, L. M. (1986). *The Art of Teaching Writing.* Portsmouth, NH: Heinemann.

Chomsky, Carol (Spring 1970). "Language Development After Six." *HGSEA Bulletin, XIV,* No. 3, 14–16.

Collins, A.; B. C. Bruce; and A. D. Rubin (February, 1982). "Microcomputer-Based Writing Activities in Upper Elementary Grades." In *Proceedings of the Fourth International Congress of the Society for Applied Learning and Technology,* Orlando, FL.

Elbow, P. (1973). *Writing Without Teachers.* New York: Oxford University Press.

Emig, J. (1971). *The Composing Processes of Twelfth Graders* (Research Report No. 13). Urbana, IL: National Council of Teachers of English.

Executive Committee National Council of Teachers of English (February 1983). "Essentials of English." *Language Arts 60,* 2, 244–248.

Fadiman, C., and J. Howard (1979). *Empty Pages.* Belmont CA: Fearon Pitman Publishers, Inc.

Fleming, M. (1985). "Writing Assignments Focusing on Autobiographical and Biographical Topics." In *Portraits: Biography and Autobiography in the Secondary School,* M. Fleming and J. McGinnis (eds.). Urbana, IL: National Council of Teachers of English.

Graves, D. H. (1983). *Writing: Teachers and Children at Work.* Portsmouth, NH: Heinemann Educational Books.

Hipple, M. (March 1985). "Journal Writing in Kindergarten." *Language Arts, 62,* 3, 255–261.

Murray, D. M. (1982). *Learning by Teaching.* Montclair, NJ: Boynton/Cook.

Naisbitt, J. (1984). *Megatrends.* New York: Warner Books.

National Assessment of Educational Progress (1986). Denver, CO: National Assessment of Educational Progress.

Perl, S. (1979). "Unskilled Writers as Composers." *New York Education Quarterly, 10.*

Rico, G. L. (1983). *Writing the Natural Way.* Los Angeles: J. P. Tarcher Inc.

Smith, F. (1982). *Writing and the Writer.* New York: Holt, Rinehart and Winston.

Stallard, C. K., Jr. (1973). *An Analysis of the Writing Behavior of Good Student Writers.* DAI 33.

Stoodt, B. (1986). "A Study of the Writing Behavior of Disabled Readers." Unpublished study.

Tiedt, I.; S. Bruemmer; S. Lane; P. Stelwagon; K. Watanabe; and M. Williams (1983). *Teaching Writing in K-8 Classrooms.* Englewood Cliffs, NJ: Prentice-Hall.

Yatvin, J. (1981). *A Functional Writing Program for the Middle Grades.* Urbana, IL: National Council of Teachers of English.

Chapter **Eight**

Building a Writing Program

CHAPTER OVERVIEW

Teachers' roles in the writing process are explored in this chapter. These roles include creating a writing setting, modeling writing, motivating writing, developing students' understanding of the qualities of good writing, encouraging and supporting writing, and evaluating writing (reading and responding to writing). In classrooms students do both private and public writing. Private writing includes writing that students may or may not share with others, while public writing is read by others. The text includes strategies for teachers to use as they fulfill each instructional role.

Anticipation Guide

Think about these questions and ideas before reading this chapter. How did you learn to write? Did you have teachers who engaged in extensive use of the red pencil? How did that make you feel? Did it improve your writing skills? Do you remember any of your elementary school writing assignments? Did they make you want to write?

1. What can teachers do to help students develop writing skills?

2. What assignments are most helpful to students?

3. How can teachers evaluate writing?

4. Should teachers evaluate students' writing?

Key Concepts

practical writing   personal writing

primary trait scoring   holistic scoring

INTRODUCTION

Teachers have the important task of building writing programs for people living in an age of information. In order to do this they must write themselves. Writing gives them the indispensable advantage of confidence in their own ability to write. When teachers discover enjoyment and satisfaction in writing, they can teach with enjoyment and satisfaction. Calkins admits:

> Writing is the hardest thing I do. I let my children know this. I tell them that, after a long weekend of writing, my whole jaw aches from being clenched. And at school, I write alongside my children. They see my struggles. They notice the pile of crumpled starts on the floor beside me. They watch as I wrestle to find a way to tackle my subjects. They watch, and they begin to understand. Writing is not magic; it's hard work. (1986)

When building a writing program, today's teachers can rely on a large body of writing research. Shirley Haley-James (1981) identified the following points of agreement among writing authorities.

1. Children learn to write by writing.

2. Even very young school age children, whose knowledge of letter formations and spelling patterns is limited, can and should write.

3. Writing frequently on self-selected topics is important for developing skill in writing.

4. When children feel a need or a desire to write for some purpose or audience, they write more effectively.

5. Children should write from their experiences, and expectations for their writing should be in line with their stage of experiential and mental development.

6. Oral language processing of the ideas and content being expressed should precede writing and occur during writing.

7. Real and varied audiences for their work are important for children to develop as writers and to their incentive to write.

8. A writing purpose and a developing concept of audience lead children to a logical need for revising selected pieces of their writing.

9. Formal study of grammar should be delayed until grade eight or nine; until then revising writing in view of the audience for the writing should be the basis of grammar-related language study.

10. Teacher and peer conferences with the writer are appropriate means of helping children process their writing orally and progress from first drafts, in which primary concern is with getting meaning out on paper, to improved drafts.

11. Holistic and **primary trait scoring** are useful means of assessing both the progress of groups of children and the effectiveness of writing programs.

Teachers can use the preceding points as a research base for developing writing programs, lessons, and instructional strategies.

WRITING INSTRUCTION VIGNETTE

Mary Lee looked up from her third-grade lesson plans and reflected on the changes in writing instruction that she had experienced over the last decade. When she was a young student teacher, her cooperating teacher really did not teach writing, but used workbooks, ditto sheets, and chalkboard exercises that required children to fill in blanks. Then as a beginning teacher she had attended workshops for "cute," motivating, writing ideas and story starters, and at the time she was excited about these ideas. But she found that she didn't know what to do after the story starters. She didn't know how to keep the students writing and she was told in the workshop that she should not evaluate the children's papers or they would be afraid to write. Nevertheless, the children became bored with her file of story starters and she was frustrated because their writing seemed to be static. They were not developing; in fact, their writing looked the same as it had during the first months of school.

Then she heard about a writing institute at a local university and enrolled. The institute opened many doors for Mary; she read books by Donald Graves, Lucy Calkins, and Donald Murray. She was excited about writing again. She designed writing instruction that included prewriting, drafting, revising, and editing. Her students were engrossed in student-teacher conferences and they found peer conferences instructive. Best of all, the students were writing more and better than ever before. She felt that her writing instruction had form and substance—she was *teaching* writing.

Vignette Discussion

You will notice that Mary has grown into writing instruction. Teachers learn and grow in the teaching profession—earning a degree does not automatically make one a teacher. A degree is the beginning of learning. Teachers learn from their students, and the most astute teachers observe their students carefully, so they are sure to learn. Mary went through a stage that many teachers experience; she went from following recipes for writing to teaching writing. This growth was based on understanding both the writing process and children. The balance of this chapter builds on the preceding chapter to help you acquire these same understandings, which will be honed to a fine point by your early years of teaching.

TEACHERS AND THE WRITING PROCESS

Teachers function in many roles when they teach writing. Each teaching function is discussed in subsequent sections.

They create a setting in which students can write.

They model the writing process.

They explain writing assignments.

They motivate students to write.

They encourage and support students' writing.

They help students understand the qualities of good writing.

They read and respond to students' writing.

They evaluate final writing products.

Teachers Create a Setting for Writing

Writing is not a sedentary activity; therefore the classroom setting and organization should permit children to move around and to talk with one another. Of course, they should speak in low tones and avoid interrupting each other when they are engrossed in composing. The adults in the environment should value questioning and exploring children's ideas. Provision should be made for regular small group and partner activities, as well as student-teacher conferences.

A routine should be established for handling common problems. Students should know what to do when they are stuck for a topic, what to do when they cannot think of what they want to say next, or how to find a listener to hear their composition. They should also know how to handle editing problems—for example, what to do when they cannot spell a word or what to do when they are not sure of the correct punctuation. Teachers and students should discuss these situations and develop ways of coping with such problems.

Classroom arrangement can facilitate the composing process. Each classroom should have a writing center containing a table, chalkboard, dictionaries, thesaurus, literature, lists of writing ideas, large sheets of paper for language experience, and writing materials. The classroom should have many bulletin board displays, books, pictures, and models to stimulate children to write. Writing materials should be readily available to students, so they do not have to interrupt the teacher.

Primary students need a wide variety of writing materials. They need stapled writing paper for journals and large sheets of paper for language experience activities. Spiral bound notebooks or sketch pads make good journals. Supplies like sharpened pencils, paper, crayons, and magic markers should be placed so children can get them as the need arises. Supplies should be checked and replenished once a week. Book binding materials should be available; however, these should be used only with teacher supervision. Children may need writing folders for filing drafts. Because primary children write larger and use large paper, their writing files must be larger. Some teachers use paper bags or large manila folders that the children can decorate.

Middle-grade children use composition books rather than stapled writing paper. Composition books can be used for journals as well. They need the same kinds of writing materials as primary age children including sharpened pencils. Book binding materials should be available for binding those books they decide to publish. Figures 8.1 and 8.2 show you how to bind hard- and soft-cover books and identify the necessary materials. Middle-grade writing folders are made from manila file folders, although each youngster may want to decorate his or her own folder. These folders should be filed so they are

COVERING THE CHIPBOARD

1. Cut 2 pieces of chipboard 6" x 9" and 2 pieces of wallpaper 8" x 11".

   Center chipboard on wallpaper and trace around it.

   Glue chipboard on wallpaper.

2. Fold the four corners of wallpaper onto the chipboard. Repeat with the second piece.

   Cut off the corners approximately 1/8" outside the fold line. Repeat with the second piece.

3. Put rubber cement along all edges of wallpaper and chipboard. Allow to dry completely.

   Fold side edges of wallpaper over tightly. Fold top and bottom edges over tightly (tucking corners under (first).

BINDING THE COVER

4. Place binding tape (3" x 11") on flat surface, sticky side up. Using a ruler, measure in 1¼" from both sides. Mark a dot. Do this approximately 3" from top and bottom.

   Leaving a space (½") on the tape, line up the covers beside the dots.

   Fold over the ends of the tape.

SEWING THE PAGES

5. Fold (individually) 2 sheets of construction paper and 8 sheets of filler paper in half. Stack all sheets inside of construction sheets.

   Punch 3 small holes in fold of paper with ice pick.

6. Sew pages with single thread (approx. 1 yd.):
   - a) up from back center (leave 6" tail)
   - b) down from inside top
   - c) up from back bottom
   - d) down from inside center

   Tie knot in back around center thread.

FINISHING THE BOOK

7. Secure spine of pages along center of tape.

   Glue the first page onto the inside front cover.
   Glue the last page onto the inside back cover, tilting cover slightly.

   Make sure construction paper does not buckle when book is closed.

8. Write an exciting story in your book and share it with a friend!

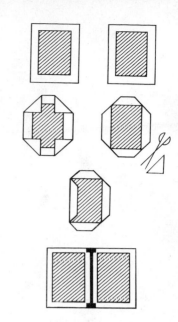

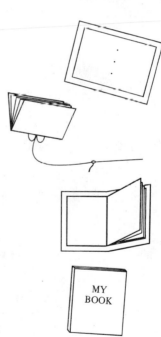

Figure 8.1 Making a hardback book.

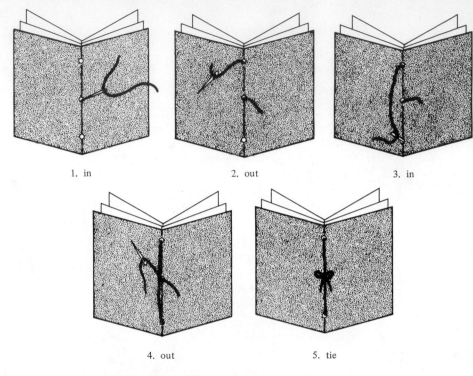

1. in   2. out   3. in

4. out   5. tie

Use string or yarn. May use construction paper for cover sheet.
1. Go in middle hole and leave a tail for tying.
2. Bring the string out the top hole.
3. Bring the string in the bottom hole.
4. Bring the string out the middle hole.
5. Tie the two ends in a knot or bow.

Figure 8.2 Making a softback book.

accessible to the children for filing compositions and recovering works in progress.

Teachers Model the Writing Process

Teachers model the writing process in two ways. They share their thoughts while writing and revising (as described in Chapter Seven), or they can write while the children are writing. Journal writing time is an especially good time for teachers and students to write because the teacher does not have to help the children with journal writing. Children who observe their teacher writing understand that the teacher values and enjoys writing.

Teachers Explain Writing Assignments

Teachers develop students' readiness for writing assignments. Students need to understand what is expected of them if they are to write successfully. The purpose of the assignment governs writing form. Some assignments are reports which are written in an expository form, others might be organized differently, such as stories which have plots, themes, and characterizations.

Preparing students to write involves identifying the audience for whom students are writing because they have to explain more to an audience that knows very little about the topic; on the other hand, if they are writing in their own journal they do not have to include the same amount of details. Writers must be aware of their audiences' interests, understandings, and expectations. Writing assignments should lead students to experiment with various approaches to a topic. Students' awareness of audience can be heightened by class discussions that explore differences in the way one treats a subject when the audience is a boy, a girl, an old person, a person from another planet, and so forth. Reading and discussing literature written from various perspectives helps students acquire a sense of audience. For example, *Bunnicula* was written by a dog who handles his subject differently than a cat might.

Writing topics should be familiar to students or the teacher should develop background for students. This gives students the confidence to write. The list below includes examples of appropriate writing assignments. Writing assignments do not differ significantly from grade level to grade level; however, students respond to the assignments according to their own level of development. For example, a first grader writing about his or her feelings following the death of a pet will express them differently from a sixth grader writing on the same topic, but the assignment is equally important to each.

1. Students may write, revise, edit, and bind books for the school library.

2. They may write school or classroom rules.

3. They may talk with adults about cooperation and respect for the rights and feelings of others and write a summary of the discussion.

4. They may work with the parent-teacher association (PTA), sending representatives to the meetings and writing up the association's activities.

5. They may write letters to newspapers regarding concerns.

6. They can write about their feelings regarding the death of a pet, moving to another school, or holidays.

7. Students can write fiction which may vary from a short story to a full novel. A few students have been known to write a series of books.

8. Students in all grades can keep journals.

9. Students can extend their understanding of the content areas through interactive journals. At the end of a class session, the teacher may tell them to write a summary of what they have learned that day, then the teacher reads and responds to the students' ideas.

10. Students can write communications such as letters, thank-you notes, memos, or telegrams.

11. They can write public notices, posters, and newspaper advertisements.

12. They can write how-to instructions for games or crafts.

13. They can write biographies and autobiographies.

14. They can create concept books such as: round is, funny is, happy is, red is, etc.

15. They can write greeting cards, comic strips, plays and skits, and captions.

Teachers sometimes give students more detailed assignments like the following detective story. Some students may find such an activity overwhelming, but when the assignment is divided into smaller tasks, students feel it is manageable. The detective story assignment is modeled after one described by Jack Wilde and Thomas Newkirk (1981).

 EXAMPLE: DETECTIVE STORY ASSIGNMENT

The teacher reads detective stories to the children or they may read these stories independently. These books establish readiness for the assignment and provide a writing model.

Three Policemen by William Pene Du Bois
The Alligator Case by William Pene Du Bois
The Horse in the Camel Suit by William Pene Du Bois
Maximillian Does It Again by Joseph Rosenbloom
Encyclopedia Brown, Boy Detective by Donald Sobol
Encyclopedia Brown Takes the Case by Donald Sobol
Encyclopedia Brown Tracks Them Down by Donald Sobol

The teacher explains that the students will have three constraints when they write.

1. The criminal should be as smart as the detective.

2. The clues should not point directly at the criminal.

3. The clues should lead to a logical solution.

Each step in the assignment can be completed on different days.

1. Make a list of crimes that you might write about. These do not have to be serious crimes; some of them might be funny. Think about the list of crimes and decide on one crime to write about.

2. Make a list of characters. Decide what characters to include in your story. Write character descriptions. You may consult our classroom lists of body parts, adjectives for describing body parts, comparisons that can be used to describe body parts, personality traits that characters might have, and personal habits.

3. Make a list of settings for the story and decide on one or two. Write a description of the setting or settings. Be sure to list the details of the scene of the crime.

4. Describe the crime and the discovery of clues. Before writing about the clues, you may make a list of possible clues and then decide which clues to include in the story.

5. Work out a solution. The solution should explain how the detective figured out the crime.

6. Use the drafts created in each step to create a detective story.

7. Read the story to a peer editor.

8. Revise the story as many times as necessary to make it the way you want.

9. Write or type the story. Bind the story into a book. Put a library card into the book, so your friends can check your book out and read it.

Teachers Motivate Students to Write

Authentic, functional writing assignments motivate children. "For writing to come to life, a writer must feel involved, must feel a commitment and want to say something" (Tway, 1985). Writing is a complex and strenuous thinking process, and until the student is engaged with something significant any writing done is likely to be perfunctory. As stated earlier children (people) have a need to write, but some factors mitigate against writing. A blank piece

Teachers motivate writers.

of paper is intimidating. The fear of failing—failing to find the words, of spelling the words, of thinking of something to say—is scary. Fearing that the things one has to say hold no interest for others can stifle motivation. By helping children overcome these fears a teacher releases their writing energies.

Indeed children should write about their experiences and their truth because for writing to be good it must be about something that matters to the writer. Writers search for truth. Gardner describes this search when he says, "Fiction seeks out truth . . . the writer's joy in the fictional process is his pleasure in discovering, by means he can trust, what he believes and can affirm for all time" (Gardner, 1984). Nancy Martin claims that when children transform the events and feelings of their lives into a story, it makes those elements of their lives more knowable and more distant (Martin, 1983). We do not usually attribute such lofty thinking to children, but children like all people in the community of writers are motivated when they have something to say that matters to them.

Personal Writing   **Personal writing** includes writing to communicate messages, to keep records, to express feelings, to share ideas, or to find out more about what we know or feel about something. Children do not automatically understand what writing can do for them. They learn this from experiences and from teachers who model the satisfactions of writing. Once children experience the satisfactions of writing, they become self-motivated, self-propelled writers. They sense the power that comes from knowing they *can write!*

Journals   Journals are personal writing. The sources lie almost wholly within the individuals, and their personal taste is the important factor. Journal writing helps students acquire vocabulary and writing fluency.

Personal writing is not graded and children should have the freedom to choose whether or not to share it with others. Children who want to share their journals can ask the teacher to read a specific entry; they can clip parts not to be read to show they are "off limits." Some teachers have a drawer in which students place things they want him or her to read. Teachers show their respect for students' privacy when they ask permission if they wish to use students' writing in class as examples. Teachers should not share personal information read in children's writing with others because it becomes gossip and causes them to lose faith in teachers.

Journals should be a daily part of the classroom schedule. Children put themselves into their writing when they know that they can rely on a specific period of time to write. Journal writing should not be an activity that children can do when they have completed all of their other work. Students should be alerted when the journal writing period is drawing to a close, so they can conclude their writing.

Over a period of time journal writing can become quite pedestrian. Some children may write statements like the following, "The sun is shining.

Two boys are absent from school today. I like school." When this is the kind of writing that appears daily it is time to liven up the journals. This can be achieved in several ways. Teachers can create a model for journal writing by reading aloud from literature that models journal, diary, and letter writing. Children's books that can be used for this purpose include:

A Gathering of Days by Joan Blos. New York: Scribner, 1979 (grades 5 and 6).

Dear Mr. Henshaw by Beverly Cleary. New York: Morrow, 1983 (grades 3 and 4).

Harriet the Spy by Louise Fitzhugh. New York: Harper & Row, 1964 (grades 5 and 6).

My Side of the Mountain by Jean George. New York: Dutton, 1959 (grades 4 and 5).

Letters to Horseface by F. N. Monjo. New York: Simon and Schuster (grades 3 and 4).

Me and Willie and Pa by F. N. Monjo. New York: Simon and Schuster, 1973 (grades 3 and 4).

West from Home by Laura Ingalls Wilder. New York: Harper & Row (grades 5 and 6).

Books like the following show children how to write about everyday activities in interesting ways.

Beverly Quimby Age Eight by Beverly Cleary. New York: Morrow, 1984.

Anastasia Krupnik by Lois Lowry. Boston: Houghton Mifflin, 1980.

Interesting assignments can jazz up journals so children do not write the same "old stuff." Teachers may suggest topics like the following:

The best thing that happened to me this week.

The best thing that has happened to me today.

The worst thing that happened to me this week.

The worst thing that has happened to me today.

The thing about which I know the most.

The things that make me smile.

The things that make me frown.

The things that make me cry.

The things I like about my best friend.

Use as many descriptive words as possible when you write today.

Write about your day or week in terms of colors.

What did you learn about yourself this week?

What worries you the most?

What cheers you up?

Public Writing   Public writing is writing that is intended for an audience; therefore, they must think about expressing their thoughts and ideas for others to understand. Like all writing assignments, public writing should give children a purpose that releases their energy for writing. Many writing authorities frown on the notion of giving children writing assignments or story starters because of their concern for children's self-expression. This concern is appropriate; however, many children (and adults) need help to get started. Once children have gained confidence in their own ability to write, they will not need assignments or story starters. Teachers should be alert for those children who never need this assistance and for those who have developed the independence to write without assignments, so their writing development is not limited. We should remember that many professional writers do write specific assignments given by their editors.

Although gimmicky writing ideas are not a real answer to motivating students, teachers should have an extensive collection of writing starters and writing ideas that relate to children's experiences. Good writing ideas are ones that children feel they have something to say about. These ideas should tap children's writing energies and stimulate their desire to write. Motivational writing ideas are especially useful during the early part of the school year when teachers are introducing children to writing. Following are some motivating writing suggestions. Please keep in mind that these ideas should be tailored to meet the needs of specific classes and students. An idea that is motivating for one group or student may not stimulate another. Whenever possible give children choices in their writing assignments.

Children's Literature as a Writing Motivator   Literature is one of the best writing motivators. Children are attracted to stories and characters and they may want to write another character or to think of other events that could have occurred in the story. For example, primary grade children who enjoy the *Little Bear* books by Else Minarik can create an entire series of their own "Little Bear" stories. Middle-grade children who enjoy *A Wrinkle in Time* by Madeline L'Engle can create additional adventures for the characters.

Children can write or dictate stories to accompany their favorite wordless picture books. Mercer Mayer has created some of the best wordless picture books for young children. Among his best books are *Frog Where Are You?* and *Frog Goes to Dinner.* Pat Hutchins, John Goodall, and Paula Winter have also written excellent wordless picture books for young children. Remy Charlip created the complex wordless picture book *Thirteen* for middle-grade children.

Children enjoy writing patterned stories based on books like *Fortunately* by Remy Charlip. Cumulative stories like John Burningham's *Mr. Grumpy's Outing* and *Mr. Grumpy's Motorcar* and *Drummer Hoff* by Ed Emberley create writing models for children. Folktales also provide writing patterns like *Chicken Little* and *The Little Red Hen.*

Writing lists is motivating for many people. A class can create a book of lists that incorporates writing from all of the students. Such book could be titled *The Fourth-Grade Book of Lists* after the famous one created by the Irvings. Some very creative approaches to lists are reflected in these books: *What Do You Do with a Kangaroo?* by Mercer Mayer; *Who Wants a Cheap Rhinoceros?* by Shel Silverstein; *The Temper Tantrum Book* by Edna Mitchell Preston; *Bored with Being Bored!* and *How to Beat the Boredom Blahs* by Jovial Bob Stine and Jane Stine.

Many children enjoy writing riddle books which is another opportunity to create a class book like *The Great Third-Grade Riddle Book.* Books like *The Carsick Zebra and Other Animal Riddles* by David Adler, *The Riddle Book* by Roy McKie, and *Beastly Riddles* by Joseph Low are models for riddle book writers.

Traditional literature naturally attracts children because it is simple, direct, and uncluttered with extensive description. They can create their own *pourquoi* (why stories), like "How the Elephant Got a Long Trunk" or "How the Rabbit Got a Short Tail." Children enjoy writing modern versions of folktales. After reading a book like *Jim and the Beanstalk* by Raymond Briggs, they may create modern versions of "Little Red Riding Hood," "Goldilocks and the Three Bears," or "The Three Little Pigs." Another interesting writing assignment is to write folktales from a different point of view. "Cinderella" can be written from the point of view of a wicked stepsister, or "Little Red Riding Hood" from the wolf's point of view, or "The Three Billy Goats Gruff" from the Troll's point of view.

After studying biographies like *A Proud Taste for Scarlet and Miniver* by Elaine Konisburg, *Mr. Revere and I* by Robert Lawson, and *Ben and Me* by Robert Lawson, children may be newly motivated to write biographies.

Social studies is enlivened when children study books like *George Washington's Breakfast* or *If You Lived When Abraham Lincoln Lived.* Children can learn about historical figures in new ways.

Teachers may find motivating writing ideas in the following books and journals.

Children's Writing: An Approach for the Primary Grades by Leonard Sealey, Nancy Sealey, and Marcia Millmore. International Reading Association.

Language Arts, a journal published by the National Council of Teachers of English (NCTE).

Sparkling Words: Three Hundred and Fifteen Practical and Creative Writing Ideas by Ruth Kearney Carlson. National Council of Teachers of English.

Teaching Writing in the Content Areas: Elementary School by Stephen Tchudi and Susan Tchudi. National Education Association.

Teaching Writing in the Content Areas: Middle School/Junior High by Stephen Tchudi and Margie Huerta. National Education Association.

They All Want to Write Fourth Edition by Alving Treut Burrows, Doris C. Jackson, and Dorothy O. Saunders. Hamden, CT: Library Professional Publications, 1984.

Practical Writing　**Practical writing** refers to expository (informational writing). Everyone reading this text has written many reports during their educational career. No doubt some reports were copied directly from encyclopedias or trade books, in spite of your teacher's admonition to "write it in your own words." Some students develop considerable creativity in report writing. This author came home one day some years ago to discover her fifth-grade daughter perusing an encyclopedia and a thesaurus. When queried about her purpose, she responded, "writing a report, but I can't write it exactly like the encyclopedia, so I am using the thesaurus to replace the words in the encyclopedia." An ingenious approach, but not what her teacher intended. Unfortunately, students do not learn from such assignments. In order to learn, they must think about ideas and synthesize information to reach conclusions. Copying from an encyclopedia is a mechanical process that does not even require students to read. Practical writing instruction can prevent many of students' problems with report writing.

Practical writing comes naturally to many children. Children in kindergarten, first grade, and second grade often write attribute books that attempt to tell "all about" a topic or an event. These are the precursors of practical writing. A young child wrote this report after a week at the beach.

> We wnt to the bech. Thar wuz a bg strm, a hrecan at the bech. The wavs were hi and ther wernt any shelz. The wind wuz strg. We plad in the sand and we had fn.

This spontaneous writing is reminiscent of children's writing in science, social studies, and mathematics student logs. In logs, students have a place to examine ideas, to write their thoughts, questions and notes. They can also map content chapters and identify key concepts in their logs. In a class where interactive logs are assigned, the teacher responds to students' writing regularly, answering their questions and directing their attention to important concepts. The following example was taken from the mathematics log of a third grader.

How is multiplication like addition?

What are the uses of multiplication?

What problems should I watch out for when I am multiplying?

What new terms are used in multiplication?

Writing in the Content Areas   When teachers use writing as a means of learning, they make content the center of the writing process. This approach to learning gives *clarity of content* top priority (Tchudi and Tchudi, 1983). Content area writing activities should help students structure and synthesize their knowledge, not merely regurgitate it (Tchudi and Tchudi, 1983). Structuring the content writing process and content writing activities helps students avoid the pitfalls of copying from encyclopedias. Calkins (1986) suggests the following cycle for practical writing.

> Choosing a research area and beginning to focus on a specific topic for writing.
>
> Becoming an expert on the topic (taking notes).
>
> More focusing of one's topic, early analysis of incoming information.
>
> More research.
>
> Readiness for writing: reading, studying models, rehearsing for writing.
>
> Drafts, conferences, redrafts, confering, editing, publishing.
>
> Cycling back for more research with a new focus.

"What can I write about?" is the students' lament. Choosing a topic for writing is not easy. Content textbooks provide a logical starting place for identifying topics. Carefully selected topics make students want to write and want to write well, using their subject matter knowledge in the process (Tchudi and Tchudi, 1983).

Students tend to choose topics that are too broad, such as a third grader who writes a report about birds and attempts to tell all about all of the birds in the world. Recently, a kindergarten neighbor brought home instructions to write a report on 15 different birds in his own handwriting. This is an instance of an assignment that covers too broad a topic. When teacher and pupil remember that the writer should become an "expert" on the topic, their expectations are altered. They recognize that one cannot become an expert on 15 birds, but one can learn about robins. When children select topics on which they would like to become expert, they study and write with greater enthusiasm. Years ago, I remember a sixth grader who decided to become an expert on "black holes." This led to a year-long study including writing that fascinated friends and relatives. That young person has never lost his fascination with "black holes" and is now studying science at a major university.

This list of example content writing topics will help teachers understand how to state writing topics that are interesting to students, as well as sufficiently focused to facilitate writing.

1. Identify three cleaning products found in your home such as laundry detergent, bathroom cleanser, and window cleaner. Make a list of ingredients from each label. Then, based on the unit in your science text, write an explanation of how each product works.

2. Examine insecticides used at home and make a list of the ingredients found on two of these products. Use information in your science text and write an explanation of the cautions that should be exercised in using these products.

3. Read a biography of Jonathan Muir. Identify the incident in his life that you consider the most important and write a short story about it.

4. How did the volcano in Africa cause 1500 people to die? Write a newspaper article explaining how they could have protected themselves from this danger.

5. A class is preparing to bury a time capsule. What objects do you think should be included? Why? Your classmates will study your composition to determine the objects that will be included in the capsule.

6. Make a list of questions about your mathematics unit.

7. Explain how you can use the ideas that you learned in Unit Three of your mathematics text.

8. Study the great sea turtle and write an article that explains why they are almost extinct and how they can be saved.

9. Study the school menus for a week to determine whether they are well balanced. Write a notice or poster for your classmates explaining why they should or should not eat in the cafeteria.

10. Think about your favorite bird. Read about this bird and write a paragraph that explains to one of your friends why this is your favorite bird.

11. After planting a bean seed that doesn't come up, write a paper that explains why it did not grow.

Becoming an Expert   How does one become an "expert" on a topic? By reading, talking, researching, viewing television, movies, and filmstrips, and by interviewing and writing. Student experts state what they have learned in their own words and use their research data to support their conclusions. Students' expertise enables them to communicate understanding rather than reporting a series of facts.

Thaiss (1986) describes a teacher whose third-grade students write to learn. Each student in this class studied one dinosaur. Their research period began with the whole class discussing "research questions" posed by the students. Class members helped each other locate information. Following the discussion, class members generated individual lists of questions to guide their research. The questions lead students to systematically explore their topics rather than haphazardly going from book to book. One student's research questions include: "How tall was the Tyrannosaurus Rex? How many teeth did it have? Where on earth did it live?" (Thaiss, 1986) As students answer their original questions, they usually discover new questions which are added to their lists.

After researching topics of interest, students can write answers to their research questions and to add any other significant facts and data. After a research session, students share their discoveries with a group of four or five which gives them opportunities to rehearse their understanding prior to writing. Subsequent to sharing, students evaluate their own work, scoring their notebooks from one to five, with five meaning "I learned something new and I did a lot of looking" (Thaiss, 1986). Students continue to research until they are "expert" enough to write about their topic.

Informational books can motivate and model practical writing. Following is a list of some excellent informational books that give students an excellent writing model.

Oceanography

Brindze, Ruth. *The Rise and Fall of the Seas; The Story of the Tides.* Harcourt Brace Jovanovich, 1964.

Fichter, George S. *The Future Sea.* Sterling, 1978.

Fisher, James. *The Wonderful World of the Sea.* Doubleday, 1970.

Foster, John. *The Sea Miners.* Hastings, 1977.

Stephens, William. *Come with Me to the Edge of the Sea.* Messner, 1972.

Wolfe, Louis. *Aquaculture: Farming in Water.* Putnam's, 1972.

Mixed Topics

Cole, Joanna. *A Frog's Body.* Morrow, 1980.

Dickinson, Alice. *Carl Linnaeus: Pioneer of Modern Botany.* Watts, 1967.

Kiefer, Irene. *Underground Furnaces: The Story of Geothermal Energy.* Morrow, 1976.

McClung, Robert M. *America's Endangered Birds.* Morrow, 1979.

Milne, Lorus, and Margery. *Gadabouts and Stick-at-Homes.* Scribners, 1980.

Selsam, Millicent, and Jerome Wexler. *Eat the Fruit, Plant the Seed.* Morrow, 1980.

Simon, Seymour. *The Secret Clocks: Time Sense of Living Things.* Viking, 1979.

Readiness for Writing and Drafting   Dorothy Grant Hennings (1982) suggests a variety of strategies to ready students for writing and drafting including:

1. Factstorming

2. Categorizing facts

3. Collaborative drafting of paragraphs on related information and sequencing these paragraphs into a cohesive whole and drafting introductions and conclusions

Factstorming occurs after students have developed expertise regarding their topic through research. In factstorming students randomly call out words and phrases that come to mind on a topic while several students record these on chart paper or on the chalkboard in the order given. For example, a factstorming of pioneer life in America could produce the following list:

walking	wagons	ax
rifle	cow	canoes
rafts	horses	flat boat
logs	tools	cooking utensils
flour	sugar	spinning wheel
flax	wool	linsey-woolsey
deerskin	corn	turkey
mush	porridge	hogs

This prewriting activity would enable many children to write; however, a categorizing strategy can be used after factstorming.

Categorizing helps students organize and relate the collected facts. When categorizing the above information, a teacher could ask students to identify only the items that tell the foods that pioneers ate. Subsequently, they could identify modes of travel, objects that pioneers used, or foods and clothing.

After students organize the data, they can work in writing teams to draft paragraphs for each category on the chart. One member of the team writes the sentences for the paragraph. The paragraphs thus produced will be sequenced into a cohesive report. While the writing teams draft, the teacher circulates and asks questions and provides guidance when it is needed. The writing teams work together to revise and edit their piece once they finish composing. Strategies like the preceding help students learn to draft their own individual pieces later.

Observation   Observation is an important aspect of writing in both fiction and nonfiction. Children learn to write conversation by listening to conversation and observing people as they talk. They learn about creating plots by reading and watching television, but they also learn about plots as they live them. Observation is certainly important in scientific writing and contributes greatly to all other forms of writing. Teachers can stimulate and guide children in using their senses as a tool for writing.

Teachers can bring objects and animals into the classroom for students to see, hear, smell, touch, and when appropriate, taste. Students may use their senses, make notes, and write about their experiences. They may also complete charts as a form of note taking.

	Smell	Touch	Taste	Hear	See
Shells					
Crabs					
Shrimp					
Fish					
Seaweed					

Writing Poetry   Poetry may be either public or private writing. Students may feel that some of their poetry is so personal they do not wish to share it, while there may be other poems they want to share. Poetry is a distillation of ideas and feelings; poets communicate the essence of their subject. Poems are terse, using a few words to convey complex thoughts. Poetry is the ideal medium for examining thoughts and feelings. Children often produce poetic language unintentionally simply because it communicates what they want to say.

As teachers we lead children into writing poetry through reading it aloud, so that they enjoy and appreciate it. Poetry and poetry selection is presented in greater depth in Chapter Nine. Students' experiences with poetry gives them a sense of poetic language, a model for writing poetry. Teachers must provide students with the time to write, read, and rewrite until they shape the poem to their liking. Finally, students should have opportunities to read their poetry aloud, if they choose, to an appreciative audience of classmates and teachers. The appreciation expressed by the important people around them will motivate children to write more poetry.

Writing poetry in the classroom usually falls into two major categories. First, is poetry written on a theme, such as color, feelings, humor, a book, a season of the year, a historical figure, and a concept. Second is the particular form of poetry, such as Haiku, Tanka, and Cinquain. Examples of these are included in this section, as is a lesson plan for writing theme poetry.

Poetry may take many forms. The more common forms that you may choose to use with elementary students are explained in subsequent paragraphs.

Couplets are the simplest type of rhymed verse. Many children produce couplets as they experiment with language. For example, "Pink, pink, she drank some ink." Many jump rope jingles are couplets. The only difficulty in writing couplets is finding rhyming words, and children need to understand that some words do not have rhymes. Couplets are a good poetic form for class compositions and for choral reading.

LESSON PLAN FOR WRITING THEME POETRY

OBJECTIVE:

To write humorous poetry as part of a unit of study of the things that make us laugh.

INTRODUCTION:

Read the following poems from *The New Kid on the Block* by Jack Prelutsky.

"The New Kid on the Block"

"Louder than a Clap of Thunder"

"I'd Never Eat a Beet"

Discuss where the students laughed as they listened to the poems. What do they find funny in television shows?

INSTRUCTION:

Students will choose a funny idea to write about. They may reread the introductory poems or other funny poems to help them form their ideas and communicate them. They may return to these poems over a period of days or weeks as they refine them.

MATERIALS:

The New Kid on the Block by Jack Prelutsky and other humorous poetry that the children enjoy.

SUMMARY: (SYNTHESIS AND EVALUATION)

Ask children who would like to share their poems. You may make a class book of humorous poetry or individual students may create books of humor, incorporating poetry, jokes, stories, etc.

Quatrain is a commonly used verse form which follows the following pattern (Tiedt and Tiedt, 1967).

1. Quatrains contain four lines.

2. The lines are of uniform length.

3. There is rhyme.

4. The rhyme pattern varies.

This poem about Thomas Jefferson is a quatrain.

I was a leader of people as President.
But first I was an author and innovator.
Who proudly established many a precedent.
But most of all I was a bookworm and educator.

Haiku is an unrhymed poetry form created by thirteenth-century Japanese poets, and very popular with American school children. You can find books of Haiku in most libraries and examples of it in most basal readers. Haiku consists of three lines totaling 17 syllables.

Line 1: 5 syllables

Line 2: 7 syllables

Line 3: 5 syllables

The subject of Haiku is usually nature. There is no rhyme, and few pronouns or articles are used. The goal of Haiku is to contrast ideas in a subtle fashion. Children experience more success with Cinquain and Haiku when ideas rather than form are emphasized. In writing these forms of poetry, children should identify the idea they wish to communicate first and to write this idea. They then can play with language until it expresses what they want to say in the selected form.

Cinquains are poems of five lines, although there are many varieties of this invented form. Cinquain is related to Haiku and the stress should be on the thought expressed in the unrhymed lines of cinquain. The five lines are supposed to fit these guidelines:

First line: One word which may be the title

Second line: Two words that describe the title

Third line: Three words that are an action

Fourth line: Four words that are a feeling

Fifth line: One word that refers to the title

Red
Exciting color
With energy jumping
Singing in my head
Glorious

Tanka are also Japanese poems. They contain five lines and these lines include a Haiku in the first three lines. Tanka is also unrhymed and follows a defined pattern with a total of 31 syllables in the five lines.

Line 1: 5 syllables

Line 2: 7 syllables

Line 3: 5 syllables

Line 4: 7 syllables

Line 5: 7 syllables

Teachers Encourage and Support Students' Writing

Through the appreciation we express for children's writing, through listening to them read it and responding appropriately, we encourage students to continue writing. Without an appreciative, responsive audience, many children would not be motivated to write and revise and edit their work. The writing process is arduous and it is important that children stick with it to develop and refine their skills.

The student-teacher conferences discussed in Chapter Seven are another way teachers can support and encourage students writing. Conferences give teachers a means of helping students focus on the topic, a way of getting beyond writer's block, and revising their work until it communicates the way they want it to.

Teachers Help Students Understand the Qualities of Good Writing

Children need to recognize the qualities of good writing, so they will understand the goal of the writing process. Certainly, our students will not all become professional writers, but understanding the qualities of good writing will help them improve the quality of their own writing. Getting children to write is a goal of writing instruction. Students should strive to improve the quality of written expression.

One of the best ways to help children learn about the qualities of good writing is to immerse them in literature of all types. The literature should span the whole of human experience and knowledge and should include all forms of literature; therefore, fiction, nonfiction, picture books, poetry, and drama are significant parts of the reading program.

Literature immersion can be accomplished in a variety of ways. Teachers can and should read aloud to children daily. Children can share excerpts from their favorite authors' writings in the reading-aloud program. Choral reading and creative dramatics are additional ways to expose children to outstanding literature. Another way of exploring literature is to study authors' backgrounds through the booklets and pictures distributed by the publishers. Information about authors is found in reference books like *Books Are by People* (Citation Press, 1969); *The Junior Book of Authors* (eds. S. Kunitz and H. Haycraft; H. W. Wilson, 1953); *More Junior Authors* (ed. M. Fuller; H. W. Wilson, 1963);

and *From Writers to Students; The Pleasures and Pains of Writing* (ed. M. Jerry Weiss; International Reading Association, 1979).

A good way to introduce a study of the qualities of good writing is to ask children to think about the best book they have read (Calkins, 1986). Then the class can identify what characteristics make a book a favorite. Donald Murray, writing about the qualities of good writing, says, "I would prefer it if the standards of good writing and the elements of a good subject arose from the evolving text within the class. A good subject is one that interests first the writer, and then the reader. Good writing is what makes the reader feel or think and the best writing is what makes the reader feel and think (Murray, 1982). Murray identifies six qualities of good writing.

1. Meaning: There must be meaningful content.

2. Authority: Good writing includes specific, accurate, honest information.

3. Voice: Good writing has an individual voice.

4. Development: The writer should satisfy the reader's desire for information.

5. Design: Good writing has form, structure, order, focus, coherence.

6. Clarity: Good writing is marked by simplicity.

A character development lesson for middle-grade students could develop along these lines. The teacher alerts children to the fact that character development is important in fiction. Students identify their favorite fictional characters. Then they explore how the author revealed the character's personality. At this point, students should begin to notice that authors do not just describe characters, they show them—through actions, thoughts, conversations, as well as through their interactions with other characters. Students can find examples of characterization in literature that has well-drawn characters like the following.

The Great Gilly Hopkins by Katherine Paterson. Crowell, 1978.

Call it Courage by Armstrong Sperry. Macmillan, 1941

Anastasia Krupnik by Lois Lowry. Haughton Mifflin, 1979.

Frozen Fire by James Houston. Atheneum, 1970.

Tough Chauncey by Doris Buchanan Smith. Morrow, 1974.

Characterization writing assignments include making comparisons of characters, identifying a character and explaining why you would enjoy having that character for a friend; and explaining why, or projecting what a character will be like as a grown-up.

Young children can study characterization in picture books. In planning picture book lessons, teachers should be sensitive to the fact that characterization is revealed by both pictures and words. However, the techniques for revealing characterization in picture books are the same. The following books can be used for this lesson: *Swimmy* by Leo Lionni (Pantheon, 1963); *Bread and Jam for Frances* by Russell and Lillian Hoban (Harper & Row, 1964), and *Rosie and Michael* by Judith Viorst (Atheneum, 1974).

Teachers Read and Respond to Students' Writing

Evaluation should be a positive response to children's writing that assesses students' progress toward successful communication. The response process is concerned with identifying individuals' strengths and weaknesses at a specific time. Evaluation encourages growth because students who are aware of their strong points will duplicate them and work to overcome their weaknesses (Tiedt et al., 1983).

Evaluation teaches students to judge quality and helps them develop their own standards. Hillocks reports research that shows children who were taught to apply specific criteria made significant gains in the quality of writing revisions and in the frequency of revisions. Hillocks also notes that "as a group, these studies indicate rather clearly that engaging young writers actively in the use of criteria, applied to their own and to others' writing, results not only in more effective revisions but in superior first drafts" (1986). Evaluation helps children become responsible for their revision and editing.

Writing is hard to evaluate because the creative process is uniquely individual. Students differ in maturity, knowledge, and style and these differences are manifested in their compositions. "The students are individuals who must explore the writing process in their own way, some fast, some slow, whatever it takes for them, . . . to find their own way to their own truth" (Murray, 1982). But remember that evaluation is necessary because it helps students develop and refine writing skills.

Formative and Summative Evaluation   Evaluation exists in many forms and for many purposes. In the final analysis all writing evaluation is concerned with the question, "Did the words convey the thought or feeling that the writer intended?" Writing evaluation should be both formative and summative.

Formative evaluation occurs during the writing process. Formative evaluation is concerned with children's growth in the writing process. For instance, are they improving in organizing their thoughts during the prewriting process? How well do they compose, revise, and edit their writings? The prewriting, writing, revising, and editing phases of the writing process all offer opportunities for the teacher and other students to help individual writers. Much formative evaluation takes place during writing conferences with formative data coming from the writer, peers (peer conferences), and teachers in the form of open-ended questions such as, "What is your main point?" or "Can you think of another way to say that?" Formative evaluation does not result in a grade, but it provides encouragement for growth.

Summative evaluation is concerned with judging fully revised writing. In summative evaluation student writers are graded on what they have produced at the end of the writing process. This means that students should choose writing from their folders that they wish to revise and edit to the publishable stage. Summative evaluation should address students' final products. Materials that have not been edited and revised to their satisfaction should not be evaluated.

Teachers Evaluate Final Writing Products

Evaluation techniques should ensure successful writing. Teachers need to suggest interesting and relevant topics and they should allow students to self-select topics. Assignments should be clearly explained. "For example, if the writing is to be in narrative form, review the elements of narration so that students will submit the correct form. Share the criteria for evaluation with the students. Knowing what to include and what to edit for will guide the students appropriately" (Tiedt et al., 1983). Every composition is not evaluated. Children learn to write from the process of exploring, thinking, and experimenting with language; therefore instructional goals can be achieved without evaluating everything children write. Teachers can obtain sufficient evaluative information to guide children's learning through reading samplings of children's compositions. Furthermore, children need to have opportunities to experiment as they write without the pressures of assessment.

Teachers and peer editors should read and respond to writing rather than criticizing it. Whatever form of evaluation is used, students' strengths and weaknesses need to be identified. Teachers and/or class members may tell what they like best and ask questions to clarify points that are unclear. Teachers' and peer editors' positive and negative comments can be written on notes and placed at appropriate places on students' papers; editors call these notes flags. This is a professional approach to editing that demonstrates appropriate respect for children's work.

Comments such as the following illustrate the kinds of positive responses that teachers may make regarding students' writing.

I like the sound of your words.

Your use of the word _____ is very effective.

Your story has lots of action which makes it very interesting.

Your words express meaning very well.

I can picture this description.

You write conversation very well.

Your beginning is especially good (could be middle or end that is good).

Your piece of writing has a beginning, a middle, and an ending.

I know how you felt in this situation.

The example you used here makes your point clearly.

This is a very good paragraph because you have a main idea that you explained with details.

The following comments can be used to indicate that students' need to revise their writing.

Where does this story happen?

Can you give me an example here?

Can you think of another way to say the idea in this sentence?

You have used the word *this* eight times. Can you think of a way to change it in three of these places?

Look at the first two sentences and see if you can think of a word to leave out?

Can you find two sentences that you could leave out?

Holistic Scoring   When using **holistic** scoring essays are given a numerical score representing the rater's opinion of the overall quality of the essay. The rater or raters are instructed to read the essay quickly and to score it as a whole without pondering the parts. However, when teachers evaluate writing as a basis for helping students they need to supplement holistic evaluation with analytic scoring to help pinpoint specific strengths and weaknesses. In this instance, a scale of criteria and ratings called a *rubric* is used to guide evaluation and to ensure objective judgments. Table 8.1 is a rubric that demonstrates holistic scoring criteria for narrative.

Table 8.1   Holistic Scoring Criteria for Narrative

Name _____   Date _____

Analytic Scale for Holistic Scoring

	Low		Average		High
Wording	1	2	3	4	5
Ideas	1	2	3	4	5
Organization	1	2	3	4	5
Syntax	1	2	3	4	5
Usage	1	2	3	4	5
Spelling	1	2	3	4	5
Punctuation	1	2	3	4	5

Evaluator _____

Primary Trait Scoring   Primary trait scoring assesses predetermined features that are crucial to the success of a particular writing task. For example, instructions from a teacher must be logical and unambiguous if readers are to follow them. The primary trait of written directions is an unambiguous, sequential, and logical progress of instructions. Successful writing will exhibit that trait while unsuccessful writings will not. When using primary trait scoring, everything is ignored except the primary trait that was announced for the writing assignment. Primary trait writings are usually evaluated with a numerical score that ranges from 1 to 4 with 4 being the highest score. An example of primary trait scoring follows.

Assignment: Pretend it is your birthday and your mother invited your friends for a surprise party. Write about how you feel. What happens at your party? How do you feel about the activities and presents?

Primary trait: Expression of feeling through elaboration of a role.

1 = No established role. The student writes about a party, but does not assume the role of a birthday child. Does not relate to the party activities.

2 = Little or no elaboration of role. No distinctive character or personality emerges. Reports activities, but does not relate feelings.

3 = Good elaboration of role. Expresses attitudes and feelings. Develops party activities, games, presents. May include some irrelevant details.

4 = Inventive and consistent elaboration of role. Use of vivid and creative details to sustain the role. Does not lapse out of role. Includes few if any irrelevancies.

Other = Illegible, illiterate, misunderstood task, writes on a different topic or responds "I don't know."

Children's Scoring   Whatever scoring strategy is used students should have opportunities to respond to the scoring of teachers or peers. They may explain some criticisms and make needed changes when appropriate. Conferences give teachers a chance to share their evaluation of students' writing and to help them use the evaluation data to improve their writing. Children should have opportunities to evaluate their own writing. Although, self-evaluation is difficult it is valuable for students (Tiedt et al., 1983). Figure 8.3 shows a self-evaluation form for children.

TROUBLESHOOTING

One of the most common questions teachers raise about writing is how to correct errors in grammar, spelling, and punctuation. Teachers realize that they can inhibit children's writing when they identify errors, but at the same time they feel that ignoring mistakes will cause children to develop sloppy writing habits. Conferences between teachers and students, as well as peer conferences help writers revise and edit until their writing meets conventional standards. Teachers must realize that writing will improve with time

---

SELF-EVALUATION

Name _____ Date _____

Title _____

Why I wrote this paper (no more than two sentences) _____

_____

The best thing about my composition is _____

_____

_____

The hardest thing about writing this paper was _____

_____

I can make my paper better if I _____

_____

I think my grade should be _____

Figure 8.3   Self-evaluation guide for writing.

and practice. Children do not develop into writers in one day or one year. They develop gradually toward the goal of communicating their ideas and feelings.

Many teachers express writing "aversion" and avoid writing. Teachers who have negative attitudes toward writing find it difficult to motivate children to write. They also have difficulty writing with their students in spite of the fact that authorities like Donald Graves (1983) recommend this practice. In order to develop more positive attitudes toward writing, teachers may keep journals or write reviews of movies and television shows. They may enroll in writing institutes or courses.

Grading children's compositions presents problems for many teachers. They do not want to inhibit children's writing through evaluation, but they feel that evaluation is their responsibility. Teachers should experiment with holistic scoring, analytic scoring, and primary trait scoring, keeping in mind that they do not need to evaluate every piece of writing. Using a variety of scoring techniques, reading content aloud, scheduling revision conferences during the writing process, and grouping for peer evaluation help give children the evaluative data they need to improve their writing without making children feel that they are incompetent.

Writer's block is a problem for some students. Writer's block may occur at the beginning of a writing session or in the middle of a session. Some writers are helped when the teacher tells them to write "I can't think of anything to write" until they think of something to write. In other instances, brainstorming and writing words that are related to the topic help students get the momentum to write. Reading books, especially those written by other children, stimulates some children; these may be compositions by classmates or published materials like those in *New Births New Breaths* published by the North Carolina Council of the International Reading Association. Teachers can find many useful suggestions in the book, *Sparkling Words: Three Hundred and Fifteen Practical and Creative Writing Ideas* by Ruth Kearney Carlson.

Many teachers feel that they do not have enough time for children to write every day in spite of the fact that they recognize the importance of writing for children. They feel pressured to teach the skills that are assessed on standardized testing instruments and teaching these skills does not leave much time for writing. There are no easy solutions to such a complicated problem, but children can learn quite a bit about writing when they write daily for 10 or 15 minute segments (this writing plan is further explicated in the following item). A carefully planned writing program can be implemented without an investment of an hour each day. Children may write in their daily journals if they have individual time during the school day. Compositions can be revised and edited for homework, thus saving classroom time. Teachers and parents should remember that children think and learn through their writing; therefore children should write in every subject area. This will increase their subject matter understanding, as well as their writing competence.

A pressing problem for some teachers is how to initiate a writing program when the children have no writing experience and/or the teacher lacks experience in teaching writing. In such situations, teachers may initiate a two-week writing program by following the suggested schedule, which is designed to ease students and teachers into daily writing while addressing all aspects of the writing process. This program starts students thinking about audience, initiates writing conferences, and lays a foundation for evaluation. Writing topics are suggested for this program; however, children who indicate that they would like to self-select topics should be encouraged to do so. The goal of all writing programs is for students to choose their own topics.

 WRITING PROGRAM—WEEK ONE

MONDAY

Demonstrate the composing process with an overhead projector or a large piece of paper. The teacher selects a topic that is familiar and demonstrates to students prewriting, composing, and revising. Think aloud during boardwork. This permits students to observe their teacher working through the writing processes, as well as making mistakes, selecting the appropriate word to express an idea, crossing out words and moving sentences around to better express ideas. Demonstrate dating and signing compositions, so that students develop this habit at the outset. Students who observe the teacher working through the writing process understand what they are supposed to do when they write. They also learn that compositions do not flow from the pen in finished form. Teachers of young children demonstrate the writing process every time they compose a language experience chart. They can make the most of these activities by talking about their thought processes as they write.

TUESDAY

On this day the teacher demonstrates how to create written conversations. The teacher writes a question on an overhead transparency or a large piece of paper and invites a student to respond to the question. After the student writes a response, the teacher writes another question and the student writes a response. This continues until the conversation reaches a conclusion. After the demonstration, pair students to write conversations with one another. In classrooms where computers are available or in computer labs, students can write their conversations on the computers.

WEDNESDAY

The assignment is a group story. The teacher identifies a topic that is familiar to the students and tells the students to think of a sentence related to the topic. This is their prewriting period. After two to three minutes the teacher tells the students to write their sentences. The teacher begins the group composition by writing the main idea on the chalkboard and then asks students to contribute sentences that fit into the composition. If there is a computer in the classroom, the composition can be done on the computer. When the group compositions are completed, give each student a file folder for their writing. They may decorate their files as they wish. These files are placed in a file drawer; if there are no file drawers available then make one from a box.

THURSDAY

Today's assignment is to write for ten minutes on their favorite subject. Explain they should get their ideas on paper, and that punctuation, spelling, and capitalization will be taken care of as they revise and edit. Some students may have trouble getting started, so the teacher should be prepared to confer with them about favorite books, television shows, hobbies, and vacation trips to get them going. If all else fails, have them write, "I can't think of anything to write" until they think of something to write. The teacher writes while the students are writing. This composition should be placed in their folder.

FRIDAY

The students write about five things that make them feel good today. While the students are writing the teacher should circulate around the classroom conferring with children who need assistance. These compositions are placed in their folders.

WRITING PROGRAM—WEEK TWO

MONDAY

The writing topic today is "foods I like." Brainstorm the topic with the children. Write the words they brainstorm on the chalkboard (prewriting). Allow the students a minute and a half to think about their own ideas. Then start writing, allowing the children 15 minutes to write. When the students are finished, ask if anyone would like to read their composition aloud. If too many children volunteer, place their names in a box and draw out as many as you have time to hear. If no one volunteers to read, do not force them. When the reading is completed have the children put the compositions in their writing folders.

TUESDAY

"How I am different from my best friend" is today's writing subject. During the prewriting session, discuss comparison and contrast. You may read some examples of this writing style. Follow up with students brainstorming contrasts such as things that are fast and slow like a turtle and a kangaroo. Then have students make a list of ways they are different from their best friend. If you are doing this activity in grades four, five, or six, you may carry the activity over to the next day. However, primary grade teachers will probably have the children write their compositions on the same day as the prewriting session.

WEDNESDAY

Middle-grade students may write their contrast composition today. Primary grade teachers can bring objects into the classroom like: a smooth stone, an irregular piece of an eraser, a glass marble, a piece of sandpaper, a piece of metal, a shell, or a small piece of driftwood. The teacher may read a book like *Swimmy* by Leo Lionni to the class to prepare them to write interesting descriptions. After reading the book, ask the children to think of words that describe the way that the objects look, feel, and sound. Write the words on the chalkboard. Then ask the students to describe one of the objects by comparing it to other objects, colors, or sounds. Explain to the students that the person reading their composition should be able to visualize the object after reading the composition. This writing goes in their folders.

THURSDAY

Today's topic is "The most important thing that happened to me this week." After a three-minute prewriting period, give the children ten minutes to write. Then pair the children and ask them to read their compositions to each other. Place this writing in their folders.

FRIDAY

Assign each youngster a peer editor. Then have each student choose one piece of writing that they would like to revise and edit for publication. They should spend this period revising and conferring with peer editors. The teacher should have as many student conferences as time permits.

SUMMARY

Teachers play a major role in developing writing skills. They help students understand writing, and they model writing through their own writing. Among the ways that they guide students' writing development are: helping students select and focus topics; helping students become experts on their topics; publishing, reading, and responding to students' writing; and guiding students into writing in various forms such as journals and poetry.

Literature provides both a model and a motivator for writing. Writers learn how to write from reading literature; therefore, teachers should read poetry, fiction, and nonfiction to their students to create writing models. Some literature stimulates children to write new episodes, new characters, and/or new endings.

Although it is not necessary to evaluate all of children's writing, identifying students' strengths and weaknesses helps them refine their writing skills. Two general approaches are used to evaluate children's writing—holistic and primary trait. Writing can be self-evaluated as well as evaluated by teachers and peers. Evaluative information can be given to students in conferences and through written comments.

Teachers regularly encounter problems in teaching writing, which fall into the following categories: motivating students to write; writer's block; evaluation of students' writing; teachers' aversion to writing; time to write; and teachers and students who are inexperienced writers.

Thought Questions

1. What are the major themes in this chapter?

2. Compare holistic evaluation with primary trait evaluation. Which do you prefer? Why?

3. How can evaluation improve writing?

4. Discuss the teacher's role in developing children's writing competence.

5. How do professional writers help us understand the writing process?

6. What is the relationship between the language conventions (spelling, handwriting, punctuation, capitalization, and grammar) and writing (composition)?

Enrichment Activities

1. Plan a writing lesson using literature as a writing model. Teach this lesson if possible.

2. Visit an elementary classroom and obtain examples of children's writing. Evaluate the writing using holistic evaluation and holistic analytic evaluation. What are each writer's strengths and weaknesses?

3. Use the directions in this chapter to make a bound book.

4. Interview children at various grade levels to determine how much writing they do in class and whether they enjoy writing.

5. Start your own journal, making sure that you write in it each day.

6. Read two of the related readings. How do the authors' ideas compare to those expressed in this chapter?

Selected Readings

Burrows, A.; D. Jackson; D. Saunders (1984). *They All Want to Write* (4th ed.). Hamden, CN: Library Professional Publications.

Carlson, R. K. (1979). *Sparkling Words: Three Hundred and Fifteen Practical and Creative Writing Ideas.* Geneva, IL: Paladin House Publishers.

Cooper, C. R., and L. Odell (1977). *Evaluating Writing.* Buffalo, NY: State University of New York.

Daniels, H., and S. Zemelman (1985). *A Writing Project: Training Teachers of Composition from Kindergarten to College.* Portsmouth, NH: Heinemann.

Graves, D. H. (1983). *Writing: Teachers and Children at Work.* Portsmouth, NH: Heinemann.

Hansen, J.; T. Newkirk; and D. Graves (eds.) (1985). *Breaking Ground: Teachers Relate Reading and Writing in the Elementary School.* Portsmouth, NH: Heinemann.

Hillocks, G. (1986). *Research on Written Composition.* Urbana, IL: National Conference on Research in English.

Mosenthal P.; L. Tamor; and S. Walmsley (1983). *Research on Writing.* New York, NY: Longmans.

Sealey, L.; N. Sealey; and M. Millmore (1979). *Children's Writing: An Approach for the Primary Grades.* Newark: DE: International Reading Association.

Stewig, J. (1975). *Read to Write.* New York: Hawthorne Publishers.

Tiedt, I.; S. Bruemmer; S. Lane; P. Stelwagon; K , Watanabe; and M. Williams (1983). *Teaching Writing in K-8 Classrooms.* Englewood Cliffs, NJ: Prentice-Hall.

Tway, E. (1985). *Writing is Reading.* Urbana, IL: National Council of Teachers of English.

Weiss, M. J. (ed.) (1979). *From Writers to Students: The Pleasures and Pains of Writing.* Newark, DE: International Reading Association.

Wolfe, D., and R. Reising (1983). *Writing for Learning in the Content Areas.* Portland, MA: Weston Walch, Publisher.

Ziegler, A. (1981). *The Writing Workshop.* New York, NY: Teachers and Writers Collaborative.

References

Calkins, L. M. (1986). *The Art of Teaching Writing.* Portsmouth, NH: Heinemann.

Gardner, J. (1984). *The Art of Fiction.* New York: Alfred A. Knopf.

Graves, Donald H. (1983). *Writing: Teachers and Children at Work.* Portsmouth, NH: Heinemann Educational Books.

Haley-James, S. (1981). "Twentieth-Century Perspectives on Writing in Grades One through Eight." *Perspectives on Writing. In Grades 1–8,* S. Haley-James (ed.). Urbana, IL: National Council of Teachers of English.

Hennings, D. (1982). *Communication in Action: Teaching the Language Arts* (2d ed.). Boston: Houghton Mifflin.

Hillocks, G. (1986). *Research on Written Composition.* Urbana, IL: National Conference on Research in English.

Martin, N. (1983). *Mostly About Writing.* Montclair, NJ: Boynton/Cook.

Murray, D. M. (1982). *Learning by Teaching.* Montclair, NJ: Boynton/Cook.

Tchudi, S., and S. Tchudi (1983). *Teaching Writing in the Content Areas: Elementary School.* Washington DC: National Education Association.

Thaiss, C. (1986). *Language Across the Curriculum in the Elementary Grades.* Urbana, IL: National Council of Teachers of English.

Tiedt, I., and S. Tiedt (1967). *Contemporary English in the Elementary School.* Englewood Cliffs, NJ: Prentice-Hall.

Tiedt, I.; S. Bruemmer; S. Lane; P. Stelwagon; K. Watanabe; and M. Williams (1983). *Teaching Writing in K-8 Classrooms.* Englewood Cliffs, NJ: Prentice-Hall.

Wilde, J., and T. Newkirk (March 1981). "Writing Detective Stories." *Language Arts* 58 (3), 286–292.

Chapter **Nine**

Children's Literature

CHAPTER OVERVIEW

Literature is one foundation of the English language arts. Literature is the content of the language arts and a form of art because authors express their perspectives of the world through literature. Fiction, nonfiction, and poetry should be an important part of the language arts curriculum because they have so many values for students. Literature contributes to language development, sense of story, experience, knowledge, aesthetic and creative development, and multicultural education. Teachers need to choose books that children will enjoy and appreciate, so they will be motivated to read. Literature should be incorporated in classroom activities through reading to children, book discussions, writing, and aesthetic activities.

Anticipation Guide

Think about these following questions before reading this chapter. Can you remember your favorite book or story from elementary school? What was it? What did you like about it? Did you ever have a teacher who read to you regularly? What do you remember about him or her? Read the following questions and try to answer them as you read this chapter.

1. What are the values of literature for elementary children?

2. How is literature related to speaking, listening, reading, and writing?

3. What are the structural elements of fiction?

Key Concepts

plot	story grammar
setting	theme
style	characterization
story structure	

INTRODUCTION

Why is literature so vital to the language arts? Researchers show that children take over the language they hear and read and use it as part of their own (Cazden, 1972; Chomsky, 1972; White, 1984). "Children make literary language part of their own language because it is memorable" (Cullinan, 1987). Good stories make children listen, talk, read, and write. This is an important factor in teaching the language arts, since they are learned through use. Literature should permeate language arts instruction. "You can't teach reading comprehension if you don't have a good story to work with" (Cullinan, 1987). Literature provides strong language models. Hearing and reading good stories helps build vocabulary, sharpens language sensitivity, and develops students' sense of writing style.

A SIX-YEAR OLD EXPERIENCES LITERATURE

Ann Williams took her six-year old daughter, Ginny, to the public library last Monday evening. Ginny chose three picture books, *Clifford The Big Red Dog, Regards to the Man in the Moon,* and *Red Is Best.* When they arrived home, Ginny asked her mother to read *Red Is Best* aloud. Ann asked Ginny why she chose that book first and Ginny responded, "Because I like red best of all."

Ginny pointed out words she recognized as Ann read.

> But how can I be Red Riding Hood in my blue jacket? I like my red jacket the best. I like my red boots the best. . . . my red boots take bigger steps. I like my red boots the best. . . . my red pyjamas keep the monsters away when I'm sleeping. I like my red pyjamas the best. . . . juice tastes better in the red cup. I like the red cup best. . . . my red barrettes make my hair laugh. I like my red barrettes best. . . . red paint puts singing in my head. I like the red paint best. (Stinson, 1982).

Ginny clapped her hands and laughed, "That girl's just like me. I like red best too." As she went to bed, she sang, "Red is best, red is best, it puts singing in my head." The next day Ginny took *Red Is Best* to school so she could retell the story for "Talking Time." Later during "Writing Time" she decided to create her own book about red. Ginny wrote and illustrated the following book that expressed her thoughts about red.

> I lik red best. I lik my red drs and my red shz and my red blnkt. I lik red flerz and red carz. My fren Kelly likz blue. I lik red.

Literature and Ginny

Ginny's experiences with *Red Is Best* illustrate the value of literature for language arts development. Literature is both an end and a means. The entertainment that literature provides makes it an end in itself, but literature also extends listening, speaking, reading, and writing skills. Ginny enjoyed the book her mother read. She listened and pointed to words. Ginny understood (comprehended) the feelings the author expressed because she related them to her own experiences with red. Ginny responded to the book *Red Is Best* in singing and repeating her favorite words and phrases from the story. Later, she spoke as she retold the story to her classmates.

Ginny wrote her own version of *Red Is Best* which involved semantics, syntax, spelling, handwriting, and punctuation; then she read and reread her draft. Her writing demonstrated that she understood how to express her ideas in written language. She drew pictures to illustrate her book.

CHILDREN'S LITERATURE

The preceding vignette demonstrates the powerful force of literature in the language arts and makes us aware that literature in its various forms is the content of the language arts. Children talk about, listen to, read, write, and appreciate literature. The National Council of Teachers of English (1983) tells us that literature is "one of the primary means by which a culture transmits itself. The reading and study of literature add a special dimension to students' lives by broadening their insights, allowing them to experience vicariously places, people, and events otherwise unavailable to them, and adding delight and wonder to their daily lives."

Children's literature is literature that appeals to children, that addresses their experiences and interests. It has all of the qualities of adult literature. "The skilled author does not write differently or less carefully for children just because he thinks they will not be aware of style or language" (Huck et al., 1987).

Literature is a form of art, wherein an author creates a unique statement through careful and precise use of language. This verbal expression of the human imagination is apparent in the language of a book like Leo Lionni's *Swimmy.* Swimmy, a small black fish is saddened when his school of fish is gobbled up by a hungry tuna:

> He swam away in the deep wet world. He was scared, lonely and very sad. However, his spirits brightened as he saw the marvels in the ocean depths. He saw a medusa made of rainbow jelly . . . a lobster, who walked about like a water-moving machine . . . a forest of seaweeds growing from sugar-candy rocks . . . an eel whose tail was almost too far away to remember . . . (Lionni, 1963).

Byrd Baylor, an artist indeed, makes us hear the rocks in *The Other Way to Listen*:

Of course
their kind of singing
isn't loud.

It isn't
any sound
you can explain.

It isn't
made
with words.

You couldn't
write it down. . . . (Baylor, 1978)

Poets and storytellers are artists, but so are the practical writers who express their art through informational books. Tomie de Paola makes information very interesting in books like *The Popcorn Book, The Cloud Book, The Quicksand Book, The Kids' Cat Book,* and *The Family Christmas Book.* In *The Popcorn Book* he informs us that the American Indians liked popcorn and had a variety of ways to pop it.

One way was to put an ear of corn on a stick and hold it over a fire. . . . Another way was to throw the kernels right into the fire by the handful. The popcorn popped out all over the place, so there was a lot of bending and running around to gather it up.

WHAT LITERATURE DOES FOR CHILDREN

The preceding sections have alerted you to some of the ways that children's literature contributes to students' lives. In this chapter we are largely concerned with children's language development, their sense of story, their experiences, their storehouse of knowledge, their aesthetic and creative development, and multicultural education. Subsequent sections in this chapter will explore these aspects of literature in greater detail.

Literature Extends Language

Literature is a source of mature, expressive language for children who are learning language. They build a storehouse of linguistic possibilities from listening to and reading literature. Children listening to stories like *Swimmy* are exposed to richer language than that which they hear in everyday conversation. They use the language they hear to construct the grammar, or rules, of language, which enables them to generate language.

Written language differs from oral language. Authors use more compound and complex sentences when they write, as you can see in the following excerpt from *Miss Maggie*:

Miss Maggie tended a garden alongside the old log house. But what with cows, dogs, and boys occasionally passing through, Miss Maggie's garden didn't grow a lot. Still, there was always a potato or two to boil. Nat would see Miss Maggie rising up from the soil, her brown, wrinkled face partly hidden by a faded blue bonnet (Rylant, 1983).

Children learn about English word order and how to impart information in English sentences when they listen to selections like the preceding.

Chomsky (1972) found that young children who were read a large number of linguistically complex books realized significantly greater linguistic development than did children who did not have this experience. In this study, the positive relationship between linguistic development and exposure to literature was true for young children who listened to stories and for older children who read their own stories. The young children who exhibited greater linguistic complexity had heard more books—and more linguistically complex books—each week than had the children who manifested lower linguistic development. Cohen (1968) also found that reading literature aloud and participating in follow-up activities caused significant improvement in second graders' word knowledge and reading comprehension. After examining related research the Commission on Reading concluded, "The single most important activity for building the knowledge required for eventual success in reading is reading aloud to children" (Anderson et al., 1985).

Clearly, teachers and parents should read literature aloud to children every day. Reading aloud to children should not be limited to young children; sixth graders benefit as much from listening to stories as do first graders. Suggestions for selecting books and reading aloud are introduced later in this chapter.

Learning Words   The majority of English words represent concepts; for instance, the words, horse, mountain, and freedom each are labels for concepts. Thus when children expand their vocabulary, they are usually expanding their store of concepts. Learning concept labels (words) also enables children to communicate their ideas to others. Words in isolation have no meaning. When we hear the word *run,* the meaning is not apparent until we read the context to determine whether it is a *run* in a stocking or a *run* performed by a person whose legs are moving. Children acquire word meanings from reading literature because the words appear in context that gives them meaning.

Whenever children read, they are expanding and refining word meanings; however, some books emphasize word meanings. For example, *Snake In, Snake Out* by Linda Banchek explores prepositions such as "in" and "out." The story line is concerned with an old lady's efforts to get rid of a snake. Students can look at the illustrations and tell what is happening by using the word at the bottom of the page; the illustrations show several instances of each concept. In Kathy Stinson's book *Big or Little?,* a boy voices his feelings about "big" and "little."

> You know, sometimes I feel so big.
> When I can tie my shoes,
> and zip my jeans
> and button my shirt all by myself,
> that means I'm big.
> But sometimes I feel so little.
> When I can't reach the button when I go and visit my friend,
> that means I'm little (Stinson, 1983).

The author and illustrator of *Busy Day,* Betsy and Giulio Maestro, show an elephant and a man, who are the protagonists of the story, engaging in the action that the verb describes. For "washing" the man is at a sink, wiping his bald head with a wet washcloth. The elephant creates his own shower by spraying himself with his trunk. The illustrations give a context for the verbs and they tell a story about the man and the elephant who are circus performers. *I Think I Thought and Other Trick Verbs* by Marvin Terban explores 30 irregular verbs like "blow," "break," and "bring." The author relies on alliteration and illustrations to interest children as you can see from the following quotation.

Charlie *chooses* chowder, not chop suey.
Chiquita *chose* cheesecake that was gooey.
Celia Seagull *sees* sailors in the sea.
Simon Salmon *saw* a ghostly jamboree.

Homonyms include words that sound alike (homophones) but differ in meaning, such as "blue" and "blew," and words that are spelled alike but are pronounced differently and have different meanings (homographs), such as "wind the clock" and "the wind is blowing." Terban combines riddles and homonyms in his book, *Eight Ate A Feast of Homonym Riddles.* The fun in Emily Hanlon's book *How a Horse Grew Hoarse on the Site Where He Sighted a Bare Bear* begins with the title and escalates as one reads. Bernice Hunt also explores homonyms in her book *Your Ant Is a Which.*

Words, Words, Words by Mary O'Neill can help children develop concepts of word meanings, as well as concepts of language, grammar, and words. The poet explores the essence of such words as "contentment" and "happiness." Middle-grade students may write their own notions of the concepts presented in this volume.

Letters and Numbers in Literature   Alphabet books and counting books are naturally interesting to young children and they are vehicles for developing concepts, words, and sounds. Following are some alphabet and counting books that are popular with children.

Alphabet Books

Chess, Victoria. *Alfred's Alphabet Walk.* Greenwillow, 1979.

Crowther, Robert. *The Most Amazing Hide and Seek Alphabet Book.* Viking, 1978.

Emberley, Ed. *Ed Emberley's ABC.* Little, Brown, 1978.

Munari, Bruno. *Bruno Munari's ABC.* Collins-World, 1960.

Piatti, Celestino. *Celestino Piatti's Animal ABC.* Atheneum, 1966.

Yolen, Jane. *All the Woodland Early: An ABC Book.* Collins-World, 1979.

Counting Books

Bayley, Nicola. *One Old Oxford Ox.* Atheneum, 1977.

Sendak, Maurice. *Seven Little Monsters.* Harper & Row, 1977.

Yolen, Jane. *An Invitation to the Butterfly Ball: A Counting Rhyme.* Parents, 1976.

In addition to the books mentioned in this section, a number of authors write rhyming narratives that preschool and primary-grade children enjoy. These authors include Byrd Baylor, Ludwig Bemelmans, Margaret Wise Brown,

Lucille Clifton, Janina Domanska, Aileen Fisher, Virginia Kahl, Jack Prelutsky, and Rosemary Wells. Middle-grade children will enjoy the work of
poets David McCord, Eve Merriam, and Clyde Watson.

Figurative Language   Figurative language can be problematic for children
and for people who are learning English as a second language. However, social
interaction with others who use figurative language encourages children to do
the same (Cullinan, 1981). Children who are exposed to numerous examples
of figurative language are more likely to master it. Children's literature is an
obvious source of examples because authors so often use figurative language
in writing for children.

Swimmy, which was discussed earlier in this chapter, is an excellent
source of figurative language for class discussion. In *A Wet and Sandy Day*
Joanne Ryder makes extensive use of figurative language which children
understand because it relates to their experiences. Katherine Paterson and
Natalie Babbitt who write for middle-grade students frequently use figurative language to evoke mental images, especially in Babbitt's *The Eyes of the
Amaryllis.*

> The beaming sea lay far out, at low tide, much as it had the afternoon before,
> and it sparkled in the early sunshine, flicking tiny, blinding flashes of light into
> the air. The horizon, impossibly far away, invited her. This was a mermaid
> morning—a morning for sitting on the rocks and combing your long red hair
> (Babbitt, 1977).

In *Bridge to Terabithia,* Katherine Paterson describes Jesse's feelings as
"mad as flies in a fruit jar" and bubbling inside him "like a stew on the back
of the stove," while she describes Gilley's mother as "a flower-child gone to
seed" in the *Great Gilley Hopkins.* These rather homely images extend students'
understanding of the author's ideas and of language.

Idioms are a picturesque use of figurative language that confuse the
literal minded reader. In Fred Gwynne's books *The King Who Reigned, A Chocolate
Moose for Dinner,* and *A Sixteen Hand Horse* we see a king who is raining and a
car pool (cars in a swimming pool). Peggy Parrish's *Amelia Bedelia* is a literal
minded maid who makes clothing for a chicken when she is instructed to
"dress a chicken" and she draws pictures of drapes when she is told to "draw
the drapes." After reading books like the preceding many children enjoy
illustrating idioms or creating their own books of idioms.

Language Exploration   All of the books discussed in the language section
contribute to a playful attitude toward language. In addition to the books
discussed in preceding sections, books of tongue twisters, riddles, jokes, and
puns add to children's language play. For example, young children enjoy the
language play in Naomi Bossom's turnabout book, *A Scale Full of Fish and Other
Turnabouts.* A turnabout is "race for a train," and its opposite "train for a race."
After the children grasp the pattern they can guess the turnabouts. In *Big Pig,*

Dennis Nolan describes overweight animals with rhyming words like "Whopper Grasshopper" and "Fat Bat." Steven Kroll says, "Edward clumped out of bed . . . fumbled over his flippers and splashed to a roar" in *Gobbledygook*, while Nicola Bayley uses alliteration and internal rhyme in *The Patchwork Cat.* The rhythm, rhyme, and sound repetition in Mother Goose rhymes is good language play for youngsters.

Rhythm and rhyme

Tom, Tom, the piper's son,
Stole a pig, and away he run.
The pig was eat, and Tom was beat,
And Tom went roaring down the street.

Alliteration

Peter Piper picked a peck of pickled peppers
A peck of pickled peppers Peter Piper picked;
If Peter Piper picked a peck of pickled peppers,
Where's the peck of pickled peppers Peter Piper picked?

Repetition

Polly put the kettle on,
Polly put the kettle on,
Polly put the kettle on,
    We'll all have tea.

Sukey take it off again,
Sukey take it off again,
Sukey take it off again,
They've all gone away.

Children enjoy the repeated patterns of sounds, words, and phrases in some books. Wanda Gag does this in *Millions of Cats;* Asphyr Slobodkina uses this technique in *Caps for Sale;* as does Julia Scheer in *Rain Makes Applesauce.* Ruth Kraus creates splendid language play in her book *A Very Special House.*

I know a house—
it's not a squirrel house
it's not a donkey house
—just like I said—
and it's not up on a mountain
and it's not down in a valley
and it's not down in a hole

. . .

oh it's right in the middle—
oh it's ret in the meedle—
oh it's root in the moodle of my head head head (Kraus, 1953).

Additional books that encourage language exploration include:

Bishop, Ann. *Oh Riddlesticks.* Whitman, 1976.

Juster, Norton. *The Phantom Tollbooth.* Random House, 1961.

Keller, Charles. *Ballpoint Bananas and Other Jokes for Kids.* Prentice-Hall, 1973.

———. *Daffinitions.* Prentice-Hall, 1976.

———. *Glory, Glory, How Peculiar.* Prentice-Hall, 1976.

———. *Going Bananas.* Prentice-Hall, 1975.

Rees, Ennis. *Pun Fun.* Abelard-Shuman, 1965.

Sarnoff, Jane. *The Monster Riddle Book.* Scribners, 1975.

Schwartz, Alvin. *A Twister of Twists, A Tangler of Tongues.* Lippincott, 1972.

Seuss, Dr. *Horton Harches the Egg.* Random House, 1957.

———. *Yertle the Turtle and Other Stories.* Random House, 1958.

Language Patterns   Patterned language is frequently found in literature and it has a particular appeal to children. In fact, children enjoy the language play of repeating language patterns they hear in stories like *Henny Penny,* and they enjoy chanting the refrain from such stories. *The Little Engine That Could* is a long-time favorite and many people immediately remember the line "I think I can," which the little engine repeats going up the mountain and the refrain "I thought I could" that the engine repeats coming down the mountain. Another old favorite that can be read, sung, or chanted is *I Know an Old Lady.* The old lady swallowed a fly, and she keeps swallowing larger and larger animals to eliminate the fly. All the while, the spider that she first swallowed to catch the fly continues to squirm and wriggle inside her.

The book *Fortunately* is based on a pattern of opposites like those found in traditional literature and frequently seen in contemporary television shows. In this book, Ned is invited to a birthday party, but unfortunately the party is in Florida.

> Fortunately, a friend lent him an airplane.
> Unfortunately, the motor exploded.
> Fortunately, there was a parachute in the airplane.
> Unfortunately, there was a hole in the parachute.

This book can be used as a basis for writing activities, drama, and art.

Mercer Mayer used a pattern in creating *What Do You Do with a Kangaroo?* Throughout the story, the protagonist deals with a variety of obstreperous animals and queries "Well, what do you do when a kangaroo jumps in your bed and starts to boss you around? Or a llama starts trying on your blue jeans? Or a tiger takes over your tricycle?" The fierce little girl in this book asks

"What do you do?" but she seems to know what to do. Children enjoy thinking of their own ways to handle such aggravating animals and creating surprise endings like Mercer Mayer did. Shel Silverstein uses a similar pattern when he asks, *Who Wants a Cheap Rhinoceros?* In this book he cites the things a cheap rhinoceros can do like eating bad report cards before parents see them. Children can choose an animal and write their own book; for example, they might ask "Who Wants a Cheap Giraffe?

Literature Develops a Sense of Story Structure

Children acquire a concept of narrative or **story structure** from listening to and reading stories. They use their concept of narrative structure to tell stories, listen to stories, read stories, and write stories. The concept of narrative structure is also called a "story schema" which is a cognitive structure identifying the components of and the structure of stories (Stein and Glenn, 1979). For example, stories include plot, setting, and characterization (Applebee, 1978; Stein, 1979). Children who have repeated exposures to literature develop concepts of what goes into a story. After hearing over and over stories that have characters, students will expect a story to have characters. When they hear a new story, they will be ready to assign someone to the role of character. "Story schemas" enable students to anticipate that new stories will have the same components as the stories they have listened to and read.

Story grammars are concerned with the network of relationships among the components of stories. Experienced readers realize intuitively that there is a relationship between the setting and the characters' actions in many stories. In the book *Swimmy*, Swimmy is the main character who loses his family to a hungry tuna. Swimmy then explores the ocean floor and sees many marvels. His actions are determined by the setting in this story.

Virtually all stories told in the Western culture share certain elements which include *a character, a setting, a problem, an attempt or attempts to overcome the problem,* and *a conclusion.* In most stories, the problem, the attempts to overcome the problem, and the conclusions become *episodes.* Some stories have only one problem, attempt, conclusion sequence (episode) while others have several episodes. Following is a chart identifying the components of a story and the story grammar (relationships among the aspects of the story) in *Regards to the Man in the Moon* by Ezra Jack Keats.

Setting	Junkyard
Characters	Louie Louie's parents Susie
Problem	The children are laughing at Louie because his father is a junk dealer.
Attempt (action)	Louie and his parents get to work and build the "Imagination I."

	Louie and Susie go out of the world in the "Imagination I." Their vehicle is powered by imagination.
	They see many wondrous things as they travel.
	They are halted by Ziggie and Ruthie who decided to follow them, but they used up all of their imagination and are stuck.
	Susie and Louie help them rediscover their imagination, and they are able to return home.
Resolution	Soon all the kids were ready to take off. The children stopped laughing.

Students use their sense of story. In order to tell a story they need to include the components of story and to build a logical relationship among the components of story. For instance, children who understand stories usually tell stories that build logically from one event to the next. Students also use their sense of story to listen to stories. Their understanding of a story enables them to follow a story they hear. Researchers have found that both beginning readers and efficient mature readers rely on story structure to guide their reading comprehension (Marshall and Glock, 1979). Children who do not develop story grammars often experience reading comprehension problems. Children also use their story knowledge to write stories. This understanding enables them to write the appropriate components of a story and to relate the components appropriately.

Information like the preceding suggests that teachers should read many well-structured stories to children, and that children should read many well-structured stories themselves. This will enable students to develop the story grammars necessary to guide their listening and reading comprehension and writing ability.

Literature Develops a Sense of Nonfiction Text Structures

Children need to learn about the structure of nonfiction as well as fiction. The majority of nonfiction is structured as descriptive writing, expository writing, or persuasive writing. Descriptive writing portrays a character or a situation. It describes how an object appears to the senses, or how someone feels, or what a particular setting looks like. The main purpose of expository writing is to explain—to tell how something is done. Persuasive writing is structured to influence readers. The various forms of writing may be combined; for example description is often combined with narrative. Description may be used to influence readers; an instance of this combination is found in *When I Was Young in the Mountains* by Cynthia Rylant. Ms. Rylant describes her life in the mountains in the following excerpt.

When I was young in the mountains, we walked across the cow pasture and through the woods, carrying our towels. The swimming hole was dark and muddy, and we sometimes saw snakes, but we jumped in anyway.

Her descriptions convince us that she loved her mountain childhood (Rylant, 1985).

Children must be exposed to the language of nonfiction if they are to understand this structure and style of writing. Through hearing and reading nonfiction over and over, children will begin to recognize the language and organizational patterns of these books. As a result, children will be better able to listen to, discuss, read, and write nonfiction. To provide this experience, teachers should regularly read carefully selected nonfiction to their students.

Children's literature can add depth, meaning, and elaboration to the content areas. Students studying the Middle Ages will have a better sense of this period through a book like *Chanticleer and the Fox* than they will from recounting dates and details in a social-studies text. Trade books like the following will help students understand the times and places of history.

Blades, M. *Mary of Mile 18.* Tundra Books, 1971. This book portrays life in northern British Columbia.

Bulla, C. *Squanto: Friend of the White Men.* Crowell, 1954. This book is about the Indians and settlers and particularly addresses the life of Squanto.

Cameron, E. *Julia and the Hand of God.* Dutton, 1977. This story is set in California during the 1920s.

Clark, A. *All This Wild Land.* Viking, 1976. Frontier life in Minnesota is the subject of this book.

Dalgleish, A. *The Courage of Sarah Noble.* Scribners, 1954. Children will understand frontier life after reading this book.

Edmonds, W. *Bert Breen's Barn.* Little, Brown, 1975. Turn-of-the-century life is described in this book.

Lobel, Arnold. *On the Day Peter Stuyvesant Sailed into Town.* Harper & Row, 1971. Lobel pictures New Amsterdam and Peter Stuyvesant's campaign to clean up the city.

Monjo, F. N. *The House on Stink Alley: A Story About the Pilgrims in Holland.* Holt, Rinehart and Winston, 1977. The author tells us about Pilgrim life in Holland.

Literature Imparts Knowledge, Information, and Concepts

Both fiction and nonfiction impart knowledge and information to children which supports their conceptual development and intellectual development. For example, primary-grade children who are studying metamorphosis can enrich their concept through hearing and seeing books such as *The Very Hungry*

Caterpillar by E. Carle (Philomel, 1969), and *Ten Little Caterpillars* by B. Martin (Holt, Rinehart and Winston, 1983) (Spiegel, 1986). Books like *The Quicksand Book* by Tomie de Paola and *Digging Up Dinosaurs* by Aliki will activate primary-grade children's interest in expository writing and motivate them to acquire additional information on these topics. Interests grow out of experience and information; therefore, students are usually more interested in familiar topics.

Middle-grade students have many interests that can be elaborated and deepened by reading nonfiction. The following nonfiction books will motivate them to further reading and research.

Barth, Edna. *Turkeys, Pilgrims, and Indian Corn: The Story of the Thanksgiving Symbols.* Seabury, 1975.

Knight, David. *Harnessing the Sun: The Story of Solar Energy.* Morrow, 1976.

Lauber, Patricia. *Tapping the Earth's Heat.* Garrard, 1978.

Lefkowitz, R. *Save It! Keep It! Use It Again! A Book About Conversation and Recycling.* Parents, 1977.

Schneider, Tom. *Everybody's a Winner: A Kid's Guide to New Sports and Fitness.* Little, Brown, 1976.

Literature Stimulates and Models Thinking

Literature stimulates children's intellectual development and provides models for thinking. Specifically, literature contributes to students' concept development, to their skill development in the areas of observation, classification, and the difference between real and make-believe.

Many children's books include characters who demonstrate thinking skills as they solve problems. When using these books in the classroom, teachers at both the primary- and middle-grade levels should have students identify the problem, brainstorm possible solutions, and evaluate solutions. The following books could be used in thinking activities. In *Where Did My Mother Go?* by Edna Preston, Little Cat has a problem; he can't find his mother. He does solve the problem. Warton the toad had a big problem in *A Toad for Tuesday* by Russell Erickson. He is captured by an owl who plans to eat him on Tuesday. Warton examines his problem and thinks of various solutions, but you will have to read the book to find out his solution. The book *Jumanji* by Chris Van Allsburgh presents a totally different kind of problem that is caused by a board game.

Middle-grade children may read many books that identify and solve problems. *The Journey of the Shadow Bairns* by Margaret Anderson is based on Elspeth MacDonald's problem, which is to prevent her brother from being separated from her. Students reading *Switching Tracks* by Dean Hughes have opportunities to participate in a number of problem-solving activities. Mark's life changes as a result of his father's death, which leads to a number of problem situations. Students may discuss how they would have reacted in a specific situation and what they would have done differently.

Concept Development   Concepts are acquired over an extended period of time and are generalized from students' experiences. Books like *Over, Under and Through,* and *Fast-Slow High-Low* by Jana Hoban contribute data to support specific concepts that young children must develop. Other concepts like freedom, courage, and honesty are developed through reading stories. As students read stories that express specific concepts like freedom, honesty, or courage, they gradually acquire the data needed to refine and extend this concept. Students who read *Call It Courage* by Armstrong Sperry, *Shadow of a Bull* by Mara Wojciechowska, and *Island of the Blue Dolphins* by Scott O'Dell can explore the courage expressed in each story. Teachers can help students acquire concepts through literature by encouraging them to compare stories they read.

Observation   Books alert children to the need for observation as well as the kinds of things to look for as they observe. The book *Wild Mouse* by Irene Brady is written in a diary format; the author has recorded the growth and development of three white-footed mice for a two-week period. The descriptions are accompanied by sketches. Students could observe plants or animals in the classroom and dictate or write their observations. They can make drawings to illustrate their observations like the author of *Wild Mouse* did. *The Biggest Bear* by Lynd Ward is fiction, but the author builds readers' suspense and observation skills by showing the bear as a cub, then showing what the bear did rather than showing the bear—finally readers see a gigantic bear.

Real and Make-Believe   Young children must learn to discriminate between events and characters that are real and those that are make-believe. One of the best ways to do this is to compare a book that has make-believe characters and situations with a book that has real characters and situations. Children in a first-grade classroom might compare the mice in *Wild Mouse,* which are real, with those in *Frederick,* by Leo Lionni, which are make-believe. The make-believe mice tell stories, dream, and talk; of course the mice in *Wild Mouse* do not do this. However, there are some similarities between the mice that should cause children to think more carefully than they would if there were no points of similarity.

Literature Stimulates Creativity and Imagination

Literature educates the imagination according to Northrup Frye (1968). When students read books like *Regards to the Man in the Mood* by Ezra Jack Keats, *Conrad's Castle* by Ben Schecter, and *Where the Wild Things Are* by Maurice Sendak, they are getting the message that using one's imagination is a very good thing to do. The authors of these books demonstrate how one can build things in one's imagination. Conrad builds a castle in his imagination, while

Louie and Susie fly away in the "Imagination I" whose energy source is imagination and the author goes on to state that their friends couldn't move until they got their imagination going. Max in *Where the Wild Things Are* escapes from his room to the land of the wild things where he has a grand time until he returns to the warmth and security of his very own room.

Literature stimulates creativity and imagination in other ways. For example, the playful attitude toward language expressed in Ruth Krauss's *A Very Special House* and *Red Is Best* by Kathy Stinson stimulates children to play with language. Such books give children a model of creativity.

Robert McCloskey talks of his imagination in the film *The Lively Art of the Picture Book,* when he says he has one foot firmly planted in reality and the other foot on a banana peel. Writers like Robert McCloskey help us exercise our imagination on every day events. We see this kind of imagination in the books *Alexander and the Terrible, Horrible, No Good, Very Bad Day* by Judith Viorst and *If You Give a Mouse a Cookie* by Laura Numeroff. In each of these books the authors are writing about the daily events in youngster's lives, but after reading these books, these daily experiences will never seem quite the same again because we have seen them through the eyes of imagination.

Wordless picture books tell stories through pictures. Many of these books are very interesting and they stimulate children to tell and write stories. These are examples of excellent wordless picture books:

Mayer, Mercer. *One Frog Too Many.* Dial, 1975.

Mayer, Mercer. *Hiccup.* Dial, 1978.

Goodall, John. *The Adventures of Paddy Pork.* Harcourt Brace Jovanovich, 1968.

Winter, Paula. *The Bear and the Fly.* Crown, 1976.

Literature stimulates us to speak, listen, read, and write creatively. Therefore this topic is explored in the chapters addressing these topics. You may refer to Related Readings in Chapters Four, Five, Six, and Seven for stimulating creativity in the language arts.

Literature Helps Students Understand Themselves and Others

Literature gives students an opportunity to explore various roles. It enables them to walk in another person's shoes for a little while and there is no better way to understand another person. Books help students understand their peers, the handicapped, and people from other cultures.

For instance, a common problem in children's lives is disagreeing and quarrelling with friends. Nothing hurts them so much as rejection by friends or a disagreement with their "best friend." Reading about such problems can help students cope with these experiences and feelings of grief, loneliness, and frustration. Books like the following will help students cope with these experiences and will help students understand themselves and their peers.

Burch, Robert. *D. J's Worst Enemy.* Viking, 1965.

Clifton, Lucille. *The Times They Used to Be.* Holt, Rinehart and Winston, 1974.

Cohen, Miriam. *Will I Have a Friend?* Macmillan, 1967.

Little, Jean. *One to Grow On.* Little, Brown, 1969.

Sharmat, Marjorie. *Getting Something on Maggie Marmelstein.* Harper & Row, 1971.

Stolz, Mary. *A Wonderful, Terrible Time.* Harper & Row, 1967.

Literature can help students understand handicapped people. As they gain insights about the handicapped, children are more likely to treat them with respect. Books like the following help them acquire important insights.

Blume, Judy. *Deenie.* Bradbury, 1972. (wearing a brace)

Crane, Caroline. *A Girl Like Tracy.* McKay, 1966. (mentally retarded)

DeGering, E. *Seeing Fingers: The Story of Louis Braille.* McKay, 1962. (blindness)

Little, Jean. *From Anna.* Little Brown, 1972. (blindness)

Southall, Ivan. *Let the Balloon Go.* St. Martin's, 1968. (spastic)

There are a large number of books available today to help children understand the aged person. Books like the following will lead children to more enriching experiences with the older members of their families.

Blue, Rose. *Grandma Didn't Wave Back.* Watts, 1972.

Borack, Barbara. *Grandpa.* Harper & Row, 1967.

Fox, Paula. *A Likely Place.* Macmillan, 1967.

Lundgren, Max. *Matt's Grandfather.* Putnam, 1972.

Snyder, Zilpha. *The Witches of Worm.* Atheneum, 1972.

Bishop (1987) points out that literature can help us understand that we are connected to one another through our emotions, our needs, and our desires, because these are experiences common to all people. Books also can help us understand, appreciate, and value the differences among us—the uniqueness of each cultural group that enriches us all. Finally, literature can be used to develop an understanding of the effects of social issues and forces on the lives of ordinary individuals. When teachers share literature that extends our cultural understanding they are transmitting cultural values—they are letting youngsters know what we consider important.

Multicultural understandings are developed through fiction, nonfiction, and poetry. Listening to stories, dramatizing events and historical incidents, role playing cultural events, and writing about thoughts helps students grow to new levels of understanding. The following references will help you select materials to develop multicultural understanding.

Educational Resources Center. *Discovering India: A Guide for Use in American Schools.* Albany, NY: State University of New York and NYS Department of Education, 1970.

Highwater, Jamake. *Many Smokes, Many Moons: A Chronology of American Indian History Through Indian Art.* Lippincott, 1978.

Sims, Rudine. *Shadow and Substance: Afro-Americans in Contemporary Children's Fiction.* National Council of Teachers of English, 1982.

Tway, Eileen, ed. *Reading Ladders for Human Relations* (6th ed.). National Council of Teachers of English, 1981.

Wagoner, Shirley. "Mexican-Americans in Children's Literature." *Reading Teacher, 36,* 10 (December 1982), 274–79.

TURNING CHILDREN ON TO LITERATURE

How do you turn children on to literature? You start showing them the joys of reading during the first year of life. You read to them daily. Reading to children is one of the most important things parents and teachers can do. Jim Trelease (1985) devised the following formula for building children's interest in reading books.

1. You read to children while they are still young enough to want to imitate what they are seeing and hearing.

2. You make sure the readings are interesting and exciting enough to hold their interest while you are building up their imaginations.

3. You keep the initial readings short enough to fit their attention spans and gradually lengthen both.

Read to infants! Yes, Dr. T. Berry Brazelton (1979) says that the new parents' most critical task during the early months of life is learning how to calm the child, how to bring the child under control so the youngster learns to look around and listen and pay attention. The human voice is one of the most powerful tools that parents and teachers have and reading aloud to children gives them a chance to hear a human voice.

Will reading aloud to children really make a difference? Yes! Yes! Yes! The children who are read to during the first year of life consistently enjoy reading and become excellent students. Dorothy Butler (1980) demonstrated this thesis in her book *Cushla and Her Books.* Cushla's parents began reading to her when she was four months old. By nine months of age she responded to the sight of certain books and indicated to her parents that these were her favorites. By age five she could read by herself, in spite of the fact that her doctors had previously diagnosed her as "mentally and physically retarded" and recommended institutionalization. After observing her skills at the age of five, psychologists pronounced her above average in intelligence and socially well-adjusted. In a massive research study, Benjamin Bloom (1964) studied the developmental profiles of 1000 children and demonstrated that 50 percent of the intelligence a child will have at maturity is already formed by age four. Reading to children can stimulate that intellectual development.

Many parents feel they do not have time to read aloud because of the demands of their employment. Many teachers feel that they do not have time to read aloud because they must teach the skills and competencies that are measured on standardized tests. As a result, children are not hearing good literature anyplace. Then we wonder why television is replacing reading. Children really do not have an opportunity to experience the joys of reading.

Prospective teachers in undergraduate children's literature courses reflect this trend. The majority of these young people report that they have not been read to nor do they have knowledge of children's literature. They do not even know such classic children's literature as *Where the Wild Things Are* and *Charlotte's Web.* Research shows that 60 percent of the third- and fourth-grade teachers do not read aloud regularly to their classes. By sixth grade, 74 percent of the teachers reported that they did not read regularly to their classes (Tom, 1969).

Studies of early readers over the past 25 years indicate that four factors are present in the home environment of nearly every early reader (Durkin, 1966; Clark, 1976; Forester, 1977).

1. The child is read to on a regular basis. This activity is extremely important to early readers. Every one of the children in Durkin's research was read to. In addition, the parents were avid readers who served as examples for their children. Early readers had families who read books to them, but they also read packages, street signs, and billboards.

2. Many reading materials were available in the homes of these children.

3. Paper and pencil were readily available for the children. These children showed an early interest in scribbling and drawing. They enjoyed copying objects and letters of the alphabet.

4. The family stimulated children's interest in reading and writing by answering endless questions and praising efforts at reading and writing. Books were available for children. In many cases parents wrote the stories children dictated and displayed their work in the home.

Jim Trelease (1985) identifies the value of children's literature in the following quotation: "Children's literature arouses their imaginations, emotions, and sympathies. It awakens their desire to read, enlarges their lives, and provides a sense of purpose and identity for children."

SELECTING BOOKS FOR CHILDREN

The books read to and by children should represent the best in children's literature. Once teachers and parents are committed to reading aloud, they have to learn how to select literature. The task of selecting from among the more than 3000 children's books published each year is a formidable one. Teachers who are knowledgeable about children's books can help parents identify books to purchase and read.

Teachers may refer to book reviews in journals like the *Horn Book Magazine, School Library Journal,* and *Language Arts,* and to reference works like *The Elementary School Library Collection, Bibliography of Books for Children, The Read Aloud Handbook,* and *Children's Books Too Good to Miss* for assistance. But they must also read widely and evaluate children's books themselves. Children's books like adult's books are analyzed through the elements of literature: plot, characterization, setting, theme, and style. When each of these elements unfolds naturally and is integrated we have a well-written story.

What Is a Good Fictional Book?

A good children's book is an enjoyable experience, a literary experience. A fictional book should have a theme suitable for the child's age and characters who come alive. There should be action which claims the child's attention, with a well-rounded plot. Some sort of climax and satisfactory resolution will induce a feeling of total satisfaction in the whole experience (Butler, 1980)

Good books entertain.

Plot   The **plot** of a story is the plan of the story, what happens in the story. A good plot tells an interesting story. Ordinarily, plots begin with an introduction that lets the readers know what is happening. In *Bunnicula,* by James and Deborah Howe, the authors tell readers about the Monroe family, Harold the dog, and Chester the cat. Bunnicula is introduced into the family under mysterious circumstances, thus building suspense.

The plot builds naturally and logically after readers accept the fact that the rabbit is found in a theater with an unreadable note tied to its neck. Chester the cat immediately takes note of Bunnicula's unusual markings. The suspense mounts when mysterious white vegetables with fang marks appear around the house. Chester is convinced the rabbit is the source of the problem. He stalks Bunnicula, believing he is a vampire. Chester despairs for the safety of the Monroe family and is convinced that he must warn them about the vampire rabbit. The authors build a plausible series of events with each event creating a foundation for the next event and exacerbating the suspense. When the Monroes seem oblivious to Chester's warnings, he decides to demonstrate what the rabbit is doing by pretending to sink his teeth into Harold's neck. Poor Chester only succeeds in convincing the Monroes that he has a problem. This episode is the climax of the plot, the peak of the suspense.

The denouement or falling action which ties the story together occurs when the Monroes take all three animals to the veterinarian. The vet gives Bunnicula carrot juice because he is starving, he sends Chester to a cat psychiatrist, and gives Harold a treat. However, Chester's psychiatrist does not cure him of his fears about Bunnicula which leads the reader to the sequel *The Celery Stalks at Midnight.*

Bunnicula is a fantasy, but fantasies are evaluated in the same way as other forms of fiction. The major difference is that the author must introduce any fantastic elements in acceptable ways. Fictional picture books are similar to other forms of fiction except that the story is told through pictures, as well as words.

Characterization   **Characterization** is the way the author portrays the characters in the story. Some characters are so well portrayed that readers feel that they would know them if they were to meet. Gilley in the *Great Gilley Hopkins* is one such character. Gilley is memorable because readers know her strengths and weaknesses. We know what she likes and dislikes and we can anticipate how she will behave in most situations. Her personality is multidimensional with some aspects that we like and some that we do not like. Authors reveal their characters through their thoughts, words, and deeds, and through the thoughts, words, and deeds of the other characters. Some characters change, grow, and develop as a result of story events, while others remain much the same.

The multifaceted characters in *Bunnicula* are Harold the dog and Chester the cat. Harold is an easy-going character who is most concerned with the rattle of cellophane in the kitchen. Like most dogs he is more concerned with his stomach than anything else. He translated the note written in a dialect of the Carpathian Mountain region. Harold describes events with the detail that help the reader visualize the action. He does not get excited over Chester's hysterics, but he is often innocently drawn into situations.

Chester the cat was a birthday gift to Mr. Monroe along with a first edition of Dickens' *A Tale of Two Cities,* so he developed a taste for reading early in life. Mr. Monroe, a professor, uses Chester as a sounding board for his lectures. Chester is a direct contrast to Harold. He is nervous, excitable, and intellectual. The moment he saw Bunnicula's unusual markings, he jumped to the conclusion the rabbit was a vampire. The vampire stories he read contributed to his fears for the Monroes.

Both Chester and Harold are well-developed personalities; however, they retain cat and dog characteristics. The Monroes and Bunnicula are presented in a rather sketchy fashion because they are the foils for Chester and Harold.

Setting   Setting is where and when a story takes place and it should be an integral part of the plot. The authors create a mysterious mood at the beginning of the story with the description of a cold, wet, dreary night. Most of the story takes place in the Monroe family home. Although the setting is not precisely labeled, the reader is left with the impression that it is a suburban area.

Theme   The **theme** is the statement underlying the story. Common themes in children's literature are courage, growing up, friendship, and individuality. At times the author states the theme very specifically; the theme of *Summer of the Swans* is "growing from an ugly duckling into a swan." In some instances, the theme identified in a book depends on the reader and the reader's experience. As readers, we bring meaning to the stories we read.

Some books for young children do not have a clearly defined theme. These books might be called "a slice of life" because they present everyday events in children's lives. *The Snowy Day* by Ezra Jack Keats is one such book.

Style of Writing   Writers create moods and symbols through the words they use and the arrangement of words into sentences. The writing **style** of the Howes in *Bunnicula* has several important characteristics. First, they tell the story from Harold's point of view. Harold explains the dialog and background information in asides to the reader. As the story progresses, Harold makes comments like the following, "No thank you, I'd rather be stretched out on my favorite rug in front of a nice, whistling radiator." The second characteristic of their style is the use of description to create mood. For example, "Well, it was cold, the rain was pelting the windows, the wind was howling and it felt pretty good to be indoors." Third, the Howes use action to advance the plot. For example, loud crashes, music in the night, and the appearances of white vegetables move the story along.

Selecting a Nonfiction Book

Teachers and parents should read both fiction and nonfiction to children; therefore, nonfiction trade books should be analyzed as carefully as fiction. Well-written nonfiction is as interesting as fiction. When evaluating nonfiction you should consider these factors: accuracy of information, inclusion of all significant facts, support of generalizations with facts, identification of facts and opinions, presentation of differing points of view, and avoidance of racism and sexism.

Accurate Information   Well-written nonfiction is carefully researched and gives accurate information. The first criteria for an information book is accuracy. In the book, *Germs Make Me Sick!* Melvin Berger explains that germs are tiny, tiny living things. He goes on to explain that "a line of one thousand germs could fit across the top of a pencil," thus giving readers a context for understanding how very tiny germs are. Berger then explains that bacteria are small plants, and viruses are tinier than bacteria. The author accurately explains how germs, bacteria, and viruses get into the body. And he goes on to explain that doctors do not have drugs to cure diseases caused by viruses which is appropriate, since authors should indicate that some information is not known about the topic. The excellent, accurate illustrations enhance this book and clarify the information. Although this book is short and relatively simple, readers learn a lot of accurate information from it.

Carol and Donald Carrick use language effectively in their book, *The Blue Lobster: A Life Cycle.* For example:

> The last rays of the sun melted across the floor of the summer sea. They glowed on a rock ledge where a mother lobster had taken shelter.
> She glided out on the tips of her slender legs, her body heavy with the thousands of ripe eggs she had carried for a year and a half (Carrick, 1975).

Notice how accurately they describe their subject and how the information is integrated into the narrative, so that it is not merely a cataloging of information.

Include All Significant Facts   Authors of informational books usually do considerable research. Since they cannot tell their readers all the facts, they include all the *significant* facts. For instance, in the book *Germs Make Me Sick* the author included the significant facts that a youngster could absorb and understand, but there are medical books full of more facts that the author could have included.

Support Generalizations with Facts   An author's generalizations must be fact-based. An author's generalizations must be supported by valid data. For an audience to accept the generalization that aerobic exercise is deleterious to their health, an author should provide facts regarding individuals whose health was damaged by aerobic exercise. It may be that the people who were injured by aerobic exercise did not perform the exercises correctly.

Discriminate Between Fact and Opinion Authors of informational books should clearly identify the statements of fact and the statements of opinion. For example, an author who has the opinion that aerobic exercise is harmful to our health should state, "In my opinion . . . ," because this is not an established fact.

Present Differing Views on Controversial Subjects There are different points of view regarding almost every subject in the world; therefore, no topic should be presented in a single dimension. Readers have the right to know that there are several theories or points of view. For example, there are several theories regarding the origins of the world.

Avoid Racism and Sexism Authors should avoid racism and sexism in all forms of literature. Our society is multicultural and names and pictures in a book should reflect this. Any discussion of culture, values, beliefs, and so forth should reflect the full range of our culture.

Sexism is primarily concerned with pronouns *he* and *his* as opposed to *she* and *her*. Sexism also occurs in situations where doctors and scientists are portrayed as men, while nurses and teachers are women. A balanced approach would show men and women in professions, as well as men and women taking care of children and the home.

Poetry

Children grow into poetry as they hear it read aloud. Identify those poems that are most appealing to your students and regularly reread these poems. After they have heard a poem several times, many students will join in when the teacher reads. Poetry choices should be varied, so that children have an opportunity to appreciate several kinds of poetry.

These guidelines will help you select and share poetry with children.

1. Select poems that both you and the children appreciate.

2. Read the poetry in advance to get a feeling for it.

3. Have a good anthology or two at hand so you can use poetry in conjunction with classroom events (birthdays, the first robin of spring, etc.).

4. Collect poems that you enjoy and that you think the children will enjoy.

5. Read poetry aloud after scanning it.

6. Write poetry on charts and use choral reading and chanting to develop students' interest and their ability to read poetry aloud.

7. Do not analyze the meaning of poetry.

8. Enjoy poetry!

Children Enjoy the Rhythm and Rhyme of Poetry Children are initially attracted to poetry because of its rhythm and rhyme. These characteristics are found in popular Nursery Rhymes and poems. An illustration of the rhythm of rain is seen in "The Umbrella Brigade" by Laura E. Richards. You may wish to read this poem aloud so that you can hear this rhythm.

Poets Communicate Poets love language and they express this love in a compact form of writing. One might even say it is terse because every word counts. Poetry is elusive. Poetry communicates through language—it may communicate humor or tell a story. Poetry is personal—what appeals to one person does not to another. Poets try to convey the essence of their subject through carefully chosen and arranged words that appeal to our emotions. Edward Lear communicates about himself in his poem "How pleasant to know Mr. Lear," which is a comical self-portrait.

Poetry Has a Sensory Quality Poets appeal to all of the senses as they strive to create different effects. For instance, in "Down the Rain Falls," by Elizabeth Coatsworth, the poet has a "crackling fire" and a "tick tock" clock. Christopher Morley appeals to the sense of smell in "Smells (Junior)."

Finding the Right Book for Each Child

Teachers turn children on to reading when they direct them to books that are interesting and meet their needs. Interests are individual entities that are related to our experiential background; therefore, each individual's interests differ from those of another individual. Helen Huus states that interest is based on a peculiar combination of factors that includes developmental state, experience, and curiosity (Huus, 1979). Children's experiences with being read to and learning to read form a basis for their attitudes about literature. Children whose teachers read interesting stories and who encourage them to read books that give them pleasure will develop positive attitudes toward literature. In order to motivate children to feel positive about reading, teachers must know not only what interests children at different stages of development, but also the interests of individual students in the class.

Children enjoy stories about characters and experiences that are understandable. Some stories appeal to children because their experiences enable them to follow the plot. Other stories are interesting simply because they make children laugh.

Children's preferences in literature are as diverse as the children themselves because a book cannot be considered as a separate entity. A literary work comes to life when readers interact with the text. Readers use their experiences and the author's words to create meaning. This is why children understand stories that are related to their experiences. Readers actively select aspects of the text to remember, filling in the gaps in the text with data derived from their experiences. By making inferences about characters, plot, setting, theme, and author's style the reader provides a personal meaning.

There is a body of research regarding children's choices of books to read. However, this research must be analyzed carefully. The preferences indicated in a research study may simply reflect the fact that those were the books available to children. Perhaps if they had opportunities to read a greater variety of books, they would make different choices. Literary quality is more important than the topic of the book.

During the early grades children enjoy the sound of the language and the illustrations most of all. They enjoy representational illustrations and bright colors. Primary-grade children enjoy literature about animals, nature, and daily experiences.

PRESENTING LITERATURE TO CHILDREN

After selecting interesting, appropriate literature teachers should present it enthusiastically. Teachers may present literature in a variety of ways, such as through media, booktalks, reading aloud, and uninterrupted sustained silent reading. Of course, students can always read independently.

Media

Teachers may tell stories using visual aids like flannel boards and pictures. Of course, puppets are a long-time favorite for presenting stories to children. Records, films, filmstrips, and video cassettes are vehicles for sharing literature, although teachers need to carefully evaluate the quality of commercially prepared media. Children may use blank filmstrips or slides to prepare a media presentation. Middle-grade students can create a media presentation that incorporates mood music as a background, while an individual or group does a reader's theater presentation.

"Reading Rainbow"   "Reading Rainbow" is a PBS-TV network broadcast designed to motivate children to read. This show presents television and movie personalities reading children's books. Children enjoy the programs very much and they successfully motivate students to read; however, many children do not have a chance to see these shows. Teachers may consider calling parents' attention to the programs and create displays of "Reading Rainbow" selections. Most local libraries have lists of the "Reading Rainbow" selections and many local bookstores display the selections. Teachers may want to videotape the programs for classroom viewing. This is legal, as long as the teacher uses the videotape of a broadcast with just one class. The tape may be run twice for the purpose of teaching and reinforcement but both showings must take place within ten days of the original broadcast.

Another way to benefit from "Reading Rainbow" is to use it as a format for classroom productions. Students can read and discuss literature in the same style as the television program (Goodfriend and Gogel, 1987). The programs can be videotaped for the students' use and for other classes.

Junior Great Books   The Junior Great Books Program is a literature program that follows a specific format and philosophy. Discussion leaders must attend training courses conducted by the Great Books Foundation. This program is usually reserved for more able students although less able students enjoy participating in the discussions. Great Books Programs are often after school programs. For information about this program write to: Great Books Foundation, 40 East Huron Street, Chicago, Illinois 60611.

The Junior Great Books format can be used as a model for developing schoolwide literature discussion programs. Teachers can serve as discussion leaders with each teacher leading the discussion of an individual book and the students selecting the book discussion they want to participate in. This kind of program gives children a chance to know other teachers and to see them as models of reading.

Booktalks

Booktalks are effective strategies that require a minimum of preparation. The goal of a booktalk is to motivate students to read the book. It highlights the book and excludes the climax. A booktalk is more effective when the teacher displays the book while telling about it. On occasion, visual aids are used to enhance booktalks. In selecting books to talk about, be sure to choose ones that you enjoy as it is difficult to be enthusiastic about a book otherwise.

Read Aloud Guidelines

Throughout this chapter, the importance of reading aloud has been stressed. When reading aloud these principles should be kept in mind.

1. Select books that children cannot or do not choose to read for themselves.

2. Select quality literature.

3. Plan each day's selection in advance.

4. Tell students the title, the author, and the topic to introduce the book. Hold the book so that children can see the cover.

5. Group the children close together in the primary grades. Have them sit on the floor, carpeting, or pillows.

6. You should be familiar with the story, so that you can maintain eye contact with children while you are reading the story.

7. Hold picture books so that children can see the illustrations.

8. Guide students' listening with listening purposes. For example, ask the class to listen to the story to identify where the story happened or to identify the protagonist's problem.

9. Read with a natural voice, using pitch, stress, and tone of voice to express meaning. Do not overdo the sound effects or you will distract the students from attending to the story.

10. Conduct a follow-up discussion that includes discussion of the listening purposes and student responses to the reading. Children should be encouraged to raise their own questions and ideas about the story. The teacher should encourage and respect each youngster's contribution.

Uninterrupted Sustained Silent Reading

Uninterrupted sustained silent reading (USSR) is an activity that stimulates silent reading of literature. During this period everyone in the classroom and/or school reads including teachers, visitors, secretaries, cafeteria staff, and custodians. At the outset, the reading period may be only five minutes long, but this time should be gradually extended. A kitchen timer may be useful for timing reading. USSR provides everyone in the school with opportunities to read for pleasure. Linda Gambrell (1978) suggests the following guidelines for such a program:

1. Lay the groundwork for the program by promoting student interest before exercises actually begin.

2. Collect interesting materials, such as books, magazines, and newspapers.

3. Everyone should read during the period, including teachers.

Colorful bulletin board displays on books, authors, and story characters is a way of presenting literature to students. An attractive classroom reading corner might persuade children to relax and read. Rugs, rocking chairs, and overstuffed chairs will invite children to relax and enjoy a good story.

RESPONDING TO LITERATURE

Teachers need to know how to offer activities that will extend students' responses to literature in ways that will foster the growth of imagination and understanding. Imaginative responses to literature may take many forms ranging from introspection to discussion, writing, dance, art, and drama. Students may respond to fiction, nonfiction, and poetry in the modes suggested in this section. The form of literary response that appeals to children depends on individual interests and talents. Some children are too shy to respond orally, but they may write gifted responses to the literature they read. Since response to literature is individual, no two responses will be exactly alike.

Writing

Books with repetitive structure inspire children to write in the same pattern. For example, *The Pancake* and *If You Give A Mouse A Cookie* have such

Children respond to literature.

structures. Children who read *Old Macdonald Had an Apartment House* may be inspired to modernize folktales as Judith Barrett did in this book. Children who read *Bunnicula* may be inspired to write a story from the point of view of an animal. *Ben and Me* and *Mr. Revere and I* are also written from animals' perspectives. Chapters Seven and Eight include many writing response activities.

Drama

Some books inspire drama. Children who read stories like *Words by Heart* or *Bagthorpes Unlimited* will want to dramatize their favorite episodes. Poems like "Bam, Bam, Bam" by Eve Merriam is an excellent one for dramatization. Young children enjoy dramatizing stories like *Stone Soup* and *Frederick* because they are good stories involving an almost unlimited number of characters and incorporating considerable action. Puppets are another form of dramatization that children enjoy very much. They can create their own puppets and their own puppet play. Chapter Five includes a number of drama activities. Choral reading, puppets, reader's theater, and pantomime are all forms of dramatization that offer students opportunities to respond to literature. Classroom dramatizations can be videotaped for future use. Playing back these dramas gives children opportunities to appreciate the literature and to self-evaluate. Drama is discussed in greater detail in Chapter Four.

Cooking

Literature can also lead to cooking. Books like *Rain Makes Applesauce, Blueberries for Sal, If You Give a Mouse a Cookie, The Popcorn Book, Stone Soup,* and *The Pancake* naturally make children (and teachers) hungry. A poem like "Smells" by Aileen Fisher will enhance the sensory experience of cooking. *Chicken Soup with Rice* by Maurice Sendak is a poem that children enjoy cooking. Children may be inspired to combine cooking and writing by writing their own recipes and recipe books.

Art

Literature frequently inspires art. Children who listen to *Swimmy* are bound to draw fish and their teachers may create bulletin boards or mobiles from this artwork. Children enjoy creating friezes and murals that show the scenes from books they have read. They can make clay models of their favorite characters. Diaramas, three-dimensional scenes from stories, may be created in shoeboxes. *The Borrowers* lends itself well for a diarama because the Borrowers used everyday objects in their home. Some children enjoy making wall hangings about literature. Papier-mâché, models, slides, filmstrips and videotapes are all media that children can use to respond to literature.

Discussions

Book discussions provide additional opportunities to respond to literature. Teachers should plan units of books that are related in some way. These books may have similar themes, similar subjects, similar characters, similar plots, or the same author. After reading books like *Red Is Best* and *Hailstones and Halibut Bones* children can discuss their favorite colors and the way their favorite colors make them feel. They could create a bulletin board that expresses their feelings about color.

Middle-grade children can compare the mothers in *Nobody's Family Is Going To Change*, *The Cat Ate My Gym Suit*, and *Representing Super Doll*. The discussants should address the problems faced by each mother, the possible alternatives, and the action taken. Discussions are valuable to literary response because meaning in literature is such a personal response.

Discussion Guidelines Class or group discussions give students opportunities to respond to the literature they are reading. For primary- and middle-grade students use questions to guide their discussion of the basic story they have read.

1. Who are the main characters?

2. What words are used to describe them?

3. When did this story take place? Find the words that tell when it happened.

4. What was the main character's problem?

5. What happened to the main character? Did he or she solve the problem?

A discussion that develops students' response to the story elements (plot, theme, characterization, setting, and style) and the relationships among these elements could be developed with the following questions.

1. What kind of a person is this character? How do you know?

2. Do the characters in this story act as you expect them to based on what you know about their personalities?

3. Did the characters change during the story? How? Why?

4. What did the main character learn in this story?

5. Did the setting play an important role in this story? How?

6. Why did the author write this story?

7. Does the title have any special meaning?

Some discussions should focus on comparing two stories. When presenting the stories to primary children, the teacher should read the stories aloud. On the other hand, middle-grade children can read the stories silently and then participate in a discussion. One way to compare stories is to compare characters. For example, Gilley in *The Great Gilley Hopkins* could be compared with Harriet in *Harriet the Spy*. Plots can be compared—for example, the plot of *The Mixed Up Files of Mrs. Basil E. Frankweiler* with the plot of *Julie of the Wolves*. The settings of the preceding books make an interesting comparison also. Questions like the following can be used to guide story comparison.

1. How are these stories alike?

2. How do these stories differ?

3. Do the stories have the same theme? If so what is it?

4. Can you think of any other stories that are similar to these stories? If so, what stories?

There is a great deal of excellent nonfiction available for children today, and it is a good source of discussion material. The following discussion questions can be used as a guide.

1. What is the subject of this book or selection?

2. What did the author say to you about this subject. Can you state an idea or point of view that is being conveyed?

3. Did the author support this point of view or main idea?

4. Identify the author's statements of fact.

5. Does the author explain causes and effects?

6. What conclusions and generalizations are made?

7. What was the author's purpose for writing this piece?

Story Web

A web is a planning device for developing a specific book or concept. Figure 9.1 is an example of a story web. Teachers should keep in mind that all of the activities in a web would not be used in class because doing all of them would make even the best book seem dull. A web simply shows the possibilities for developing a work of literature.

Evaluation of the Literature Program

Formal assessment has no place in the literature program. However, teachers should observe their students to determine the amount of reading they do. How often do they read for pleasure? Do they choose quality literature to read? Do they mention books that they have enjoyed reading? What are their responses on the interest inventory? This data should be combined with reading assessment to determine whether students can read and understand fiction and nonfiction and whether they can read and appreciate fiction, nonfiction, and poetry. Students who have difficulty may be experiencing problems as a result of poor reading skills, lack of background experiences, or lack of interest.

TROUBLESHOOTING

The major problem that teachers experience in relation to literature is motivating students to read. Many children cut their teeth on television and prefer this passive activity to the more demanding activity of reading. Many children feel that they do not have time to read because they go to daycare facilities after school and have homework when they arrive home. Home-

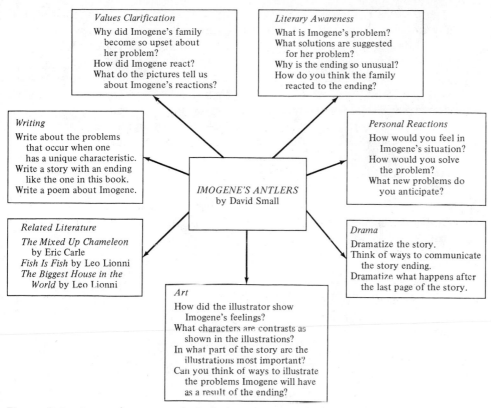

Figure 9.1 A sample story web, based on *Imogene's Antlers* by David Small.

work may occupy their time until bedtime. This means that teachers must set aside school time for recreational reading or children will not have the time to read.

SUMMARY

Literature is both an end and a means. Literature provides entertainment and escape, but it also develops speaking, listening, reading, and writing abilities. Teachers must learn about books and children so they can give children rewarding reading experiences that will nurture their love of literature. Parents should start reading to children as soon as they are born and teachers should start reading to them as soon as they come to school. This early introduction to quality literature is important in developing lifelong readers.

Teachers may refer to journals and reference books to select literature for children. However, they must develop their own literature evaluation skills. In fiction, plot, theme, characterization, setting, and style are examined as a basis for selecting quality literature. Nonfiction should present information in an accurate fashion, support generalizations, and separate fact from opinion. Poetry should be read aloud by a fluent reader. Children enjoy the rhythm and rhyme of poetry, its communication, and the story element.

Literature can do many things for children. It expands and supports language development in speaking, listening, reading, and writing.

Oral reading is the most common way to present literature to children. However, silent reading, booktalks, art, music, displays, movies, records, and drama are all modes of presenting literature to children.

Readers interact with literature to create meaning; this meaning is individual because each individual brings different experiences to the literature. Children respond to literature through speaking, listening, reading, and writing. In addition they may manifest their response to literature in art, music, and drama.

Teachers use story maps to organize their presentation of literature and students' responses. A web is a form of brainstorming the activities and materials related to a topic. Teachers do not expect students to complete all of the activities included in a web.

Thought Questions

1. How is literature related to language arts instruction?

2. What values does literature have for language development?

3. What are some of the ways that children can respond to literature?

4. How are fiction and nonfiction alike? How are they different?

5. How do students acquire a sense of story?

6. Discuss the relationship between literature and cognitive development.

Enrichment Activities

1. Select a picture book to read to a kindergarten or first-grade class. Use the guidelines in this chapter for presenting the book to the children.

2. Read "Bookwatching: Notes on Children's Books" in *Language Arts.* Then read one of the books reviewed. Do you agree with the reviewer's comments regarding the book?

3. Administer the interest inventory in this chapter to a group of middle-grade students. Then summarize their responses. What generalizations can you make about this class?

4. Select an issue of the *Horn Book Magazine* and read the entire issue. What did you learn?

5. Select an author or illustrator who appeals to you. Study his or her life through reading reference materials as well as the *Horn Book Magazine* and *Language Arts.*

6. Create a map for use in the primary grades or the intermediate grades.

7. Visit a school and ask the children at each grade level to select their favorite book.

8. Prepare a booktalk and present it to a group of children.

9. Compare two reviews of the same book. Reviews of children's books appear in *Language Arts, Horn Book Magazine, Bulletin of the Center for Children's Books, School Library Journal,* and *Booklist.*

10. Write a review of a picture book or a novel for middle-grade students that could be sent to parents to help them select books for their children.

11. Prepare a summer reading list for one grade level.

12. Have a child retell a story that you have read to him or her.

Selected Readings

Butler, D. (1980). *Cushla and Her Books.* Boston: Horn Book.

Cullinan, B. E., and C. W. Carmichael (eds.) (1977). *Literature and Young Children.* Urbana, IL: National Council of Teachers of English.

Cullinan, B. E. (1981). *Literature and the Child.* New York; Harcourt Brace Jovanovich.

Glazer, J. (1986). *Children's Literature for the Young Child* (2d ed.). Columbus, OH: Charles Merrill.

Hopkins, Lee B. (1980). *The Best of Books Bonanza.* New York: Holt, Rinehart and Winston.

Huck, C. E. (1979). *Children's Literature in the Elementary School* (3d ed.). New York: Holt, Rinehart and Winston.

Larrick, N. (1975). *A Parent's Guide to Children's Reading.* New York: Doubleday.

Lukens, R. J. *A Critical Handbook of Children's Literature* (3rd Ed.). Chicago: Scott-Foresman.

Roser, N. and M. Frith, Eds. (1983). *Children's Choices: Teaching with Books Children Like.* Newark, DE: International Reading Association.

Tiedt, I. (1979). *Exploring Books with Children.* Boston: Houghton-Mifflin.

Trelease, J. (1985). *The Read Aloud Handbook.* New York: Viking Penguin.

Children's Books

Aaron, Chester. *Spill.* Atheneum, 1977.

Alexander, Anne. *Noise in the Night.* Rand McNally, 1960.

Aliki. *Digging Up Dinosaurs.* Crowell, 1981.

Allsburg, Chris Van. *Jumanji.* Houghton-Mifflin 1981.

Asimov, Isaac. *The Moon.* Follett, 1966.

Asimov, Isaac. *Stars.* Follett, 1968.

Atwood, Ann. *Haiku: The Mood of Earth.* Scribners, 1971.

Babbitt, Natalie. *The Eyes of the Amaryllis.* Farrar, Straus, & Giroux, 1977.

Baylor, Byrd and Peter Parnall. *The Other Way to Listen.* Scribner's, 1978.

Berger, Melvin. *Germs Make Me Sick!* Harper & Row, 1985.

Brady, Irene. *Wild Mouse,* Scribners, 1978.

Bridwell, Norman. *Clifford the Big Red Dog.* Scholastic, 1979.

Brown, Joseph. *Wonders of a Kelp Forest.* Dodd, Mead, 1974.

Brown, Marcia. *Stone Soup.* Scribners, 1947.

Carrick, Carol and Donald. *The Blue Lobster: A Life Cycle.* Dial, 1975.

Conford, Ellen. *Eugene the Brave.* Little, Brown, 1978.

Cresswell, Helen. *Bagthorpes Unlimited.* Macmillan, 1978.

Crowe, Robert. *Clyde Monster.* Dutton, 1976.

Danziger, Paula. *The Cat Ate My Gym Suit.* Delacorte, 1974.

Daughtry, Duanne. *What's Inside?* Knopf, 1984.

de Paola, Tomie. *The Quicksand Book.* Holiday House, 1977.

de Paola, Tomie. *The Popcorn Book.* Holiday House, 1978.

Domanska, Janina. *If All the Seas Were One Sea.* Macmillan, 1971.

Erickson, Russell. *A Toad for Tuesday.* Lothrop, Lee, and Shepard, 1974.

Fenner, Carol. *Tigers in the Cellar.* Harcourt Brace, 1963.

Fisher, Aileen. *In the Middle of the Night.* Crowell, 1965.

Fisher, Leonard Everett. *The Death of Evening Star: The Diary of a Young New England Whaler.* Doubleday, 1972.

Fitzhugh, Louise. *Nobody's Family Is Going to Change.* Farrar, Straus & Giroux, 1974.

Fox, Siv Cedering. *The Blue Horse and Other Night Poems.* Seabury, 1979.

Fritz, Jean. *George Washington's Breakfast.* Coward-McCann, 1969.

Gans, Roma. *Birds at Night.* Crowell, 1968.

Goudy, Alice. *Houses from the Sea.* Scribners, 1959.

Goudy, Alice. *The Day We Saw the Sun Come Up.* Scribners, 1961.

Haig-Brown, Roderick. *The Whale People.* Morrow, 1963.

Hoban, Tana. *Over, Under and Through.* Macmillan, 1973.

Holling, C. *Seabird.* Houghton-Mifflin, 1948.

Hopkins, Lee Bennet. *Go to Bed! A Book of Bedtime Poems.* Knopf, 1979.

Howe, Deborah and James. *Bunnicula: A Rabbit-Tale of Mystery.* Atheneum, 1979.

Hoyt, Edwin. *From the Turtle to the Nautilus.* Little, Brown, 1963.

Hutchins, Pat. *Rosie's Walk.* Macmillan, 1968.

Keats, Ezra Jack. *Regards to the Man in the Moon.* Collier, 1981.

Kellogg, Steven. *The Island of the Skog.* Dial, 1973.

Kellogg, Steven. *The Mysterious Tadpole.* Dial, 1979.

Krauss, Ruth. *A Very Special House.* Scholastic, 1953.

Lifton, Betty Jean. *Good Night, Orange Monster.* Atheneum, 1972.

Lionni, Leo. *Frederick.* Pantheon, 1967.

Lobel, Arnold. *The Pancake.* Greenwillow, 1978.

Mayer, Mercer. *There's a Nightmare in My Closet.* Dial, 1968.

Mayer, Mercer. *What Do You Do with a Kangaroo?* Scholastic, 1973.

McCloskey, Robert. *Blueberries for Sal.* Viking, 1963.

McGovern, Ann. *If You Grew Up with Abraham Lincoln.* Scholastic, 1966.

Meader, Stephen. *Whaler 'Round the Horn.* Harcourt Brace Jovanovich, 1950.

Numeroff, Laura Joffe. *If You Give A Mouse A Cookie.* Harper & Row, 1985.

Paterson, Katherine. *The Great Gilly Hopkins.* Crowell, 1978.

Peck, Richard. *Representing Super Doll.* Viking, 1978.

Rinard, Judith. *Creatures at Night.* National Geographic, 1977.

Rylant, Cynthia. *When I Was Young in the Mountains.* Dutton, 1982.

Rylant, Cynthia. *Miss Maggie.* Dutton, 1983.

Scheer, Julian. *Rain Makes Applesauce.* Holiday, 1965.

Schubert, Ingrid and Dieter. *There's a Crocodile Under My Bed.* McGraw-Hill, 1981.

Scott, Jack D. *Loggerhead Turtle: Survivor from the Sea.* Putnam, 1974.

Sebestyen, Ouida. *Words by Heart.* Little, Brown 1979.

Selsam, Millicent. *Night Animals.* Four Winds Press, 1979.

Sendak, Maurice. *Chicken Soup with Rice.* Harper, 1962.

Silverstein, Shel. *Who Wants a Cheap Rhinoceros?* Macmillan, 1983.

Sperry, Armstrong. *Call It Courage.* Macmillan, 1940.

Spier, Peter. *Crash! Bang! Boom!* Doubleday, 1972.

Spier, Peter. *Gobble, Growl and Grunt.* Doubleday, 1972.

Stephens, William. *Come with Me to the Edge of the Sea.* Messner, 1972.

Stinson, Kathy. *Red Is Best.* Annick Press, 1982.

Stinson, Kathy. *Big or Little?* Annick Press, 1983.

Thiele, Colin. *Storm Boy.* Harper & Row, 1978.

White, Ann Terry. *The Sea Around Us.* Golden Press, 1958.

Wolfe, Louis. *Aquaculture: Farming in Water.* Putnam, 1972.

References

Anderson, R., E. Hiebert, J. Scott, and I. Wilkinson (1985). *Becoming a Nation of Readers.* Bloomington, IN: The Center for the Study of Reading.

Applebee, Arthur (1978). *The Child's Concept of Story.* Chicago: University of Chicago Press.

Auten, A. (January 1984). "Understanding Other Cultures Through Literature." *Reading Teacher, 38,* 4, 416–419.

Bishop, Simms R. (1987). "Extending Multicultural Understanding Through Children's Books." In *Children's Literature in the Reading Program,* B. Cullinan (ed.). Newark, DE: International Reading Association, 60–67.

Bloom, Benjamin (1964). *Stability and Change in Human Characteristics.* New York: Wiley.

Brazelton, Berry (1979). In an interview in *Options in Education,* a production of National Public Radio and the Institute for Educational Leadership of the George Washington University.

Butler, Dorothy (1980). *Cushla and Her Books.* Boston: The Horn Book.

Cazden, C. (1972). *Child Language and Education.* New York: Holt.

Chomsky, C. (1972). "Stages in Language Development and Reading Achievement." *Harvard Educational Review, 42,* 1–33.

Clark, Margaret M. (1976). *Young Fluent Readers.* London: Heinemann.

Cohen, D. H. (February 1968). "The Effect of Literature on Vocabulary and Reading Achievement." *Elementary English, 45,* 209–213.

Cullinan, Bernice E. (1981). *Literature and the Child.* New York: Harcourt Brace Jovanovich.

———. (1987). "Inviting Readers to Literature." In *Children's Literature in the Reading Program,* B. Cullinan (ed.). Newark, DE: International Reading Association, 2–14.

Durkin, Dolores (1966). *Children Who Read Early.* New York: Teachers College Press.

Forester, Anne D. (November 1977). "What Teachers Can Learn from Natural Readers." *Reading Teacher, 30,* 160–166.

Frye, N. (1968). *The Educated Imagination.* Bloomington: University of Indiana Press.

Gambrell, L. (December 1978). "Getting Started with Sustained Silent Reading and Keeping It Going." *Reading Teacher, 32,* 3, 328–331.

Glazer, Joan I. (1986). *Literature for Young Children* (2nd Ed.). Columus, OH: Charles Merrill.

Goodfriend, P., and M. Gogel (January 1987). "Schoolwide Public Relations for the Reading Teacher: A Primer." *Reading Teacher, 40,* 4, 428–432.

Huck, C. E. et al (1987). *Children's Literature in the Elementary School* (4th Ed.). New York: Holt, Rinehart and Winston.

Huus, H. (1979). "A New Look at Children's Interests." In *Using Literature and Poetry Affectively,* J. Shapiro (ed.). Newark, DE: International Reading Association.

Marshall, Nancy, and Melvin Glock (1979). "Comprehension of Connected Discourse." *Reading Research Quarterly, 16,* 10–56.

Meyer, Bonnie (1977). "The Structure of Prose: Effects on Learning and Memory and Implications for Educational Practice." In *Schooling and the Acquisition of Knowledge,* Richard Anderson and Rand Spiro, eds. Hillsdale, NJ: Lawrence Erlbaum.

National Council of Teachers of English, Executive Committee (February 1983). "Essentials of English." *Language Arts, 60,* 2, 244–248.

Spiegel, D. (October/November 1985). "A Story Grammar Approach to Reading and Writing." *Reading Today,* 3.

Stein, N. L. (1979). "How Children Understand Stories: A Developmental Analysis." In *Current Topics in Early Childhood Education* (Vol. 2), L. Katz (ed.). Norwood, NJ: Ablex.

Stein, N. L., and C. G. Glenn (1979). "An Analysis of Story Comprehension in Elementary School Children." In *New Directions in Discourse Processing,* R. O. Freedle (ed.). Norwood, NJ: Ablex.

Tom, Chow Loy (1969). "What Teachers Read to Pupils in the Middle Grades." Unpublished doctoral dissertation. Columbus: Ohio State University.

Trelease, Jim: (1985) *The Read-Aloud Handbook.* New York. Penguin Books.

White, D. (1984). *Books Before Five.* Portsmouth, NH: Heinemann.

Part THREE

The Conventions of Language

Chapter **Ten**

Spelling the English Language

CHAPTER OVERVIEW

Spelling is one of the conventions of written language. Spelling is acquired developmentally. Spelling instruction should have two major facets: teaching students to spell specific words and teaching them to study words systematically. Teachers can help students who have difficulty spelling by identifying their stage of spelling development and teaching to their needs at the level of development. In order to do this, teachers need to know the nature of English, the developmental stages of learning to spell, and how to teach students to spell words systematically. Teachers may choose an informal or a formal spelling program.

Anticipation Guide

Read the following questions and think about them before you read this chapter. How well do you spell? What do you do when you don't know how to spell a word? How did you learn to spell? Do you proofread papers before handing them in to an instructor? Now read the following questions and try to answer them as you read this chapter.

1.   What are the developmental stages of spelling?

2.   Describe an informal spelling program.

3.   What steps are included in a systematic approach to learning spelling words?

Key Concepts

within word pattern   syllable juncture
spelling conscience   invented spelling
letter name

INTRODUCTION

Spelling is one of the conventions of written language which means there are generally accepted ways of spelling words. The conventions of language, spelling, grammar, punctuation, and capitalization give written language the consistency that enables us to communicate. Earlier in our history, we did not have spelling conventions; therefore, any word might be spelled in many different ways. For example, *cat* might have been spelled *kat, katt,* or *caat.* It is not unusual to see a word spelled three or four different ways on a single page written by Queen Elizabeth I. Readers in those days had to figure out what the writer intended a written word to represent. After the printing press was invented, the conventions of written language developed to help printers know what to print. Children today learn to spell so they can communicate their thoughts without forcing readers to guess what they intended to say.

Spelling is important in daily life. We regularly make judgments about people's education and intelligence based on their ability to spell the words they use in job applications, reports, and letters. Spelling errors seem to jump out at the reader causing him or her to conclude the writer is not very bright. Spelling difficulties interfere with written expression because students often use words they can spell rather than the words that best express the intended meaning.

The purpose of the elementary spelling program is to teach children to spell English words. As you read the following vignette, identify the strategies this teacher uses for spelling instruction in this fourth-grade class.

SPELLING IN A FOURTH-GRADE CLASSROOM

Myra Peterson looked over the new spelling list as she prepared her lesson plans for the following week. She has been teaching fourth grade for the past five years and uses a fairly traditional textbook approach. On Monday, she introduced the spelling list from the adopted program and the students completed the word meaning activities in the text. She expanded on these when she observed that the students needed to better their understanding of specific words. Then the students took a "trial" test on Tuesday to identify the words they could spell and those that required additional study. On Wednesday Myra's students spent fifteen minutes on word study, guided by a worksheet that she had devised. The worksheet looked like this:

	STUDY SHEET					
Words to Study	Pronounce word	Word meaning	Word parts	Close eyes visualize	Write word	Check word

The students continued word study on Thursday, and on Friday they were tested on the words they were unable to spell correctly on Tuesday. Myra felt that her students were doing reasonably well in spelling, although she was considering a program like the one her friend Susan Miller had developed. Susan did not use a spelling text. She used lists of difficult words derived from research and the words that her students regularly missed in their writing. Myra thought Susan's program made sense, but she was afraid that she would have difficulty managing such a program.

Vignette Analysis

This vignette reflects contemporary spelling instruction in the United States. Some teachers, like Myra, follow an adopted spelling program because they like the security of a systematic program. They believe that they are more likely to include all of the appropriate words and instructional strategies with a spelling text. Other teachers, like Susan, have sufficient teaching experience and spelling knowledge to choose to develop their own program. The teachers who develop an independent spelling program must plan to invest more time because they must identify words, plan exercises, sequence spelling skills, and teach children a method of spelling unknown words; however, many teachers find an individually tailored spelling program very satisfying.

SPELLING

English is a complex language. Spelling English words is also complex. This complexity was generated by history. English is a "borrowing language" which has adopted words from many other languages (McCrum, Cran, and MacNeil, 1986). The Anglo-Saxons were unable to read and write, but they had a sophisticated oral tradition. When the Romans invaded England, they brought both Latin and Christianity. The natives borrowed extensively from both. Next, the English borrowed from the Vikings who raided their villages along the coast. In 1066 the Normans invaded England bringing French with them and of all the languages that English borrowed from, French had the greatest impact. What has all of this to do with spelling? History changed English spelling.

History and Spelling

Eighty percent of the words in the English language are of foreign origin (McCrum, Cran, and MacNeil, 1986). After borrowing the words, the English needed to write them. English tongues had difficulty pronouncing the sounds of the new words. We write words the way we say them, and so some English spellings reflect pronunciation differences. In some situations, the foreign spelling was adopted along with the word, but transferring spelling from one language to another does not always result in a logical spelling in the new language. In some other instances, the foreign spelling was adopted, but the word was given an English pronunciation, creating a mismatch between written and spoken word. In addition to these factors, the "great vowel shift" occurred in English which altered the sounds of long and short vowels. We have sounds like the silent "h" in *honor* and "r controlled" vowels as in *word.* Although English spellings appear inconsistent, the relationship between letter and sound is systematic not random. Therefore, with systematic study, children can learn to spell English.

One of the greatest difficulties in spelling English is the fact that we have 26 letters and 44 sounds in English. This means that some letters must represent several sounds. Three tiers of order govern English spelling: letter, pattern, and meaning. Children acquire the system for spelling English, gradually over a period of years (Henderson, 1985).

What Do Teachers Need to Know About Spelling?

Our inconsistent spelling system can be intimidating, but we can teach children to spell. In order to do this, teachers must know the following things, all of which are included in this text.

1. They must understand the English language.

2. They must know the developmental stages of learning to spell.

3. They must know how memory and thinking operate in learning to spell.

4. They must know suitable methods of teaching spelling.

5. They must be able to integrate the preceding information to create a spelling program.

FOUNDATIONS OF SPELLING

The goal of spelling instruction is to develop students' ability to communicate in written language. Spelling programs need to provide for individual differences. Some children learn to write words easily, but most children need direct instruction in order to acquire the spelling skills necessary to do this. Spelling programs have two focal points. First, they should guide children in learning how to spell specific words. Many of these words will be memorized through repeatedly reading and writing them. Spelling principles like vowel patterns help in spelling words that have more regular symbol-sound relationships. Second, they should teach children how to systematically study words (Rule, 1982). Usually, students are taught a set of steps for learning unknown words. The spelling program must provide students with opportunities to practice the words, principles, and spelling system. Spelling practice is most effective when it involves actual writing situations.

There are two important trends in spelling instruction. The first is *meaning.* Language arts authorities and teachers are beginning to recognize that students must understand words—have a meaning for them—if they are to spell and remember the words. Therefore, spelling activities should have a basis in meaning. Students should associate meanings with the words they are learning and all of the practice activities should be meaningful to the students.

The second trend is to incorporate what we know about the *developmental stages* of spelling into classroom reading instruction. How do the stages of spelling development relate to spelling instruction? Knowing the sequence of spelling acquisition stages helps teachers know how to develop students' readiness for the next stage. For example, knowing that children need a concept of the word before formal spelling instruction means that spelling instruction should develop the concept of the word. Students need to know the difference between a word and a letter. The interrelatedness of the language arts is quite apparent in spelling; students are learning to write words, but they need the language concept of the word to do this—they need to be able to read words to spell them, they need to know word meanings in order to learn and remember how to spell words. Associating spoken and printed words helps develop a concept of word in both reading and writing. As you read this chapter, notice the many interrelationships among the language arts and spelling.

Teachers can use their knowledge of the stages of spelling to diagnose and remediate spelling problems. To identify the student's stage of spelling development, the teacher analyzes his or her errors (**invented spellings**), which are the spellings children "invent" or create when they do not know how to write a word. Invented spellings are based on the child's stage of development. After identifying the stage, the teacher helps the child develop the skills and understandings to perform successfully at the next stage of development. For instance, Steve, a third-grade student, was having problems. A diagnosis revealed that he spelled *each* as *ech, even* as *evn,* and *other* as *uther.* These spellings are characteristic of stage three; therefore, Steve needs to work on within word letter patterns. Stage specific instruction does improve spelling performance.

The following section summarizes the stages of spelling development.

Developmental Stages of Learning Spelling

Spelling is a developmental skill, which means that it is learned gradually over an extended period of time. Since spelling is developmental, children who are novice spellers make judgments about how to spell words that are qualitatively different from those of adults who are mature spellers (Read, 1971). Researchers studied the errors (invented spellings) that normally developing children made as they attempted to spell words in order to identify the stages of spelling development. They found that children move through five predictable stages as they acquire spelling skill (Read, 1971; Bissex, 1980; Henderson and Beers, 1980; Henderson, 1981).

The developmental stages of spelling reflect the developmental stages of learning about words. Henderson (1985) says, "The concept of word is a benchmark in the advent of literacy. . . . until the word as a concrete object is conceptualized, children cannot examine words systematically, think about them, and begin to note the inner workings of their form." Children need to have much practice listening, writing, and reading written language to acquire a concept of word. Spelling instruction cannot move ahead until the students have a concept of word.

These developmental stages of spelling are summarized in this section. Note the overlap of ages in the stages to indicate the varying maturation of individuals.

Stages One Through Five   *Stage 1*—The **Prereading** Stage spans the ages of one through seven for average children. During this stage children scribble, draw, and imitate writing. Through these activities they realize that letters are used to write words, so they group letters together which do not relate to the actual spelling of the word. For example, children at this step may write ABDG to represent the name *Kathy,* or TRM to represent the word *dog.* Instruction for this stage should focus on language, listening to stories, telling stories, identifying symbols, and pictures, learning letters, scribbling, drawing, and imitating writing.

Stage 2—The **Letter Name** Stage occurs between the ages of five and nine for average children. These youngsters have a concept of word and the alphabetic principle of writing; therefore, they can learn to spell any word they can speak. The fact that they begin to spell words with consonants correctly indicates they are discriminating sounds. They tend to use only direct letter-to-sound matches. Early in this stage children may use one consonant letter to represent an entire word. Then they begin to write all or most of the consonants in a word. Children in this developmental level might spell the word *cat* as *kt* or the word *get* as *gt.* When they begin to write vowels, they write long vowels more than short vowels. During this stage children should learn sight words, read aloud, and begin to understand the basic form of stories. Following are examples of stage two spellings for the word *boat* that occurred at the beginning, middle, and end of this developmental stage.

Stage 2 (early)-*b*

Stage 2 (middle)-*bt*

Stage 2 (end)-*bot*

Stage 3—The **Within Word Pattern** of spelling development occurs between the ages of six and twelve. This stage is called "the within word" stage because children are ready to learn about the within word vowel patterns of English spelling and the relationship between these patterns and English word meaning. Children in this stage use vowels, although they may use an incorrect vowel to represent a sound. A youngster in this stage might spell *rain* as *rane, many* as *mene,* and *trip* as *trep.* Their invented spellings use more vowels than in previous stages. In order to move to the next stage of development children need to understand how letter groups work as units and relational thinking (Henderson, 1985). Children in this stage of development need to read orally and silently, to acquire word meanings, and to continue rapid word acquisition. Sorting activities where they categorize words by spelling patterns help students achieve the cognitive development they need to proceed to the next stage of spelling.

Stage 4—**Syllable Juncture** appears between the ages of eight and eighteen. Invented spelling errors tend to occur at juncture and schwa positions. The core principle of this stage is that of doubling consonants to mark the short English vowel. Children learn this principle after they master the basic vowel patterns, including the silent *e* marker. They recognize the need to double consonants, but they are unsure when to apply this generalization. This characteristic is exhibited by the youngster who spelled *rider* as *ridder* and *gate* as *gaett*. However, *sitting* was spelled correctly. Youngsters in this stage may exhibit difficulty with the silent *e* and digraphs. For example, a youngster in this stage might spell *make* as *maik* and *little* as *litl*. The most common errors during this stage occur in spelling the *schwa* sound. Teaching children to walk through words, which involves speaking words naturally, defining syllable divisions, noting affixes, and recognizing meaning units, extends students' maturity in this stage of spelling development.

Stage 5—The **Derivational** Stage occurs between the ages of ten and one hundred. A ceiling age of one hundred indicates that we continue to learn how to spell words throughout our lives. In stage five, children are aware of the conventions of English spelling. These youngsters have three major understandings about spelling words. One understanding is when to double consonants as in *happy*. The second understanding is knowing the various forms of words that are based on the same root. Children in this stage associate a word with one having a similar meaning in order to spell it. Students who know how to spell *govern* use that knowledge to spell *government*. Third, students have become sufficiently acquainted with syntax (grammatical structure) to understand when a word requires endings such as *-ly* as in *quickly*, or *-ed* as in *wanted*.

Language Readiness

In kindergarten and first grade, most children need readiness experiences that will enable them to emerge as competent spellers. Some older children who have not achieved the readiness necessary for successful spelling also need these activities. The following concepts should be developed in the language readiness program.

1. A concept of word.

2. Word meanings (concepts represented by words).

3. The components that distinguish one word from another.

4. Awareness of the syntactic patterns in English.

5. The upper- and lower-case letters of the alphabet.

6. Letter-sound relationships.

Beginning readers and writers must develop a stable *concept of word* so they can focus on individual words within a line of text. A concept of word enables them to develop a sight vocabulary and to attend to the visual patterns of words in text. Children cannot recognize words if they do not understand that words are printed units; they cannot match written words with spoken words if they do not understand that words are bounded by white spaces.

Kindergarten and first-grade teachers may use many activities to help children develop a stable concept of word. One of the best activities is reading aloud to children. Children memorize nursery rhymes and simple poems from hearing them read and then the spoken words can be associated with written words. For instance, introduce a nursery rhyme such as: *Jack be nimble, Jack be quick, Jack jump over the candlestick.* Read the nursery rhyme to the children. Write it on a chalkboard or on chart paper. Then read it aloud as you point to each word (preserve the rhythm as you read). Ask the children to join you in reading, creating a choral reading situation (continue to point to the words as the group reads). Then individual children may take turns reading and pointing to the words as they read. The teacher may ask individual children to point out target words suggested by the teacher.

The previously described activity develops a concept of word, a model of reading, and memory for text. A similar activity can be developed by having children dictate a language experience story that is written by the teacher and used as text for choral reading, pointing out target words and individual reading.

Tracing models of words on the chalkboard or on work sheets that have dotted lines for students to follow helps develop a concept of word and how to write the word. Children can use magnetic or wooden letters to form words also. Manipulative letters are helpful in developing concepts of words and letters.

Word meanings are also developed by the preceding activities. Categorizing activities are excellent for developing word meanings. For example, young children may group words that represent fruits and vegetables or pets and wild animals. As children build associations for words, they find it easier to remember written words. Young children enjoy making picture dictionaries for the words they are learning. They can draw the pictures or cut them from magazines and catalogs.

The components that distinguish one word from another are developed through oral and written language. Children must be able to tell the difference between words such as *bell* and *ball* in order to spell and read words. As children use language and listen to others they hear likenesses and differences in words (auditory discrimination). Talking and listening activities facilitate auditory discrimination. Comparing and contrasting written words on charts and in books helps children learn to examine words for such distinguishing characteristics (visual discrimination) as length, beginnings and endings, double letters, ascending letters such as *t* and *l* and descending letters such as *g* and *p*. Writing words on the chalkboard and on paper, as well as watching the teacher write dictated stories, develops these abilities.

Awareness of syntax, the structure and pattern of language is developed through reading, writing, speaking, and listening. As children experience each of these aspects of language they develop a sense of meaningful word order in sentences. They develop an understanding of words that require an *-ing* ending as in coming, an *-ed* ending as in wanted, or an *-s* ending as in wants in order to make sense in a sentence. When children dictate experience stories which are written by the teacher they have an opportunity to develop these understandings. Reading rhymes and stories also develops a sense of the structure and pattern of language. The experiences discussed in the preceding paragraphs, as well as those in earlier chapters develop these experiences. Published spelling programs frequently include activities that require students to fill in blanks in sentences and paragraphs to develop this ability. These programs also include activities that instruct children to write sentences and paragraphs which develop a sense of the structure and pattern of language.

Knowledge of the upper-case and lower-case letters of the alphabet is developed in primary reading, handwriting, and spelling programs. The need for this skill is obvious since children must use the letters of the English alphabet to write words. Alphabet books, identifying letters in advertising materials, learning to write names, and letter matching activities help children acquire this knowledge.

Awareness of letter-sound relationships refers to understanding how to write sounds such as /b/ which is the first sound in the word *boy*. This awareness is developed through all types of language experiences. Beginning reading and spelling programs include many activities that stress sound-symbol relationships. Teachers may use informal activities such as asking children to find all of the words that begin with a /b/ in an experience chart, a trade book, or on the front page of the newspaper. Classification activities that require students to find pictures of objects that begin with a sound identified by the teacher also stimulate development of this skill. Making illustrated alphabet books is a motivating activity for many students.

Oral and written language activities develop the concepts students need as they learn to spell. Student journals are particularly valuable for kindergarten and first-grade children because they contribute to all of the spelling readiness skills identified in this section.

Phonics and Spelling

Phonics has been the focus of many recent spelling programs, because letter-sound relationships are related to spelling. However, competent spellers cannot rely totally on phonics. Phonics rules knowledge helps children spell no more than 50 percent of the words they use. Such information supports the belief that phonics is only one aspect of spelling rather than a total approach.

The following phonics principles offer the most consistent value in spelling.

1. The association between consonant sounds and the letters that represent these sounds is more consistent than vowel sounds.

2. Words ending in silent *e* usually drop the *e* before adding a suffix beginning with a vowel. When adding a suffix beginning with a consonant, the *e* is retained (*bake-baking, like-likely*).

3. When a word ends in a consonant and a *y*, the *y* is changed to *i* before a suffix is added unless the suffix begins with an *i* (*candy-candies*).

4. Words ending in a vowel and *y* do not change the *y* to *i* when adding a suffix beginning with a vowel (*play-played*).

5. The letter *q* is usually followed by *u* (*quit, quart*).

6. The plurals of most words are formed by adding *s* (*boy-boys*).

7. When a noun ends with *s, x, sh,* or *ch* the plural is usually formed by adding *es* (*boxes, buses, churches, bushes*).

Primary-Grade Spelling Instruction

Initially, primary spelling instruction focuses on readiness. Language arts instruction in first grade develops student readiness for spelling. Daily speaking, listening, reading, and writing activities develop spelling knowledge. Many first graders have developed a stable concept of word, which enables them to learn sight words. They memorize sight words from seeing them in print and associating meaning and pronunciation with print. Knowing words gives students a means of looking at details within words, which helps them learn the patterns of letters in words. By the end of first grade many children have incidentally memorized the visual image of sight words so they can spell them. Auditory discrimination is important throughout the primary grades because discerning the sounds in words helps students spell them.

Primary-grade children who match consonant letters to phonemes (sounds) are ready to study vowel spelling patterns concurrently with their studies of sight words and word meanings. This stage is usually achieved in second grade. Most primary spelling programs include consonants and consonant blends in first grade. By second grade the focus of instruction shifts to vowels and vowel spelling patterns. Word sorts that direct students' attention to the common vowel patterns will help them master these patterns. Locating examples of words that fit vowel patterns in their reading materials also helps reinforce the patterns.

By third grade, most children have learned to spell the common sight words they learned to read previously. They have learned to read many words with inflected endings of *-ed, -ing, -s,* and *-es.* Inflected endings are associated with English syntax and third-grade children understand syntax well enough to anticipate when a word will be inflected. Thus, they are ready to learn to spell inflected endings. Two-syllable words occur with greater frequency in third grade reading content, so they are ready to spell longer words. Two-syllable words are more likely to include prefixes or suffixes, so students can learn to spell common affixes. Compound words appear with greater frequency in second- and third-grade reading materials, which means they should be included in these spelling programs.

In addition to stressing meaning, spelling activities should help students identify the words comprising a compound word and the affixes that form words. Visual identification of these word parts aids spelling mastery. Children may use known words to form compound words. They can also use affixes with known roots to form words.

Middle-Grade Spelling Instruction

Most middle-grade students encounter many polysyllabic words. To spell these words they need to understand syllables and syllable junctures. Of course, meaning is central to the middle-grade spelling program. Students use their word knowledge to infer the spelling of related words. During these grades the spelling curriculum includes the rules for dropping *e* and when to double consonants with *-ed* and *-ing.* The major syllable patterns in English such as vowel-consonant-consonant-vowel and vowel-consonant-vowel are explored. Although they have learned these patterns in reading, students must learn to use them for encoding (writing) words rather than decoding. They also memorize words that are irregularly spelled. Students' command of prefixes and suffixes is considerably expanded.

This section explored the spelling knowledge and understandings developed in the elementary grades. The next section examines the words to be learned in elementary school.

What Words?

The preceding section examined the spelling principles that children need to learn in elementary school. This section addresses the question of what words to learn. Spelling words have been researched many times over the years. Horn (1926) studied words that were frequently used in writing, Rinsland (1945) examined words that students used both in and out of school, and Fitzgerald (1951) studied the words that children used in and out of school as they grew from childhood to adulthood. Each of these studies was concerned with word frequency, which means identifying words that are used often. The idea behind this approach is that words students use most often should be the ones that they learn to spell.

Frequency   Research in the frequency of words in various types of materials has helped in identifying spelling words used in current spelling lists. Jacobson (1974) studied the frequency with which words occur in children's writing, while Harris and Jacobson (1972) studied the words occurring in basal readers. Green (1955) identified the words that are likely to be spelled correctly at various grade levels, while Gates (1937) studied the most probable misspellings for selected words at various grade levels. Five thousand words account for about 95 percent of the running words in everyday adult writing (Henderson, 1985). Therefore, it seems logical to include these frequently occurring words in the spelling curriculum. You may wish to study the lists of words referred to above, as well as sight word lists like the Dolch list (1948), Dolch's list of 95 common nouns (1945), Johns' revision of the Dolch list (1976), and Durr's (1973) list of the 188 words that occur most frequently in popular trade books. You may wish to compare the words introduced in commercial spelling programs with those on frequency lists.

Researchers have also examined words that are particularly difficult for students to spell. These words are often called "spelling demons." A list of spelling demons for elementary students follows.

about	decorate	knew	read	there
address	didn't	know	receive	they
advise	doctor	laid	received	though
again	does	latter	remember	thought
all right	early	lessons	right	through
along	Easter	letter	rough	tired
already	easy	little	route	together
although	enough	loose	said	tomorrow
always	every	loving	Santa Claus	tonight
among	everybody	making	Saturday	too
April	favorite	many	says	toys
arithmetic	February	maybe	school	train
aunt	fierce	minute	schoolhouse	traveling
awhile	first	morning	several	trouble
balloon	football	mother	shoes	truly
because	forty	name	since	Tuesday
been	fourth	neither	skiing	two
before	Friday	nice	skis	until
birthday	friend	none	some	used
blue	fuel	o'clock	something	vacation
bought	getting	off	sometime	very
built	goes	often	soon	wear
busy	grade	once	store	weather
buy	guard	outside	straight	weigh
children	guess	party	studying	were
chocolate	half	peace	sugar	we're
choose	Halloween	people	summer	when
Christmas	handkerchief	piece	Sunday	where
close	haven't	played	suppose	which
color	having	plays	sure	white
come	hear	please	surely	whole
coming	heard	poison	surprise	women
cough	height	practice	surrounded	would
could	hello	pretty	swimming	write
couldn't	here	principal	teacher	writing
country	hospital	quarter	tear	wrote
cousin	hour	quit	terrible	you
cupboard	house	quite	Thanksgiving	your
dairy	instead	raise	their	you're
dear				

SOURCE: The New Reading Teacher's Book of Lists by Edward Bernard Fry, Ph.D., Dona Lee Fountouki-dis, Ed.D., and Jacqueline Kress Polk, MA. Copyright © 1985. Used by permission of the publisher, Prentice-Hall, Inc., Englewood Cliffs, NJ.

Spelling Patterns   In many basal spelling textbooks, the words in the weekly lessons are organized by spelling patterns. For example, one lesson might include words like *took, hood, book,* and *cook* because these words represent a specific spelling principle. Words in this kind of program are selected to illustrate and reinforce spelling patterns that frequently occur in English. Specific lists might include words ending with a silent *e* or words that end with a specific spelling pattern like (consonant) *le,* such as *tremble* and *humble.*

Word Meanings   Some textbooks group the spelling words according to concepts and meanings. For example, a weekly lesson for young children might include animal words like *cat, dog,* and *bear.* The words for older children might be categorized as government related, such as *congress, legislature,* and *senator.*

Word meanings are very imortant in spelling because students must learn to read words before they attempt to learn to spell them. Children can learn to spell words they do not know, but like all rote memorization, they will be quickly forgotten. Spelling lists should be comprised of words that students know how to read. These words should have meaning for students so they can retain the spellings.

Personal Spelling Lists   Because children vary in their ability to spell words, each student should have a personal spelling list that includes words that he or she misspells in writing. The student may refer to this list as he or she writes and as a source of spelling words.

In addition to learning to spell words that children use in their personal writing, it is helpful if they learn to spell what Hillerich (1977) calls a "security list," comprised of words commonly used in writing English. Hillerich points out that a carefully selected security list will enable correct spelling of 96 percent of all words anyone will write in a lifetime.

Another way of tailoring spelling lists to meet individual needs is to identify words in content textbooks that the students need to learn to spell. These words are a good challenge for good spellers. They may be too difficult for students who are developmentally below the fourth level.

A System for Learning Spelling Words

At the outset of this chapter, you learned that the spelling program should teach children specific words and a system for learning words they do not know how to spell.

Spelling instruction must focus on helping children learn to write words; therefore, effective spelling instruction gives children many opportunities to write words in meaningful situations. For instance, classroom compositions and reports, letters, and invitations are natural writing situations that give students spelling practice. "Spelling is for writing. It is not to develop skills in alphabetizing, recognizing double consonants, or identifying affixes and inflectional endings. These activities may contribute to greater word sense or a wider vocabulary, but the odds are that they do not contribute to greater power in spelling" (Graves, 1985). Graves reviews research showing that when words are applied in writing, children are more likely to spell them correctly. Furthermore, when spelling is isolated from the mainstream of writing, children get the impression that spelling is for exercises rather than writing.

Certainly, the more students know about words and word meanings, the more likely they are to learn to spell those words successfully. Many words must be memorized. Writing helps students visualize the internal patterns of letters in words, thus helping them memorize the sequence of letters within words. Phonics instruction has limited value in spelling instruction due to the irregularities of spelling English words. The phonics principles that have the greatest utility in spelling were listed earlier in this chapter.

Generally speaking, spelling instruction is based on giving students a test (trial test or pretest), followed by instruction and opportunities for students to practice and apply correct spellings, followed by a final test on the words that were missed in the trial test. The goal of the trial test is to identify the words that students should study for that week.

Testing (evaluation) must be an integral part of spelling instruction because it helps teachers and students identify the words they need to learn and because correcting their own tests provides for the immediate feedback which is so important to students who are learning to write words. Horn (1947) found that students improved spelling knowledge when they corrected their own pretests, because this facilitated immediate feedback. However, many teachers believe that they should recheck students' papers to be certain they did not overlook any errors. You may have students check with a specific colored pencil or magic marker to separate their checking from yours.

SPELLING INSTRUCTION

According to Hillerich (1977) the following word study method is recommended in most spelling programs.

1. Look at the word and say it to yourself.

2. Close your eyes. Try to see the word as you spell it to yourself.

3. Check to see if you were right. If not, go back to step 1.

4. Cover the word and write it.

5. Check to see if you were right. If not, go back to step 1.

6. Repeat steps 4 and 5 two more times.

Proofreading

During the editing stage of the writing process, children must learn to read their written material to identify misspelled words that they need to correct. Spelling is a problem-solving activity. Students may not know the correct spelling of a word they want to write, but they can approximate a word by spelling it as well as they can so they do not interrupt their flow of thought to look up the word. Experts agree that such approximations or misspellings do not lead to memorization of mistakes (Read, 1971; Bissex, 1980). If students realize that they do not know how to spell a word, they can code the word by underlining or circling it for later checking.

Proofreading our own written content for spelling errors can be a difficult task, because we tend to see what we expect to when we read our writing, thus overlooking our errors. Older children can benefit from using a professional secretary's approach to proofreading. They read typed materials backward across the lines to identify misspelled words.

Proofreading is related to **spelling conscience**. A spelling conscience simply means that the student feels responsible or accountable for spelling words correctly. When editing their compositions, they realize that poor spelling reflects on the quality of their work. Students who have a spelling conscience realize that poor spelling can inhibit communication.

Dictionaries are commonly used for finding correct spellings. Of course, one of the problems with this is finding words in a dictionary when one does not know how to spell them. Some teachers overcome this problem by teaching students to think of various ways to spell a word and to look up those spellings. This is a form of educated guessing. A better approach is to use a word book rather than a dictionary. Word books only list words written by syllables; therefore more words are on a page and the reader can quickly skim to locate a correct spelling. Two word book examples are listed below.

20,000 Words (7th Ed.) by Louis A. Leslie, McGraw-Hill.

The Word II, by Kaethe Ellis, Houghton-Mifflin.

Formal and Informal Spelling Instruction

Spelling instruction may be formal or informal. For formal spelling instruction, schools usually employ a basal spelling program. Basal spelling programs offer weekly spelling lists and activities that are intended to help students learn to spell the words. Formal spelling programs can be developed without the use of basal materials. In these formal programs spelling lists, activities, and methods are stipulated. These formal programs may be based on local spelling needs and materials.

Informal spelling instructions are incidental. They are largely based on the words that children misspell in their written work. The children study these words and the teacher may teach them spelling principles as the need arises. In some regards, an informal program is similar to language experience reading, and the children may keep a word bank or a notebook of words they are learning.

Selecting words to teach may be a local decision or a matter of following a prescribed program. Nevertheless, teachers must identify the proper placement for students. They need to identify their stage of spelling development and/or an appropriate grade level spelling list.

Spelling Placement

The first step in determining spelling placement is to ask students to read the list of words. Any words they cannot read should be eliminated. If they cannot read 6 words out of 25 they probably are at too difficult a level.

To diagnose a spelling stage, students' invented spellings should be analyzed. Students who spell largely with consonants are in stage 1; these students might spell *what* as *wt*, *cup* as *cp* and *dog* as *dg*. A youngster in stage 2 might spell *what* as *whot*, *cup* as *cop*, and *dog* as *dg*.

In identifying word list placement, students should be placed in word lists where they can already spell 50 to 75 percent of the words included in the list. Children who consistently miss more than 50 percent of the words presented on the pretest are in a list which is too difficult. These children should be placed in an easier list where they are able to spell a higher percentage of words correctly. You may discover that they need more readiness because a 50 percent error rate indicates that they have not learned to spell basic sight words, they have not learned the principles of spelling words, and they do not have a system for learning new words.

Spelling Schedule

Formal spelling programs ordinarily begin in second grade because kindergarten and first-grade students usually are in a readiness stage. There are many variations in spelling instruction and scheduling; the following examples are merely illustrative, they are not intended to prescribe a spelling program.

The first aspect of the weekly spelling schedule is the **pretest** (sometimes called the trial test) which is usually administered on Monday of the school week. The pretest is administered before the students look at the spelling list in order to discover which words on the list need to be studied. The children should write the words in column form as they are dictated. When pronouncing the spelling list the teacher should follow the following procedure:

1. Pronounce the words distinctly.

2. Use the word in a meaningful sentence to help students understand the meaning of the word.

3. Pronounce the word again.

When the students complete spelling the dictated words, the teacher says the correct spellings while showing the correct spellings on an overhead projector or writing them on the chalkboard. This permits the children to hear and see the correct form as they correct their papers. When a word is misspelled, the students should write the correct spelling beside the misspelled word. The teacher may wish to check these lists since we recommend that children study only the misspelled words and that their final test include only the words misspelled on the pretest.

On Tuesday of the school week children usually begin to study the words they misspelled on the pretest. They may study words through activities that develop word meaning, understanding of language structure and word structure, and in some instances sound-symbol relationships. Crossword puzzles, filling in blanks in sentences, categorizing words, and writing sentences are commonly used word study strategies. Children should be encouraged to use a study method. Fifteen minutes is usually enough time to devote directly to word study since children are working with words and language throughout the school day. Word study may be conducted in either a small group setting or on an individual basis.

Fifteen minutes a day on Wednesday and Thursday may be devoted to word study utilizing activities such as those described in the preceding paragraph or those that are provided in the spelling textbook. This amount of time is usually adequate when children are working on a list of spelling words which is at an appropriate level of difficulty, in other words they are not struggling with a lengthy list of unknown words.

The final test is presented on Friday. This test is presented in the same manner as the pretest and it is scored in the same fashion. Testing in this fashion helps children identify their own trouble spots. The teacher will need to collect these test papers so that he or she can record the students' grades.

The approaches used to help students learn to write words should focus on the aspects of words that will help children learn to spell words or proofread for misspellings. Table 10.1 shows a spelling schedule.

AN ALTERNATIVE SPELLING SCHEDULE

Marge Greer teaches 27 fourth graders. Spelling is a part of the language arts block in her classroom. She has divided her students into four spelling groups, each with a different spelling list. Each group has 15 minutes of direct spelling instruction and/or practice each day, including word meanings, learning words, and learning a system for spelling new words. All the children in this class write at least 15 minutes a day, and twice a week they have a longer composition period.

One group includes the five lowest students. Two of these students are developmentally at stage two and the others are almost at stage three. She is teaching them sight words in reading and focusing on vowel spelling pattern activities in spelling instruction. Their spelling list is comprised of common sight words that they have learned to read.

Table 10.1 Weekly spelling schedule

Monday	Tuesday	Wednesday	Thursday	Friday
Trial test	Word study 15 minutes	Word study 15 minutes	Word study 15 minutes	Final test

The second group includes seven students who are stage three spellers. They are spending time doing vowel pattern activities including sorts and finding words in their reading books and trade books that fit patterns identified by the teacher. Their spelling list includes reading sight words, words that fit vowel patterns, and words that are related in meaning.

The third group enrolls nine students. These students are developmentally at level four. Their instruction focuses on syllable patterns like VCV, VCCV, and VCCCV. Their spelling list is derived from a fourth-grade basal spelling text and it is enriched by adding two or three words from the content text each week.

The fourth group enrolls six students. These students are advanced. They are at the fifth level of development. Their instruction consists of words they have misspelled in their own writing, new words they encounter in textbooks and tradebooks, and words that they want to learn to spell. These students tend to come up with long lists of words from their content textbooks and the words they want to learn to spell.

Madge or an aide pronounces the spelling lists for students. Then they show the correct spelling on the overhead projector or on the chalkboard. Students correct their papers and hand the papers in. She analyzes the errors and teaches the needed principles or words to the group if necessary or to individuals when errors are individual.

SELECTING AND USING SPELLING MATERIALS AND STRATEGIES

Spelling textbooks are used in many classrooms as the basis for instruction and offer an organized, sequentially developed program that can be adapted to the individual needs of students. When selecting spelling textbooks, teachers should determine whether the published program addresses the following:

Provides lists of words commonly used in children's writing

Stresses word meanings in activities

Includes writing activities

Teaches letter patterns within words

Stresses syntax (word order) in activities

Stresses word structure in activities

Teaches a method for learning new words

Includes some work with sound-symbol relationships

Spelling textbooks can be adapted to individual needs by altering the word lists; for example, a word list may be shortened for some students. On the other hand, students who know many of the words on the pretest may need to learn words from their private lists, so these can be added to the list of words to learn. Teachers may decide to eliminate activities in some lessons that do not address students' needs. For example, many current spelling texts overstress phonics; some of these activities may be eliminated. Teachers may decide that their students need additional writing experiences and include writing activities in spelling lessons. When using a published spelling program teachers can use the spelling schedule in Table 10.1 or the one suggested in a basal text.

Spelling Bees

Spelling bees are used in many schools, and of course there is a national spelling bee. Spelling is more a visual skill than an oral skill; therefore, this activity has limited value for developing students' ability to write words. Spelling may be adapted to a written format by having students write the words pronounced on the chalkboard rather than spelling them aloud. In fact, when a student asks you how to spell a word it is better to write the word than to spell it aloud.

Another weakness of spelling bees is that the students who most need spelling practice get the least. Poor spellers are eliminated early in the game; therefore, strong spellers have more opportunities to spell words, which gives them more practice.

Typewriters

Typewriters are very useful spellings aids for some children. Children who have very poor handwriting, poor coordination, or who are handicapped often find a typewriter very helpful. Sometimes words are marked wrong on their spelling papers due to poor handwriting rather than poor spelling. These children's difficulty in writing clearly may prevent them from developing a clear image of the words they write. Apparently, selecting the keys on the typewriter and sequencing the keys to form a word helps them focus on word form and thus aids their spelling development. This also helps the teachers who have to read their handwriting and evaluate their spelling. Typing skill is so useful both for writing and using a computer that typewriters should be placed in elementary classrooms. The popularity of electric typewriters has made mechanical typewriters more affordable for classroom purchase.

Newer electronic typewriters have spelling programs like those of computers. These programs enable children to check and correct their spelling.

Computers

Computers are important for writing; therefore they impinge on spelling. Children who write with a word processing program have an opportunity to proofread their writing on the computer monitor before it is printed. This provides an opportunity for writing without interruptions to look up correct spellings, and students have an opportunity to correct misspellings before the content is printed, thus reducing the work of recopying.

Spelling programs are incorporated into most word processing software today. These spelling programs will check the spelling in text written on the computer by comparing every word in the text with the dictionary in the spelling program. After the checking is completed, each word that does not conform to the dictionary is pulled up on the screen so that the writer can determine whether the word is misspelled or whether the word is simply not in the program dictionary. The program will then mark any misspelled words, so the writer can reenter the text and correct them. This program offers several options for the writer; for instance, the writer may add desired words to the program dictionary or the writer may opt to type in correct spellings and have the computer replace the incorrect spellings. Computers do not provide the correct spellings but they do make proofreading much easier.

DICTIONARY SKILLS

Dictionary skills are appropriately related to all of the language arts, but they will be included with spelling because dictionaries are so often related to writing words correctly. The most important task of an elementary dictionary is to enter and define terms that students are likely to encounter in the course of their school activities and life experiences. Therefore, a dictionary should be based on a carefully selected word list appropriate to students in the elementary grades.

Dictionary and Thesaurus Skills

Dictionaries are the source of word meanings, spellings, pronunciation, synonyms, and word history for old words. A thesaurus gives synonyms and antonyms for words, as well as spellings. A thesaurus is especially valuable to students during the composition process. Since a thesaurus is organized in dictionary style today, the skills identified for dictionary study will also help students use the thesaurus.

Locating words

Finding word meanings

Pronouncing words

Using the dictionary as an aid to spelling

Using the dictionary as a writing tool

Locating Words

Locating words in the dictionary calls three skills into action—alphabetizing to the fourth letter, identifying guide words, and dividing the dictionary into fourths.

The role of alphabetizing in dictionary use is obvious because the words are arranged in alphabetical order. There are many opportunities during the school day to practice alphabetizing. For instance, children can alphabetize their spelling words; this activity will enhance spelling because it encourages students to examine spelling words carefully. Students also use alphabetical order in the library card file (unless the library has a computerized card file). Children may alphabetize the words in their word banks. Spelling textbooks, reading textbooks, and language arts textbooks all include alphabetizing exercises.

Dividing the dictionary into fourths helps you narrow the search for the guide words that will lead you to the word you are looking up. You can use strips of paper to divide the dictionary into fourths—generally speaking part one will include the letters A, B, C, D; part two will include the letters E, F, G, H, I, J, K, L; part three includes the letters M, N, O, P, Q, R; while part four includes S, T, U, V, W, X, Y, Z. This will enable you to locate the section for the first letter in the word you are looking up. Then the guide words will narrow the search to the page the word is on. Guide words are the two words at the top of the dictionary page in heavy black type that help students quickly locate words in the dictionary. Guide words show the first and last entry words on the page. For example, if you were looking up the word *major* would it be on the page that has the guide words *mainsail* and *make,* or the guide words *make-believe* and *mallet*?

Finding Word Meanings

Words in the dictionary may have one or more definitions. Each definition is usually followed by a colon (:), then by a sentence with the word in italic type. The sentence helps students know how the word may be used in a sentence—that is, it provides context clues to word meaning. When words have more than one meaning, each meaning is numbered. The most common meaning is first, the next most common meaning is second, and so on. Students have to identify the meaning that is appropriate to the context in which he or she originally read the word.

Pronouncing Words   Dictionaries provide pronunciation keys to help students pronounce the words in the dictionary. The key shows all the letters, marks, and symbols that represent sounds in words. Usually the pronunciation of words is in parentheses after the meaning.

Spelling   Finding a word in the dictionary when you do not know how to spell it is very difficult and can be time-consuming. However, during the editing of compositions, students need to check the accuracy of any uncertain words. Sometimes, words can be spelled in more than one way, such as *good-by* or *good-bye*. The first spelling listed in the dictionary is usually the preferred one.

Writing   Dictionaries are useful in writing because students can look up information about their writing ideas. In order to vary their sentences and vocabulary, students can look up word meanings to identify synonyms that could be used in place of the word.

Dictionary Instruction

Dictionary lessons should be given once or twice a week for about 20 minutes each time. Immediately after instruction, students should have opportunities to practice these skills in purposeful classroom situations. Dictionary skills should be reviewed and extended at every elementary grade level. Teachers can create informal inventories of dictionary skills to diagnose the status of students' understanding. Those students who have perfected their dictionary skills should not have to continue studying them.

EVALUATION

Evaluation of spelling progress and achievement is a necessary aspect of teaching. Assessment helps teachers assign spelling grades, measure progress, diagnose spelling problems, and analyze students' developmental stages.

A number of sources provide the information needed to evaluate students' spelling progress. Weekly spelling tests, teacher constructed or part of an adopted spelling program, provide information for student assessment. However, periodic review tests, administered every month or six weeks and covering previously taught words, help teachers assess students' retention of spelling words. If students immediately forget the spelling words they are taught, the program needs to be altered to meet individual needs.

Standardized tests usually are designed for students to identify the correct spelling of a word among a number of choices available. Some very excellent spellers find this a difficult task, while some poor spellers score high on this type of test. Standardized tests tend to be unreliable sources of information regarding spelling progress since the nature of the spelling task on these instruments differs from the skills required to write words.

TROUBLESHOOTING

The spelling problems that teachers most frequently encounter in elementary classrooms are discussed in this section.

1. Students who spell words correctly on the weekly spelling tests may misspell many words in their written compositions. A number of factors can contribute to this problem. Students often forget how to spell those words that are in their reading vocabulary and for which there are no associated meanings. Therefore, activities that stress word meanings will help overcome this problem. Another source of difficulty could be that the student does not regularly use many of the words on the spelling list, so they lack the reinforcement necessary to overlearn the words which makes them "stick" in memory. You may want to compare the words on the spelling list with the

words that the youngsters use in their compositions. If there is a significant discrepancy, you may need to use a different source for spelling words.

2. Children who spell the words correctly on the weekly spelling tests, but who cannot spell them on the periodic review tests. This problem suggests that students are not reading or using the words enough to remember them. One solution is to analyze their reading materials and motivate them to read more sophisticated content. Also, reduce the amount of time between weekly tests and the periodic review tests. Instead of administering review tests every four or five weeks, give them every two weeks. This provides additional reinforcement.

3. Children who are afraid to attempt to spell words when they are writing. They may sit and stare at the paper, use a word they know how to spell or ask the teacher how to spell the word. In response to requests to spell words, you should encourage students to say the word over to themselves, trying to hear the phonemes (sounds) in the word, and to write a letter for the first sound, then the next sound, and so forth. Some students will be able to spell only the first letter in a word, but this is an initial step toward spelling independence. When they are able to spell only one or two letters in a word encourage them to draw a line to represent the rest of the word. For example, if the child were writing the word *cookie,* she might write c_____ to show the word has more letters.

Praise children's efforts to spell words, even when they are able to spell only one letter. If we reserve praise for correct spellings, children will be afraid to invent spellings in order to communicate their ideas in written language.

4. Students who refuse to proofread their material is one of the most difficult spelling problems. There are two possible solutions for this problem. First, students can proofread one another's compositions. Second, give each student a checklist (see Figure 10.1) to complete as he or she proofreads.

I have read all of the words in this composition twice after revising it.

                                                     yes   no

I have read all of the sentences in this composition twice after revising it.

                                                     yes   no

I have checked all of the capital letters in this composition.

                                                     yes   no

I have checked all of the punctuation in this composition.

                                                     yes   no

---

Figure 10.1   Spelling checklist.

Teachers may use a self-made checklist to aid in summarizing students' spelling progress and to analyze their errors. A spelling checklist is shown in Figure 10.2. Through analyzing the words missed over a period of time, teachers can determine whether students need instruction regarding a partic-

Spelling Word	Error: ou	Error: r-controlled vowel — ur	Error: ay	Error: schwa	Error
course corse	✔				
Thursday Thrsda		✔	✔		
period prud		✔		✔	
Summary (1 point for each error)	1	2	1	1	

Name _____   Date _____

Problems to remediate: _____

_____

_____

Figure 10.2 Diagnostic spelling summary sheet.

ular aspect of spelling. For instance, some children may consistently have difficulty with irregular plural nouns or with possessive nouns. When teachers identify specific spelling problems, they may select units of study from a spelling text to help the student or they may develop games or chalkboard work to help students understand the reasons they are misspelling words.

SUMMARY

Spelling is an integral part of the writing process. It should be taught and learned through writing words. Researchers have discovered that spelling is a developmental skill and that children move through a continuum of development as they move toward competent spelling. Competent spellers know how to spell many words, but they also know how to proofread and correct spelling errors. Spelling readiness is built on a sense of word, word meanings, knowledge of the upper- and lower-case letters of the alphabet, understanding of the structure of language, and understanding the features that distinguish one word from another. Both published spelling programs and informal spelling programs should stress word meanings, language structure, word structure, and consistent phonic information. Both kinds of spelling programs should incorporate words that the students use regularly in their own writing. The spelling schedule should include a pretest, word study, and a final test. Assessment of spelling progress helps teachers assign grades, diagnose students' spelling problems, assess students' retention of previously taught spelling words, and analyze students' stages of development.

Thought Questions

1. How will the use of computers influence spelling instruction in the future?

2. Why does the author of this text state that spelling is one of the easiest language arts skills to integrate instructionally with the other language arts?

3. Briefly explain the developmental stages of spelling.

4. Discuss the aspects of word knowledge that are most helpful to students learning to spell.

5. Discuss how to adapt a published spelling program to individual needs.

6. Discuss the relationship between writing and spelling.

Enrichment Activities

1. Administer a spelling test to a group of children and evaluate the various stages of development found within the group.

2. Develop a file of spelling activities.

3. Examine a published spelling series and compare it with the guidelines provided in this chapter. Identify its strengths and weaknesses.

4. Obtain a set of sample of writing papers from a classroom teacher and identify the stages of development and diagnose specific spelling problems.

5. Make two word sorts that could be used for spelling instruction.

Selected Readings

Beers, J., and C. Beers (February 1980). "Vowel Spelling Strategies Among First and Second Graders: A Growing Awareness of Written Words." *Language Arts, 57,* 2, 166–172.

Bissex, G. (1980). *GYNS AT WRK: A Child Learns to Write and Read.* Cambridge, MA: Harvard University Press.

Gentry, R. (January 1981). "Learning to Spell Developmentally." *Reading Teacher, 34,* 2, 378–81.

Henderson, E. (1985). *Teaching Spelling.* Boston: Houghton-Mifflin.

Henderson, E., and J. Beers (eds.) (1980). *Developmental and Cognitive Aspects of Learning to Spell.* Newark, DE: International Reading Association.

Hillerich, R. (March 1977). "Let's Teach Spelling—Not Phonetic Misspelling." *Language Arts, 54,* 3, 301–307.

Hodges, R. (1981). *Learning to Spell.* Urbana, IL: National Council of Teachers of English.

Lutz, E. (November 1986). "ERIC/RCS Report: Invented Spelling and Spelling Development." *Language Arts, 63,* 7, 742–744.

Marino, J. (February 1980). "What Makes a Good Speller?" *Language Arts, 57,* 2, 173–177.

Morris, D. (September 1981). "Concept of Word: A Developmental Phenomenon in the Beginning Reading and Writing Processes." *Language Arts, 58,* 6, 659–667.

Nicholson, T., and S. Schachter (October 1979). "Spelling Skill and Teaching Practice—Putting Them Back Together Again." *Language Arts, 56,* 7, 804–809.

Rule, R. (April 1982). "Research Update: The Spelling Process: A Look at Strategies." *Language Arts, 59,* 4, 379–384.

Sorensen, M., and K. Kerstetter (October 1979). "Phonetic Spelling: A Case Study." *Language Arts, 56,* 7, 798–803.

Templeton, S. (October 1979). "The Circle Game of English Spelling: A Reappraisal for Teachers." *Language Arts, 56,* 7, 789–797.

Zutell, J. (October 1978). "Some Psycholinguistic Perspectives on Children's Spelling." *Language Arts, 55,* 7, 844–845.

References

Bissex, G. (1980). *GYNS AT WRK: A Child Learns to Write and Read.* Cambridge, MA: Harvard University Press.

Dolch, E. (1945). "A Basic Sight Vocabulary of 220 Words." In *A Manual for Remedial Reading.* Champaign, IL: Garrard Publishing.

————. "Ninety-Five Nouns Common to Three Word Lists." In *Problems in Reading*. Champaign, IL: Garrard Publishing.

Durr, W. (1973). "A Computer Study of the High Frequency Words in Popular Trade Juveniles." *Reading Teacher, 27,* 14.

Fitzgerald, J. (1951). *A Basic Life Spelling Vocabulary*. Milwaukee, WI: Bruce.

Gates, A. (1937). *A List of Spelling Difficulties in 3876 Words, Showing the "Hards-Spots," Common Misspellings, Average Spelling-Grade Placement, and Comprehension Grade Ratings of Each Word*. New York: Bureau of Publications, Teachers College, Columbia University.

Graves, D. (1985). "Spelling and Other Language Arts." *Spelling Progress Quarterly, 2,* (1), 15–16.

Green, H. (1955). *The New Iowa Spelling Scale*. Iowa City: Bureau of Education Research and Service, University of Iowa.

Harris, A., and M. Jacobson (1972). *Basic Elementary Reading Vocabularies*. New York: Macmillan.

Henderson, E. (1981). *Teaching Children to Read and Spell*. DeKalb: Northern Illinois University Press.

Henderson, E. (1985). *Teaching Spelling*. Boston: Houghton-Mifflin.

Henderson, E., and J. Beers, Eds. (1980). *Developmental and Cognitive Aspects of Learning to Spell*. Newark, DE: International Reading Association.

Hillerich, R. (1977). "Let's Teach Spelling—Not Phonetic Misspelling." *Language Arts, 54,* 3, 301–307.

Horn, E. (1926). *A Basic Writing Vocabulary—10,000 Words Most Commonly Used in Writing*. University of Iowa Monographs in Education, First Series, no. 42. Iowa City: University of Iowa Press.

Horn, T. (1947). "The Effect of the Corrected Test on Learning to Spell." *Elementary School Journal, 47,* 277–285.

Jacobson, M. (Spring 1974). "Predicting Reading Difficulty from Spelling." *Spelling Progress Bulletin,* vol no?, 8–10.

Johns, J. (1976). "Updating the Dolch Basic Sight Vocabulary." *Reading Horizons, 116,* 2, 104–111.

McCrum, R.; W. Cran; and R. MacNeil (1986). *The Story of English*. New York: Viking.

Read, C. (1971). "Preschool Children's Knowledge of English Phonology." *Harvard Educational Review, 41,* 1–34.

Rinsland, H, (1945). *A Basic Vocabulary of Elementary School Children*. New York: Macmillan.

Rule, R (April 1982). "Research Update: The Spelling Process: A Look at Strategies." *Language Arts, 59,* 4, 379–384.

Sulzby, E. (1980). "Word Concept Development Activities." In *Developmental and Cognitive Aspects of Learning to Spell,"* E. Henderson and J. Beers (eds.). Newark, DE: International Reading Association.

Chapter **Eleven**

Handwriting

CHAPTER OVERVIEW

Handwriting often is taken for granted. However, it is an important skill that is basic to communication and to success in all subject areas. This chapter examines prewriting skills and manuscript and cursive handwriting instruction, including the sequence for teaching these skills. The methodology for teaching both manuscript and cursive writing includes providing students with a perceptual model so they can visualize the handwriting stroke or letter, practicing the stroke or letter, and writing letters in the context of words. The principles and methods of teaching handwriting, materials for handwriting and remedial handwriting instruction are examined in this chapter.

Anticipation Guide

Think about these ideas and questions before you read this chapter. How would you rate your handwriting? Good, fair, poor? Do you think your handwriting is good enough to serve as a model for children who are learning to form letters correctly? Which style of handwriting is easiest for you, manuscript or cursive? Try to answer the following questions as you read this chapter.

1. Why are children taught manuscript writing and then introduced to cursive?

2. What is the newest form of handwriting?

3. Is handwriting an obsolete skill?

Key Concepts

Manuscript   Cursive
D'Nealian

INTRODUCTION

Fluent, legible handwriting enables students to do justice to their knowledge. Awkward handwriting that lags behind the writer's thoughts and illegible handwriting that cannot be read inhibit communication. In both instances the writer has failed to communicate his or her thoughts. In contemporary society, literacy is highly valued; a person who cannot read or write is looked down on by others and usually has a negative self-concept.

Failure to write legibly reduces employability, decreases self-esteem and the respect of others, contributes to underachievement in related academic subjects, and costs business and government millions of dollars annually (Barbe, Lucas, and Wasylyk, 1984). Thousands of tax returns are delayed each year because Internal Revenue Service representatives cannot read the illegible handwriting on the forms. The postal service is also hampered by illegible handwriting. Each year over 38 million pieces of mail wind up in the dead-letter office at a cost of nearly $4 million a year for extra handling (Wasylyk, 1984).

Why do students need handwriting instruction in this era of computers, electronic typewriters, and tape recorders? Because handwriting is a basic language arts skill. Students continue to need legible, flowing handwriting in order to take class notes, to complete forms, to label, to write personal letters and notes, to take tests, and to draft compositions. Furthermore, Markham (1976) found that handwriting legibility influences teachers' evaluation of students' work. Even students who have access to computers in classrooms and homes usually have to share these computers with others; therefore, they must draft their compositions so they can make the most efficient use of the computer when they gain access to it.

Handwriting is basic to other subject areas. Knowledge of subjects like social studies, science, and mathematics are demonstrated through handwriting. Students write words to demonstrate their spelling skills. Researchers have found that about 20 percent of spelling errors are due to poor handwriting (Barbe, Lucas, and Wasylyk, 1984). In mathematics, illegible numbers, symbols, and signs add confusion to the subject. Copying numbers from one step of a problem to another is a source of errors for many students. Yet, legible handwriting is available to the majority of students. "Handwriting, more than any other subject, can be improved through instruction and practice" (Barbe, Lucas, and Wasylyk, 1984).

Handwriting is a motor skill that must be learned in order for children to communicate effectively in writing. Mina Shaughnessy (1977) found that poor handwriting was a significant barrier to good writing. Research with young writers shows they lose out on effective composing because of the slowness with which they put words on paper (Graves, 1978). Poor handwriting inhibits spontaneous productivity because holding a pencil for more than five minutes or sequencing letters across a line in a set space is simply too great a demand (Graves, 1978). In short, poor handwriting is a disabling nuisance that creative productive people can ill afford (Arena, 1968).

Handwriting instruction is described in the following vignettes. As you read these sketches, think about the teachers' objectives, methods, and materials.

KINDERGARTEN WRITING

After the milk break, Kathy Christopher called her kindergarten students to order. She was ready to review the *top to bottom* stroke and the *left to right* stroke they learned last week, and to teach them the *slant right* stroke which is used in manuscript letters like *N, M,* and *W.* The manuscript alphabet was exhibited on a bulletin board in front of the classroom. A chart on the other side of the classroom showed the strokes necessary for writing manuscript letters. In addition, the students had a copy of the alphabet taped to each desk; they also had a strip of masking tape on the desks to indicate where to lay their writing paper.

Kathy wrote the review strokes on the chalkboard and asked them to find the letters in the manuscript alphabet that used these strokes. The children quickly identified *l, i, l, and H.* Kathy told them to take their chalkboards and chalk from their desks. She directed the children to practice writing the review strokes; then she demonstrated the new stroke and the children practiced making it.

After the children practiced the strokes, Kathy handed them sheets of unlined newsprint which the children lined up with the masking tape on their tables. Then, Kathy directed them to take their pencils out of their desks. Mary raised her hand and asked, "Should I use my 'fat pencil' "? Her teacher responded, "No, use a regular pencil." "Where do we hold our pencils, boys and girls?" In unison, the children said, "on the painted part." "Hold your pencil up so I can see whether you are holding it correctly. Jimmy, move your fingers up on the pencil a little bit. Shelley, move your fingers down on the pencil slightly."

"Today, you are going to practice the slant right stroke that we use to write upper-case *N.* Look at the alphabet on your desk and find the upper-case *N.* Watch while I write the slant right stroke. Now, write three slant right strokes." While the children wrote the strokes, Kathy walked around watching them and adjusting their paper as necessary.

HANDWRITING IN A FOURTH-GRADE CLASSROOM

Jim Reeves prepared to introduce a handwriting lesson to his fourth-grade students. He wrote the letters *b, e, f, h, i, j, p, r, u, w.* How are these letters alike? After considerable thought, Sandy responded, "They all have an undercurve." Jim wrote the *undercurve* stroke on the chalkboard and said, "How many letters can you find in the cursive alphabet chart that use this stroke?" The students identified the letters *b, e, f, h, i, j, k, l, p, r, s, t, u, w.* "This is an important stroke because it is used to write so many letters."

"Practice writing this stroke on your writing paper. Then write all of the letters that use this stroke. After you finish them, choose a character from the list on the chalkboard and write four words that describe the character. Then choose a setting from the list of story settings and write four words that describe that setting. Write a paragraph using the words that you have chosen." The chalkboard looked like the following.

Character	Setting
scientist	Mars
football player	imaginary world
sailor	spaceship
king	baseball field
rock star	mucky swamp
pilot	sinking ship

Vignette Analysis

Both teachers recognize that children do not automatically acquire handwriting skill as they mature, thus handwriting instruction is necessary. The teachers in these vignettes were teaching different forms of writing—manuscript and cursive—to students at varying stages of development, but their instruction had many things in common. Both teachers had charts in their classes that gave students visual images of the letters. Both teachers encouraged students to compare letters and strokes which adds to their visualization of the letters. In both classrooms, students learned to write the strokes that are necessary to write letters. All students practiced the strokes before writing the letters. The writing assignments in these classrooms were purposeful, so the students were not forced to complete routine, meaningless activities.

The kindergarten classroom is a contrast to the fourth-grade classroom in some regards. The kindergarten children wrote on individual chalkboard and on unlined newsprint. Kathy uses the chalkboard to teach handwriting because the tactile sensation created when children move the chalk across the chalkboard aids their learning and because kindergarten children find it easier to write with chalk. Kathy prefers using unlined newsprint while the children are learning to form letters correctly. Kathy has learned that children who have to write on lined writing paper at the same time they learn letter formation are confronted simultaneously with two difficult tasks. Furthermore, the majority of young children do not have the pencil control necessary to avoid going over the lines. Then their teachers use a red pencil to identify every instance of line crossing. This discourages many children from learning to write. Children who learn letter formation before having to use lined paper learn to write better and they do so with less effort. Kathy uses standard pencils for handwriting because her students use them at home and the traditional "fat" pencils are awkward for most students.

Jim did not use the chalkboard in this particular lesson, although he does frequently have the students practice their writing skills on the chalkboard. He regularly combines handwriting instruction with composition and with spelling to help his students recognize the functional nature of handwriting.

HANDWRITING READINESS

There are prewriting skills just as there are prereading skills. Handwriting readiness skills are quite similar to the language arts readiness skills. Young children must be able to perceive letters and to identify the likenesses and differences in letters in order to write them. They need to have oral language skills and the understandings that will enable them to follow directions and observe their teachers' handwriting models. In order to learn handwriting, children need to develop large muscle control. Scribbling and drawing are vehicles for developing pencil control, as well as the understanding that writing and drawing can represent objects and ideas (Goodnow, 1977). Clay (1975) found that early drawings and scribbling lead children to discover how to form letters. For instance they may accidentally form an *O* which becomes the basis for *a, d, and e.* By the age of three, children who have opportunities to scribble and draw learn that scribbles go up and down and that these scribbles are called writing, while pictures are not called writing (Gibson and Levin, 1975). After developing these understandings, they learn that print has distinctive features. Learning to write one's own name is a significant step toward learning what words are (Clay, 1975). They learn that this invariant group of letters consistently represents their name.

The following list identifies skills students should acquire before teachers initiate formal handwriting instruction.

1. Small muscle development.

2. Adequate eye-hand coordination.

3. Ability to hold a writing tool.

4. Distinguish top from bottom.

5. Follow left-to-right progression.

6. Recognize basic shapes (circle, square, and triangle).

7. Reproduce basic shapes.

8. Recognize basic strokes: top-to-bottom line, left-to-right line, slant-left line, slant-right line, backward circle, and forward circle.

9. Trace and write the basic strokes.

10. Recognize the upper- and lower-case letters and the numerals 0–9.

11. Reproduce upper- and lower-case letters and numerals 0–9.

HANDWRITING CURRICULUM

The major objective of the handwriting curriculum is to develop children's handwriting legibility for communication. First children should learn correct letter formation; then they should develop writing fluency, so they can quickly and accurately communicate ideas and information. Handwriting is a medium for expressing ideas and feelings. In order to achieve these skills, students must develop prewriting skills, manuscript writing skills, and develop cursive writing skills.

Prewriting skills (these skills are identified in the following section) should be developed prior to actual handwriting instruction. Students' prewriting skills should be assessed to determine whether they are ready to learn manuscript writing. These skills can be assessed by observing children's skill mastery as they participate in classroom activities. Children are ready to learn manuscript writing strokes and manuscript writing after they acquire prewriting skills.

Manuscript writing has several advantages for young children. It is easy for young children to write manuscript letters legibly because only six strokes are necessary to prepare them to write upper- and lower-case manuscript letters. Manuscript letters also parallel the print that children see in basal readers. Furthermore researchers have found that children who learn manuscript in the early grades have better spelling, handwriting, reading, and composition skills than students who never received manuscript instruction (Barbe, 1980).

Cursive writing is not introduced until children have mastered manuscript letter forms and achieved fluency in writing these forms. When cursive writing is introduced too early, it interferes with children's ability to communicate in writing. The new D'Nealian approach to handwriting instruction introduces young children to disconnected cursive during initial handwriting instruction. The long-term impact of this method on mature handwriting and reading is not yet determined. The D'Nealian approach is discussed later in this chapter.

Cursive writing is usually introduced in the latter part of second grade or in third grade, as an additional skill rather than as a replacement for manuscript writing. Both writing styles should both be maintained throughout the school years. Manuscript is generally more legible than cursive and many printed forms like driver's license applications, magazine subscription forms, and so forth, request that respondents "please print." Furthermore, the widespread use of computers displaying manuscript print provides another reason for maintaining manuscript writing skills. Throughout the years, educators have suggested that there is no need for cursive writing in modern society (Hildreth, 1960). However, tradition dies hard, and at the present time it appears that cursive writing will be a part of the curriculum for some time to come.

Skills Sequence

The first stage of handwriting is the prewriting stage which many children develop before coming to school. However, children who have not had opportunities to play with puzzles, pencils, crayons, and magic markers during the preschool years will need to explore these materials in kindergarten before formal handwriting instruction commences.

Formal handwriting instruction is usually initiated with teaching students how to form the basic strokes that make up manuscript letter forms. Children must learn to form these strokes before they learn the letter forms. Later when cursive writing is introduced, the students will learn the basic strokes comprising these letters before learning to form the cursive alphabet.

The sequence of handwriting skills for elementary school students is given below.

A. Prehandwriting skills

B. Strokes for manuscript
  1. horizontal
  2. vertical
  3. backward circle
  4. forward circle
  5. slant right
  6. slant left

C. Manuscript alphabet

D. Application of manuscript in assignments

E. Strokes for cursive
  1. slant
  2. undercurve
  3. downcurve
  4. overcurve

F. Cursive alphabet

G. Application of cursive in assignments

H. Maintain manuscript and cursive

HANDWRITING INSTRUCTION

As stated earlier, the goal of handwriting instruction is to develop efficient, legible writers. To meet this goal, handwriting must be taught in an organized, sequential manner. The following principles which were adapted from Graham and Miller (1980) should be used to guide handwriting instruction.

1. Handwriting instruction is direct not incidental. Students do not acquire handwriting skills as a result of maturation.

2. Handwriting is taught in planned, short, daily lessons.

3. Teachers practice lessons prior to presentation and are able to write a "model" hand.

4. Handwriting skills are overlearned in isolation and then applied in meaningful context.

5. Teachers stress the importance of handwriting and do not accept slovenly work.

6. Students are encouraged to evaluate their own handwriting.

7. Students do develop their own individual handwriting style while maintaining legible handwriting.

8. The handwriting program is planned, monitored, and modified on the basis of assessment information.

Prewriting Skills

Many prewriting skills are developed through reading readiness activities. Routine daily activities such as buttoning and preschool skills such as cutting with scissors promote coordination and muscle control. Such control is necessary to properly hold writing utensils and to write on lined and unlined paper.

Developing Visual Acuity   In reading readiness activities young children learn the top of the page from the bottom of the page, they learn to scan the page from left to right, they learn to identify shapes, letters, and numerals. Matching activities are included in reading readiness programs to help develop children's visual perception skills, as well as letter, word, and numeral perception. A matching activity is illustrated in Figure 11.1. Coordinating handwriting and reading enhances both skills. When children learn to make handwriting strokes and to form letters, they are learning how to "look" at letters, words, and numerals. Their hand and eyes work together to send messages to their brains that develop visual perception.

Small Muscle Coordination   Young children need small muscle coordination in order to hold a pencil. Activities with manipulative toys such as Legos, Tinker Toys, and snap beads are excellent for small muscle development. Playing with toy cars and trucks, miniature gas stations, barns, and dollhouses also requires children to use their small muscles. Modeling with clay, sand, play dough, putty, and paper mache develops small muscles. Many daily activities promote coordination—buttoning, zipping, sewing, screwing caps on jars, cutting with scissors, drawing, and painting.

Eye-hand Coordination   Eye-hand coordination refers to the ability to make the eyes and hands work together which enables children to make pencils, crayons, and paints to go where they want them to. A variety of activities develop this skill. These activities include finger painting, pasting, folding paper, cutting with scissors, stringing beads, popsicle stick art, jumping rope, following dots, and completing mazes.

Directions: Draw a circle around all of the letters that look like the first one in each row.

A	A	B	A	A	K	X	A	R	A	T
b	b	r	b	b	c	t	b	e	k	b

Figure 11.1   Sample matching activity.

Holding Writing Implements Many children can hold writing implements before coming to school; however, some children are not familiar with writing materials. These youngsters need opportunities to develop this skill in kindergarten. Activities that permit children to play with sponges, straws, squeeze bottles, sticks, shovels, eggbeaters, chalk, and crayons will develop their ability to hold writing tools.

There is a hierarchy of difficulty in using writing implements. Pencils are one of the most difficult tools to manipulate. If you doubt this, give your students an opportunity to write with chalk, a felt-tip marker, a pencil, and a crayon (Lamme, 1979). Then ask them which tool was the easiest to use. In most classrooms, children overwhelmingly chose markers as the easiest to use. Children can make marks easier with magic markers than with crayons and pencils. Therefore, it is wise to begin actual handwriting instruction with markers and felt-tip pens. Once children have gained confidence in their ability to form letters and are holding writing tools in a relaxed manner, pencils can be introduced. Chalkboards should not be overlooked during writing instruction. Children enjoy writing on chalkboards and the strong tactile sensation of the chalk on the chalkboard helps children learn correct letter formation.

Once children graduate to using pencils, teachers must determine the appropriate pencil for them to use. Traditionally, young children have used "fat" pencils; however, there is no particular advantage to the large child-sized pencils. In fact, some children write better using regular adult-sized pencils from the start (Lamme, 1979).

Children should learn how to hold writing utensils properly during the prewriting period and continue using the skill whenever they write. Figure 11.2 shows the correct way to hold a pencil (or pen) for both right-handed and left-handed children. Loosely grip the writing implement above the shaved tip about an inch from the tip. The index finger remains on top of the pencil. Teachers should observe children's writing habits to prevent them from holding the pencil too tightly because this will make them tire quickly. Tense writers also make strokes that are very dark and they make tears in the writing paper. Teachers' efforts to teach children the correct way to hold their pencils should not contribute to their tension or they are creating a self-defeating situation.

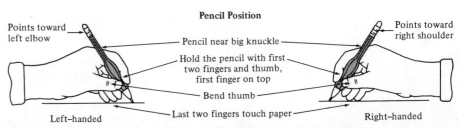

Figure 11.2 Paper positions for right- and left-handed writers.

During the prewriting period left-handed students should be taught the correct pencil grip, so they can avoid a left-handed "hook." It is better to teach them the correct way to hold a writing implement at the outset than to attempt to correct a bad habit later.

Unlined Paper   Kindergarten and first-grade children should use unlined paper to learn manuscript letter formation. As stated earlier in this chapter, children who learn correct letter formation on lined paper face two difficult tasks simultaneously. Children are ready for lined paper when they master manuscript letter formation and when their writing has achieved a consistent height on unlined paper (Lamme, 1979). Children do not find it easier to write on wide-lined paper than on regular adult paper with narrow spaces for writing (Halpin and Halpin, 1976).

Children should practice using the correct paper position every time they write, so they habitually use the correct position. Paper position helps both right-handed and left-handed children write better. However, teachers should use common sense in teaching paper position. Children should be able to sit comfortably while writing. (Figure 11.6 will show correct paper positions for cursive writing.)

Teaching Manuscript Strokes

The basic strokes of manuscript writing can be developed through activities like drawing, painting, finger painting, playing in sand, and coloring. Books like Ed Emberley's (1979) drawing books and *Harold and the Purple Crayon* (Johnson, 1955) give children drawing activities that help them acquire these strokes. In the early stages of handwriting, children are transitioning from drawing to handwriting; therefore drawing activities are a natural vehicle for developing the basic manuscript strokes.

Teaching the Manuscript Alphabet

Three basic strategies are important to successful handwriting instruction. First students need to acquire a clear perceptual image of the letter forms to serve as a model in the muscular formation of the letter (Furner, 1969). Second, they should copy the stroke or letter while looking at a model. Finally, students should apply the skill in the context of a word.

Letter or numeral imagery is developed by looking at the letter on charts and in books. Alphabet books like the following are very helpful in developing visual imagery of the alphabet.

Alexander, Anne. *ABC of Cars and Trucks.* Doubleday, 1956.

Baskin, Hosea, Tobias, and Lisa. *Hosie's Alphabet.* Viking, 1972.

Duvoisin, Roger. *A for the Ark.* Lothrop, 1952.

Eichenberg, Fritz, *Ape in a Cape.* Harcourt Brace Jovanovich, 1952.

Garten, Jan. *The Alphabet Tale.* Random House, 1964.

Grossbart, Francine. *A Big City.* Harper & Row, 1964.

Munari, Bruno. *Bruno Munari's ABC.* World Publishing, 1960.

Piatti, Celestino. *Celestino Piatti's Animal ABC.* Atheneum, 1966.

Shuttlesworth, Dorothy. *ABC of Buses.* Doubleday, 1965.

Zacks, Irene. *Space Alphabet.* Prentice-Hall, 1964.

Alphabet Books for Older Children

Cahn, William, and Rhoda Cahn. *The Story of Writing.* Harvey House, 1963.

Charlip, Remy. *Handtalk: An ABC of Finger Spelling and Sign Language.* Parents Magazine Press, 1974.

Farber, Norma. *I Found Them in the Yellow Pages.* Little, Brown, 1973.

Gasiorowicz, Nina and Cathy. *The Mime Alphabet Book.* Lerner, 1974.

Gourdie, Tom. *The Puffin Book of Lettering.* Penguin Books, 1961.

Ogg, Oscar. *The Twenty-Six Letters* (Rev. Ed.). Crowell, 1971.

Scott, Joseph, and Lenore Scott. *Hieroglyphs for Fun.* Van Nostrand Reinhold, 1974.

Teachers can assist children in developing visual perception through asking questions like the following.

What size is the letter? (tall or short, wide or slim)

Where does the letter begin?

Where does the letter end?

Are there any slant lines in the letter?

Are there any circles in the letter?

How many curves are in the letter?

How many strokes are required to make the letter?

Is there a lift? (lift means the pencil is lifted from the paper)

Which stroke is written first?

After discussing the letter or numeral, the teacher should demonstrate how to write the letter on the chalkboard while the children watch. Having the teacher model correct letter formation is very important in handwriting instruction; therefore, teachers should frequently write on the chalkboard using correct letter formation. The language experience approach to reading (see Chapter Six) is especially helpful in developing both reading, writing, and handwriting skills because the students see the teacher writing their ideas and words. Children need to "read" songs, stories, and verses from charts and class books that they have seen their teacher write in the classroom.

The next step in developing handwriting skills requires students to practice writing the letter they are learning. After they have finished writing the letter three times, the teacher asks them to compare their letters to the model and draw a circle around their best letter. At this time, the teacher should help any children who are experiencing difficulty. These youngsters may need to trace models or have the teacher guide their hand to help them develop a better image of the letter.

The children who have formed the letter acceptably should write words that contain that letter. This will give them additional practice, so they will not forget the letter formation. Some teachers combine handwriting and phonics instruction so children can list words that include both a phoneme they are studying and a letter in the manuscript alphabet. Children should make books (Chapter Nine), greeting cards, pictures, charts, maps, letters, and signs. These activities create a functional context for handwriting skills, while making handwriting an integral part of the language arts program.

Reversals

Reversals occur frequently during the early stages of handwriting. Most reversals are the result of inexperience in reading and writing letters. Children are simply not aware of the details that distinguish one letter from another. In most cases, reversals are *not* a symptom of learning problems. Youngsters who are inexperienced in dealing with print had a chance to orient themselves to letters and their placement. During their preschool years, they recognized a toy truck whether it was upside down, on its side or had a wheel broken off; but looking at letters, a *b* becomes a *d* when it is turned around. In this spatial orientation is significant. With experience, children learn to read details in letters and words. Many reversals disappear during though some children continue reversing in second grade. Such reversals should not cause alarm because most of them are insignificant and gradually disappear as children acquire more experience.

Teachers can help prevent reversals. First, they should avoid mutually interfering discriminations. Letters and words that are very similar like *b* and *d*, or *saw* and students are more likely to confuse similar words and letters introduced together therefore, teachers must avoid letters and words at same time. Instead, introduce letter until they know it may take several weeks have students practice or words that are easily well that they cannot same level understanding students thoroughly at the same time. fused, introduce th presenting mater

Learning correct letter formation helps children avoid reversals. Correct letter formation is reinforced when students see teachers demonstrate the correct beginning point, the correct direction of motion, and correct sequence of multipart letters when they write on chalkboards and charts.

D'NEALIAN HANDWRITING

D'Nealian handwriting is a recent development in handwriting systems. The D'Nealian alphabet is shown in Figure 11.3. The lower-case letters in this system are similar to cursive lower case, so that when students make a transition from manuscript to cursive they can merely join the letters to-

See for yourself how easy it is!

xperience how easy it is to write D'Nealian manuscript tters. Using a felt-tip pen or grease pencil, trace the

D'Nealian alphabet on the acetate overlay. Arrows and stroke numbers offer guidance in direction and sequence.

re's the transition?

With D'Nealia
That's the feat
the favorite of

's hardly *any* transition.
his handwriting method
coast. All you do is

add a few simple joining strokes (shown in red) and—presto—you're writing in D'Nealian cursive!

Figure 11.3 D'Nealia

gether. Research shows that D'Nealian students reverse fewer letters (Farris, 1982; Trap-Porter, 1984). In the D'Nealian approach, the upper-case letters are more like the manuscript upper-case letters.

PARENTS AND INITIAL HANDWRITING INSTRUCTION

Many children who learn to write at home are more prolific writers when they enter school. Parents are important to the handwriting curriculum (Hall, Moretz, and Statom, 1976). Therefore, teachers should make a special effort to communicate with parents regarding correct letter formation, appropriate writing materials, and what to expect from their children. Parents who understand the goals of the handwriting curriculum and what children can do are able to help their children get a good start in handwriting. Some teachers and principals send ideas home each week or each month. These ideas may include reading, literature, writing, and handwriting activities in which both parents and teachers can participate.

CURSIVE HANDWRITING INSTRUCTION

The word **cursive** means "flowing," or writing that is joined together. Cursive writing is done with a continuous motion that is interrupted only by pauses within letters and a lift of the pen after each word. Cursive has long been the hallmark of a mature and educated writer and has come to be expected of adults (Wasylyk, 1984). Children think of cursive writing as a major step toward maturity, a "grown up" form of writing. In an effort to appear more grown up, young children often attempt to produce cursive writing before they are taught cursive letter formation. The cursive alphabet is shown in Figure 11.4.

Teaching Cursive Writing

Cursive writing is usually introduced during the second half of second grade or during third grade. Pupils differ in their readiness for this skill; readiness is achieved when students can write the manuscript letters from memory, and when they are able to read cursive writing. However, the later this transition is made, the quicker and easier children find the change. Youngsters who fluently write manuscript find cursive writing easier to learn.

Cursive writing is usually introduced over a four- to six-week period with daily instructional periods from 15 to 20 minutes. During the transition period children may write class assignments in manuscript and gradually move to cursive after they learn to form all of the upper- and lower-case letters.

Cursive Instruction Before cursive handwriting instruction begins a model of the cursive alphabet should be exhibited in the classroom for stu-

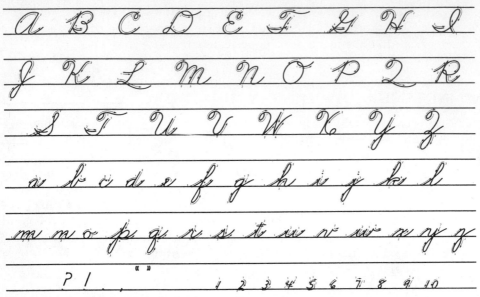

Figure 11.4 Cursive alphabet.

dent reference. In addition, each student should have an individual copy of the cursive alphabet. The teacher should have students practice their own cursive handwriting until they develop firm, bold, and precise handwriting.

Whenever it is introduced, cursive writing represents considerable change for children. Cursive instruction follows the same pattern as manuscript instruction. First, students must develop a visual image of the strokes and the letters they comprise. Then they should practice the stroke after the teacher's demonstration. After they practice the stroke or letter, they should compare their efforts with a model. The next step is writing the stroke or letter in the context of a word. Finally, they should practice writing cursive letters in purposeful writing situations.

For most students individual handwriting style begins to emerge at about fourth grade. Teachers should anticipate this development and accept the stylistic flourishes adopted by many children during this period, so long as the handwriting is legible. A variety of styles of handwriting are acceptable.

The strokes used in cursive writing differ significantly from manuscript strokes. In cursive writing there are four basic strokes: slant, undercurve, downcurve, and overcurve (see Figure 11.5). These strokes are the building blocks for cursive letter forms.

Paper and Pencil Position

The quality of handwriting is influenced by paper position and by the way the pencil is held. Paper is placed differently for right-handed students than it is for left-handed students. Figure 11.6 illustrates the paper position for right- and left-handed children. Masking tape should be placed on students' desks to

LESSON PLAN FOR CURSIVE HANDWRITING

OBJECTIVE:

Given the word *run,* the students will form the letter *r* correctly and join it to the succeeding letter.

INTRODUCTION:

Show students a model that illustrates the correct formation and joining of *r.* Explain that correct formation and joining will make their handwriting more legible.

INSTRUCTION:

1. Have students visualize the *r* by asking questions like the following: Which stroke is made next? How do you join it to the next letter in the word *run?* When do you lift the pencil?

2. Have students make three or four *r*'s, and ask them to describe the process as they write the letters.

3. Practice by having students write as many words as they can think of that begin with the lower-case *r.*

MATERIALS:

Standard pencils, handwriting paper, model of correct formation of lower-case, cursive *r.*

SYNTHESIS AND EVALUATION:

Encourage students to self-evaluate by comparing their letters to the model *r* and answering the following questions: Which of my *r*'s is the best? Why is it best? How is it like the model? How is it different from the model? How can I improve my *r*? (This activity contributes both to synthesis and evaluation.)

show them correct paper placement. Masking tape or a purchased pencil grip can be placed on students' pencils to show them where to hold the pencil.

LEFT-HANDED STUDENTS

Our handwriting system works better for right-handed students than it does for left-handed ones, which is unfortunate because research has revealed that 11 percent of the pupils in grades one through six preferred the left hand

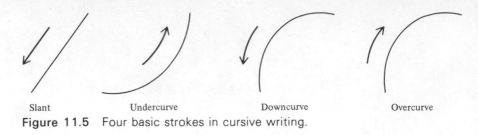

Slant   Undercurve   Downcurve   Overcurve

Figure 11.5 Four basic strokes in cursive writing.

Paper position
for
cursive writing

Left–handed

Right–handed

Pull toward
left elbow

Pull toward
midsection

Figure 11.6 Paper position for cursive writing.

(Enstrom, 1962). Among this group, 12.5 percent of the boys preferred the left hand while 9.7 percent of the youngsters preferring the left hand were girls. Teachers must make specific instructional provisions to meet the needs of left-handed pupils. Reversing the way that you teach right-handed students will not meet the needs of lefties; in fact such instruction causes them to write illegibly (Harrison, 1981).

Enstrom's (1962) observational research revealed that left-handed students' handwriting adjustments fell into two categories. The first group attempted to write with the writing hand below the writing line and the second group approached from the left side of the paper hooking their wrists in order to write. Within the two groups students adjusted their paper placement and hand position in order to achieve what they viewed as greater legibility. Overall, left-handed students wrote more clearly than did right-handers.

Teaching handwriting to left-handed students involves three basic adjustments (Howell, 1978):

1. Paper position

2. Pencil grip

3. Handwriting slant

Paper Position

Enstrom's research revealed that the most legible handwriting was produced when students did not hook. Therefore, students should learn to position their paper to avoid hooking, which also causes them to smear the paper as their hands drag over the written material.

Left-handed students should slant their paper to the left. The exact paper position will depend on the individual child. Things like body size, sitting position, and desk influence the best paper position. Children should be encouraged to adjust the paper slightly (still slanted to the left) until they can identify the best position for them. After identifying a good paper position, the teacher should place masking tape on the desk or table for the student to use as a guide for lining up handwriting paper in the future.

Pencil Grip

Left-handed students should hold their pens or pencils so that they point over the shoulder of their left arms. They should grip the pencil an inch or more higher than right-handed students. This permits them to see what they are writing and to avoid smearing the writing with their hand.

Slant

Left-handed students should not be expected to develop the same slant as right-handed students. They should be permitted to write vertically. Some left-handed students are most comfortable slanting their writing to the left, which is acceptable so long as the slant is not so extreme as to inhibit reading. Harrison (1981) recommends permitting students to slant between vertical and 45 degrees to the left.

Instruction for Left-Handers

In teaching left-handed students keep in mind that they usually write more slowly than do right-handed students. Be certain that they have left-handed desks or writing tables that are large enough to permit the adjustments they need in paper position. The chalkboard is a boon to left-handed students because they can write on it without concern for paper position. Therefore, the chalkboard is an ideal place for them to learn letter formation.

Teachers often find that grouping left-handed students together for instruction enables them to meet the needs of students, as well as avoid the confusion that occurs when left-handed and right-handed students are taught together. You may choose to teach them at the same time, but group the left-handed students together at a table in the classroom. This permits you to give them instructions as a group and they can see other left-handed students rather than being confused by sitting next to a student who is working from the right-handed perspective.

ERASERS

Erasers are a continuing problem for teachers and students. Teachers should remove erasers from students' pencils immediately. This avoids black erasure marks and holes that are erased in papers. Students should learn to cross out errors rather than erase them, which is both neater and more professional than erasing.

CALLIGRAPHY

Recently, there has been a growing interest in calligraphy as a hobby. In some places classes are offered to develop this skill, while kits are widely available in hobby stores. Calligraphy kits can be used in classrooms to spark middle-grade students' interest in this skill. Some of the children's books listed earlier in this chapter can be used in conjunction with calligraphy activities.

EVALUATION

Handwriting is mastered when the student writes the letters with the correct strokes, correct alignment, proportion, and line quality. Handwriting evaluation should be twofold. First, students should self-evaluate their handwriting by comparing their own writing with the model provided in their handwriting textbook or with a handwriting scale. Handwriting scales help teachers objectively evaluate students' handwriting. Figure 11.7 illustrates a model for

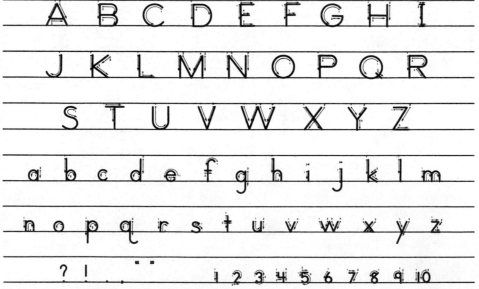

Figure 11.7   Model for manuscript writing.

manuscript, while Figure 11.4 (see page 342) illustrates a cursive handwriting model.

Children find it easier to evaluate their own handwriting if they frame the letters with a file card from which a circle or square is cut. The hole can be placed over a letter, thus focusing attention on a single letter (see Figure 11.8).

Children may self-evaluate manuscript and cursive handwriting by answering questions like the following:

1. Is my paper positioned correctly?

2. Did I hold my pencil correctly?

3. Did I visualize the letters correctly?

4. Did I form the letters correctly?

5. Did I make the spaces between the letters correctly?

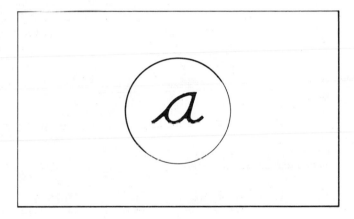

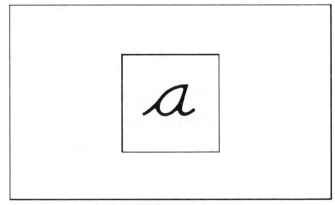

Figure 11.8   Self-evaluation of handwriting style.

6. Did I make the spaces between the words correctly?

7. Did I write the punctuation marks correctly?

8. Did I make correct line quality?

Teachers must also evaluate children's handwriting. Evaluation enables teachers to plan instruction to meet individual needs. Once specific weak areas are identified teachers can plan lessons that will remediate students' specific difficulties.

Teachers may use handwriting scales and questions like the preceding examples when they evaluate children's handwriting. Speed or rate of handwriting is an additional means of evaluating handwriting, although speed is only relevant when it is considered in relation to legibility. Handwriting speed cannot be evaluated unless the handwriting is legible. The following guidelines are estimates of speed by grade level (Barbe, 1980).

Grade 2	30 letters per minute
Grade 3	40 letters per minute
Grade 4	50 letters per minute
Grade 5	60 letters per minute
Grade 6	67 letters per minute
Grade 7	74 letters per minute
Grade 8	80 letters per minute

THE CHALKBOARD AS AN INSTRUCTIONAL AID

The chalkboard is very useful because it offers a large surface and brings into use the larger arm and shoulder muscles (Lucas, 1976). Chalkboard writing offers children freedom of movement which helps them develop smooth handwriting. Writing on the chalkboard gives children opportunities to develop eye-hand coordination, as well as large and small muscle development. The chalkboard gives children a kinesthetic experience which speeds learning for most children. Hearing the letter and the strokes, saying them aloud, writing them, and seeing them strengthens the mental image. According to Virginia Lucas (1976), chalkboard writing offers the following benefits:

1. Enables the teacher to more easily demonstrate the sequence of strokes or other instructional tasks.

2. Simplifies writing conditions.

3. Provides easy viewing for other students as well as for the teacher.

4. Easier to evaluate and make corrections.

5. Economical.

6. Permits multi-experiences.

One type of lesson that is frequently offered on the chalkboard is direct instruction in the mechanics of letter formations. In this kind of lesson, the teacher demonstrates the skill and explains the procedures to follow. The teacher writes a model and explains how to make the particular stroke or letter. Teachers can focus students' attention on a specific stroke or letter part by erasing all of the letter but the part being emphasized. When practicing on the chalkboard students should write one stroke or letter at a time, and they should practice by following the teacher's specific directions. After students have learned to form letters correctly, they should write the letter from recall without a model to follow. Students should locate the best letters or words on the chalkboard and explain why they are the best.

Writing on the Chalkboard

Teachers must learn to write well on the chalkboard because they frequently use it for demonstrating letter formation, for instructional purposes in all subject areas, for writing information, for writing instructions, and for writing homework.

When demonstrating on the chalkboard, the teacher should stand to one side while writing or write the letters high enough on the chalkboard so that the class can see them clearly. The teacher may also demonstrate by sitting in a chair facing the chalkboard and writing above his or her head (Lucas, 1976). When demonstrating cursive writing the teacher may write slightly to the left or right of center. The teacher should reach only as far as is comfortable when writing on the chalkboard. The teacher should hold an eraser in one hand for easy use.

When writing manuscript, it is best to write directly in front of the eyes. Students should face the board and stand about an arm's length from the chalkboard when writing manuscript. When the first line is written at eye level, it serves as a guide for keeping the following lines straight. Children should hold an eraser in their left hand for easy use (left-handed children hold the eraser in the right hand).

Chalk   In the primary grades, large chalk is used for manuscript writing and the chalk should be at least a half-length piece. Children should hold the chalk like a primary crayon about one inch from the writing end. The first finger is on top of the chalk. The end of the bent thumb is placed against the chalk. The top of the chalk points in the direction of the shoulder. The elbow should be held close to the body.

After third grade, children should use regular size chalk. Chalk that is broken evenly will not break while children are writing on the chalkboard. The writing end of the chalk should be blunt and rounded. This is achieved by turning the chalk frequently. This helps avoid screeching noises when writing on the board. The chalk should be held with the thumb, index, and third fingers near the writing end (Lucas, 1976).

TYPEWRITING AND COMPUTING

Many elementary schools are introducing typewriting because computers and typewriters are frequently used in schools today. The keys on electronic typewriters and on computers are closer together than on conventional typewriters; therefore, young children can reach the keys and learn touch typing. They can eliminate the mechanical difficulties of forming letters—freeing children to express their ideas without having to cope with the difficulties of remembering how to form letters, words, and punctuation marks. Children are motivated to use these mechanical devices; typing skills can thus enhance composition, reading, spelling, and handwriting. These skills enable students to produce written reports, class newspapers, booklets, and their own trade books.

A number of typewriting books are available to teach touch typing to elementary school students, such as D. D. Lessenberry et al., *Introductory Typewriting,* and Mary Ellen Switzer's *Typing Fun.* In classrooms where typewriters are not available, students may use plastic overlays to practice their keyboard skills.

TROUBLESHOOTING

As a result of extensive research, Enstrom (1966) concluded that most handwriting difficulties were the result of poor instruction or no instruction. Only one of every 10 schools requires its teachers to have some kind of handwriting training (King, 1961). Handwriting is an unpopular subject with teachers (Greenblatt, 1962), and student teachers rank handwriting last among subjects they feel prepared to teach (Groff, 1962). This data suggests that troubleshooting handwriting problems must begin with teachers. Teachers must develop legible, fluent handwriting before they can teach it. Furthermore, teachers should prepare to provide handwriting instruction for their students.

Handwriting problems fall into two general categories: letter formation problems and fluency problems. In remediating handwriting, letter formation should come first. Students should learn correct letter formation and practice until they can automatically form the letter or letters. Then speed is gradually increased by having students apply and practice the skills in functional written assignments.

A number of methods have been developed for correcting letter formation difficulties. For example, the Visual Auditory Kinesthetic Tactile Approach (VAKT) (Graham and Miller, 1980) is explained in the following steps.

1. The teacher writes the letter with crayon while the student observes the process.

2. The teacher and student both say the name of the letter.

3. The student traces the letter with the index finger, simultaneously saying the name of the letter. This is done successfully five times.

4. The student copies and names the letter correctly three times.

5. Without a visual aid the student writes and names the letter correctly three times.

Some remedial handwriting methods require the student to trace dotted representations of the letter, while others involve using a highlighter to identify incorrect parts of the letter formation. All of the remedial handwriting methods involve the use of letter models which students trace.

Handwriting fluency can be increased through motivational, functional practice. Students may apply handwriting skills during spelling instruction, in writing letters and notes, in making lists, and in composition. When students practice to achieve fluency, they should compare their writing to a handwriting scale to determine their progress and to identify letters or letter parts that require additional work.

SUMMARY

Good handwriting is important even in an electronic era. The goal of handwriting instruction is fluent, legible handwriting that permits students to express their ideas. The handwriting curriculum includes prewriting skills, manuscript writing, and cursive writing. Children usually learn manuscript writing in kindergarten and then progress to cursive writing in second or third grade. However, manuscript writing is maintained throughout students' school careers. Young children find it easiest to write with magic markers and most difficult to write with large pencils. Both manuscript and cursive writing are taught in similar ways. First students visualize the stroke or letter they are learning to write; then they learn the basic stroke or strokes that comprise the letter; then they watch the teacher form the stroke or letter; then students practice writing the letter or stroke three or four times; finally they apply the stroke or letter in handwriting practice. Paper position and pencil grip contribute to handwriting legibility. Left-handed students' paper should be positioned differently than right-handed students' paper. Students should practice self-evaluation by comparing their letters to those on a handwriting scale. Both teachers and students should use handwriting scales and questions to evaluate handwriting. Both teachers and students should use the chalkboard for handwriting instruction.

Thought Questions

1. Discuss the relationship between handwriting and composition. Explain how handwriting can facilitate or deter composition.

2. Compare manuscript handwriting with D'Nealian handwriting. What are the strengths and weaknesses of D'Nealian handwriting?

3. Discuss the use of unlined paper and regular pencils in early handwriting instruction.

4. Discuss the pros and cons of eliminating cursive handwriting from the curriculum.

5. Do you think that computers and typewriters will eliminate the need for handwriting instruction? Why or why not?

6. Is your own handwriting a good model for elementary school students? If not, how can you improve your handwriting?

Enrichment Activities

1. Collect handwriting papers from elementary school students. Evaluate them using the questions suggested in this chapter and compare them to appropriate handwriting scales.

2. Examine a handwriting series. Compare the methods suggested with those discussed in this chapter. How are they alike and how are they different?

3. Practice writing on the chalkboard. Did you write well enough to be a good model for your students?

4. Practice both manuscript and cursive handwriting until you can achieve the standards suggested for teachers in this chapter.

5. Observe a class (second or third grade) that is learning cursive writing. What problems did the children exhibit?

6. Create a lesson plan for a transition class based on the model lesson plan in this chapter.

7. Find a children's book you could use to teach handwriting, like an alphabet book.

8. Visit a first-grade classroom and conduct a study of handwriting implements. Allow children to choose from a "fat" pencil, a regular pencil, a magic marker, and chalk. Have the children vote to decide which implement allows them to write most fluently and legibly.

9. Interview elementary teachers to determine the best time for transitioning to cursive writing.

10. Obtain a calligraphy kit and practice calligraphy.

Selected Readings

Askov, E., and M. Peck (1982). "Handwriting." In *Encyclopedia of Educational Research* (5th ed.), H. Mitzel, J. Best, and W. Rabinowitz (eds.). New York: Free Press.

Barbe, W.; V. Lucas; and T. Wasylyk (1984). *Handwriting: Basic Skills for Effective Communication.* Columbus, OH: Zaner-Bloser.

Harrison, S. (1981). "Open Letter from a Left-handed Teacher: Some Sinistral Ideas on the Teaching of Handwriting." *Teaching Exceptional Children, 13,* 116–120.

Howell, H. (May, 1978). "Write on Your Sinistrals!" *Language Arts, 55,* 852–856.

Koenke, K. (November 1986). "Handwriting Instruction: What Do We Know?" *Reading Teacher, 40,* 2, 214–216.

References

Arena, John (1968). "Handwriting: Must It Be a Learning and Instructional Enigma?" *Academic Therapy, 4,* 5–6.

Barbe, W.; V. Lucas; and T. Wasylyk (1984). *Handwriting: Basic Skills for Effective Communication.* Columbus, OH: Zaner-Bloser.

Barbe, Walter (November 1980). "The Right Way to Write in the Primary Grades." *Early Years,* 84–86.

Bryant, Dale (April 1965). "Some Principles of Remedial Instruction for Dyslexia." *Reading Teacher, 18,* 7, 567–572.

Clay, Marie (1975). *What Did I Write?* Auckland: Heinemann Educational Books.

Drummond, H. (February 1959). "Suggestions for the Lefties." *National Elementary Principal, 38,* 18–25.

Emberley, Ed (1979). *Ed Emberley's Big Green Drawing Book.* Boston: Little, Brown.

Enstrom, A. (1966). "Handwriting: The Neglect of a Needed Skill." *Clearing House, 40,* 168–169.

Enstrom, E. (1962). "The Relative Efficiency of the Various Approaches to Writing with the Left Hand." *Journal of Educational Research, 55,* 283–298.

Farris, P. (1982). *A Comparison of Handwriting Strategies for Primary Grade Students.* Arlington, VA: ERIC Document Reproduction Service.

Furner, Beatrice (November 1969). "The Perceptual-Motor Nature of Learning in Handwriting." *Elementary English, 46,* 127–136.

Gibson, E. and H. Levin (1975). *The Psychology of Reading.* Cambridge, MA: The MIT Press.

Goodnow, Jacqueline (1977). *Children Drawing.* Cambridge, MA: Harvard University Press.

Graham, Steve, and Lamoine Miller (October 1980). "Handwriting Research and Practice: A Unified Approach." *Focus on Exceptional Children, 13,* 2.

Graves, Donald H. (March 1978). "Handwriting Is for Writing." *Language Arts, 55,* 3, 393–399.

Greenblatt, E. (1962). "An Analysis of School Subject Preferences of Elementary School Children of Middle Grades." *Journal of Educational Research, 55,* 554–560.

Groff, P. (1962). "Self-estimates of Teaching Ability in Elementary School Subjects." *Journal of Teacher Education, 13,* 417–421.

Hall, M. S. Moretz, and J. Staton (May 1976). "Writing Before Grade One—A Study of Early Writers." *Language Arts, 53,* 582–585.

Halpin, G., and Halpin, G. (1976). "Special Paper for Beginning Handwriting: An Unjustified Practice?" *Journal of Educational Research, 69,* 267–269.

Harrison, S. (1981). "Open Letter from a Left-handed Teacher: Some Sinistral Ideas on the Teaching of Handwriting." *Teaching Exceptional Children,* 13, 116–120.

Hildreth, G. (May 1960). "Manuscript Writing After Sixty Years." *Elementary English,* *37,* 3–13.

Howell, H. (May 1978). "Write on Your Sinistrals!" *Language Arts, 55,* 852–856.

Johnson, Crockett (1955). *Harold and the Purple Crayon.* New York: Harper & Row.

King, F. (1961). "Handwriting Practices in Our Schools Today." *Elementary English, 38,* 483–486.

Lamme, Linda (1979). "Handwriting in an Early Childhood Curriculum." *Young Children 35,* 1, 20–27.

Lucas, Virginia (1976). *Chalkboard Techniques and Activities for Teaching Writing.* Columbus, OH: Zaner-Bloser.

Markham, Lynda (Fall 1976). "Influences of Handwriting Quality on Teacher Evaluation of Written Work." *American Educational Research Journal, 13,* 4, 277–284.

Shaughnessy, M. (1977). *Errors and Expectations: A Guide for the Teacher of Basic Writing.* New York: Oxford University Press.

Trap-Porter, J.; J. Cooper; D. Hill; K. Swisher; and L. LaNunziata (July/August 1984). "D'Nealian and Zaner-Bloser Manuscript Alphabets and Initial Transition to Cursive Handwriting." *Journal of Educational Research, 77,* 343–345.

Wasylyk, T. (1984). "The Cursive Alphabet." In *Handwriting: Basic Skills for Effective Communication.* W. Barbe, V. Lucas, T. Wasylyk (eds.) Columbus, OH: Zaner-Bloser.

Chapter **Twelve**

Grammar, Usage, Dialect, and Punctuation

CHAPTER OVERVIEW

Grammar, usage, and dialect are the subjects of this chapter. Grammar is the structure of English, while usage is concerned with appropriate ways of expressing ideas in English and attitudes toward various forms of usage. Standard English is the preferred usage, while nonstandard usage is that which deviates from the preferred. Dialect refers to language variations that are based on geography, socioeconomic status, education, and sex. Formal grammar instruction should be reserved for seventh and eighth grade because it requires the abstract thought that students generally develop about the age of 12. But children can learn quite a lot about standard English from speaking, listening, reading, and writing it. This chapter explains traditional grammar, descriptive (structural) grammar, transformational-generative grammar, and functional grammar. Research is introduced to help teachers sort out the "why," "when," "what," and "how" of grammar instruction. Teaching suggestions include reading and listening to literature, sentence combining, sentence expansion and rearrangement, revising and editing, and model sentences.

Anticipation Guide

Think about these ideas before you read this chapter. What do you know about formal grammar? Can you diagram a sentence? Do you speak standard English? Can you identify a grammatical sentence? Can you explain why it is grammatical? Do you speak a dialect? How do you feel about your spoken grammar? As you read this chapter, try to answer the following questions.

1. Why is grammar controversial?

2. How is English grammar related to the language arts?

3. How is the Ann Arbor decision related to grammar?

4. What grammar activities are appropriate in the elementary grades?

5. What is the purpose of punctuation?

Key Concepts

grammar
contextual approach
descriptive (structural) grammar
inflected language
kernel sentence

dialect
traditional school grammar
functional grammar
transformational-generative
  grammar

INTRODUCTION

Grammar is at once the most controversial of the aspects of the language arts and the least understood. Teachers must understand how grammar fits into the elementary language arts curriculum if they are to design effective instruction. In fact, teachers must understand more about grammar than they will teach their students. It is no simple matter to determine the appropriate role of grammar in the language arts curriculum. Should formal grammar be in the curriculum? When should grammar instruction begin? How much grammar should be taught? What type of grammar should be taught? How should grammar be taught? Then there are the people who believe that the current trend toward minimizing formal grammar instruction in elementary schools has led to the demise of "good" language.

There are those who would have us believe that if teachers would only teach grammar, all of the world's ills, including war, greed, famine, and hatred would be cured. The grammar issue is further complicated by the fact that almost everyone who speaks English has an opinion about teaching it and feels compelled to make pronouncements about instruction.

As you learned in preceding chapters, language is a human communication system. We first "own" spoken language; later we learn about its grammatical structure (Genishi and Dyson, 1987). Language is comprised of *phonemes,* the sounds of language; *morphemes,* the meaning-bearing clusters of sound; *semantics,* the meaning system of language including definitions of words and meaningful combinations of words; and *syntax,* the organization of words within sentences. *Grammar* describes the structure of language. In this book, grammar is defined in two ways. The first defines grammar as the underlying rules that speakers have intuitively grasped for comprehending and producing their language (Malmstrom, 1977); this aspect of grammar was discussed in Chapters Three and Four. Grammatical rules enable English speakers to generate an almost infinite number of sentences. The second meaning of grammar is the written explanation and description of the underlying language rules (Malmstrom, 1977) and is the focus of this chapter. **Correctness** is adherence to accepted conventions or rules.

The *mechanics* of language includes punctuation and capitalization, which are discussed in subsequent sections of this chapter. *Usage* refers to common acceptable uses of language (Smelstor, 1978). Appropriate language usage depends upon the communication situation, the language context. Language that is appropriate on the playground may not be appropriate in the classroom. Young children do not understand complex, abstract words that are foreign to their experience, so teachers use language they will comprehend. There are always several ways to express an idea, although some ways are more appropriate than others in a given situation. For example, the utterance "she done it" is nonstandard usage which is unacceptable in many situations, while "she did it" is standard usage and more acceptable in most contexts.

The interrelatedness of the language arts is further illustrated through grammar, mechanics, and usage. We use these aspects of language to express meaning in oral language, to understand spoken and written language, and to communicate thoughts in written language. Noyce and Christie (1983) recommend integrating grammar study with reading and writing, and Shirley Haley-James (1981) suggests integrating grammar instruction with the revising and editing stages of the writing process. As you read the following quotation from *The Cry of the Crow* by Jean George (1982) notice how the author uses sentence structure and semantics to create a mood.

> The rainy season began in late May. After sunny bright mornings, white puffy clouds would form, pile into huge thunderheads, and pour rain in the late afternoon and night. The waters of the Glades began to rise, and the white egrets and wood storks hunted the grasses of the Everglades. Fish and small water animals flourished wherever there was water.

Now, experiment with this paragraph. Use synonyms for the words, combine sentences and reduce others to kernel sentences. What happens? Does the writing have the same impact? Why is water in its various forms discussed so much? What role does sentence structure play?

Many grammars have been developed to explain the structure of English. In this chapter we will discuss traditional grammar, descriptive (structural) grammar, transformational-generative grammar, and functional grammar, because they explain current teaching practices, as well as terms and concepts that teachers meet in their textbooks and professional reading.

GRAMMAR IN THE SECOND GRADE

Jackie O'Conner settled down on the sofa to read the grammar exercises that her second-grade students had completed earlier in the day. She sighed and shook her head as her frustration mounted. "What's wrong with these kids?" she muttered. Verbs didn't seem so difficult. They used them correctly when they talked. Then to make matters worse, she realized that this was the fourth ditto sheet that she had given her students, after teaching the lesson in their textbook and completing a workbook page in class. She paused over Chris Kirk's paper.

> The little dog *done* a trick.
>
> He has *did* the trick before.
>
> The tall clown *give* me two balloons.
>
> I have *give* the red balloon away.

"Well, that settles it; I have to find some more work sheets on verbs." One of the second-grade grammar objectives is "To use the verbs *did, done, gave,* and *given* correctly in sentences and they simply can't do it."

SIXTH-GRADE GRAMMAR VIGNETTE

Jim Royer looked thoughtfully at his students and wondered why they hadn't absorbed more grammar. He taught the basic components of grammar in the sixth-grade curriculum, but the students continued to make so many errors. Oh, well, time to start class. Jim called his sixth-grade class to attention for grammar. He wrote the words *singular* and *plural* on the chalkboard. Then he asked the students to think of a meaning for each word. Josh responded first, so Jim asked him to give his definition for singular. Josh answered *one* and Jim said, "Yes, that's an excellent answer; now who can give a meaning for *plural.*" Cindy said, "I know." Jim said, "All right, tell us." Cindy replied, "more than one." "Good."

"We're going to study singular nouns and singular verbs and plural nouns and plural verbs. When you speak and write, you should use singular verbs with singular nouns and plural verbs with plural nouns. Now, can someone give me a singular noun?" Jerry said, *"teacher."* Jim wrote *The teacher* on the chalkboard and said, "Now give me a singular verb to go with the noun." "Is *watch* a verb?" queried Sam. "Yes, *watch* is a verb sometimes, but it depends on how it is used in a sentence. Try *watch* with the noun phrase, *The teacher;* does it sound right?" "No, it doesn't sound right," Sam replied. . . . "Now read the sentence on the board to yourself, does it sound right to you? Yes it does because the sentence has a plural noun (subject) and a plural verb (predicate)."

"Now I am going to put some sentences on the overhead. These sentences were taken from the papers you turned in on Monday." The first sentence he put on the overhead was, *They are going to the concert.* "Is the subject plural or singular.?

Grammar and language go together.

Vignette Analysis

Jackie O'Conner is obviously a conscientious teacher who is determined that her students will learn the "good" grammar prescribed in the curriculum. Clearly, she fits Newkirk's (1978) description of language teachers as people who teach grammar and mark up students' papers for not conforming to the rules. Jackie taught grammar and the students practiced this grammar when they completed exercises by writing words in blanks. She reflects a traditional or formal grammar approach to grammar instruction.

Jim Royer's philosophy of grammar instruction appears to combine direct instruction with integrated language instruction, as illustrated with his teaching of noun and verb agreement in the vignette. He demonstrated understanding of the interrelated language arts when he drew on students' language to further their understanding. After reviewing the concept of noun and verb agreement, Jim selected sentences from students' compositions so they could apply their understanding to revising sentences.

TYPES OF GRAMMAR

Over the years three major types of grammar have developed: traditional school grammar, descriptive grammar, and transformational-generative grammar (Smith, Goodman, and Meredith 1976). However, Smelstor (1978) includes a fourth type of grammar: functional or contextual grammar. Each of these views of English grammar contributes to our understanding of the English syntactic system. Each approach is discussed in the following sections.

Traditional School Grammar

Traditional school grammar was borrowed from Latin school grammar in England (Smith, Goodman, and Meredith 1976), thus forcing English into a Latin mold. English does not fit a Latin paradigm because the two are different types of language. Latin is an **inflected language**—one that depends on word endings; the grammatical functions are supplied by case endings. Word placement in a Latin sentence is flexible, since word function is signaled by the case endings. For example, the Latin word *appellabat* means *he called* in English. The letters *bat* in the word *appellabat* tell readers how the word functions in a sentence. Modern English is not an inflected language, although Old English (Anglo-Saxon) was. In modern English, grammatical functions are indicated by position—the subject, predicate, and object of a sentence are indicated by their position in the sentence. Consider the sentence, "The girl killed the snake." There would be an entirely different meaning if the word order were altered to, "The snake killed the girl."

Imposing Latin grammar on modern English resulted in awkward rules that were inconsistent with actual language use. An instance of this is seen in the Latin-based rule of grammar that states a sentence should never end in a preposition. Avoiding prepositions at the end of sentences often results in stiff or awkward sentences like the sentence, "Not ending sentences with a preposition is foolishness up with which I will not put," which is attributed to Winston Churchill.

Traditional school grammar relied heavily on rules and definitions that *prescribed* "correct" grammar for speakers and writers. In traditional grammar there are usually eight parts of speech, phrases, clauses, and three sentence types—simple, compound, and complex. By contrast, linguistic grammarians *describe* the ways that people use language rather than set up rules to determine (prescribe) the way language "ought" to be. Baron (1982) points out that many Americans have "linguistic insecurity," which is the feeling that their language is somehow not up to snuff. Linguistic insecurity drives otherwise ordinary people to watch their grammar in the presence of English teachers. Linguistic insecurity is derived from traditional grammar and drives students in college-level descriptive grammar courses to demand that they be taught prescriptions for what ought to be, that they be told where to put their commas. As Baron (1982) also notes, linguistic insecurity creates silence because the afflicted are afraid to make mistakes; therefore, they are reluctant to communicate.

Descriptive (Structural) Grammar

Descriptive (structural) grammar emerged from empirical studies of English as it is used. Structural grammarians emphasize basic sounds and meaning units as they study the whole of language including phonemes, morphemes, and syntax. In this view of language, any grammatical arguments would be settled by studying spoken language.

In English, four systems operate: pattern and sentence order, word classes and functions, inflectional changes, and function or structure words. Structural grammarians examined a corpus of sentences to identify basic sentence patterns and to describe the form and function of words in each pattern. Although descriptive linguists disagree regarding the number of basic sentence patterns in English, Lefevre (1964) lists four basic patterns with variations:

Pattern	Example
Noun-verb	Girls run.
Noun-verb-adjective	Carnations smell spicy.
Noun-verb-adverb	Girls run fast.
Noun-verb-noun	Girls run races.
Noun-verb-noun-noun	The boy gave the trophy to Linda.
Noun-linking verb-noun	The girl is a runner.
Noun-linking verb-adjective	The runner is beautiful.

Descriptive grammarians have studied the functions of words in sentences and identified four word classes that are defined by their positions in patterns. For example, the pattern of the following sentence indicates that nouns should be used to fill the blanks. *The _____ walked the _____.* Some grammarians use the traditional terms (noun, verb, adjective, adverb) to identify the four form classes in descriptive linguistics, while others call them class 1 (nouns), class 2 (verbs), class 3 (adjectives), and class 4 (adverbs). The words in these four classes have meaning because they have a referent or represent a specific idea, while structure words are empty words having little or no meaning. Structure words are syntactic signals. Examples of function words include:

Type of Function Word	Example
Noun markers	*The* dog ran.
Verb markers	She *is* coming.
Negative	She is *not* coming.
Intensifier	She is *very* happy.
Conjunctions	The cat *and* dog are biting *and* kicking.
Phrase markers	Jan will come *into* the house.
Question markers	*Who* will come?
Clause markers	They should call *before* they come.

Descriptive grammarians also study the signals that pitch, stress, and juncture give to language. Speakers of English use variations in stress, pitch, and juncture to alter meaning. This aspect of language is discussed in Chapter Three.

Transformational-Generative Grammar

Transformational grammarians who study the process of grammar emphasize word units in sentence context, such as noun phrases and verb phrases. Transformational grammarians recognize that English speakers can generate an almost infinite number of sentences which they have neither heard nor spoken previously. They are interested in the generative process—the rules that enable speakers to produce novel sentences that other speakers can understand. Noam Chomsky (1965) is a leading transformational-generative grammarian.

Transformational-generative grammar is based on the notion that sentences have *surface structure* and *deep structure*. *Surface structure* refers to sentence form—what is spoken or written. *Deep structure* refers to the meaning of the sentence—the structure underlying the language used in the surface structure. For example, *Susan hit the ball* and *The ball was hit by Susan* have different surface structure, but the deep structure is the same. The second sentence is a transformation of the first.

This view of grammar is based on *kernel sentences,* phrase structure rules, and transformational rules that explain how sentences are generated. **Kernel sentences** are basic language units, simple, active, declarative sentences from which all other sentences are formed. *The dog ran* is a kernel sentence comprised of a noun phrase and a verb. *Phrase structure rules* are used to generate basic language units. *Transformational rules* are used for rearranging and combining basic language units into different forms or surface structures. A basic set of phrase structure rules is shown below.

1. Noun phrase + verb phrase = Sentence (NP + VP = S)

2. NP   determiner + common noun
               proper noun
               pronoun

3. VP   auxiliary + verb expression

4. Examples of common sentences:

The baby cried.
The boy is a scholar.
The boy scared his mother.
The man has jogging shoes.
Cake is good.
She bought the dog a leash.
The jogger seems tired.

The words in basic sentences are in a fixed order. The subject is followed by the predicate. A basic sentence diagram looks like the following.

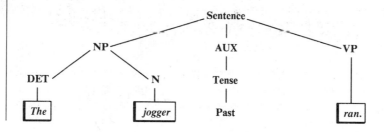

Functional or Contextual Grammar

Functional grammar instruction is process oriented because it is concerned with acceptable usage and mechanics as needed for speech and writing, rather than with rules in isolation (Smelstor, 1978). This means that in the context of a conversation among friends an individual would use informal language, while he or she would use more formal expression to communicate an oral report. This approach is thus called "contextual" (or functional). In this approach, students acquire an understanding of grammatical correctness through expressing their own ideas in written and spoken language. In such an approach to grammar, it is important to emphasize that students' ideas are important enough to warrant communication that is coherent and free of distracting errors (Holbrook, 1983). Appropriate language is gradually achieved as students grow and develop, speaking, listening, reading, and writing standard English. For instance, Shirley Haley-James (1981) recommends helping students understand the grammar of their own writing as they work through the revision aspect of the writing process. Practicing desirable language forms is more effective than memorization of rules (Kolln, 1981).

The impetus for a functional approach to grammar grew out of the current emphasis on "whole language," as well as from research which showed that formal grammar instruction had little value for students. Newkirk (1978) examined research dating back to 1902 and concluded that "there is no evidence that grammar, as it is traditionally taught, has a noticeable effect on writing improvement." Elley, Barham, Lamb, and Wyllie (1975) studied three approaches to communicating in writing over a three year period and found that formal grammar instruction had virtually no influence on language growth. Stein and Glenn (1978) posit the idea that learning how to parse the language or analyze language as one does when studying formal grammar may be a totally different process, unrelated to the effective use of language. There is a difference between learning information about English grammar and communicating.

Furthermore, the red inking of errors that often accompanies formal grammar instruction does no good and causes many students to fear writing more than anything else they do (Farrell, 1977). These individuals develop writing apprehension, a general avoidance of writing and situations that might involve writing (Daly and Miller, 1975).

USAGE

Usage refers to the pronunciations, words, and grammar that individual speakers use to communicate. Usage reflects speakers' dialect. As you probably know, some dialects have greater prestige and are socially more acceptable than others. For example, a Boston dialect has greater prestige than many other dialects. Standard English is highly acceptable and prestigious while the dialectical variations of standard English called nonstandard English usage have low acceptability. "In the United States standard English is in many situations the appropriate and thus powerful dialect to use" (Baugh, 1987). When we refer to the power of language, we often mean its social power—to get an answer to a question, to maintain a friendship, to help get a job (Baugh, 1987).

Usage is important because people make judgments about each other on the basis of language samples. When we hear a person say, "I ain't got no time fer restin,'' we evaluate their intelligence, education, and culture. Expressions like, "I be here," "I have ten cent," and "I am here since eight o'clock" are not acceptable and will limit students' communication and their opportunities for education and earnings.

Usage is less rigid today than it was years ago. Even English teachers are becoming more tolerant of variant forms of usage. For example, distinctions between the following words have virtually disappeared: dived/dove, hanged/hung, reared/raised.

Children acquire usage as they learn language; therefore, their usage parallels that of their parents and others in their close environment. If their parents use double negatives, the children use them. Children are not aware that their usage deviates from others until they venture outside of their natural language environment which usually occurs when they start school. They may experience some difficulty communicating if their usage (dialect) differs from that of the teacher or the other students.

Usage varies from situation to situation. For example, we use one level of usage when talking with friends, another level when talking with a clerk in a department store, and still another level when talking with a spouse. Even very young children demonstrate sensitivity to levels of usage because they vary language, using one level of usage with friends, another with parents, and still another when talking with grandparents.

The activities suggested for teaching grammar in this chapter will help children develop appropriate usage. In addition, tapes, television, records, oral story reading, dramatizations, and games will help children develop standard English usage. A large amount of oral language practice is necessary to learning a second form of usage. Class discussions of various ways to state ideas will alert children to thinking about language and word choice. These discussions should motivate children to learn another form of usage because in the final analysis children's desire to learn additional forms of usage is necessary to success.

AMERICAN DIALECT

A bag, a sack, a tote, or a poke, which one do you carry? The word that you choose depends on where you live. People from southern Ohio "warsh" their clothes and "arn" them. They plant "booshuz" when they landscape. Southern neighbors will "carry" you downtown if your car breaks down. These language differences reflect some of the regional dialects in the United States. **Dialects** are indigenous to America as to other nations. Linguists have studied and documented these differences. Studies reveal five major dialect areas in the United States. Figure 12.1 shows these dialect areas; you will notice more dialect groups in the eastern half of the United States than in the west and far west. This dialect group distribution reflects the early settlement of our country and the westward migration of the population. Dialects are modified

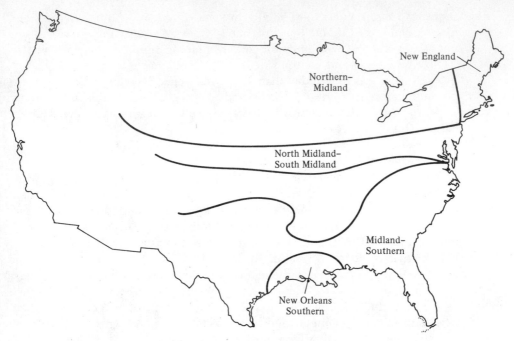

Figure 12.1   Five major dialect areas in the United States.

when they are transplanted to a new geographic area due to the interaction of the person's dialect with that of the new community.

Dialects are bona fide language systems with phonology, grammar, and semantics (Shuy, 1973). They are language variations rather than language deficiencies. Most of us are aware that geographic area influences dialect; however, other factors also have a powerful influence on dialect. These factors include speakers' age, sex, and socioeconomic status. For instance, teenagers often speak a language that can be understood only by other teenagers. Women sometimes use different vocabulary than men. Today, men participate more frequently in childcare than they once did, so their language may influence children, as well as the children's dialect influencing theirs.

Teachers are most concerned about those persons who speak dialects that vary widely from standard English. These groups include Americans like those in the Appalachians, some Blacks, children of Spanish descent (especially Chicanos and Puerto Ricans), American Indians, Alaskan Eskimos, and Hawaiians. Some examples of the differences between standard and nonstandard English are explained below.

Pronunciation

Dropping the final sounds in words—for example, pronouncing *told* as *toll* or *past* as *pass.* Another instance is overstressing the first syllable; as in *hótel* and *pólice* (Labov, 1970).

Grammar

Perfective construction, as in *I done forgot.*

Absence of the present-tense verb, as in *She walk.*

Presence of an invariant *be* category, as in *I be here.*

Extensive use of multiple negation as in *Nobody don't know nothing* (Shuy, 1973).

Vocabulary

Examples: *greens* instead of *salad, bag* instead of *sack,* and *skillet* instead of *frying pan.*

When children enter school they have virtually mastered the grammar of their dialect. They know how to use their dialect's patterns of rhythm and pitch with great subtlety (Smith, Goodman, and Meredith, 1976). They create sentences that are grammatical within their dialect. Their vocabulary reflects the experiences common to those in their culture and geographic area.

The most important thing that teachers can do when teaching students who speak a dialect is to try to understand rather than reject their variant speech. Dialect is not "good" or "bad"; nor does it inhibit learning. Researchers have found that dialect does not directly interfere with learning to read (Seitz, 1977; Rupley and Robeck, 1978). Dialect can present a major problem to language arts learning when teachers' reject students' dialect Therefore, teachers must understand and value their students' dialect and enlarge their vocabulary. The only approach that may help any large number of children is expansion; not the rejection of their mother tongue—but expansion outward from the idiolect and subcultural dialect to the expanded language of the general culture, giving up only what is no longer needed and adding to meet new needs. Teachers can be of enormous help in this process.

Attitudes toward dialect have changed in recent years. The *Ann Arbor decision* contributed to these changes. In the Ann Arbor decision, the court found that a school board had failed to help its teachers learn about Black English and how to instruct students in code switching from a dialect prevalent in the community to a standard dialect. The court found that a language barrier existed when teachers failed to recognize a language that was perfectly acceptable in the child's community. The court ordered an approach to teaching that recognized Black dialect and advocated code switching to the grammar, vocabulary, and syntax that are appropriate to the situation in which the language is used. This decision recognized the importance of learning standard English which allows students to be more generally understood. However, Black English is necessary for communication in some settings.

Young children (preschool) should have opportunities to be emersed in standard English. Their instruction should include activities like listening to stories, talking, drawing, painting, telling stories, and expanding their experiential background. These activities will help preschoolers acquire alternative dialects that enable them to switch codes.

Teachers can help children expand their language through teaching the language arts skills. Children should learn about *code switching.* We switch codes as we switch audiences; therefore, we talk to peers in one way and to an instructor in another. Children who understand that it is appropriate to use several codes because each code permits communication in a specific setting are more comfortable with their language. Teachers who model standard English, who listen with respect when their students speak, and who read literature aloud daily are encouraging children's language expansion. Teachers who encourage oral language through classroom activities and games and provide many opportunities to read, write, and listen are contributing to language growth. Teachers can read books that are written in dialect and discuss dialect differences with students. In short, teachers who richly instruct children in the language arts are helping children grow into standard English usage.

TEACHING GRAMMAR AND USAGE

The importance of understanding grammatical structures has been investigated and there is evidence that this knowledge is positively related to students' achievement in all four language processing areas (speaking, listening, reading, and writing). In other words, the more syntactic understanding students have at their command, the higher their language arts achievement. Please note that formal grammar instruction, which is not positively related to achievement is different from understanding grammatical structures.

Goals

The goal of language arts instruction is to enable students to communicate more effectively. Understanding the various ways of expressing ideas and the flexibility of English for communicating enables students to communicate more effectively. As they speak and write, language users must choose the words, phrases, clauses, and sentences that express their thoughts most effectively.

Which Grammar and Usage Should We Teach?

Children's control of the structure of their language (grammar) is largely mastered by the time they come to the first grade. During the elementary grades, their syntax becomes increasingly more complex; however, only a few new rules or structures are learned after third grade (Chapter Three). "What seems to be happening is that students do not learn new rules but become more comfortable and adept at manipulating the language rules they already know" (Straw, 1981). For instance, most children can use nouns, verbs, prepositional phrases, adverbs, and so forth, long before teachers ever introduce those terms. Heilman and Holmes (1978) suggest that, "the less emphasis there is on grammatical labels, the more the child will learn about the word patterns (syntax) that English sentences will accommodate." The elementary grammar curriculum should include opportunities to manipulate language, so that children acquire greater control and understanding of their language. The methods of encouraging language exploration are discussed in subsequent sections of this chapter.

HOW SHOULD GRAMMAR AND USAGE BE TAUGHT?

Roger Brown (1979) points out that "communication skills must in life be used with many sorts of listener and reader, and so in school students surely should practice all their language arts with one another and not just 'beam' them at the teacher." The first requirement for grammar instruction is an environment that stimulates a playful, exploratory attitude toward language. This environment should give students many different settings and purposes for using all of the language arts. Through language use children develop language comprehension, that intuitive sense of grammar that helps them function without rules. Such an environment is discussed in Chapter Two.

There seems to be little value in marking students' papers, since they apparently do not observe those marks and change their grammar accordingly. Furthermore, students who know the accepted conventions of punctuation, sentence structure, and usage do not necessarily follow those conventions in their own writing (Weaver, 1979). Weaver further notes that the structuring of activities influences students' responses. Therefore, the following strategies, activities, and materials are designed to encourage students to acquire new knowledge and to apply both new and existing knowledge.

Grammar Comprehension

When students develop grammar comprehension, they are developing an "ear" for standard English which is a sense of what sounds right. This is an intuitive understanding of language that develops from the language children hear in their environment. An intuitive grasp of grammar enables us to interpret the syntax in a nonsense sentence like, "Galdof is an amguerent blap with many trinkles." We can answer questions like, "What is a galdof?" This intuitive sense of grammar is developed through speaking, listening, reading, and writing activities that give children opportunities to manipulate and refine English.

Teachers who read literature to children daily are helping them understand standard English. Children grow accustomed to standard English grammar as they read. Literature read to children and literature for them to read should include narrative, exposition, and poetry. Folktales are especially valuable because they often include repeated patterns. For example, in the folktale "The Three Little Pigs," the wolf repeats "I'll huff and I'll puff and I'll blow your house down."

When presenting literature to children, whether it is read to them or by them, teachers can stop the reading at intervals and ask children what they think will happen next. This facilitates language comprehension because children use language and experience to anticipate story development. Many children's books develop an intuitive grasp of grammar. The following are just a few examples of good literature.

Aiken, Joan. *Arabel and Mortimer.* Doubleday, 1981. This nonsensical, hilarious book makes middle-grade students laugh and motivates them to write.

Bayley, Nicola, and William Mayne. *The Patchwork Cat.* Knopf, 1981. Alliteration and internal rhymes make this tale just right for reading aloud.

Bober, Natalie. *A Restless Spirit: The Story of Robert Frost.* Atheneum, 1981. A well-written biography that includes lines from Frost's poems as chapter headings.

Gackenback, Dick. *McGoogan Moves the Mighty Rock.* Harper & Row, 1981. This story is told in the style of an Irish storyteller, with language signaling story changes.

Joyce, William. *George Shrinks.* Harper & Row, 1985. The theme of this picturebook, dreams, is similar to *The Night Flight* and they can be used together.

Livingston, Myra Cohn. *Sky Songs.* Holiday House, 1985. Poetry for all ages.

Lobel, Arnold. *Whiskers & Rhymes.* Greenwillow, 1985. This poetry will appeal to all ages.

Ryder, Joanne. *The Night Flight.* Four Winds Press, 1985. This book has a lyric quality which makes it good to read aloud. The language in this book makes it an excellent one to contrast with *George Shrinks.*

Silverstein, Shel. *The Missing Piece Meets the Big O.* Harper & Row, 1981. Silverstein uses assonance, alliteration, and rhythm to tell a fable in poetic language. Middle-grade students will enjoy hearing it and it will stimulate writing.

Stoltz, Mary. *The Explorer of Barkham Street.* Harper & Row, 1985. Mary Stolz has created wonderful characters and vivid images in this narrative. Reading this book aloud to middle-grade students leads to rich discussions.

For children to read independently

Baker, Betty. *Rat Is Dead and Ant Is Sad.* Harper & Row, 1981. This is a Pueblo Indian cumulative story which is told with repetition, alliteration, structure, and dialog. Young child will enjoy reading it.

Fos, Paula. *One-Eyed Cat.* Bradbury, 1985. Middle-grade students will enjoy this book.

Freedman, Russell. *When Winter Comes.* Dutton, 1981. This informational book for young readers is told in a question-and-answer style.

Practice Desirable Grammar

Research shows that practicing desirable language forms improves students' usage more than memorizing rules (Kolln, 1981). Therefore, children should have many opportunities to practice speaking and writing desirable language forms. Activities such as creative dramatics, choral reading, class discussions, and writing stories, poems, and reports give students opportunities to practice language. Tompkins and McGee (1983) suggest activities that use literature to teach children standard English, and they include lists of books to use. You may refer to Chapters Four through Nine for additional ideas to develop these activities.

Sentence Combining

Sentence combining is a form of sentence manipulation that enhances grammatical understanding and communication. Sentence-combining instruction involves combining two or more sentences, often simple sentences or kernel sentences, into a single sentence that is more complex than the original sentences. For example, the sentences, "Linda has two dogs" and "Linda's dogs are frisky" could be combined into the sentence, "Linda has two frisky dogs."

Research in sentence combining has produced evidence that it is effective in developing grammatical understanding and usage (O'Hare, 1973; Combs, 1975). In more than 30 studies, the researchers concluded that sentence combining had a significant effect on productive language growth (Straw, 1981). Furthermore, studies have been conducted with many types of students including elementary and secondary, high ability and low ability, and different ethnic groups with the results showing that sentence combining practice consistently resulted in growth. Sentence combining activities produced growth whether the exercises were presented orally or in writing. Sentence combining can begin in the primary grades with oral or written activities like those illustrated on the next page. Teachers often illustrate the concept and practice oral sentence combining to prepare students for subsequent written exercises. Sentences for combining are usually provided for students in first and second grade, while students in the middle grades can compose their own sentences. Teachers also can select sentences from students' writing to use for sentence combining. This will develop writing skill, as well as language. Students find sentence combining activities more meaningful when they have opportunities to discuss how to combine sentences and why sentences are combined in certain ways.

Sentence combining exercises can be structured or unstructured. The following exercise is an unstructured activity, while the ones after it are structured.

UNSTRUCTURED SENTENCE COMBINING ACTIVITY

Directions: Combine the following sentences to make an interesting story.

There sits the black dog.
Her name is Muffin.
She wags her tail.
She eagerly barks.
She is pleading for more food.
She eats bones.
She eats meat.
She eats cookies.
She is not particular.
She eats almost anything.

Possible result:

There sits the little black dog, Muffin. She wags her tail and eagerly barks as she pleads for more food. She eats bones, meat, and cookies. Muffin is not particular, eating almost anything.

STRUCTURED SENTENCE COMBINING ACTIVITIES

Directions: Combine each set of sentences into one sentence.

1. Susan has new shoes.
   Her mother bought them for her.

   _____

2. Linda has a kitten.
   It is a yellow kitten.

   _____

3. Muffin is a dog.
   She is a mutt.
   Her hair is black.

   _____

4. Jim found a toad.
   It was big.
   It hopped away.

Students who have grasped the concept of sentence combining can create more complex sentence combinations like the following:

a. The woman went downstairs.
   The woman ate dinner.

   The woman went downstairs and ate dinner. (compound predicate)

b. The cat caught a mouse.
   The cat was sitting at the door.

   The cat, who caught a mouse, was sitting at the door. (relative clause)

c. The doorbell rang.
   No one answered it.

   The doorbell rang, but no one answered it. (coordination)

d. The rain was heavy.
   The grass grew.

   The grass grew because the rain was heavy. (subordination)

e. I am not going to play the piano.
   I am going to sing.

   I am not going to play the piano; however, I am going to sing. (sentence connection)

f. Susan has a dog.
   The dog likes to eat.

   Susan's dog likes to eat. (possessive)

g. Sharon is my older sister.
   She went to Florida.

   Sharon, my older sister, went to Florida. (appositive)

SENTENCE COMBINING ACTIVITY

Directions: What sentences were combined to make the sentence in each item?

1. I was in the yard, mowing the grass.

Possible answer:

      I was in the yard.
      I was mowing the grass.

2. I was in the orchard picking apples when it started to rain.

Possible answer:

      I was in the orchard.
      I was picking apples.
      The rain started.

Rearranging and Expanding Sentences

Students can develop an understanding of language flexibility and power through experimenting with word order. Rearranging the same set of words into different sentences as suggested in the following activity helps students' understanding.

Directions: Give each student seven word cards that have the following words written on them. Then have the students arrange the cards into as many different sentences as they can. This activity can be done at the chalkboard instead of on cards.

often   I   relax   when   I   go   home

The teacher can write sentences chosen from literature on cards or on the chalkboard and ask students to rearrange the words into different sentences. During reading class or when students are revising their compositions, teachers may ask them to rearrange the words in sentences in different ways. For example, students reading *A Toad for Tuesday* could rearrange the words in the sentence, "In the morning, when the toad woke up, the owl was gone as before" to create these sentences:

When the toad woke up in the morning, the owl was gone as before.
The owl was gone in the morning, when the toad woke up.
The owl was gone, as before, when the toad woke up in the morning.

Transformations   Sentence transformations help students grasp the flexibility of language. They may transform positive sentences into negative sentences, or negative sentences into positive ones. Declarative sentences can be changed into questions or questions into declarative sentences. Following are examples of these transformations.

TRANSFORMING SENTENCES

a. Susan went to Virginia.   Susan did not go to Virginia.

b. Linda did not go to the picnic.   Linda went to the picnic.

c. George went downtown.   Did George go downtown?

d. Will this be a long meeting?   This will be a long meeting.

SUBSTITUTING WORDS IN SENTENCES

Directions: Write a sentence on the chalkboard and have children suggest words to substitute for words identified in the sentence.

There was an *old goat.*

lazy	cow
silly	crow
scary	bat

REDUCING SENTENCES

Directions: Reduce sentences to their basic subject and verb.

Sentence: The happy, little black dog ran down the street after the cat.
Reduction: The dog ran.

Expanding Kernel Sentences Expanding kernel sentences is a way of encouraging language experimentation, as well as a way of developing writing skills. For example, the kernel sentence, "The girl ran" could be expanded to "The little girl ran fast." Of course, individual children may expand a given kernel sentence in different ways. Children may select kernel sentences from their writing for expansion, thus refining their written expression. Expansion of kernel sentences from students' own writing usually results in more interesting sentences.

LEARNING SENTENCE PATTERNS FROM LITERATURE

Literature provides many examples of English sentence patterns. Students may create sentences based on the model or they may transform sentences to questions, singular to plural, and so forth. Literature like the following illustrates English sentence patterns. Poems like *Jump or Jiggle* by Evelyn Beyer and Charlotte Zolotow's *Say It, Say It* provide simple sentence patterns for students to emulate. Cynthia Rylant models sentences that create a narrative in *When I Was Young in the Mountains.* In *Brown Bear, Brown Bear, What Do You See?* Bill Martin models questions for students; Steven Kellog uses an interesting pattern of questions and answers in *The Day Jimmy's Boa Ate the Wash.* A question format appears in Sesyle Joslin's *What Do You Say, Dear?* and *What Do You Do, Dear?*; Mercer Mayer's *What Do You Do with a Kangaroo?*; *Who Wants a Cheap Rhinoceros?* by Shel Silverstein; *The Temper Tantrum Book* by Edna Mitchell Preston; Robyn Supraner's *Would You Rather Be a Tiger?* Additional literature is suggested in Chapter Nine.

Practicing Grammar Through Revision and Editing

Revising and editing processes offer students opportunities to examine their compositions to determine whether they are communicating their ideas. Revision is more than a remedial step taken because errors have been made; it encompasses the generation, development, and refinement of language. Writers engage in revision to make sure the content is fully developed, the language is optimum, and extraneous matter is eliminated. Hillocks (1986) points out that revision is a process of choosing appropriate ways of expressing ideas; writers use their innate knowledge of grammar to make those choices. "Furthermore, students will profit much more from direct feedback and assistance in the rewriting stage than from any prior instruction in mechanics or any suggestions for consulting a handbook. The interaction with a genuine audience is crucial" (Weaver, 1979). When students revise their compositions to express their ideas, they examine and rewrite the syntax of their sentences. Thus, the revising process offers students opportunities to use grammar in functional situations.

Students find it easier to revise and edit grammar when they read what they have written aloud. They can work in pairs to help one another identify grammar revisions. They may use their language arts textbook as a handbook to help them verify their written expression. Student-teacher conferences are another vehicle for guiding students' grammar revisions: teachers can ask questions and identify sentences for students to combine, expand, and reword. Class discussions are useful for focusing students' attention on common grammar problems. You may refer to Chapter Four for further assistance.

The editing process is largely a matter of proofreading, identifying spelling, punctuation, capitalization, and grammar errors. In this situation, students are usually reading their compositions to identify usage errors, such as noun and verb agreement. Editing is an individual process since students make different errors. After editing many of their own compositions, students begin to anticipate the kinds of grammar and usage errors that they commonly make, so they can edit them out of their written work. During the editing process students may need to refer to word books, dictionaries, grammar books, handbooks, and a thesaurus.

Match Sentence Patterns

Examples of English sentence patterns can be drawn from children's writing. As stated earlier in this chapter, children learn grammar and usage through manipulating their own language; therefore having them find sentences in their compositions that match the sentence patterns introduced earlier in this chapter is a sound teaching strategy. For example, a student could match the S-V-DO (subject-verb-direct object) patterns with a S-V-DO sentence from his or her writing. A sentence like, "The cat is on the roof," exemplifies this pattern. The subject is "the cat," the verb is "is," and the direct object is the prepositional phrase "on the roof."

HOW TO USE AN ENGLISH TEXT

Many teachers must use an adopted English text for instruction, while other teachers choose to use a basal text. This section addresses appropriate adaptations of a basal English text in an elementary classroom. A sample fifth-grade lesson is shown in Figure 12.2.

In Chapter Three you learned how to survey a basal text and a chapter in a text. Let's assume that you have performed each of these tasks and have identified the example lesson as an essential one for fifth-grade students. The objective, to identify main verbs and helping verbs in verb phrases, is an important one. The motivation section of the lesson is superfluous unless the class is low achieving or immature. Average and above average students could skip the motivation section and move on through the lesson sequence. Instead of writing the practice exercises, they could select a piece of writing from their writing files and identify ten main verbs or helping verbs in that piece of writing—unless there are not ten verbs in it, in which case they should find as many verbs as they can and classify them as to present, past, or future. When this is completed they can select a trade book that they have read and examine the verbs in it, classifying them as main verbs, helping verbs, present, past, or future.

A lesson like the one described provides direct instruction while encouraging students to apply the material to their own reading and writing.

Improving Usage

Teachers model standard English usage for their students which means they must be aware of their own usage in the classroom. Children emulate their teachers' usage to a surprising degree; therefore, modeling is one of the best means teachers have to help children understand standard English. This means that teachers need to develop their usage to the point that they are excellent language models. In some instances, prospective teachers need to take additional course work to prepare for the language responsibilities of teaching.

In planning instruction for standard English usage, teachers should remember that language is an important part of ego and handle instruction accordingly. They should not attempt to replace children's language with standard English, thus implying that their language is "bad." Instead, they should plan to teach standard English usage as a second language, thus enabling children to switch from one level of usage to another when appropriate. Well-planned instruction develops children's respect for their own dialect and that of others.

Teachers and students need to identify the important usage problems in the classroom. They may make lists and charts to show the occurrence of these expressions and identify appropriate expressions for communicating their ideas. Following is an example of such a chart.

Usage Problem	Another Way to Say It
"I be here."	"I am here."
"He be here."	"He is here."
"Is this hisn or yourn?"	"Is this his or yours?"
"I have ten cent."	"I have ten cents."

Children enjoy identifying many ways of expressing their ideas. They may make a list of appropriate ways of expressing ideas like the preceding. Hennings (1986) suggests writing many variations of word choices on the chalkboard and then classifying the expressions as "everyday language" or "written language."

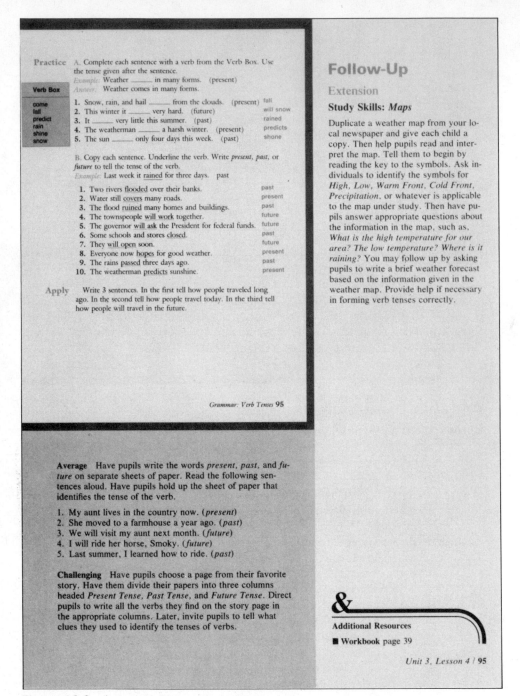

Practice   A. Complete each sentence with a verb from the Verb Box. Use the tense given after the sentence.

Example: Weather _____ in many forms.   (present)

Answer: Weather comes in many forms.

Verb Box

come
fall
predict
rain
shine
snow

1. Snow, rain, and hail _____ from the clouds.   (present)   fall
2. This winter it _____ very hard.   (future)   will snow
3. It _____ very little this summer.   (past)   rained
4. The weatherman _____ a harsh winter.   (present)   predicts
5. The sun _____ only four days this week.   (past)   shone

B. Copy each sentence. Underline the verb. Write *present, past,* or *future* to tell the tense of the verb.

Example: Last week it <u>rained</u> for three days.   past

1. Two rivers <u>flooded</u> over their banks.   past
2. Water still <u>covers</u> many roads.   present
3. The flood <u>ruined</u> many homes and buildings.   past
4. The townspeople <u>will work</u> together.   future
5. The governor <u>will ask</u> the President for federal funds.   future
6. Some schools and stores <u>closed</u>.   past
7. They <u>will open</u> soon.   future
8. Everyone now <u>hopes</u> for good weather.   present
9. The rains <u>passed</u> three days ago.   past
10. The weatherman <u>predicts</u> sunshine.   present

Apply   Write 3 sentences. In the first tell how people traveled long ago. In the second tell how people travel today. In the third tell how people will travel in the future.

Grammar: Verb Tenses **95**

Follow-Up

Extension

Study Skills: *Maps*

Duplicate a weather map from your local newspaper and give each child a copy. Then help pupils read and interpret the map. Tell them to begin by reading the key to the symbols. Ask individuals to identify the symbols for *High, Low, Warm Front, Cold Front, Precipitation,* or whatever is applicable to the map under study. Then have pupils answer appropriate questions about the information in the map, such as, *What is the high temperature for our area? The low temperature? Where is it raining?* You may follow up by asking pupils to write a brief weather forecast based on the information given in the weather map. Provide help if necessary in forming verb tenses correctly.

Average   Have pupils write the words *present, past,* and *future* on separate sheets of paper. Read the following sentences aloud. Have pupils hold up the sheet of paper that identifies the tense of the verb.

1. My aunt lives in the country now. (*present*)
2. She moved to a farmhouse a year ago. (*past*)
3. We will visit my aunt next month. (*future*)
4. I will ride her horse, Smoky. (*future*)
5. Last summer, I learned how to ride. (*past*)

Challenging   Have pupils choose a page from their favorite story. Have them divide their papers into three columns headed *Present Tense, Past Tense,* and *Future Tense.* Direct pupils to write all the verbs they find on the story page in the appropriate columns. Later, invite pupils to tell what clues they used to identify the tenses of verbs.

&

Additional Resources
■ **Workbook** page 39

Unit 3, Lesson 4 / **95**

Figure 12.2   A sample fifth-grade lesson.

Source: Ronald Cramer, Tara McCarthy, and Norman Najimy, *Language: Skills and Use* (Glenview, IL: Scott, Foresman and Company), 1986. Reprinted by permission of publisher.

Teaching

Objective

● Identify main verbs and helping verbs in verb phrases.

Motivation

Bring to class pictures of an independent worker and a worker with an assistant. For example, one picture might show a doctor; the other might show a dentist being helped by a dental assistant. Show both pictures to the class. Explain that some verbs can work alone, like the doctor. They do not need any help to show an action. These verbs consist of one word only. Other verbs need helpers, like the dentist. They use one or more helping verbs to show the action. Tell pupils they will learn more about helping verbs in this lesson.

Lesson Sequence

1. Focus   Read this section with the class. Go over each example sentence, helping pupils analyze the verb phrase. Point out the helping verb and the main verb. Make clear that the helping verbs help express the action and also show the time of the action, for example, *is* and *are* show the present tense.

2. Practice   Write the helping verbs and the tenses they signal on the board:

Present	Past	Future
am	was	will
is	were	shall
are		

Then have pupils carry out Practice A and Practice B independently. Go over the answers orally when pupils have completed the exercises.

3. Apply *(Optional)*   Have pupils notice that the content theme of the lesson is games and projects. Suggest that rereading some of the practice sentences may give pupils ideas for inventing their own games.

96 / Unit 3, Lesson 5

5 Verb Phrases

A verb can be made up of two or more words.

Focus   A verb is sometimes made up of more than one word. These verbs are called **verb phrases**. A verb phrase is made up of a main verb and one or more helping verbs. Study the example sentences below. The verb phrases are in dark type.

Present: Bob **is building** an airplane.
           Pam and Lee **are working** on a boat.

Past: Kyle **was making** a birdhouse.
           Kim and Eva **were helping** him.

Future: Debbie **will help** tomorrow.
           I **shall help** too.

In a verb phrase, the main verb tells the action happening. The helping verb tells the time of the action. Look back at the examples. The verbs *is* and *are* tell that the action is happening in the present. *Was* and *were* tell that the action happened in the past. *Will* and *shall* tell that the action will happen in the future.

Additional Activities

Easy   Write various subjects and helping verbs on one set of index cards, such as *Birds are*. On another set of cards, write several main verbs that match, for example, *singing* or *flying*. Have pupils sit in a circle or around a table. Give each player a card from the first set. Put the main-verb cards in a stack face down. Tell the first player to draw a main-verb card. If it completes the sentence begun on the card he or she holds, have that player lay down both cards and "go out." If not, have the player return the main-verb card to the bottom of the stack and have the next player draw. Continue the game until all the players have found matching cards.

Average   Duplicate or write on the board the following sentences. Have pupils rewrite each sentence by forming a verb phrase with the verb in parentheses. Tell them they will add *-ing* to the main verbs.

HOW TO PUNCTUATE_____

By Russell Baker _____

When you write, you make a sound in the reader's head. It can be a dull mumble—that's why so much government prose makes you sleepy—or it can be a joyful noise, a sly whisper, a throb of passion.

Listen to a voice trembling in a haunted room:

"And the silken, sad, uncertain rustling of each purple curtain thrilled me—filled me with fantastic terrors never felt before . . . "

That's Edgar Allan Poe, a master. Few of us can make paper speak as vividly as Poe could, but even beginners will write better once they start listening to the sound their writing makes.

One of the most important tools for making paper speak in your own voice is punctuation.

When speaking aloud, you punctuate constantly—with body language. Your listener hears commas, dashes, question marks, exclamation points, quotation marks as you shout, whisper, pause, wave your arms, roll your eyes, wrinkle your brow.

In writing, punctuation plays the role of body language. It helps readers hear you the way you want to be heard.

"Gee, Dad, have I got to learn all them rules?"

Don't let the rules scare you. For they aren't hard and fast. Think of them as guidelines.

Am I saying, "Go ahead and punctuate as you please"? Absolutely not. Use your own common sense, remembering that you can't expect readers to work to decipher what you're trying to say.

There are two basic systems of punctuation:

1. The loose or open system, which tries to capture the way body language punctuates talk.

2. The tight, closed structural system, which hews closely to the sentence's grammatical structure.

Source: "how to Punctuate," by Ruseell Baker (New York: International Paper Company), 1986. Reprinted by permission of publisher.

Most writers use a little of both. In any case, we use much less punctuation than they used 200 or even 50 years ago. (Glance into Edward Gibbon's "Decline and Fall of the Roman Empire," first published in 1776, for an example of the tight structural system at its most elegant.)

No matter which system you prefer, be warned: punctuation marks cannot save a sentence that is badly put together. If you have to struggle over commas, semicolons and dashes, you've probably built a sentence that's never going to fly, no matter how you tinker with it. Throw it away and build a new one to a simpler design. The better your sentence, the easier it is to punctuate.

Choosing the right tool

There are 30 main punctuation marks, but you'll need fewer than a dozen for most writing.

I can't show you in this small space how they all work, so I'll stick to the ten most important—and even then can only hit highlights. For more details, check your dictionary or a good grammar.

Comma [,]

This is the most widely used mark of all. It's also the toughest and most controversial. I've seen aging editors almost come to blows over the comma. If you can handle it without sweating, the others will be easy. Here's my policy:

1. Use a comma after a long introductory phrase or clause: *After stealing the crown jewels from the Tower of London, I went home for tea.*

2. If the introductory material is short, forget the comma: *After the theft I went home for tea.*

3. But use it if the sentence would be confusing without it, like this: *The day before I'd robbed the Bank of England.*

4. Use a comma to separate elements in a series: *I robbed the Denver Mint, the Bank of England, the Tower of London and my piggy bank.*

Notice there is no comma before *and* in the series. This is common style nowadays, but some publishers use a comma there, too.

5. Use a comma to separate independent clauses that are joined by a conjunction like *and, but, for, or, nor, because* or *so: I shall return the crown jewels, for they are too heavy to wear.*

6. Use a comma to set off a mildly parenthetical word grouping that isn't essential to the sentence: *Girls, who have always interested me, usually differ from boys.*

Do not use commas if the word grouping *is* essential to the sentence's meaning: *Girls who interest me know how to tango.*

7. Use a comma in direct address: *Your majesty, please hand over the crown.*

8. And between proper names and titles: *Montague Sneed, Director of Scotland Yard, was assigned the case.*

9. And to separate elements of geographical address: *Director Sneed comes from Chicago, Illinois, and now lives in London, England.*

Generally speaking, use a comma where you'd pause briefly in speech. For a long pause or completion of thought, use a period.

If you confuse the comma with the period, you'll get a run-on sentence: *The Bank of England is located in London, I rushed right over to rob it.*

Semicolon [;]

A more sophisticated mark than the comma, the semicolon separates two main clauses, but it keeps those two thoughts more tightly linked than a period can: *I steal crown jewels; she steals hearts.*

Dash [—] and Parentheses [( )]

Warning! Use sparingly. The dash SHOUTS. Parentheses whisper. Shout too often, people stop listening; whisper too much, people become suspicious of you. The dash creates a dramatic pause to prepare for an expression needing strong emphasis: *I'll marry you—if you'll rob Topkapi with me.*

Parentheses help you pause quietly to drop in some chatty information not vital to your story: *Despite Betty's daring spirit ("I love robbing your piggy bank," she often said), she was a terrible dancer.*

Quotation marks [" "]

These tell the reader you're reciting the exact words someone said or wrote: *Betty said, "I can't tango."* Or: *"I can't tango," Betty said.*

Notice the comma comes before the quote marks in the first example, but comes inside them in the second. Not logical? Never mind. Do it that way anyhow.

Colon [:]

A colon is a tip-off to get ready for what's next: a list, a long quotation or an explanation. This article is riddled with colons. Too many, maybe, but the message is: "Stay on your toes; it's coming at you."

Apostrophe [']

The big headache is with possessive nouns. If the noun is singular, add *'s: I hated Betty's tango.*

If the noun is plural, simply add an apostrophe after the *s: Those are the girls' coats.*

The same applies for singular nouns ending in *s,* like Dickens: *This is Dickens's best book.*

And in plural: *This is the Dickenses' cottage.*

The possessive pronouns *hers* and *its* have no apostrophe.

If you write *it's,* you are saying *it is.*

Keep cool

You know about ending a sentence with a period (.) or a question mark (?). Do it. Sure, you can also end with an exclamation point (!), but must you? Usually it just makes you sound breathless and silly. Make your writing generate its own excitement. Filling the paper with !!!! won't make up for what your writing has failed to do.

Too many exclamation points make me think the writer is talking about the panic in his own head.

Don't sound panicky. End with a period. I am serious. A period. Understand?

Well . . . sometimes a question mark is okay.

Usage can be improved by having children substitute expressions for trite, overused expressions like, "white as snow." Students may search the thesaurus, as well as synonym-antonym dictionaries, for words, that more precisely express "walking" or "sleeping." The students in my sixth-grade class frequently filled the chalkboard with alternate words to express a particular word. For example, for *walking,* they might suggest words like *skipped, lumbered, strolled, shuffled,* and *tripped.*

PUNCTUATION

Punctuation is an aspect of written communication. Through punctuation we express the aspects of communication that are expressed orally as pauses, stress, and pitch. Punctuation is summarized in the box on pages 380–381.

Punctuation, like the other aspects of language, is learned through use. As students punctuate their own work, they develop a better understanding of its function. You may have students examine the punctuation used by various authors, and students may compare and contrast the ways that different authors punctuate.

SUMMARY

English grammar is concerned with syntax, the structure of language. Three forms of grammar are commonly used to explain English grammar. Traditional grammar which is based on Latin grammar prescribes the rules for creating sentences. Descriptive (structural) grammar describes grammar as English speakers use it. Transformational-generative grammar is based on the rules that enable speakers to produce an unlimited number of sentences. A fourth approach to teaching grammar is the functional or contextual approach. Formal grammar should not be taught until students are in seventh or eighth grade. However, elementary school children can explore language through listening to, speaking, reading, and writing standard English grammar. Activities like listening to oral literature, silently reading literature, sentence combining, sentence expanding, and revising and editing compositions develop children's understanding of English grammar.

Thought Questions

1. How is grammar related to revision in the writing process?

2. How are grammar, usage, and dialect related?

3. Explain the contributions of traditional grammar, descriptive grammar, and transformation grammar to our understanding of language.

4. What are three synonyms for grammar?

5. How can reading be used to teach grammar?

6. Explain the intuitive grasp of grammar.

7. Discuss formal grammar instruction in the elementary school, including the what, when, why, and how of grammar instruction.

8. Why does Weaver say that children do not use the grammar they know?

Enrichment Activities

1. Tape an informal discussion. Analyze the tape and identify the various grammatical structures used. You may also identify various forms and levels of usage, as well as dialects used.

2. Read a book written in a dialect. Lois Lenski's books are excellent examples of this kind of writing. List the characteristics of the dialect found in the book. Was the book easier to read or more difficult than books written in standard English?

3. Collect and analyze several examples of children's writing. Identify any expressions that are examples of dialect.

4. Obtain a teacher's manual for one grade level of a language arts text. Identify all of the grammar rules that are introduced. How are they taught (is sentence combining used, sentence expansion, etc.)?

5. Make a lesson plan for teaching sentence combining at the grade level of your choice.

6. Identify the dialect that you speak and the characteristics of that dialect. Research your dialect to learn all that you can about it.

Selected Readings

Cordeiro, P.; M. Giacobbe; and C. Courtney (March 1983). "Apostrophes, Quotation Marks, and Periods: Learning Punctuation in the First Grade." *Language Arts, 60,* 3, 323–332.

Holbrook, Hilary Taylor (February 1983). "Whither (Wither) Grammar?" *Language Arts, 60,* 259–263.

Kean, John (1981). "Grammar: A Perspective." In *Research in the Language Arts,* Victor Froese and Stanley Straw (eds.). Baltimore: University Park Press.

Nilsen, D. (May 1977). "Dr. Seuss as Grammar Consultant." *Language Arts, 54,* 5, 567–571.

O'Hare, Frank (1973). *Sentence Combining: Improving Student Writing Without Formal Grammar Instruction.* Urbana, IL: National Council of Teachers of English.

Smelstor, Marjorie, ed. (1978). *A Guide to the Role of Grammar in Teaching Writing.* Madison, WI: University of Wisconsin.

Smith, E. Brooks; Kenneth Goodman; and Robert Meredith (1976). *Language and Thinking in School* (2d ed.). New York: Holt, Rinehart and Winston.

Smith, Nila B. (November 1975). "Cultural Dialects: Current Problems and Solutions." *Reading Teacher, 29,* 2, 137–141.

Straw, Stanley (1981). "Grammar and Teaching Writing." In *Research in the Language Arts,* Victor Froese and Stanley Straw (eds.). Baltimore: University Park Press.

Weaver, Constance (1979). *Grammar for Teachers: Perspectives and Definitions.* Urbana, IL: National Council of Teachers of English.

References

Baines, H. V. H. (1975). *An Assessment and Comparison of Syntactic Complexity and Word Associations of Good and Poor Readers in Grades Four, Eight, and Twelve.* Unpublished doctoral dissertation, University of Georgia.

Baron, D. (1982). *Grammar and Good Taste.* New Haven: Yale University Press.

Baugh, J. (February 1987). "Research Currents: The Situational Dimension of Linguistic Power in Social Context." *Language Arts, 64* (2), 234–240.

Braddock, R. Lloyd-Jones, and L. Schoer (1963). *Research in Written Composition.* Champaign, IL: National Council of Teachers of English.

Brown, Roger (May 1979). "Some Priorities in Language Arts Education." *Language Arts, 56,* 5, 483–484.

Chomsky, Noam (1965). *Aspects of the Theory of Syntax.* Cambridge, MA: MIT Press.

Combs, W. (1975). "Some Further Effects and Implications of Sentence-Combining Exercises for the Secondary Language Arts Curriculum." *DAI, 36,* 1266-A.

Daly, J. (1979). "Writing Apprehension in the Classroom: Teacher Role Expectancies of the Apprehensive Writer." *RET, 13,* 37–44.

Daly, J., and M. Miller (1975). "Apprehension of Writing as a Predictor of Message Intensity." *Journal of Psychology, 89,* 175–77.

Elley, W., I. Barham, H. Lamb, and M. Wyllie (May 1975). "The Role of Grammar in a Secondary School English Curriculum." *New Zealand Journal of Educational Studies, 10* (1), 26–42.

Entwisle, D., and N. Frasure (1974). "A Contradiction Resolved: Children's Processing of Syntactic Cues." *Developmental Psychology, 10,* 852–857.

Farrell, K. (1977). "A Comparison of Three Instructional Approaches for Teaching Written Composition to High School Juniors: Teacher Lecture, Peer Evaluation, and Group Tutoring." *DAI, 38,* 1849-A.

George, J. (1982). *The Cry of the Crow.* New York: Harper & Row.

Genishi, C., and A. Dyson (April 1987). "Research Currents: On Issues That Divide Us." *Language Arts, 64* (4), 408–415.

Guthrie, J. (1973). "Reading Comprehension and Syntactic Responses in Good and Poor Readers." *Journal of Educational Psychology, 65,* 294–299.

Haley-James, Shirley, ed. (1981). *Perspectives on Writing in Grades 1–8.* Urbana, IL: National Council of Teachers of English.

Heilman, A., and E. Holmes (1978). *Smuggling Language into the Teaching of Reading.* Columbus, OH: Merrill.

Hennings, Dorothy Grant (1986). *Communication in Action* (3d ed.). Boston: Houghton-Mifflin.

Hillocks, G., Jr. (1986). *Research on Written Composition.* Urbana, IL: National Conference on Research in English.

Holbrook, Hilary Taylor (February 1983). "Whither (Wither) Grammar." *Language Arts, 60,* 259–263.

Kolln, Martha (May 1981). "Closing the Books on Alchemy." *College Composition and Communication, 32,* 139–150.

Labov, W. (1970). *The Study of Nonstandard English.* Champaign, IL: National Council of Teachers of English.

Lance, D. M. (1977). "What Is Grammar?" *English Education, 9,* 1, 43–49.

Lefevre, C. (1964). *Linguistics and the Teaching of Reading.* New York: McGraw-Hill.

Lesgold, A. M. (1974). "Variability in Children's Comprehension of Syntactic Structures." *Journal of Educational Psychology, 66,* 333–338.

Loban, Walter (1976). *Language Development: Kindergarten Through Grade Twelve.* NCTE Research Report No. 18. Urbana, IL: National Council of Teachers of English.

Malmstrom, J. (1977). *Understanding Language: A Primer for the Language Arts Teacher.* New York: St. Martin's Press.

McCrum, R., W. Cran, and Robert MacNeil (1986). *The Story of English.* New York: Viking.

McNeil, D. (1970). "The Development of Language." In *Carmichael's Handbook of Child Psychology,* P. Mussen (ed.). New York: Wiley.

Newkirk, T. (1978). *Grammar Instruction and Writing: What Does Research Really Prove?"* ERIC Document Reproduction Service ED 153 218.

Noyce, R., and J. Christie. "Effects of an Integrated Grammar Instruction on Third Graders' Reading and Writing." *Elementary School Journal, 84,* 63–69.

O'Hare, F. (1973). *Sentence Combining: Improving Student Writing Without Formal Grammar Instruction.* NCTE Research Report No. 15. Urbana, IL: National Council of Teachers of English.

Rupley, William, and Carol Robeck (February 1978). "ERIC/RCS: Black Dialect and Reading Achievement." *Reading Teacher, 31,* 598.

Seitz, Victoria (1977). *Social Class and Ethnic Group Differences in Learning to Read.* Newark, DE: International Reading Association.

Shackford, H. (1976). *Junior High-School Students' Knowledge of Grammatical Structure and Its Relation to Reading Comprehension.* Unpublished doctoral dissertation, Boston University.

Shuy, Roger W. (1973), "Nonstandard Dialect Problems: An Overview." In *Language Differences: Do They Interfere?"* James L. Laffey and Roger Shuy (eds.). Newark, DE: International Reading Association, 91–100.

Slobin, D. (1966). "Grammatical Transformations and Sentence Comprehension in Childhood and Adulthood." *Journal of Verbal Learning and Verbal Behavior, 5,* 219–227.

Smelstor, Marjorie, ed. (1978). *A Guide to the Role of Grammar in Teaching Writing.* Madison, WI: University of Wisconsin.

Smith, E. Brooks; Kenneth Goodman; and Robert Meredith (1976). *Language and Thinking in School* (2nd Ed.). New York: Robert C. Owen Publishers.

Stein, N., and C. J. Glenn, (1978). "An Analysis of Story Comprehension in Elementary Children. In *Advances in Discourse Processing, Vol. II: New Directions,* R. Freedle, (ed.). Norwood, NJ: Ablex.

Straw, Stanley D. (1981). "Grammar and Teaching of Writing: Analysis Versus Synthesis." In *Research in the Language Arts,* Victor Froese and Stanley Straw (eds.). Baltimore: University Park Press.

Tompkins, G., and L. McGee (April 1983). "Launching Nonstandard Speakers into Standard English." *Language Arts, 60* (4), 463–469.

Van Hook, Beverly (March 1979). "Grammatical Surgery." *Teacher, 96,* 78, 80.

Weaver, Constance (1979). *Grammar for Teachers: Perspectives and Definitions.* Urbana, IL: National Council of Teachers of English.

Part **FOUR**

Meeting Students' Needs

Chapter *Thirteen*

Children with Special Needs in the English Language Arts

CHAPTER OVERVIEW

Classroom teachers instruct students who have a variety of special needs. Special needs students may include: students whose native language is not English, students who are deaf, language-delayed children, students who are blind or partially sighted, or students who learn more slowly or more rapidly than average. In order to plan instruction, teachers must understand these special needs and how to meet the special needs of those students who are mainstreamed into the regular classroom.

Anticipation Guide

Think about these ideas before you read the chapter. What do I know about children who are learning English as a second language? How would I feel if the teacher did not speak my language? How many "special" children will be in my classroom? As you read, try to answer the following guiding questions.

1. What special needs students am I most likely to encounter in my classroom?

2. What are the characteristics of children who are learning English as a second language?

3. What factors should teachers consider when teaching children who are mainstreamed in their classrooms?

Key Concepts

ESL (English as a second language)
EMH (educable mentally
 handicapped)
PL 94-142
gifted

mainstreaming
individualized educational
 plan (IEP)
language delayed

INTRODUCTION

Children with special needs are youngsters who have needs that differ from the majority of students in regular classrooms. They have special needs in the areas of language, mental ability, physical development, and social or emotional behavior. School practices must be modified to help them develop to their full potential. In the past, special needs students were segregated from the "regular" school population for specialized instruction. However, in the majority of schools today, many special needs students are **mainstreamed**— that is, they spend part of the school day with a specialist who is educated to address their special needs and they spend the balance of the school day in a regular classroom with a teacher who is not specifically educated to meet their needs.

Classroom teachers are more prepared to teach special populations than they realize. Effective teachers can instruct many types of students because effective instruction is based on the same principles whether the students learn slowly or rapidly, or whether their native language is English or Spanish. Special needs children are more like other children than they are different. They exhibit a wide range of individual differences; therefore, we must avoid labeling these students and treating them as if they are all exactly alike.

The instructional strategies suggested throughout this text will work with special students. Special students need the same language skills as other children, although teachers must tailor their instruction to their unique needs. For instance, Spanish-speaking students need opportunities to express their ideas in written English and exposure to literature that will help them learn about the culture. Slow learning children need slower paced, concrete instruction. **Gifted** children need vertical rather than horizontal enrichment. Horizontal enrichment means that students spend more time at a specific level, overlearning the skills at that level and gaining fluency. Vertical enrichment means that the students move into more difficult work as soon as they acquire the skills at a level. Gifted students are less likely to need the overlearning and fluency that average students require; they will be more challenged by vertical enrichment. However, there is no "magic bag of tricks" that teachers need to acquire in order to instruct special needs populations.

As you read the following vignette, identify the aspects of language arts instruction that appear to be usual and those that appear to be unique to the population that is learning **English as a second language (ESL).**

ESL VIGNETTE

Madge Greer looked up as Kim opened the door to her fourth-grade classroom. Kim was returning from the ESL class that she had attended since kindergarten. In third grade, she expressed ideas so well in both written and spoken English that she spent half of the school day in the regular classroom. And this year she was in fourth grade three-fourths of the day. Later in the day, Tron, another Vietnamese student would join the class. Tron and Kim had been in the ESL classroom the same number of years, but Tron's language skills had not progressed as far. Therefore, she spent only one hour a day in fourth grade. Kim and Tron appeared equally intelligent; they simply differed in language learning facility.

Initially, Madge was apprehensive about having bilingual students mainstreamed into her class because she did not speak their language. But, she found that she was enjoying the girls and they were diligent students. She asked Kim and Tron to teach their classmates Vietnamese words and they often wrote labels for bulletin board displays. She read the book *To Stand Against the Wind* by Ann Nolan Clark to help the students understand more about the Vietnamese culture. Then the class discussed the book and asked Kim and Tron questions. This led Kim to share some of her writings with the class. Tron had greater difficulty sharing her thoughts because she did not value them as much as she did the workbook pages and the exercises she copied from the chalkboard.

Vignette Discussion

Kim and Tron demonstrate the diversity one finds in ESL students. Even students who come from the same country and are the same age often learn a new language at very different rates. For some children, learning a second language takes just a few years; within two or three years they are virtually indistinguishable from native speakers of the language. Many others, however, take considerably longer. There is mounting research evidence (Swain and Lapkin, 1982; Wong Fillmore, 1983; Cummins, 1984) that even under the best of circumstances, it takes most children from four to six years to achieve the level of proficiency needed for full participation in school (Wong Fillmore, 1986). Until ESL students are prepared for full participation in the school, they are **mainstreamed** for a portion of the school day in the regular classroom. ESL students are mainstreamed to provide opportunities to use their English language skills and to extend their understanding of English culture and curriculum.

In this vignette, Madge demonstrated her appreciation for the girls' language and culture. She demonstrated to the students that knowing two languages is more useful than knowing only one (Perez, 1979). This is important for developing a strong self-concept in ESL students. If they are not allowed to use their own language in the classroom they develop low self-concepts. The problem of low self-concept is exacerbated when the teacher does not understand their culture. When Madge learned that she was going to have Kim and Tron in class she read books recommended by the ESL teacher. Even though she could not speak the Vietnamese language, she learned a few words and asked the girls to help with her pronunciation.

This vignette demonstrates the more enlightened attitude of parents, teachers, and legislators toward the education of exceptional children. One manifestation of this change is the federal legislation reflected in Public Law **94-142** (Education for All Handicapped Children Act). This law has several implications for language arts teachers. First is the mandate that children will receive instruction in "the least restrictive environment" which implies that special need students will be integrated with the regular school population. This allows students to learn ways of functioning within the larger society. Language arts teachers must teach all children to communicate with one another. In doing this, they should promote interaction among all of their students in as many different situations as possible. Mainstreamed children may participate in class discussions, drama, role playing, listening activities, composition, and reading. Literature is particularly important for special need students. They learn about language and culture through listening to the teacher read aloud.

The second implication of PL 94-142 relates to evaluation procedures. This law dictates that evaluation will not discriminate against students and that it will provide an accurate means of planning programs and evaluating progress. The evaluation will focus on identifying the strengths and weaknesses of individual students. Evaluation strategies suggested in the process chapters of this text will help you evaluate the progress of special need students, as well as the other students in your classroom.

The third mandate of PL 94-142 is that each handicapped student will have an **individualized educational plan (IEP)**. The IEP is a team effort of the special education teacher, classroom teachers, principal, and parents. The IEP identifies the present level of functioning and lists short- and long-term goals, objectives, and activities. It serves as an instructional guide for structuring the learning environment, sequencing language arts skills, modifying instruction, and instructional materials.

Students with special needs are not necessarily handicapped, but the attention to students' individual needs engendered by PL 95-142 has encouraged educators to look at all students as individuals.

LEARNING ENGLISH AS A SECOND LANGUAGE

The United States is admitting more immigrants than any other nation in the world. Between World War II and 1972, 14 million people immigrated to the United States. The immigrants now primarily come from Asia, the East Indies, Mexico, South America, and Southern Europe. Spanish is the second most frequently spoken language in the United States. Nearly one out of every 20 persons in this country is now of Hispanic birth or ancestry. Of the 11 million living in the United States, 6.6 million are Mexican American, 1.8 million are Puerto Rican, and 2.4 million are Cuban, Central American, or South American (Perez, 1979). These statistics suggest that no matter where they live elementary teachers are very likely to teach children whose native language is not English.

Bilingual education has been controversial in recent years (Baker and de Kanter, 1981); however, a recent thorough analysis of bilingual education research identified significant, positive effects for Spanish bilingual education programs (Willig, 1985). Students in Spanish bilingual programs scored higher in language arts skills, mathematics, and social studies. The students in these programs also manifested better attitudes toward themselves and school.

What Is the Purpose of ESL and Bilingual Instruction?

The purpose of ESL instruction differs from state to state. In many states, bilingual education programs were established to give ESL students instructional support in their native language. But their major purpose is to teach the language skills needed for survival as quickly as possible so they can enter regular school classes. In fact, these programs are often evaluated on the basis of how expeditiously the ESL students are mainstreamed into the regular classroom (Wong-Fillmore, 1986).

In contrast to this stance, advocates of bilingual education believe its purpose is to give ESL students a chance to learn the academic content and skills they are supposed to learn in school, no matter how long it takes them to learn English (Cummins, 1984; Hakuta, 1985; McLaughlin, 1985; Wong-Fillmore, 1986). Proponents of this approach believe children should learn to comprehend and appreciate reading content rather than focusing on accuracy in reading words. In writing they should learn to communicate ideas in written form rather than focusing on accuracy in spelling, punctuation, and grammar (Wong-Fillmore, 1986). So you see the goals of bilingual or ESL instruction are basically the same, although they differ in their means of achieving this goal.

The goals of bilingual education have been expanded to include biliteracy in some areas of the southwestern United States. This means that students will be taught to read and write fluently in two languages—Spanish and English. Such an approach helps students develop pride in their native culture thus enhancing their self-concepts.

How Do Classroom Teachers Instruct ESL Students?

Classroom teachers must realize that students who are linguistically and culturally different are not deficient persons. They bring a rich background in culture and language; therefore our long-term expectations for culturally different children should be no different than for children who speak the dominant language. ESL students need an education that prepares them for life in an increasingly complex world. They need basic language and literacy skills, as well as information about the world. Following are guidelines for classroom teachers who have ESL students mainstreamed in their classrooms.

1. Children cannot be expected to read and understand material in a language that they have not mastered in the oral form (Lopez, 1978).

2. Children whose language is other than English cannot be expected to master the language and the scope and sequence of the school curriculum at the same time and at the same rate as native speakers of English (Lopez, 1978).

3. An English as a second language (ESL) or teaching English to speakers of other languages (TESOL) approaches are not sufficient for the nonspeakers or limited speakers of English. These approaches provide for the acquisition of English as a language. However, while children are learning English as a language they fall behind academically, resulting in academic retardation (Lopez, 1978).

4. Children cannot acquire, form, or develop concepts through the medium of a language that they have not mastered orally (Lopez, 1978).

5. Children learn to read only once. They transfer academic and literacy skills learned via their native language to the second language once the second language has been sufficiently mastered (Lopez, 1978).

6. ESL students should have opportunities to use their native language in the classroom. This engenders a respect for the language and culture.

7. ESL students should learn language in the context of meaningful communication. They acquire it most readily when they try to understand and use language in the course of learning about things that are of interest to them (Wong Fillmore, 1986).

8. Curricular content should be available to these children, even while they are acquiring basic language skills. However, some of this content should be taught in their native languages (Wong-Fillmore, 1986).

The concept of biliteracy was introduced in the preceding section. Oritz and Engelbrecht (1986) studied the methods used in developing biliteracy in the Southwest noting instructional strengths and weaknesses. For example, they observed widespread use of oral Spanish, which is the strength of the program because historically children in the Southwest were punished for using Spanish in the school setting (Oritz and Engelbrecht, 1986). They found that written Spanish was not introduced in authentic, purposeful ways although this is a principle of all language instruction. In their observations, they noted that students generally turned to English when they read and wrote. These researchers questioned that permitting students to use English exclusively for reading and writing gives English more prestige than Spanish. They point out that children who are becoming biliterate need meaningful uses in the community for their developing skills.

Sound biliteracy instruction should take place in a print environment that exposes students to both languages under study. Many books in both languages should be available in libraries. Surprisingly, Oritz and Engelbrecht (1986) found few Spanish books in the libraries of the schools they studied. You may refer to bibliographies such as the one constructed by Wagoner (1982) for suggested literature to use with Mexican-American children. Students should have many opportunities to express their own ideas in written language rather than focusing on filling in blanks and copying exercises from the chalkboard. ESL students should have real uses for language rather than practice exercises. Language instruction should avoid fragmenting either language studied.

Organization of ESL Instruction

Several approaches are used in organizing ESL instruction. Many younger students are in self-contained classrooms with teachers who speak their native tongue. They are mainstreamed as they acquire control of English. Lopez (1978) describes these major approaches to bilingual education.

1. The alternate day approach. Instruction is given in English one day and in the native language the next.

2. The alternate discipline approach. Instruction is given in native language for one subject and in English for the next. Care should be taken that all subjects are taught in both languages at some time.

3. The alternate half-day approach. Instruction is given half the day in English and half the day in the native language. Again, all subjects should be taught in both languages at some time.

4. The alternate week approach. Instruction in English one week and entirely in the native language the next.

5. The student is totally immersed in one or the other language for six weeks at a time or even longer.

When teachers have ESL students mainstreamed in their classrooms they should consult with the ESL teacher who can give them suggestions for teaching these youngsters. Classroom teachers also will find assistance in the Selected Readings at the end of this chapter.

TEACHING LANGUAGE-DELAYED STUDENTS

Language delay is a condition in which a child's language development is significantly below his or her chronological age (Hubbell, 1977). **Language-delayed** children may speak in markedly childlike phrases that are much more primitive than those of their peers. Myklebust (1973) observed that average children acquired an adult level of syntax facility by age 11, but children who experienced language disorders did not achieve this level of development until age 15. They seem to lack the ability to use language purposefully (Scofield, 1978). In new situations, they may talk very little. Apparently, they lack many concepts and basic labels that are a part of daily instruction. Bain (1976) studied the writing of learning disabled students and found they used fewer words per sentence, fewer complex sentences, and infrequently used adjectives, adverbs and conjunctions. Their writing exhibited punctuation errors, inappropriate use of word endings and misuse of the article, *a*.

Language-delayed children need intensive experience with language in order to grow (Scofield, 1978). However, the standard school curriculum and school structure may constitute an alien environment for these children (Bernstein, 1972). The relationship between teacher and students is important because this relationship can give children the confidence to speak spontaneously. Scofield (1978) recommends the following approaches to teaching language-delayed children.

1. Provide language-delayed children with systematic instruction. They need direct, planned, intensive language instruction (Wiig and Semel, 1976). Systematic programs are tightly sequenced and move ahead in small steps.

Distar Instructional System (Evans, 1975) provides a highly patterned and programmed language drill. The Peabody Language Development Kit contrasts with Distar; it stimulates language is less patterned ways. Hart and Risley (1975) recommend incidental teaching as a means of stimulating language growth. In this kind of program, the teacher uses the children's experiences as means of teaching language concepts, syntax, labeling, and so forth.

2. Language-delayed children need experience with a range of language functions (refer back to Chapter Three). Children learn language as they learn its functions (Halliday, 1975). As they use language to communicate in classroom situations, they begin to acquire a sense of the ways that language functions in their lives. Language-delayed children can carry messages to the principal or school secretary. They need to rehearse what they are going to say when they deliver the message; this rehearsal gives them confidence to perform the errand. Participation in choral reading activities exposes them to a different language function plus giving them structured language activity.

3. Language-delayed children need opportunities for spontaneous speech in genuine communication situations. Spontaneous speech grows out of informal, conversational style activities. The teacher can encourage spontaneous interchanges between children. Such communication is reinforced when the teacher listens carefully to the children and discusses their interests.

Donald and Leah Johnson (1978) recommend teaching reading and writing simultaneously rather than as separate subjects. This approach to language arts instruction develops visual perception of letters and words, auditory perception of the sounds of words, and tactile perception is derived from writing words. This, in turn, helps them learn grapheme-phoneme correspondences, spelling patterns, and sentence structure. Of course, this approach is like the language arts instruction recommended for the regular classroom.

LANGUAGE ARTS FOR HEARING-IMPAIRED OR VISION-IMPAIRED STUDENTS

Children who are hearing or vision impaired have distorted sensory input. Hearing-impaired children do not receive the oral input they need to learn language without special instruction. A vision impairment prevents them from seeing written language; therefore they must have instruction to meet their special needs. Children with these impairments exhibit a full range of individual differences like other children. Their impairments may range from moderate to severe, while their experiential background, family, interests, intelligence, and motivation varies just as much as that of other individuals. Thus, teachers should see each youngster as an individual.

Teaching Deaf or Partially Hearing Students _____

Children whose hearing is impaired have distorted or incomplete auditory input; thus they lack the basis for learning language. They have not had the auditory input necessary to acquire English phonology, syntax, or semantics. Often there are difficulties producing and understanding speech sounds. For example, words like *Dan* and *tan* confuse children who do not hear sounds clearly enough to discriminate between them. In some programs for the deaf, students are taught to talk, while others rely on sign language for communication. Since sign language does not use structure words, deaf students often have difficulty understanding these words in written language. Students with hearing impairments often have difficulty understanding sentences that are grammatically complex. Multiple meanings are puzzling because they have not had the language input that would sensitize them to words that have more than one meaning.

Deaf children need many opportunities to explore language and to develop concepts of language. Earphones and/or hearing aids enable some hearing-impaired children to listen to stories that can contribute to their language development. Since deaf children have frequent need to communicate in written language, they should have early and frequent opportunities to explore written language. As you read previously in Chapters Seven and Eleven, children learn about written language through drawing and scribbling and dictating stories that the teacher writes for them. Hearing-impaired children learn in the same way, so young deaf children should draw, scribble, and dictate stories to learn about written language. Manson (1982) reports success with such an approach.

Teaching Visually Impaired Students _____

Visually impaired students do not have access to the visual data they need to develop written language concepts. They need to develop certain essential concepts of print including (McGee and Tompkins, 1982):

How to handle a book to turn pages from front to back

The left to right progression of print

Word consciousness

Understand that print has meaning

These concepts are vital to language development and can be developed in a variety of ways (McGee and Tompkins, 1982). Visually impaired children need to have many opportunities to explore concrete objects with their senses of smell, touch, taste, and hearing. Tactile books can be purchased or made from fabric, yarn, buttons, and zippers. Pockets can be placed in these books to hold cardboard or plastic shapes. Exploration should include discussion and descriptions of their experiences. Braille labels can be used for objects in the classroom.

The children should have opportunities to dictate language experience stories that are printed in Braille so they can learn the connection between written and spoken language. Teachers need to read many books and children should have opportunities to relate the stories they hear with books. They should learn about signs, newspapers, and so forth, so they learn about the functions of written language. Some visually impaired students can see when large print is used; therefore these books can be used to introduce written language. Increasing numbers of large-print books are available for use in teaching visually impaired children. With activities like the preceding, visually handicapped children can develop language arts skills. With the exception of Braille use, these activities routinely occur in classrooms.

EDUCABLE MENTALLY HANDICAPPED (EMH) STUDENTS

Educable mentally handicapped (EMH) students are youngsters developing at one-half to three-fourths slower than average children. This slowed development is reflected in their conceptual and perceptual abilities and lower intelligence quotients than average children of the same chronological age. For instance, a six-year-old youngster who has an IQ of 75 has a mental age of four and one-half (Kaluger and Kolson, 1978). Slower intellectual development results in lower overall achievement for EMH students. Even when

Special students need language.

these youngsters are given a slower paced program over a longer period of time, their peak achievement will be lower than that of average students.

Teaching EMH Students

When EMH students are mainstreamed into regular classrooms, teachers should talk with the special education teacher to learn about the individual students strength's and weaknesses. This will help them plan appropriate instruction while integrating the students into their classrooms.

Following is a summary of the major cognitive functioning characteristics of EMH students which should be considered when planning language arts instruction. EMH students often:

Learn more slowly

Are concrete learners rather than abstract learners

Are distractable

Have short attention spans

Have poor memories

Cannot transfer learning from one situation to another

EMH students need planned, direct instruction which follows the lesson plan format presented in Chapter Two. EMH students do not acquire skills incidentally; therefore, all instruction should be concrete. These youngsters do not learn through discovery because they do not understand implied or subtle relationships. For example, when teaching EMH students to compose, teachers can use concrete objects or experiences as writing stimuli rather than asking them to write about abstract imaginary experiences. EMH students are able to use the language arts processes most effectively when they are related to the students' own experiences.

EMH students need to have many opportunities for directed practice of the skills they are learning. They have poor retention of previously taught material. Thus, additional practice beyond that usually required by average students helps reinforce the skills or knowledge in their memories. Reviewing previously learned material before introducing new content also aids retention.

EMH students should have continuous feedback during the learning process. They need immediate information about their performance. When children respond appropriately, feedback reinforces this behavior. When the response is incorrect, the teacher should encourage them to repeat the task and prompt them toward an accurate response (Cohen and Plaskon, 1980). Feedback should be specific, so that students understand exactly what they are doing right. For example, when a youngster participates in a class discussion of California geography and stays on the topic giving correct information, the teacher should explain in detail why his or her comments were valuable.

Oral Language   EMH students' language is like that of younger children due to the close connection between mental and language development. Some EMH children have difficulty carrying on a conversation because they find verbal expression difficult. EMH students tend to use shorter sentences, have fewer words in their vocabulary, and have poor articulation. To lessen this, they should have many opportunities to interact. They benefit from participating in the oral language activities in the regular classroom, such as discussions, storytelling, drama, giving messages, and so forth.

Listening   EMH students find listening and understanding (auding) difficult. Their difficulties appear in all aspects of language. They have difficulty discriminating one sound from another, they cannot listen to stories and retell them; they have difficulty following oral directions. They cannot write readily from dictation; therefore teachers should plan to have them copy material rather than dictating it. Copying should be from a model on their desk rather than copying from a chalkboard which is quite difficult for EMH children. Overall they prefer visual tasks involving very little listening (Cohen and Plaskon, 1980). This suggests the use of charts, the chalkboard for direct work or demonstration, and big books and "read along books" that they can look at while the teacher reads or as they listen to a recording.

Reading   EMH students need a longer period of reading readiness prior to formal reading instruction because reading readiness is related to mental age rather than chronological age. Once they have developed basic reading skills, EMH students benefit from a systematic approach to reading instruction with skills divided into small steps that are carefully reinforced and practiced. EMH students should develop reading fluency through abundant opportunities to read each school day. Since oral reading is usually difficult for these youngsters, they should be encouraged to read all content orally. When oral reading is desirable, they need to have directed silent reading prior to oral reading. Content reading instruction is especially important for EMH students, otherwise they will be unable to learn from content textbooks.

The reading materials for EMH students should be interesting and have a controlled vocabulary. Reading materials with a controlled vocabulary reduces their frustration while giving them opportunities to apply their reading skills.

Literature is often omitted from special education programs even though these youngsters need literature as much or more than other children. Reading literature aloud to EMH students each day has the same values for them as for other children. Literature can develop their motivation to read. Furthermore, literature exposes them to ideas and information that they could not derive from the printed page independently.

Writing   The objective of writing instruction is to have children comfortably express their ideas and feelings and to generate materials that can be used to develop skills. Spontaneous written expression may be one of the most effective approaches to teaching EMH children written expression. The central core of a writing program for EMH children should be to have each child write something each day (Cohen and Plaskon, 1980). Teaching writing to EMH students is similar to teaching writing to average ones. The primary differences lie in the writing stimuli which must be concrete for EMH children and the teacher's expectations regarding students' products. As in the other language arts, EMH students will not acquire writing skills at the same pace as their age mates, but this does not mean that they cannot write.

Handwriting and spelling skills are reflected in students' compositions. Some EMH students have difficulty achieving legible handwriting which may result from poor coordination. When handwriting presents presistent difficulty for students, teachers should consider allowing them to use the typewriter or computer. In some instances, allowing EMH students to use manuscript writing rather than cursive is helpful.

Spelling is also a persistent problem for EMH students. Initially, they need to focus on writing their thoughts without concern for spelling. However, they do need to learn to correct spelling using a reference like a secretary's wordbook. In learning to spell they seem to benefit most from a kinesthetic approach which involves tracing the words they are learning.

LANGUAGE ARTS FOR GIFTED STUDENTS

Gifted students are at the opposite end of the continuum from EMH students; their special needs are usually not as obvious as those of other children so they are often overlooked in our society. They may be turned off by the normal progression through a standard curriculum. Gifted students often have a level of sensitivity to the subtleties of language and literature not possessed by typical students (Labuda, 1985). On the other hand, they have little patience for drill and routine (Labuda, 1985). They should have the intellectual stimulation that will allow them to achieve to their fullest ability.

What Are Gifted Students Like?

First of all, gifted children are children who are very much like all other children in development and basic needs. Nevertheless, their outstanding abilities enable them to achieve at high levels if school programs encourage this development. Children who are capable of high performance demonstrate achievement or potential ability in any of the following areas or in combinations of these areas (Labuda, 1974).

1. General intellectual ability

2. Specific academic aptitude

3. Creative or productive thinking

4. Leadership ability

5. Visual and performing arts

When compared to their age group, gifted children demonstrate longer attention spans, a persistent curiosity, a desire to learn rapidly, a good memory, an awareness and appreciation of people and things, a wide range of interests and problem-solving abilities (Labuda, 1985).

Gifted children exhibit a full range of individual differences. Typically, gifted children possess well-developed language skills, although those growing up in a home speaking a nonstandard dialect will learn to speak that dialect. Some gifted children learn to read early while others wait until they enter school. Many gifted children start scribbling and writing early in their lives and maintain this interest throughout their lives. In some homes, the parents teach their gifted children and encourage them to acquire knowledge and skills very early in their lives, while other parents prefer that their children have a more normal homelife. Still other parents may not realize that their children are gifted.

Language Arts Instruction for Gifted Students

As stated earlier, the lesson planning format and the instructional strategies recommended in this chapter are appropriate for all children. However, instruction should be adjusted to meet special needs. For example, gifted children need to acquire the same skills as other children, but they can do so without extensive practice.

The language arts should be approached as thinking processes. For example, they could participate in a panel discussion for science class that focused on the social impact of new scientific discoveries. Such an activity would incorporate critical speaking, listening, reading (to prepare), and writing (notes and points to be made). Teachers' questions should focus on divergent thinking that encourages open-ended, inferred responses. An instance of this is seen in a follow-up discussion of a trade book the students have read, when the teacher asks, "Did the protagonist in this story act in an ethical manner? Why or why not?" They should not deal so much with acquiring information but with interpreting, processing, and using information.

Oral Language   Gifted children should have many opportunities to participate in oral language activities. These activities will enable them to refine and extend their language skills, as well as learn to communicate with others. Oral language activities need to include both functional and creative activities. Participation in panel discussions, interviews, and class meetings will develop functional language skills, while dramatic productions, readers' theater, and puppet shows are creative activities.

Listening   Gifted children are ordinarily quite competent listeners. However, they enjoy and benefit from critical listening instruction. Critical listening instruction helps them learn to suspend judgment until they have the data to evaluate an event, situation, or a person and to look beyond the language used in propaganda. They also enjoy appreciative listening activities such as listening to poetry or a dramatic production.

Reading   One of the greatest concerns with reading instruction for gifted students is the concern that teachers will assume that such able students need no instruction. Even though their reading is fluent, they still have things to learn. In *Stages of Reading Development,* Jeanne Chall (1983) states that many people do not reach the highest stage of reading development. Which is the level of reading development at which readers construct knowledge for themselves? They use the thinking skills of analysis, synthesis, and judgment to do this. However, previous knowledge regarding the topic enables them to select and comprehend data from various sources. Readers at this level are operating at a high level of abstraction to create their own "truth" from the "truths" of others (Chall, 1983). Instruction can help gifted students reach this stage of reading development.

Gifted children who can read before they enter school should be encouraged to continue reading; however, no assumptions should be made regarding their skill development. A diagnostic approach is recommended. Informal inventories can be used to assess students' reading strengths and weaknesses. Many gifted students do need basic reading skills instruction, but they do not need the amount of skills practice that average children do. Workbooks and worksheets rarely have any value for gifted children. These activities represent skill reinforcement that they do not require. Furthermore, these activities do not ordinarily involve higher level thinking processes. Reading interesting trade books provides interesting material on which they can develop reading fluency.

Gifted students who enter school unable to read should be introduced to reading immediately. A language experience approach is an excellent way to introduce reading because the children can see the teacher write their words, the language is their own, the content is interesting to them. They can quickly learn to read with this approach. Children who are introduced to reading through language experience activities often start writing their own stories. When teaching gifted students some teachers use an individualized approach based on students' reading trade books and having teacher conferences regarding the content. Other instructors choose to use basal readers for teaching gifted students to read. The specific instructional method is not important when students are motivated to read and acquire the skills they need for reading independently.

Reading independence may come more easily to gifted students, but they do need content reading and study skills instruction. After grade three, the sophistication of content reading materials quickly escalates and readers need a way of reading, remembering, and organizing the content. Content reading and study skills instruction enables them to read efficiently.

Literature   Literature plays an enormous role in the education of gifted students. An appreciation of literature provides a chance to explore other times and places, to think, and to learn. Not only does literature challenge and stimulate gifted children, but it provides them with models for writing, thinking, and creating. The importance of excellent school media centers and classroom libraries cannot be overemphasized. The research and reading that gifted students thrive on requires books, recordings, films, pictures, video cassettes, televisions, and computers.

In addition, teachers should provide many opportunities for students to discuss the books they are reading and the television programs they are viewing. Video cassette recorders (VCRs) make it possible to tape television productions that are valuable for students and to bring them into the classroom for analysis and reaction.

Writing Gifted students should be introduced to writing early and they should write daily. In composition as in the other language arts, gifted children need stimulation and the time to explore ideas through writing. Gifted students enjoy keeping journals and many do so before they are introduced in class. Even though their writing may excel that of average students, they should experience the phases of the composing process, working through prewriting, writing, revising, and editing. Instruction should include many opportunities to share and discuss their compositions with peers. Writing instruction should include experiences with writing all forms of literature; gifted students may write plays, poems, novels, and reports.

Gifted students enjoy writing activities like the following.

1. Attending plays and writing reviews.

2. Publishing a class or school newspaper.

3. Writing letters to the editor of local newspapers regarding issues they have investigated.

4. Becoming a specialist on a certain geographic area, country, or state and writing material about the specialization.

5. Creating games and writing the directions for other students to play.

6. Analyzing an author's point of view in a book, newspaper, or magazine article.

7. Writing an article persuading another person to their point of view.

8. Writing character sketches about favorite characters.

TEACHING MAINSTREAMED STUDENTS

Teachers who have mainstreamed students in their classrooms should remember the following principles of language arts instruction.

1. Children always acquire language through real use. Therefore, mainstreamed students should have many opportunities to speak, listen, read, and write.

2. "Real" activities should stress meaning. Teachers should encourage language play and guide children as they engage in intrinsically purposeful activities (Edelsky and Rosegrant, 1981).

3. The classroom environment should stimulate children's interaction. Mainstreamed children should be seated with the other children in the classroom. If a child happens to be in a wheelchair, move furniture so he or she can sit in close proximity to the other students. This helps draw them into the group and encourages conversation as well as discussion.

4. Other children in the class can help mainstream children. They talk to them about their interests, listen to them tell about their special interests or hobbies, listen to them read, help them spell a word, and take dictation for a youngster who cannot form letters.

Integrating mainstreamed students into regular classroom instruction concerns many teachers. However, mainstreamed students do benefit from interacting with other students. When mainstreamed students become productive members of the class, their self-concept improves and the other students perceive them as an integral part of the class. Therefore, teachers should call on mainstreamed children, give them appropriate assignments, and treat them very much as they do the other students. Failure to do this will prevent mainstreamed students from being accepted in the class. The other students benefit from communicating and associating with people who are different from them. They learn that mainstreamed students are valuable members of their classes.

Teachers must communicate their expectation that all students have a responsibility to participate in class. Special students should not be ignored. Maring, Furman, and Blum-Anderson (1985) suggest the following guidelines for mainstreamed students' group participation.

1. Each member must make a serious effort to do work.

2. Each member should follow the directions for the assignment.

3. A member who disagrees with an answer to the question or item should defend that point of view, giving specific reasons based on the text or on personal experience.

4. No member dominates or withdraws from the discussion; each member must add something to the discussion.

5. Each member must display a positive and encouraging attitude toward every other group member.

SUMMARY

All children have special needs of some sort, but the children addressed in this chapter are those whose special needs must be addressed in the educational system if they are to achieve to their potential. These special needs arise from a variety of sources such as language differences, intellectual differences, and sensory differences. The majority of exceptional students receive specialized instruction; some students receive English as a second language instruction; EMH students have a special education teacher; and gifted students may have an instructor specialized in teaching bright children. Nevertheless, these students spend part of their school day in the regular classroom and participate in classroom activities. As a result, classroom teachers must be prepared to teach them as well as the other students in their classes.

Exceptional children exhibit a full range of individual differences; therefore, it is inappropriate to generalize regarding their instruction. Teachers must look at each student as an individual and plan ways to include each in classroom activities.

Instruction for special need students should follow the lesson plan format presented in Chapter Two. However, adjustments must be made within the instructional cycle to meet their special needs. Students whose native language is not English can participate in class, when the teacher is understanding and accepting. These youngsters should not be required to read and write English until they have developed an understanding of oral English. Provisions must be made to compensate for students who are visually and auditorily impaired. They need opportunities to explore language in different ways; deaf children can begin exploring written language at an early age. EMH students learn more slowly. They also learn in a very concrete fashion. They should have slow-paced instruction that provides for frequent review and considerable practice. Gifted students are at the other end of the continuum. They learn quickly with little need for reinforcement. Instruction for these youngsters should stimulate them to use their abilities to the fullest.

Thought Questions

1. Do you agree with the concept of mainstreaming? Why or why not?

2. Is the need for ESL instruction likely to change during the coming decade? If so, how do you think it will change?

3. Why are classroom teachers rarely prepared to teach students that once were classified as "special education" students?

4. In your opinion, can gifted students be challenged in the regular classroom? What provisions need to be made to ensure they are challenged?

5. Discuss ways of integrating special need students into the instructional activities of the regular classroom.

6. Compare language arts instruction for special need students with that for average students.

Enrichment Activities

1. Visit an ESL classroom and observe to determine the methods and materials the ESL teacher uses. How much of the time do the students spend in the regular classroom?

2. Interview an ESL teacher to determine the native language of the students and the recommendations they have for classroom teachers who are teaching ESL students.

3. Ask a college student from another country to describe the language problems experienced in coming to the United States.

4. Visit an elementary school and talk with the special education instructor to identify the special needs in the regular classroom.

5. Observe an EMH student during the mainstreaming portion of the day. Were the student's needs met in the classroom? To what extent was the child involved in classroom activities?

6. Develop a file of films, records, and trade books that would be useful in teaching gifted students.

7. Develop a list of language arts activities that might stimulate gifted students learning.

8. Make an annotated bibliography of trade books appropriate to read to ESL students.

Selected Readings

Bruininks, V. L. (February 1978). "Designing Instructional Activities for Students with Language/Learning Disabilities." *Language Arts, 55,* 2, 154–160.

Cohen, S., and S. Plaskon (1980). *Language Arts for the Mildly Handicapped.* Columbus, OH: Charles Merrill.

Edelsky, C., and T. J. Rosegrant (January 1981). "Language Development for Mainstreamed Severely Handicapped Non-Verbal Children." *Language Arts, 58,* 1, 68–76.

Feitelson, D., Ed. (1979). *Mother Tongue or Second Language?* Newark, DE: International Reading Association.

Labuda, M., Ed. (1985). *Creative Reading for Gifted Learners.* Newark, DE: International Reading Association.

Maring, G.; G. Furman; and J. Blum-Anderson (December 1985). "Five Cooperative Learning Strategies for Mainstreamed Children in Content Area Classrooms." *Reading Teacher, 39,* 3, 310–313.

Manson, M. (January 1982). "Explorations in Language Arts for Preschoolers (Who Happen to be Deaf)." *Language Arts, 59,* 1, 33–39.

McGee, L., and G. Tompkins (January 1982). "Concepts About Print for the Young Blind Child." *Language Arts, 59,* 1, 40–45.

McLaughlin, B. (1985). *Second Language Acquisition in Childhood,* Vol 2, *School Age Children* (2nd Ed.). Hillsdale, NJ: Erlbaum Associates.

O'Donnell, H. (October 1980). "Writing Problems of the Learning Disabled Student." *Language Arts, 57,* 7, 802–805.

Oritz, L., and G. Engelbrecht (September 1986). "Partners in Biliteracy: The School and the Community." *Language Arts, 63,* 458–465.

Perez, S. (February 1979). "How to Effectively Teach Spanish-Speaking Children, Even If You're Not Bilingual." *Language Arts, 56,* 159–162.

Piper, Terry (September 1986). "Learning About Language Learning." *Language Arts, 63,* 466–471.

Valverde, L., ed. (1978). *Bilingual Education for Latinos.* Washington, DC: Association for Supervision of Curriculum and Development.

Wong-Fillmore, Lily (September 1986). "Research Currents: Equity or Excellence?" *Language Arts, 63,* 474–481.

References

Bain, A. M. (1976). "Written Expression—The Last Skill Acquired." *An Interdisciplinary Journal of Specific Language Disability,* Vol. 26. Towson, MD: Orton Society, 79–95.

Baker, K. A., and A. A. de Kanter (September 1981), *Effectiveness of Bilingual Education: A Review of the Literature.* Washington, DC: Office of Planning, Budget and Evaluation, U.S. Department of Education.

Bernstein, B. (1972). "A Critique of the Concept of Compensatory Education." In *Functions of Language in the Classroom,* C. Cazden, V. John, and D. Hymes (eds.). New York: Teachers College Press.

Chall, J. (1983). *Stages of Reading Development.* New York: McGraw-Hill.

Cohen, S., and S. Plaskon (1980). *Language Arts for the Mildly Handicapped.* Columbus, OH: Charles Merrill.

Cummins, J. (1981). "Four Misconceptions about Language Proficiency in Bilingual Education." *NABE Journal, 5,* 31–45.

Cummins, J. (1984). *Bilingualism and Special Education: Issues in Assessment and Pedagogy.* Clevedon, England: Multilingual Matters, Ltd.

Edelsky, C., and T. Rosegrant (January 1981). "Language Development for Mainstreamed Severely Handicapped Non-Verbal Children." *Language Arts, 58,* 1, 68–76.

Evans, E. (1975) *Contemporary Influences in Early Childhood Education.* New York: Holt, Rinehart & Winston.

Hakuta, J. (1985). *Mirror of Languages: The Debate on Bilingualism.* New York: Basic Books.

Halliday, M. (1975). *Learning How to Mean: Explorations in the Development of Language.* London: Edward Arnold.

Hart, B., and R. R. Risley (1975). "Incidental Teaching of Language in the Preschool." *Journal of Applied Behavior Analysis, 8,* 411–420.

Hubbell, R. (1977). "On Facilitating Spontaneous Talking in Young Children." *Journal of Speech and Hearing Disorders, 42,* 216–231.

Johnson, D., and L. Johnson (1978). *Learning Disabilities: What Research Says to the Teacher.* Washington, DC: National Education Association.

Kaluger, G., and C. Kolson (1978). *Reading and Learning Disabilities* (2nd Ed.). Columbus, OH: Charles Merrill.

Labuda, M. (1974). "Gifted and Creative Pupils: Reasons for Concern." In *Creative Reading for Gifted Learners: A Design for Excellence,* M. Labuda (ed.). Newark, DE: International Reading Association, 2–7.

Labuda, M., Ed. (1985). *Creative Reading for Gifted Learners.* Newark, DE: International Reading Association.

Lopez, Meliton (1978). "Bilingual Education and the Latino Student." In *Bilingual Education for Latinos,* L. Valverde (ed.). Washington DC: Association for Supervision of Curriculum and Development, 1–16.

Manson, M. (January 1982). "Explorations in Language Arts for Preschoolers (Who Happen to be Deaf)." *Language Arts, 59,* 1, 33–45.

Maring, G.; G. Furman; and J. Blum-Anderson (December 1985). "Five Cooperative Learning Strategies for Mainstreamed Children in Content Area Classrooms." *Reading Teacher, 39,* 3, 310–313.

McGee, L., and G. Tompkins (January 1982). "Concepts About Print for the Young Blind Child." *Language Arts, 59,* 1, 40–45.

McLaughlin, B. (1985). *Second Language Acquisition in Childhood,* Vol 2. *School Age Children* (2d Ed.). Hillsdale, NJ: Erlbaum Associates.

Myklebust, H. R. (1973). *Development and Disorders of Written Language,* Vol. II. *Studies of Normal and Exceptional Children.* New York: Grune & Stratton.

Oritz, L., and G. Engelbrecht (September 1986). "Partners in Biliteracy: The School and the Community." *Language Arts, 63,* 5, 458–465.

Perez, S. (February 1979). "How to Effectively Teach Spanish-Speaking Children, Even If You're Not Bilingual." *Language Arts, 56,* 2, 159–162.

Scofield, S. (September 1978). "The Language-delayed Child in the Mainstreamed Primary Classroom." *Language Arts, 55,* 6, 719–723.

Swain, M., and S. Lapkin (1982). *Evaluating Bilingual Education: A Canadian Case Study.* Clevedon, England: Multilingual Matters, Ltd.

Wagoner, S. (December 1982). "Mexican-American in Children's Literature Since 1970." *Reading Teacher, 36,* 3, 274–279.

Wiig, E., and E. Semel (1976). *Language Disabilities in Children and Adolescents.* Columbus, OH: Charles Merrill.

Willig, A. C. (Fall 1985). "A Meta-Analysis of Selected Studies on the Effectiveness of Bilingual Education." *Review of Educational Research, 55,* 3, 269–317.

Wong-Fillmore, L. (1983). "The Learner as an Individual: Implications of Research on Individual Differences for the ESL Teacher." In *Pacific Perspectives on Language Learning and Teaching,* J. Clarke and J. Handscombe (eds.). Washington, DC: TESOL.

——— (September 1986). "Research Currents: Equity or Excellence?" *Language Arts, 63,* 474–481.

Glossary

Academic engaged time   The time that students spend actively engaged in learning.

Analytic language   A language in which meaning is expressed through word order. Grammar is expressed through word order.

Anaphoric terms   Words used as a substitute for a preceding word or group of words, such as *she* in "She went downtown."

Attention   The ability to focus or concentrate on a topic, an event, or an activity.

Attitude   State of mind or feeling regarding a specific entity, experience, or activity such as school, language, or reading.

Auding   Listening comprehension.

Audience   The persons who listen to, observe, and read language content.

Choral reading   Reading in unison. This activity may involve the entire group reading a selection—often poetry—in unison or the content may be divided into parts with different groups reading the various parts.

Composing   Part of the writing process in which writers express their thoughts in written language.

Compressed speech   Speech that has been speeded up to 350 words a minute for the purpose of forcing listeners to concentrate totally.

Concept of word   A requirement of literacy. Once youngsters know what a word is, they are ready to read and write. A concept of word includes knowing that words are comprised of letters, that words represent things that may or may not be present in the immediate environment, and that words are physical entities that have boundaries (beginnings and endings).

Content   The material about which speakers, listeners, readers, and writers communicate. Content is derived from experience, textbooks, class lectures and discussions, observation, and trade books. Content comprises four major aspects: ideas, words, sentences, and discourse organization.

Contextual approach   A functional approach to grammar that emphasizes ideas as well as structure. In this view, appropriate language is seen as being acquired gradually over a long period of time.

Conversation   Informal oral interaction usually occurring between two or three people.

Creative oral language   Aesthetic activities that involve talking, such as dramatics, reader's theatre, and puppet shows.

Creative or appreciative understanding   An aesthetic response to written or spoken content.

Critical understanding   Comprehension requiring readers to evaluate or make judgments about what they hear or read.

Curriculum   Planned learning experiences in schools.

Cursive   Style of handwriting featuring connected letters that is commonly used by adults in the United States.

D'Nealian   A newer style of handwriting that is very similar to cursive handwriting except that the letters are not connected.

Descriptive grammar   Also called structural grammar, this approach describes grammar as it occurs rather than prescribes what ought to be.

Dialect   Language variation often related to geographic location, although age and sex also influence language variation. For example: teenagers use different semantics and syntax than adults; men and women use different semantics.

Direct instruction   An approach to helping students learn that involves precise sequencing of content with high pupil engagement, careful teacher monitoring, and specific corrective feedback.

Discourse   A longer structure created when sentences and paragraphs are structured to express meaning.

Discussion   Oral interaction that may be more formal than conversation. A discussion may involve everyone present or, as in a panel discussion, an audience as well as the discussants. Participants in a discussion often prepare in advance for a discussion.

Editing   Part of the writing process in which writers examine the conventions of language. During editing they may correct spelling, capitalization, punctuation, and grammar.

Educable Mentally Handicapped (EMH)   Individuals who require educational programs that are adapted to their special needs. These students can also learn in the regular classroom. Earlier in our educational history these students were labeled educable mentally retarded (EMR).

English as a Second Language (ESL)   A program for students whose mother tongue is not English.

Expressive language arts   The language processes that are concerned with expressing meaning in language. The expressive language arts are speaking and writing.

Gifted   Individuals who learn more rapidly than average. Their intelligence quotient is usually above average.

Grammar   The structure of language. Grammar is more or less synonymous with sentence structure and syntax; therefore, it refers to word order, function words, and grammatical endings.

Holistic scoring   Writing evaluation based on examining a composition as a whole rather than specific aspects or parts.

Holophrases   One-word sentences that imply more elaborate structures. For example, a youngster uttering the word "drink," may be implying "I want a drink."

House Bill 94-142   Legislation designed to improve the education of "special" students. This law mandates that students be educated in the "least restrictive environment."

Idiom   Regional speech or dialect; also particular common expressions in a standard language.

Individualized educational plan (IEP)   The plan that must be created for each individual EMH student, as mandated by HB 94-142.

Informative oral language   Oral language that informs (tells) rather than provides aesthetic values.

Integrated English language arts instruction   Instruction is based on the concept that speaking, listening, reading, and writing are interrelated and reciprocal. Instruction in one language process enhances the learning of the other language processes.

Interpretation (inferring)   Filling in missing information and ideas from reader's experiences. The reader is trying to understand what the author meant by what he or she said.

Inflected language   A language depending on word endings to signal grammatical function; therefore word placement is flexible.

Instruction   Procedures or actions that teachers use to help students learn.

Invented spellings   Spellings that children create to represent words before they achieve the developmental stage of accurate spellings. Children pass through predictable developmental stages as they grow toward correct spelling.

Kinesics   Nonverbal communication signals—gestures, facial expressions, and so forth.

Knowledge   Cognitive or mental data acquired through study and experience.

Language   A system of arbitrary symbols used for communication. Included in the language system are phonemics, semantics, syntax, and discourse.

Language arts   Speaking, listening, reading, and writing processes are included in the language arts. Each of these communication skills is based on language.

Language delay   Much slower than average language development. Language delay interferes with communication.

Language functions   The ways we use language, including instrumental language, regulatory language, interactional language, heuristic language, personal language, imaginative language, and representative language.

Learning disabled   Term generally referring to individuals who have significant difficulty acquiring listening, speaking, reading, writing, or mathematical skills. There is considerable confusion regarding learning disabilities.

Letter-name stage   The second stage of spelling development. During this stage, students know the names of letters and use the letters whose names sound like the words they are writing to represent those words. The way they write words is influenced by the way they pronounce them. For example, a youngster in this stage might write *dragon* as *jragn*.

Linguist   One who studies language.

Listening   The process of understanding spoken language. Spoken language is interpreted in the brain.

Listening comprehension   The understanding of oral language. The auding or listening comprehension level is that level at which the student can listen to content and answer questions with more than 75 percent accuracy.

Literal comprehension   The recalling of stated information. This level of understanding includes remembering stated details and stated main ideas.

Main idea   The most important thought or concept in an expository selection that is supported with details. Main ideas structure exposition. They may be presented in different ways—cause and effect, comparison and contrast, chronological order, definitions, and so forth.

Mainstreaming   An educational concept that involves placing special-education students in regular classrooms for a part of the school day.

Manuscript   A form of handwriting based on circles and straight lines. This style of handwriting is used with young children, and when their muscles are more mature, usually by late second grade or beginning third grade, they are introduced to cursive handwriting.

Model   To demonstrate a skill, process, or activity. A model is an example.

Morphology   The meaningful grouping of phonemes. Morphemes are the smallest meaningful units of language.

Nonstandard English   Language that varies from standard English. Nonstandard English usage has low acceptability.

Oral language   Talk. Speakers use their physical apparatus to produce sounds (phonemes), morphemes, sentences, and discourse to communicate meanings.

Personal writing   Composing to examine one's thoughts. The writer may choose to keep such writing personal rather than share it.

Phonology   The sound system of English.

Phonemes   The smallest discrete units of sound in the language.

Plot   The story plan—what happens in the story. A plot is composed of an introductory section that lays the story groundwork and establishes setting, characters, and problem. The climax is the high point of the plot; the problem is often resolved at this place in the story, followed by the denouement or falling action.

Practical writing   Content created to fulfill functional purposes. For example, practical writing may include written directions, information, and letters.

Prewriting   The stage of the writing process in which the writer thinks about what he or she will write. The prewriting process may include organizing thoughts and/or doing research for additional information.

Preliterate   The first stage of spelling development. During this stage of development, children may "scribble-write" and write sequences of letters to represent words. These activities indicate that they are beginning to acquire *concept of word.*

Primary trait scoring   An approach to evaluating compositions that focuses on specific traits that are identified in the assignment. For example, primary trait scoring may focus on such traits as description or perspective.

Process   A systematic set of actions or activities directed toward a specific goal. For example, the writing process is comprised of prewriting, composing, revising, and editing.

Public writing   Writing intended for an audience.

Reading   The process of understanding written language. Readers use their experiences and text content to construct this understanding.

Reader's theatre   An oral presentation of drama, prose, or poetry by two or more people who read clearly and expressively. Characterization is conveyed by the reader and the narrator, and the audience is encouraged to create its own mental images of the action.

Receptive language arts   The language processes related to receiving meaning or communication from others. Listening and reading are receptive language arts.

Response to literature   Emotional reactions to written language. Response is often expressed through art, music, drama, reading, and writing.

Revising   Part of the writing process in which writers rewrite content to clarify and enrich expression.

Scaffolding   Temporary frameworks that adults create to support children in their attempts to use language successfully. Scaffolds are created through questions and statements as teachers and students interact.

Semantics   The meaning system of language. Semantics includes word meanings, the connotative and denotative meanings of words, and multiple meanings.

Sense of audience   An understanding of what the people who are listening, reading, and observing will comprehend.

Sentence combining   A form of sentence manipulation wherein writers can combine two or three simple sentences into a single sentence that is more complex than the original sentence.

Setting   The time and place of a story. The setting in story grammar includes character as well as time and place.

Skill   An acquired proficiency, ability, or expertness.

Speaking   Using speech to communicate; using oral language to express meaning.

Speaking vocabulary   Words that speakers use to communicate. Individuals have a speaking vocabulary, a listening vocabulary, a reading vocabulary, and a writing vocabulary.

Spelling conscience   A feeling of responsibility for spelling accurately.

Standard English   (also **standard American English**)   The dialect used in the media, many books, and government publications. This prestige dialect of English is usually spoken and written by leaders in social, political, and economic life in the United States, although there are a few notable exceptions, such as President Lyndon Johnson. The pronunciation and idiomatic use of standard English varies widely in practice; however, the grammatical structure is relatively uniform.

Story grammar   In this context, grammar means structure—thus story structure.

Style   The ways authors and speakers use language to communicate.

Subskills instruction   Teaching of the separate skills comprising the language arts.

Syllable juncture stage   The fourth stage of spelling development. The core principle of syllable juncture is that of doubling consonants to mark the short English vowel.

Syntax   The pattern of word order in sentences.

Synthetic language   A language that relies on a case grammar; the word endings indicate grammatical function in a specific sentence.

Telegraphic language   A language that concentrates on nouns, verbs, and descriptive adjectives, producing utterances like "See doggie."

Text structure   The way that nonfiction or exposition is structured. This structure is usually composed of an introduction, a body, and a summary or closing. Main ideas are used to structure expository content within these structures.

Traditional school grammar   Grammar was borrowed from Latin, therefore forcing English into the Latin mold. This approach is not appropriate for English because Latin is an inflected language and English is not.

Theme   The major idea conveyed by a literary work or a work of art.

Trade books   Books that are distributed to the general public. Textbooks are classified differently because they are special-purpose materials that are not in general circulation outside of schools.

Transformations   Changing sentences from one form to another. For example, a positive sentence can be transformed into a negative one or a declarative sentence can be transformed into a question.

Transformational-generative grammar   Grammar based on the concept that English speakers can generate an almost infinite number of sentences. This approach stresses the process of grammar based on noun and verb phrases.

Usage   Pronunciations, words, and grammar that individual speakers use to communicate. Usage reflects the speaker's dialect.

Visualize   To create a mental image. Listeners create visual images to accompany content that they hear. Speakers have an image that they wish to convey to their audience. Readers create images of story characters and action. Writers visualize what they wish to write. In handwriting, the writer visualizes the way to form a letter and the way to write (spell) a word.

Within-word pattern   The third stage of spelling development wherein the child is ready to learn about the "within-word" vowel patterns of English spelling and the relationship between these patterns and English word meanings.

Whole language   The simultaneous, integrated teaching of reading, writing, speaking, and listening within a context that is meaningful to the language learner.

Writing   Expressing meaning in written language.

Index